BLACK WALL STREET

100

An American City Grapples With Its Historical Racial Trauma

Hannibal B. Johnson

CENTENNIAL COMMEMORATIVE

EAKIN PRESS　Fort Worth, Texas
www.EakinPress.com

Table of Contents

Acknowledgments

No one who achieves success does so without the help of others. The
wise and confident acknowledge this help with gratitude.
Alfred North Whitehead

Special thanks to those persons who assisted with various aspects of this project, including manuscript review, editing, photography, and substantive content. Those individuals include: Dr. Vivian Clark-Adams, Jack Blair, Mayor G.T. Bynum, I. Marc Carlson, T.D. "Pete" Churchwell, Richard DeSirey, George A. Farrar, Jr., Joan Hoar, Frances Jordan-Rakestraw, Ken Levit, Darrell Mercer, Calvin C. Moore, J.D., Ph.D., Joseph L. Parker, Jr., Gary Percefull, Senator Kevin L. Matthews, Steve Wood, the 400 Years of African American History Commission,[1] and the 1921 Tulsa Race Massacre Centennial Commission.

History—inclusive, unvarnished, and authentic—is best when looked at, learned from, and leveraged. Indeed, it is not possible to blaze the trails to our future without first retracing the footsteps of our past.

This book is the culmination of years of effort, not just on the part of the author, but by many individuals and groups committed to forward momentum in Tulsa, in race relations and more broadly. I am grateful.

Prologue

Walter White, Assistant Secretary of the National Association for the Advancement of Colored People, commonly known as the N.A.A.C.P., visited Tulsa in the spring of 1921.[2] He described the city and its racial dynamics in a June 1921 magazine article.

A hysterical white girl related that a nineteen-year-old colored boy attempted to assault her in the public elevator of a public office building of a thriving town of 100,000 in open daylight. Without pausing to find whether or not the story was true, without bothering with the slight detail of investigating the character of the woman who made the outcry (as a matter of fact, she was of exceedingly doubtful reputation), a mob of 100-per-cent Americans set forth on a wild rampage that cost the lives of fifty white men; of between 150 and 200 colored men, women and children; the destruction by fire of $1,500,000 worth of property; the looting of many homes; and everlasting damage to the reputation of the city of Tulsa and the State of Oklahoma.

This, in brief, is the story of the eruption of Tulsa on the night of May 31 and the morning of June 1. One could travel far and find few cities where the likelihood of trouble between the races was as little thought of as in Tulsa. Her reign of terror stands as a grim reminder of the grip mob violence has on the throat of America, and the ever-present possibility of devastating race conflicts where least expected.

Tulsa is a thriving, bustling, enormously wealthy town of between 90,000 and 100,000. In 1910 it was the home of 18,182 souls, a dead and hopeless outlook ahead. Then oil was discovered. The town grew amazingly. On December 29, 1920, it had bank deposits totaling $65,449,985.90; almost $1,000 per capita when compared with the Federal Census figures of 1920, which gave Tulsa 72,076. The town lies in the center of the oil region and many are the stories told of the making of fabulous fortunes by men who were operating on a shoe-string. Some of the stories rival those of the 'forty-niners' in California. The town has a number of modern office buildings, many beautiful homes, miles of clean, well-paved streets, and aggressive and progressive business men who well exemplify Tulsa's motto of 'The City with a Personality.'

So much for the setting. What are the causes of the race riot that occurred in such a place? First, the Negro in Oklahoma has shared in the sudden prosperity that has come to many of his white brothers, and there are some colored men there who are wealthy. This fact has caused a bitter resentment on the part of the lower order of whites, who feel that these colored men, members of an 'inferior race,' are exceedingly presumptuous in achieving greater economic prosperity than they who are members of a divinely ordered superior race. There are at least three colored persons in Oklahoma who are worth a million dollars each; J. W. Thompson of Clearview is worth $500,000; there are a number of men and women worth $100,000; and many whose possessions are valued at $25,000 and $50,000 each. This was particularly true of Tulsa, where there were two colored men worth $150,000 each; two worth $100,000; three $50,000; and four who were assessed at $25,000. In one case where a colored man owned and operated a printing plant with $25,000 worth of printing machinery in it, the leader of the mob that set fire to and destroyed the plant was a linotype operator employed for years by the colored owner at $48 per week. The white man was killed while attacking the plant. Oklahoma is largely populated by pioneers from other States. Some of the white pioneers are former residents of Mississippi, Georgia, Tennessee, Texas, and other States more typically southern than Oklahoma. These have brought with them their anti-Negro prejudices. Lethargic and unprogressive by nature, it sorely irks them to see Negroes making greater progress than they themselves are achieving.

One of the charges made against the colored men in Tulsa is that they were 'radical.' Questioning the whites more closely regarding the nature of this radicalism, I found it means that Negroes were uncompromisingly denouncing 'Jim-Crow' [railroad] cars, lynching, peonage; in short, were asking that the Federal constitutional guaranties of 'life, liberty, and the pursuit of happiness' be given regardless of color. The Negroes of Tulsa and other Oklahoma cities are pioneers; men and women who have dared, men and women who have had the initiative and the courage to pull up stakes in other less-favored States and face hardship in a newer one for the sake of greater eventual progress. That type is ever less ready to submit to insult. Those of the whites who seek to maintain the old white group control naturally do not relish seeing Negroes emancipating themselves from the old system.

A third cause was the rotten political conditions in Tulsa. A vice ring was in control of the city, allowing open operation of houses of ill fame, of gambling joints, the illegal sale of whiskey, the robbing of banks and stores, with hardly a slight possibility of the arrest of the criminals, and even less of their conviction. For fourteen years Tulsa has been in the absolute control of this element. Most of the better element, and there is a large percentage of Tulsans who can properly be classed as such, are interested solely in making money and getting away. They have taken little or no interest in the election of city or county officials, leaving it to those whose interest it was to secure officials who would protect them in their vice operations. About two months ago the State legislature assigned two additional judges to Tulsa County to aid the present two in clearing the badly clogged dockets. These judges found more than six thousand cases awaiting trial. Thus in a county of approximately 100,000 population, six out of every one hundred citizens were under indictment for some sort of crime, with little likelihood of trial in any of them.

Last July a white man by the name of Roy Belton, accused of murdering a taxicab driver, was taken from the county jail and lynched. According to the statements of many prominent Tulsans, local police officers directed traffic at the scene of the lynching, trying to afford every person present an equal chance to view the event. Insurance companies refuse to give Tulsa merchants insurance on their stocks; the risk is too great. There have been so many automobile thefts that a number of companies have canceled all policies on cars in Tulsa. The net result of these conditions was that practically none of the citizens of the town, white or colored, had very much respect for the law.

So much for the general causes. What was the spark that set off the blaze? On Monday, May 30, a white girl by the name of Sarah Page, operating an elevator in the Drexel Building, stated that Dick Rowland,[3] a nineteen-year-old colored boy, had attempted criminally to assault her. Her second story was that the boy had seized her arm as he entered the elevator. She screamed. He ran. It was found afterwards that the boy had stepped by accident on her foot. It seems never to have occurred to the citizens of Tulsa that any sane person attempting criminally to assault a woman would have picked any place in the world rather than an open elevator in a public building with scores of people within calling distance. The story of the alleged assault was published Tuesday afternoon by *The Tulsa Tribune*, one of the two local newspapers. At four o'clock Commissioner of Police J.M. Adkison reported to Sheriff [Willard] McCullough that there was talk of lynching Rowland that night. Chief of Police John

A. Gustafson, Captain Wilkerson of the Police Department, Edwin F. Barnett, managing editor of *The Tulsa Tribune*, and numerous other citizens all stated that there was talk Tuesday of lynching the boy.

In the meantime the news of the threatened lynching reached the colored settlement where Tulsa's 15,000 colored citizens lived. Remembering how a white man had been lynched after being taken from the same jail where the colored boy was now confined, they feared that Rowland was in danger. A group of colored men telephoned the sheriff and proffered their services in protecting the jail from attack. The sheriff told them that they would be called upon if needed. About nine o'clock that night a crowd of white men gathered around the jail, numbering about 400 according to Sheriff McCullough. At 9:15 [p.m.] the report reached 'Little Africa' that the mob had stormed the jail. A crowd of twenty-five armed Negroes set out immediately, but on reaching the jail found the report untrue. The sheriff talked with them, assured them that the boy would not be harmed, and urged them to return to their homes. They left, later returning, 75 strong. The sheriff persuaded them to leave. As they complied, a white man attempted to disarm one of the colored men. A shot was fired, and then—in the words of the sheriff—'all hell broke loose.' There was a fusillade of shots from both sides and twelve men fell dead—two of them colored, ten white. The fighting continued until midnight when the colored men, greatly outnumbered, were forced back to their section of the town.

Around five o'clock Wednesday morning the [white] mob, now numbering more than 10,000, made a mass attack on Little Africa. Machine-guns were brought into use; eight aeroplanes were employed to spy on the movements of the Negroes and according to some were used in bombing the colored section. All that was lacking to make the scene a replica of modern 'Christian' warfare was poison gas. The colored men and women fought gamely in defense of their homes, but the odds were too great. According to the statements of onlookers, men in uniform, either home guards or ex-service men or both, carried cans of oil into Little Africa, and, after looting the homes, set fire to them. Many are the stories of horror told to me—not by colored people—but by white residents. One was that of an aged colored couple, saying their evening prayers before retiring in their little home on Greenwood Avenue.[4] A mob broke into the house, shot both of the old people in the backs of their heads, blowing their brains out and spattering them over the bed, pillaged the home, and then set fire to it.

Another was that of the death of Dr. A. C. Jackson, a colored physician. Dr. Jackson was worth $100,000; had been described by the Mayo brothers "the most able Negro surgeon in America"; was respected by white and colored people alike, and was in every sense a good citizen. A mob attacked Dr. Jackson's home. He fought in defense of it, his wife and children and himself. An officer of the home guards who knew Dr. Jackson came up at that time and assured him that if he would surrender he would be protected. This Dr. Jackson did. The officer sent him under guard to Convention Hall, where colored people were being placed for protection. En route to the hall, disarmed, Dr. Jackson was shot and killed in cold blood. The officer who had assured Dr. Jackson of protection stated to me, 'Dr. Jackson was an able, clean-cut man. He did only what any red-blooded man would have done under similar circumstances in defending his home. Dr. Jackson was murdered by white ruffians.'[5]

It is highly doubtful if the exact number of casualties will ever be known. The figures originally given in the press estimate the number at 100. The number buried by local undertakers and given out by city officials is ten white and twenty-one colored. For obvious reasons these officials wish to keep the number published as low as possible, but the figures obtained in Tulsa are far higher. Fifty whites and between 150 and 200 Negroes is much nearer the actual number of deaths. Ten whites were killed during the first hour of fighting on Tuesday night. Six white men drove into the colored section in a car on Wednesday morning and never came out. Thirteen whites were killed between 5:30 a.m. and 6:30 a.m. Wednesday. O. T. Johnson, commandant of the Tulsa Citadel of the Salvation Army, stated that on Wednesday and Thursday the Salvation Army fed thirty-seven Negroes employed as grave diggers and twenty on Friday and Saturday. During the first two days these men dug 120 graves in each of which a dead Negro was buried. No coffins were used. The bodies were dumped into the holes and covered over with dirt. Added to the number accounted for were numbers of others—men, women, and children—who were incinerated in the burning houses in the Negro settlement. One story was told me by an eye-witness of five colored men trapped in a burning house. Four burned to death. A fifth attempted to flee, was shot to death as he emerged from the burning structure, and his body was thrown back into the flames. There was an unconfirmed rumor afloat in Tulsa of two truck loads of dead Negroes being dumped into the Arkansas River, but that story could not be confirmed.

What is America going to do after such a horrible carnage—one that for sheer brutality and murderous anarchy cannot be surpassed by any of the crimes now being charged to the Bolsheviki in Russia? How much longer will America allow these pogroms to continue unchecked? There is a lesson in the Tulsa affair for every American who fatuously believes that Negroes will always be the meek and submissive creatures that circumstances have forced them to be during the past three hundred years. Dick Rowland was only an ordinary bootblack with no standing in the community. But when his life was threatened by a mob of whites, every one of the 15,000 Negroes

Introduction

The arc of the moral universe is long, but it bends toward justice.

Rev. Dr. Martin Luther King, Jr.

Understanding American history generally—and Tulsa history, specifically—requires an appreciation of the profound, enduring legacy of American chattel slavery,[7] including its ties to American exceptionalism.

> Out of slavery—and the anti-black racism it required—grew nearly everything that has truly made American exceptional: its economic might, its industrial power, its electoral system, diet and popular music, the inequities of its public health and education, its astonishing penchant for violence, its income inequality, the example it set for the world as a land of freedom and equality, its slang, its legal system and the endemic racial fears and hatreds that continue to plague it to this day. The seeds of all that were planted long before our official birth date, in 1776, when the men known as our founders formally declared independence from Britain.[8]

That people once passed for property posed an existential challenge to the new republic, the menacing legacy of which endures to this day.

> The United States of America, 'a new nation, conceived in liberty and dedicated to the proposition that all men are created equal,' began as a slave society. What can rightly be called the 'original sin,' slavery has left an indelible imprint on our national soul. A terrible price had to be paid, in a tragic, calamitous civil war, before this new democracy could be rid of that most undemocratic institution. But for black Americans the end of slavery was just the beginning of our quest for democratic equality; another century would pass before the nation came fully to embrace that goal. Even now millions of Americans recognizably of African descent languish in socie-

1

tal backwaters.[9]

In Oklahoma, the reach of the peculiar institution—slavery—extended beyond the white/black duality so familiar to most of us. The Five Civilized Tribes—the Cherokee, Muscogee (Creek), Chickasaw, Choctaw, and Seminole—all sanctioned chattel slavery, though relationships between Native Americans and African Americans ran the gamut from intimacy to enslavement.

Richard Franklin, a participant in the *Oklahoma Slave Narratives*, offered a window into the lesser known world of African chattel slavery among one of those tribes.

> I was born in the Creek Nation, March 1, 1856. My mother was named Thamore Franklin, she was one-fourth Creek Indian and was married to a negro slave, Fred Franklin, who was a slave of James Yargee of the Creek Nation. I am one-eighth Creek Indian and seven-eighths negro. My father was born in the Creek Nation and he, with nine other slaves, worked on the farm of Jim Yargee in the Creek Nation until 1867 when the Civil War was over. My mother was allotted one hundred and sixty acres of land near Canadian and moved on it with me when I was eleven years old. My mother drew Indian money under the Creek Treaty of 1866, when the Government agreed to pay the Creeks for all damage done in the war and also allot them land. I worked with my father until I was twenty years old and applied to the government for an allotment and they gave me one hundred and sixty acres of land in the Creek Nation. I was married to Fannie Franklin in 1876 and moved on my farm and we had seven children, two are now living, Edd and Jess, who live in Muskogee County; they are farmers. Father died in 1916 in Muskogee at the age of ninety-nine years. My mother died so long ago I don't remember what year. I was five years old when the Civil War broke out, and when Lincoln freed the slaves, some went to Kansas, some went to the army and some hid out in the woods and lived in hollow trees. The Government tried to make some go to war and did make some but we moved about one-half

mile from Fort Gibson until after the war.[10]

Throughout our history, the social construct that is race has been at the center of base acts of inhumanity. Tulsa witnessed one such emblematic event, and still grapples with its legacy.

The essential question for Tulsa in 2021, the anniversary of a defining and defiling moment in the city's history, is: What has Tulsa done in the interim between 1921 and 2021 to advance race relations and build a unified and just community?

Tulsa experienced historical trauma in 1921. The events of May 31 - June 1, 1921, affected Tulsans then, and continue to affect Tulsans in the here and now. While the wounds may not be open and apparent to all—the psychological scars hidden—they nonetheless conitue to impact the entire community, whether or not particular individuals are connected directly, or even generationally, to the source of the trauma. We are all influenced by the traumatized individuals within our midst.

Historical trauma, the cumulative emotional harm to an individual or generation caused by a traumatic experience or event, helps explain the gulf of mistrust still evident between Tulsa's African American population and its white majority. What came to be known as the 1921 Tulsa Race Riot (more commonly referred today as the 1921 Tulsa Race Massacre) represents a massive, generation-spanning fracture yet to be healed. The one-hundredth anniversary of that seminal point in Tulsa time offers an opportunity to reflect on how we have set our wound and what rehabilitative care remains.

Genocide. Slavery. Forced relocation. Destruction of cultural practices.

These experiences, shared by communities, can result in cumulative emotional and psychological wounds that are carried across generations. Researchers and practitioners call this concept historical trauma.

The effects of the traumas inflicted on groups of people because of their race, creed, and ethnicity linger on the souls of their descendants. As a result, many people in these same communities experience higher rates of mental and physical illness, substance abuse, and erosion in families and community structures. The persistent cycle of trauma destroys family and communities and threatens the vibrancy of entire cultures.

Historical trauma is not just about what happened in the past. It's about what's still happening.[11]

This book, *Black Wall Street 100: An American City Grapples With Its Historical Racial Trauma*, answers the essential question posed above, though perhaps not in a wholly satisfactory way. We, Tulsans, continue to make progress, sometimes slowly, often incrementally, but progress nonetheless.

What Dr. W.E.B. Du Bois expressed so eloquently well over one-hundred years ago about the black experience still holds true. "One ever feel his twoness—an American, a Negro; two souls, two thoughts, two unreconciled strivings; two warring ideals in one dark body, whose strength alone keeps it from being torn asunder."[12]

Segregation persists. Racial disparities—breathtaking differences in life outcomes—endure. Distrust regularly impedes understanding.

We—all of us—experience what most cities experience: The unfinished business borne of a traumatic national history around race—slavery, peonage, Jim Crow, lynching, "race riots," political oppression, economic exploitation, social isolation, mass incarceration, and so much more. By act and omission, through sanction and silence, in ways covert and overt, we are part of the institutional, systemic machinery that continues to foster disparities and inequities.

Still, we cling to one thing that makes working toward an improved, shared future in Tulsa worthwhile: hope. With that hope, we have done and are doing remarkable things that, over time, fashion the ties that bind and build the bridges that connect.

Our work remains, as does a ready pool of workers. I count myself in that number.

When Dr. Martin Luther King, Jr., visited Tulsa, he spoke of black agency—active participation in the political, social, and economic life of the community to bring about desired change.

Dr. King, then President of the Southern Christian Leadership Conference, came to Tulsa on Thursday, July 28, 1960. He spoke to more than 1,500 people at First Baptist Church, North Tulsa—the largest crowd in the church's history at the time.

Dr. King emphasized that the most important thing black Tulsans could do for civil rights is to take "the short walk to the voting booth." He continued, "You are unfair to yourselves when you have only 4,000 voters registered out of a potential 15,000."

Noting the momentous nature of the occasion, Dr. King also stressed the importance of humanitarianism, the pursuit of excellence, financial and moral support for organizations engaged in the civil rights struggle, and nonviolent direct action against the evils of segregation.

As he often did, Dr. King spoke to the imperative and power of love: "If we go into this new order with bitterness in our hearts, the new order will soon become the same as the old. Someone must have sense enough to know that love is better than hate."

Dr. King may well have been aware of the hate on full display in Tulsa just thirty-nine years earlier. He may have known that black Tulsans somehow found love during those dark, lonely days and, with that love, resurrected their famed community, dubbed "Negro Wall Street" (*a.k.a.* Black Wall Street), in remarkably short order.[13]

Untreated, the wounds of history fester like necrotizing fasciitis (*a.k.a.*, flesh-eating disease), spreading uncontrollably while feeding off our souls.[14] Knowledge is a ready, if not wholly curative, antibiotic. Foreknowledge can be an inoculation against repetition.

American chattel slavery, lynchings, "race riots," peonage, Jim Crow segregation, and all manner of white dominance and anti-black sentiments and actions persisted—indeed, to some extent, persist—in part because we woefully fail to own our past (including our colonial legacy), its relevance in our present, and its lessons for our future.

Truth. The truth. Our truth. When we seek it, claim it, and recount it, we are far less likely, in this the realm of our racial history, to repeat it.

W.E.B. Du Bois, Harvard-trained sociologist and famed civil rights advocate, pondered the purpose of history in his 1935 book, *Black Reconstruction in America*:

> If . . . we are going to use history for our pleasure and amusement, for inflating our national ego, and giving us a false but pleasurable sense of accomplishment, then we must give up the idea of history as a science or as an art using the results of science, and admit frankly that we are using a version of historic fact in order to influence and educate the new generation along the way we wish.

> It is propaganda like this that has led men in the past to insist that history is 'lies agreed upon'; and to point out the danger in such misinformation. It is indeed extremely doubtful if any permanent benefit comes to the world through such action. Nations reel and stagger on their way; they make hideous mistakes; they commit frightful wrongs; they do great and beautiful things. And shall we not best guide humanity by telling the truth about all this, so far as the truth is ascertainable?[15]

In Tulsa, truth-telling around one incident proved slow in coming. Some Tulsans still grapple with the veritable conspiracy of silence (or perhaps deafening disinterest) enshrouding the calamitous, racialized violence that gripped the city in 1921.[16]

> The 1921 Tulsa Race Riot was the worst moment in Tulsa's history. Bigotry, fear and hatred overflowed in a murderous rampage. The public safety systems that should have protected the city's black community failed completely, and the result was horrifying—a badge of shame that Tulsa will never completely live down.

> *Tulsa World*, November 18, 2008

The power in this narrative lies within the human spirit--the capacity of Tulsa's African American community members to endure and ultimately prevail in the face of long odds. Few people exemplify that human spirit better than Dr. Olivia Hooker.

One of the last survivors of the Tulsa disaster and inarguably one of its most compelling witnesses, Dr. Olivia Juliette Hooker, died at her home in White Plains, New York, on November 21, 2018, at age 103.

Dr. Hooker, a graduate of Ohio State University (bachelor's degree, 1937), Columbia University (master's degree, 1947), and the University of Rochester (Ph.D., 1961), began her professional life as an elementary school teacher. She later became the first African American woman to enlist in the United States Coast Guard and, following her military stint, embarked upon a distinguished career as a professor of psychology at New York's Fordham University.

At age six, Dr. Hooker and other black Tulsans experienced an orgy of violence as a teeming white mob invaded Tulsa's African American community, the present-day Greenwood District,[17] destroying homes, businesses, and lives in what would be called the 1921 Tulsa Race Riot.

Dr. Hooker recalled seeing men with torches storming into her family's backyard and her mother acting to protect her and her three siblings. In a National Public Radio interview, she recalled: "Our mother put us under the table. She took the longest tablecloth she had to cover four children and told us not to say a word."[18]

White hoodlums burst into the Hooker home, taking an ax to the family piano, destroying her dolls' clothes, and pillaging items of value. Meanwhile, back on Black Wall Street, roving gangs obliterated virtually everything in sight, including Samuel Hooker's clothing store [Elliott & Hooker, Clothing and Dry Goods, 124 North Greenwood Avenue]. "I guess the most shocking thing was seeing people, to whom you had never done anything to irritate, who just took it upon themselves to destroy your property because they didn't want you to have those things," she said. "And they were teaching you a lesson. Those were all new ideas to me."[19]

Dr. Hooker, in an oral history recorded in 2015 for the White Plains Public Library, referred to "the terrible catastrophe in Tulsa." She explained, "other people call it the Tulsa riot. It really wasn't a riot—we were the victims."[20]

The Hooker family migrated first to Topeka, Kansas, and then to Ohio, after the decimation of Tulsa's black community.

Dr. Hooker worked with the Oklahoma Commission to Study the Tulsa Race Riot of 1921, whose award-winning 2001 final report spurred awareness and action around the residual effects of Tulsa's calamity. She also testified about her traumatic Tulsa experience before members of the Congressional Black Caucus and others on Capitol Hill in 2005.

In 2015, at age 100, Dr. Hooker attended the commencement ceremonies at the Coast Guard Academy in New London, Connecticut. The commencement speaker, President Barack Obama, highlighted her accomplishments. "She has been a professor and mentor to her students," President Obama noted, "a passionate advocate for Americans with disabilities, a psychologist counseling young children, a caregiver at the height of the AIDS epidemic, a tireless voice for justice and equality."[21]

Though now stilled, Dr. Hooker's voice continues to resonate and inspire. Others have taken up the mantle of justice on behalf of those who suffered and died during Tulsa's darkest days.

Following are thoughts on the significance of the 100th anniversary of the "1921 Tulsa Race Riot" from various Tulsans and individuals with Tulsa ties.[22]

- *Mayor G.T. Bynum*, Tulsa Mayor, 2016 - present: "The year 1921 marks the opposite of what we want Tulsa to be: hate-fueled, divided, ignorant, unjust. The year 2021 is an opportunity for us to not just remember the lives tragically lost, but to challenge ourselves to be the kind of city we wish Tulsa had been then: motivated by love for our neighbors, united, educated, and just."

- *Senator Judy Eason-McIntyre*, former Oklahoma State Senator: "Ignoring the ugly parts of Oklahoma history benefits no one. It is imperative that the 100-year anniversary of the 1921 Tulsa Race Massacre be commemorated for two reasons: (1) It allows us to honor the victims, which requires us to be educated and to never forget; and (2) It will finally provide hope for the future for learning from the horrible experience so that we never let this kind of history repeat itself."

- *Rabbi Marc Boone Fitzerman*, Congregation B'nai Emunah:

"Tulsa tells two stories. The first is about philanthropy, entrepreneurialism, and *noblesse oblige*. The second is about violent racism and its long-lasting consequences. The second is as important as the first, and the Greenwood Massacre has to be part of the way we think about our city. The anniversary gives us another chance to tell the story with empathy as a way of honoring the victims and enfranchising their descendants."

- *Reuben Gant*, Executive Director, John Hope Franklin Center for Reconciliation: "Confronting the truth about our history is the first step towards reconciliation. Commemoration plays a far-reaching role in encouraging community-wide reconciliation."

- *Karlos K. Hill*, Ph.D., Interim Director and Associate Professor, African and African American Studies; Faculty Fellow, Dunham College, University of Oklahoma: "We should remember the Tulsa Massacre not for the violence and destruction, but rather for the black community's resilience and perseverance."

- *Senator Maxine Cissel Horner*, former Oklahoma State Senator: "It is important to commemorate the 1921 Tulsa Race Riot to acknowledge the senseless and racist attack on a thriving community. It is also imperative that we celebrate and honor Riot survivors whose voices and stories are a vital part of the Greenwood Cultural Center and the National Museum of African American History and Culture."

- *Frances Jordan-Rakestraw*, Executive Director, Greenwood Cultural Center: "This horrific event affected the lives and the culture of many people in North Tulsa. We need to know this history so that such an event will never happen again."

- *Ken Levit*, Executive Director, George Kaiser Family Foundation: "Even though a century has passed, the impact of the 1921 race massacre is experienced every day in our present lives in Tulsa. We see its results in a physical sense and feel the aftermath in our interactions as citizens in our community. A part of our very fabric, our history—its tragedies and the triumphs—creates a space for us to build relationships and experience our lives together. The work that has gained momentum in the recent decades around the 1921 race massacre has only become more relevant—not less—in our lives. 1921 will not let go of us. And it should not."

- *Rick Lowe*, Internationally-renowned artist and McArthur Fellow: "The 1921 Tulsa Race Massacre offers us the worst and the best examples of humanity. The Centennial is an opportunity to see the massacre for the evil it was and to commit ourselves to the amazing spirit of the builders of Black Wall Street, Tulsa. The Centennial is a teaching moment for all of these United States of America."

- *Oklahoma Senator Kevin Matthews*: "This is our opportunity to turn this tragedy into triumph and to show the resilience in Tulsa and the relationships that are being built, out of which untold opportunities will arise."

- *Larry O'Dell*, Director of Special Projects and Development at Oklahoma Historical Society: "The 100th anniversary of the Tulsa Race Riot is an opportunity to shine a bright light on the racial injustice of that dark moment in Oklahoma's history. Every Oklahoman should know that this horrific event happened and strive to improve egalitarianism for successive generations."

- *Mayor Rodger A. Randle*, former President Pro Tempore of the Oklahoma Senate, Mayor of the City of Tulsa, President of the University Center at Tulsa; Professor and Director of the Center for Studies in Democracy and Culture at the University of Oklahoma-Tulsa: "Our City's history is the reality that made us. The 1921 Tulsa Race Riot reminds us from where we have come, and it opens our eyes to dangers that are latent within us. For most of Tulsa's history, the riot was a story carefully buried in oblivion. Resurrecting this history has raised Tulsa's consciousness of its past and challenged us to build a more just community."

- *Representative Don Ross*, former Oklahoma State Representative: "Having been very involved in earlier efforts and having been thwarted by insincere blacks and indifferent whites—

and having missed some golden opportunities—I have chosen to retire from commemorations. I am indifferent about continuing celebration. For me, it's applauding 'going backwards.'"[23]

- *M. Susan Savage*, former Tulsa Mayor and Oklahoma Secretary of State; CEO, Morton Comprehensive Health Services: "As Tulsa approaches the 100th anniversary of the 1921 Race Massacre, the healing continues. Through the historical context created by Hannibal B. Johnson, we are reminded, individually and collectively, of the relentless effort to live together as people. The lessons learned from the tragedy of 1921 continue to teach us that our only choice is to treat one another with dignity, respect, and a sense of shared responsibility."

- *Kathy L. Taylor*, former Oklahoma Secretary of Commerce and Tourism and Tulsa Mayor: "Hannibal B. Johnson's writing continues to help each of us learn about the horrific history of the 1921 Tulsa Race Riot and the lingering economic and social divide that continues to hold our community back. His latest book should allow each of us to not only learn the history and the current impact of those events, but also understand our own biases and how each of us can work daily to change the systemic racism that exists."

O' Greenwood! Lest You Go Unheralded

Wynonia Murray Bailey, 1921 Tulsa Race Massacre Survivor (1967)[24]

She held the hopes and
future of her own
Others heard and came
to pay her homage
She was a showcase for the industrious
She stood the monument of the proud

And now, men falter midst her rubble
She symbolizes progress no more
A crone stripped of her finery
So slowly changed, so lowly bowed

Many whom she raised to dignity
Pass quickly by, all favors forgotten
Ignoring the sight of her deterioration
Aborting all thought of a second chance

Few remain to dignify her disgrace
Or fight to rescue her demise
The ghost of her better days awaits
Death rattles to intone the macabre dance

O' Greenwood! Lest you go unheralded
I sing a song of remembrance
While some of your bounty, loyal still
Place a headstone at the site of your victory.[25]

Wynonia Murray Bailey would be pleased. Her beloved Green-wood, though once brutalized and marginalized, has not gone unheralded. Indeed, people from all corners of the world, people of every stripe, now speak its name. The rich history of Tulsa's Greenwood District has become the stuff of Ph.D. dissertations, documentary films, plays, books, and even musical suites. The primary interest of the scholar, author, and the dilettante seems to lie in unmasking the horrific domestic violence that took place in 1921, the anniversary of which this work, *Black Wall Street 100, An American City Grapples With Its Historical Racial Trauma*, marks.

The imperative of setting things right—reckoning with histor-ical honesty and transparency—cannot be overstated. In so doing, we must commemorate that seminal event while being mindful of the bigger picture: the remarkable human spirit of those who envisioned, shaped, and sustained the Greenwood District up to and beyond that inflection point. We cannot fully understand the impact of the calamity and senseless violence that marked the "1921 Tulsa Race Riot" (the "riot")[26] unless we first understand the Greenwood District—Black Wall Street—prior to that cataclysmic historical marker.

Even today, the riot[27] looms large in Tulsa. Indeed, many chal-lenge the characterization of the event, referring to it with alter-native terms such as: assault, disaster, ethnic cleansing, genocide, holocaust, massacre, and pogrom. Other terms associated with the event have included: burning, calamity, catastrophe, cataclysm, eruption, Negro uprising, invasion, race war, and even civil war.[28]

A cursory examination of definitions reveals the subtlety and nuance attached to describing the events of May 31 and June 1, 1921, in Tulsa accurately. Following are some of the more commonly used labels, defined:

Assault: A physical attack.

Disaster: A sudden event, such as an accident or a natural catastrophe, that causes great damage or loss of life.

Ethnic cleansing: The mass expulsion or killing of members of an unwanted ethnic or religious group in a society.

Genocide: the deliberate killing of a large group of people, especially those of a particular ethnic group or nation.

Holocaust: Destruction or slaughter on a mass scale, especially caused by fire or nuclear war.

Massacre: An indiscriminate and brutal slaughter of people.

Pogrom: An organized massacre of a particular ethnic group, in particular that of Jews in Russia or eastern Europe.

Riot: A violent disturbance of the peace by a crowd. NOTE: A "white riot," then, would be such a violent disturbance of the peace effected by white people.[29]

The choice of one label to the exclusion of all others leads inexorably to likely unintended consequences, the most significant of which may be a version of the "chilling effect." That is, when we insist that one descriptor fully occupies the field, with no room left for other terms, we risk shutting down what might otherwise have been a rich, productive discussion. The risk is even greater when shaming follows the failure to adhere to "acceptable" terminology.

Words matter. Names matter. So, too, does critical thinking around nomenclature. "Race riot" is a term of art—a phrase with special historical context and connotation. It has existed and will continue to exist in historical and archival materials. That said, nothing prohibits us in the present from reclaiming and renaming the event as we see fit.

Questions to consider around the use and appropriateness of

that "race riot" tag include: (1) Who named the event?; (2) Who was missing from the table (*i.e.,* voiceless) at the time of the naming?; (3) What is the substantive significance of the chosen moniker?; (4) What alternative labels might one attach the event to better describe what occurred?; and (5) Should such an event occur today, how might we ensure the soundness of its naming, both procedurally and substantively?

It may well be that more than one term applies to a single event. Arguably, that is the case with respect to what historically has been known as the "1921 Tulsa Race Riot." The debate over naming should not overshadow the substantive facts surrounding the event itself which, by any measure, qualify as cataclysmic.[30]

The 1921 Tulsa Race Massacre Centennial Commission ("Centennial Commission") began as the 1921 Tulsa Race *Riot* Centennial Commission. The name officially changed on November 29, 2018. Commission Chair, Senator Kevin Matthews announced: "Although the dialogue about the reasons and effects of the terms riot [versus] massacre are very important and encouraged, the feelings and interpretation of those who experienced this devastation as well as current area residents and historical scholars have led us to more appropriately change the name to the 1921 [Tulsa] Race Massacre Commission."[31] Arguably, that change in nomenclature better characterizes the actuality of the event, which was deplorable regardless of the label one might affix to it.[32]

Like an irremovable scarlet letter, the 1921 Tulsa catastrophe, emblematic of the deadly racial tumult sweeping America at the time,[33] is a shame never fully erased. Its enduring legacy has been a gulf of racial distrust, manifest in myriad ways, some almost imperceptible; others, open and obvious.

Tulsans' inability to live down this dreadful part of our past suggests we ought to focus our energies on ways to *live up* to our potential. Now is the time to pause to ponder our past, its present legacy, and our shared future as a community; to remember, reclaim, and reconcile our history.

When the eyes of the nation——and perhaps the world—look to Tulsa in 2021, let it be known that Tulsa remembers, but no longer reflects, much of the mindset so evident in 1921. We have made significant progress in matters of race, even as we continue to struggle through the long slog toward equity.

At this, the centenary of this cataclysmic milestone, it behooves us to rededicate ourselves to healing our history, engaging in an appreciative (and searching) inquiry into our past, and reaffirming our too-often-spotty commitment to diversity, equity, and inclusion.

Where is Tulsa heading?

Dr. Martin Luther King popularized the notion of the "Beloved Community" as a society based on justice, equal opportunity, and love of one's fellow human beings. Decades later, this call for a Beloved Community remains as relevant and compelling as it did when it was first issued.

As explained by The King Center, the memorial institution founded by Coretta Scott King to further the goals of Dr. Martin Luther King, Jr.:

> Dr. King's Beloved Community is a global vision in which all people can share in the wealth of the earth. In the Beloved Community, poverty, hunger and homelessness will not be tolerated because international standards of human decency will not allow it. Racism and all forms of discrimination, bias, bigotry and prejudice will be replaced by an all-inclusive spirit of sisterhood and brotherhood; of shared humanity.[34]

Fundamental to the concept of the Beloved Community is inclusiveness—economic, political, and social. The notion that all can share in earth's bounty describes a society in which the social product is shared far more equitably than it is in the world as we know it.

The Beloved Community is aspirational. A mere aspiration without action, like faith without works, is dead. But the Beloved Community paradigm gives us both a path forward and a set of lofty goals for which to aim. What if Tulsa came to be known as a Beloved Community?

Healing our history presupposes, at a minimum: acknowledging past misdeeds; apologizing for past and ongoing harms; and atoning, as best we can, for the damage done—making amends.

When we do this, we may then engage, constructively, with one another in way-forward dialogue. It is about working through shared trauma and pain toward common understanding and shared space.

Hidden History
Hannibal B. Johnson

History as we know it...
The history we don't know.

Discovery, hegemony:
   Civilize "savages;"
   Shackle slaves.
Whitewashed history.

Colonization, conquest:
   Protect property;
   Manifest destiny.
Eurocentric history.

Victors, vanquished:
   Declare winners;
   Stifle strife.
Anodyne history.

Rights, realties:
   Proclaim equality;
   Deny dignity.
Asymmetrical history.

Foundational facts, inconvenient truths:
   Question authority;
   Pressure power.
Unvarnished history.

Fundamental freedom, real justice:
   Celebrate struggles;
   Mark movements.
Social history.

Open wounds, lasting pain:
> *Strategize solutions;*
> *Reconcile differences.*

Healing history.

New voices, untold stories
> *Live legacy;*
> *Preserve past.*

People's history.

History as we know it . . .
The history we don't know.[35]

We—Americans—seem to go out of our way to avoid tackling the too-long-avoided topic of race. The meaningful, sustained, productive conversations that could chip away at the systemic, institutional barriers giving rise to race-based disparities and inequities remain off-putting for far too many.

We will continue to struggle with issues of race unless and until we bind up the wounds of our history. For Tulsans, the most obvious such wound is the so-called 1921 Tulsa Race Riot.

The Tulsa catastrophe devastated the Tulsa's Greenwood District, the successful African-American entrepreneurial enclave dubbed "Negro Wall Street" and, later, "Black Wall Street."[36]

Scores died. Still more suffered grievous physical and psychological injuries. Property damage soared into the millions of dollars. This cataclysmic event, the worst of the many such violent, race-based incidents in twentieth century America, altered the delicate balance of race relations in Tulsa for decades to come.

In the wake of this historic trauma, psychological dynamics—shame, blame, guilt, fear, and post-traumatic stress disorder—conspired to render the community virtually silent about its sins; powerless to confront its own demons. Silence is never neutral, though. Silence always speaks.

This stubborn refusal to acknowledge, let alone reckon with, our tragic past has done harm—arguably, irreparable harm. Still, the path toward reconciliation remains in sight.[37]

The Tulsa community is still in the process of healing its history. Trust-building is key.

"Social capital," the value of social networks that bond similar people and bridge between diverse people, with norms of reciprocity, leverages individual capacities for group gains. Simply stated, it is the goodwill we leverage from our positive relationships with others, whether through sharing information and resources, providing aid and assistance, or relying upon trust built over time through meaningful, positive interactions.

Often overlooked and undervalued, social capital is among the ties that bind. Though not readily quantified and monetized, it brings inestimable value to individuals and communities. Racial reconciliation is one of many potential returns on an investment in social capital in general, and trust-building, specifically.

In Tulsa, surface calm long veiled a range of suppressed emotions that swelled over time along color lines. Among African Americans, anger, fear, sadness, post-traumatic stress disorder, and distrust took hold. Among whites, blame, shame, guilt, and regret dominated the psychological circuitry.

People scarcely whispered about those ghastly days, May 31 and June 1, 1921, as though refusing to give voice to the calamity might magically make it disappear. Local image mavens sought to sanitize—to erase the conflagration from the community's consciousness. City leaders proceeded as though the devastation, like white chalk on a blackboard, could somehow be wiped away—erased from our collective memory. In the ensuing decades, few dared to address it pedagogically, and textbooks routinely omitted references to this damnable chapter in our history.

The full dimensions of this epic tragedy, buried layers-deep in the city's community consciousness, have only been recently realized. That years-long obfuscation stunted Tulsa's growth, physically, emotionally, and spiritually. Despite progress in fits and starts, our failure to come clean about our dirty little secret undermined our ability to: understand Tulsa's role in the twentieth century American race drama; build trust across the great chasm of race; and use history as a springboard for strategic, transformational change.

The past looms large in our present. While the kind of racism so evident in 1921 no longer dominates our lives, subtle remnants of that dynamic persists. Today, it is not about blatant, in-your-face kinds of racial incidents, rather, it is about the disparities and inequities that manifest in employment, health care, education, and other arenas. It is about a curriculum that only marginally covers the vast contributions of people of color and, until recently, wholly omitted the history of Tulsa's Historic Greenwood District. It is about the salt-in-the-wound reminders of white supremacy and slavery and Jim Crow that come with schools named for the likes of Robert E. Lee, Jean-Pierre Choteau, Andrew Jackson, and Christopher Columbus.[38] Like other places around the nation, we are finally discussing how distorting—whitewashing—our history and lionizing certain individuals of dubious character inflicts real harms upon real people.

We sense our own illness, yet we seem incapable of administering more than palliative care. Though we may feel less pain, the underlying disorder—a system built on power and privilege—endures.

If we are to reach our full potential, we must take the lessons of the past, utilize them in the present, and project them into our positive, shared vision for the future. Only by stepping back into our past and reconciling with it will we be able to sprint forward toward new horizons.

Our challenge is not simply healing from the historical trauma that our racial violence wrought, but rather doing that *plus* addressing the ongoing traumas we continue to face. It is about addressing the past, attending to the present, and advancing an inclusive vision for the future.

Like healing our history, an appreciative inquiry requires a searching look in the rearview mirror. It counsels us to look back for inspiration and example—for past positives that captivate and catalyze us in the present to fashion a more favorable future. The circumstances surrounding the massacre offer just such an opportunity.

As noted, the 1921 Tulsa calamity leveled the Greenwood District—"Black Wall Street"—a storied enclave of black businesspersons on and near Greenwood Avenue who gained renown for

their entrepreneurial pluck. The Greenwood District founders envisioned lives beyond the imagination of many African Americans
of the time. Some thrived amidst deep-seated, race-based hostility
from virtually all quarters. Sometimes bloodied, but always un-
bowed, they raised the social, political, and economic bars during
a period known as the nadir of race relations in America.

The lessons and legacy of the Black Wall Street architects offer a platform from which to empower young men and women,
promote self-development and self-sufficiency, and launch a new
corps of black business owners. Historical role models matter, not
as replacements for such paragons in the here-and-now, but as
supplements to them.

That said, successful twenty-first century entrepreneurs cannot be bound by the binary racial equation of the past. At the community, state, national, and global levels, racial and ethnic diversity abounds. Our challenge is figuring out ways to leverage that
diversity for mutual advantage. We must heed the exhortation of
the legendary Cheyenne chief, Morning Star (*a.k.a.*, "Dull Knife"),
"Let us make a new way."[39]

Diversity, equity, and inclusion rest on the fundamental proposition that our shared humanity trumps all that might otherwise
separate and divide us. Our community is defined by how we
treat the least among us. In 1921, Tulsa provided a tragic but illustrative case of our capacity for inhumanity.

The saga of Tulsa's Historic Greenwood District, both in times
of triumph and tragedy, centers on the indomitable human spirit—a people's incredible capacity to be forward-thinking and nimble in the face of ever-changing circumstances. The lessons from
this rich history remain timeless.

At the five-score anniversary of Tulsa's deadly racial violence,
let us exhale, and then let us breathe freely, oxygenating our efforts on three fronts: (1) making an appreciative inquiry into our
past so as to leverage our assets and advantages for community
betterment; (2) healing our history by binding up the wounds of
our past through acknowledgement, apology, and atonement; and
(3) recommitting to diversity, equity, and inclusion—to the cardinal principle that we are only as good as our proverbial weakest
link and the shared understanding that we all matter equally. If we

do this, we will have honored the memory of our darkest days by illuminating them with a bright new light.

The Centennial Commission seeks to "leverage the rich history surrounding the 1921 Tulsa Race Massacre by facilitating actions, activities, and events that commemorate and educate all citizens." Its projects serve to "educate Oklahomans and Americans about the Race Massacre and its impact on the state and Nation; remember its victims and survivors; and create an environment conducive to fostering sustainable entrepreneurship and heritage tourism within the Greenwood District specifically, and North Tulsa generally."

The Centennial Commission's emphasis on the Greenwood District and North Tulsa highlights both a once prosperous, segregated black community worthy of elevation and the historical reality of an underserved, marginalized black population situated, in part, in these geographic areas.

In the fall of 2018, Centennial Commission members embarked upon a $30 million capital campaign to enhance the Greenwood District, adding a world-class, museum-quality experience. Other projects include: (1) a Pathway To Hope, a self-guided tour of the Greenwood District expected to include a downloadable phone app with information about various landmarks; (2) a teacher institute designed to develop teachers' knowledge about substantive Greenwood District history and skills in terms of best-practices pedagogy for teaching that history; and (3) a 100-day countdown to the centennial with a signature event marking each day.[40]

Members of the Centennial Commission and community leaders traveled to Montgomery, Alabama in the spring of 2019 seeking an opportunity to build *esprit de corps* and find inspiration in that city's remarkable history centers, the National Memorial for Peace and Justice, the Legacy Museum of African American History, and the Rosa Parks Museum. The experience offered insights into place-making, facility design, and approaches to historical narrative. Commissioners emerged reenergized and committed to telling the story of Tulsa's Historic Greenwood District in a way that connects emotionally with Tulsans and visitors alike.[41]

The Centennial Commission rose from humble beginnings in 2015. Its founder, Oklahoma Senator Kevin Matthews, recounted its origin story.

The Centennial Commission grew out of discussions with Dr. Lester Shaw of Tulsa and others who brought forth the idea of enhancing cultural tourism. We had been in discussions at the Capitol about the state of the Native American Cultural Center being built in Oklahoma City while Tulsa's Greenwood Cultural Center and other entities related to African American Culture had gone wanting of government resources and support at nearly every level. I had an Interim Study approved by the Senate Pro Tempore, the leader of the Senate, in July of 2015. The study clarified the uniqueness of this issue, as well as the potential revenue generation for the State. In December 2015, we had the first formal meeting to start the Centennial Commission, designated by me as State Senator of District 11, to do those things we ultimately memorialized in the Centennial Commission's mission statement. This took no formal resolution or a vote from the Oklahoma Legislature, although the Governor and every level of elected official agreed with the mission and thus joined the Centennial Commission. Careful collaboration, clarification, and organization, led to crafting Senate Bill 17,[42] a revolving fund held at the Oklahoma History Center and managed by the Oklahoma Historical Society, passed both the Senate and the House unanimously and was signed into law.[43]

This book, endorsed by the Centennial Commission and the 400 Years of African American History Commission, furthers the educational mission of both bodies. *Black Wall Street 100: An American City Grapples With Its Historical Racial Trauma* offers updates on developments in Tulsa generally and in Tulsa's Greenwood District specifically since the publication of *Black Wall Street: From Riot to Renaissance in Tulsa's Historic Greenwood District.*[44] This work is a window into what distinguishes the Tulsa of today from the Tulsa of a century ago. Before peering through that porthole, we must first reflect on Black Wall Street history.

Chapter One

Revisiting Our Roots

When the roots are deep, there's no reason to fear the wind.
Chinese proverb

Persons of African descent arrived in present-day Oklahoma in three principal waves: (1) with Spanish explorers in the sixteenth century; (2) with the "Five Civilized Tribes" during their forced migration from the Southeastern United States during the "Trail of Tears" era of the 1830s and 1840s; and (3) in the post-Reconstruction Diaspora from the Southeastern United States, principally in the 1880s and 1890s. It is the latter two waves that gained traction.

The African American journey with their Native American kin has been largely ignored.

"Go West, young man, and grow up with the country" is advice widely credited to Horace Greeley (1811 -1872), a nineteenth century politician and founder of the *New-York Tribune*. This admonition, consistent with the Manifest Destiny philosophy of the day, encouraged settlement of America's western lands, irrespective of the "collateral damage" to the indigenous people already there.[45]

For the southeastern United States-based Five Civilized Tribes (Cherokee, Muscogee (Creek), Chickasaw, Choctaw, and Seminole), "Go West" became not an admonition, but a command. The federal government forcibly removed these tribes to Indian Territory in the West (the eastern half of modern-day Oklahoma) in the 1830s and 1840s.[46]

The Five Civilized Tribes, all of whom practiced chattel slavery, participated in the Civil War, with combatants and supporters on both sides, but with all tribes officially aligning with the Confederacy. That wartime alignment would have significant consequences.[47]

The conclusion of the Civil War and the beginning of African American liberation it wrought seemed ripe with opportunities to stake claims to land, and thus further erode the racial caste system that limited life prospects for African Americans. Progress loomed on the horizon.

At a January 1865 meeting with Union General William Tecumseh Sherman and Secretary of War Edwin M. Stanton, a black Baptist minister named Garrison Frazier, himself formerly enslaved, responded to the age-old question, "What do the Negroes want?" Reverend Frazier noted: "The way we can best take care of ourselves is to have land, and turn it and till it by our own labor . . . . and we can soon maintain ourselves and have something to spare . . . We want to be placed on land until we are able to buy it and make it our own." Someone asked the Reverend whether the newly-freed people preferred to live among whites or in relative isolation. He opined: "I would prefer to live by ourselves, for there is a prejudice against us in the South that will take years to get over . . . ." Four days later, having sought and gained the approval of President Lincoln, General Sherman issued Special Field Order No. 15.[48]

The common refrain, "forty acres and a mule" traces back to General Sherman's Order. The Order itself calls for up to forty acres of tillable ground per family in specified parts of the South. Field Order No. 15 makes no mention of mules.[49] However, General Sherman later decreed that the Army could lend the unseasoned settlers mules—beasts of burden—to assist them on their newly-acquired land.[50]

This bold gesture of reparation swelled the hopes on many formerly enslaved African Americans. They believed and were told by various political figures that they had a right to own the land they had long worked while enslaved. They were eager to control their own property, and their own destiny.

Theirs would be a dream deferred. President Andrew Johnson, Lincoln's South-sympathizing successor, countermanded Order No. 15 in the fall of 1865, ceding the lands back to the southern planters who had waged war on the United States.[51]

Still, freed people widely expected to legally claim 40 acres of land and a mule after the end of the Civil War, long after the reversal of proclamations such as Field Order No. 15 and the *Freedmen's*

NOTICE.

Cherokee - Freedmen - Enrollment.

The Commission to the Five Civilized Tribes will continue in session at

MUSKOGEE, IND. TER.,

from April 1, 1902, until May 31, 1902, inclusive, for the purpose of hearing rebuttal and supplemental testimony with respect to the enrollment of Cherokee Freedmen.

Notice is hereby given to all Freedmen listed as doubtful claimants that after May 31, 1902, their cases will be considered as completed, and will be finally decided by the Commission and reported to the Secretary of the Interior for his approval.

Native Cherokees, Freedmen, or Claimants by adoption who have not already appeared can apply for enrollment until July 1, 1902.

Mr. George Vann,
Ft. Gibson, I.T.
Cherokee F-D-173
Register.

TAMS BIXBY,
T. B. NEEDLES,
C. R. BRECKINRIDGE,
Commissioners.

Example of a Cherokee Freedman notice of Dawes Commission hearing from 1902.[54]

Bureau Act, which also offered various assistance to these now-freed persons.

For the Freedmen in Indian Territory (part of present-day Oklahoma), the persons of African ancestry living among the Five Civilized Tribes, access to land became a real and enduring reality. The Freedmen received land allotments pursuant to their tribal relationships, based upon the *Treaties of 1866* negotiated between the Five Civilized Tribes and the federal government after the Civil War, and pursuant to the Dawes Commission allotment process that broke up communal tribal lands.[52] By act of Congress on March 3, 1893, the federal government charged the Dawes Commission, named after its chairman, Senator Henry Dawes of Massachusetts, with negotiating agreements with the Choctaw, Muscogee (Creek), Chickasaw, Seminole, and Cherokee Nations.[53]

In addition to this forced migration with Native Americans, the post-Reconstruction Diaspora brought African Americans to Oklahoma. Prominently in Kansas, then principally in Oklahoma, all-black towns founded by black visionaries and risk-takers like E.P. McCabe mushroomed in the post-Reconstruction era. Weary Southern migrants formed their own frontier communities, largely self-sustaining and self-governing. These rural, all-black towns offered hope—hope of a respite from second-class citizenship; hope of political self-determination; and hope of full participation through land ownership in the American economic dream.

African American booster E.P. McCabe and others touted Oklahoma, then divided into Indian Territory and Oklahoma Territory, as a virtual "promised land" for African Americans. McCabe dreamed of an all-black state carved out of Oklahoma Territory. He and his equally ambitious late 1800s-contemporaries sought to wean African Americans from the breast of that special form of Southern hospitality on which they had been nursed—racism.

Oklahoma attracted hordes of weary Southerners fleeing the oppression of the Jim Crow South. Though McCabe's "black state" dream never materialized, Oklahoma boasts more than fifty all-black towns throughout its history—more than any other state. These are, in part, McCabe's legacy.

The promise of Oklahoma faded significantly when it became a state in 1907. The new Oklahoma Legislature passed as its first measure Senate Bill Number 1. That law firmly ensconced segregation as the law of the land in Oklahoma. Jim Crow reigned.[55]

Despite an auspicious beginning, the all-black town movement crested between 1890 and 1910, a time when American capitalism transitioned from agrarian to urban. This seismic change, coupled with tectonic social, political, and economic shifts, ultimately sealed the fates of these unique, historic black oases. Many perished. Most faded. Only the strong survived. Those that remain serve as monuments to the power of hope, faith, and community and testaments to the indomitable human spirit.[56]

Early in the twentieth century, the black community in Tulsa—the "Greenwood District"—became a nationally renowned entrepreneurial center. In segregated Tulsa, the Greenwood District resembled an all-black-town-within-a-town.

The bulk of the Greenwood District sits on what were once Cherokee land allotments, with a small portion consisting of Muscogee (Creek) township lands set aside by the federal government. Land represents access to economic, political, and social standing--to the American Dream. For African Americans, particularly in the nineteenth and twentieth centuries, land served as the handmaiden of true freedom.

Upon this land, this parcel with Native American roots and ties, this downtown-adjacent acreage, the Greenwood District emerged.

Eli Grayson, a multiracial citizen of the Muscogee (Creek) Nation with ancestors listed as both Creek Freedmen (*i.e.,* descendants of formerly enslaved African-originated people) and Creek by blood (*i.e.,* descendants of people with ethnic Native American ancestry), bemoaned the lack of focus on the role of Creeks of Indian and African descent in creating the relative wealth in Tulsa's Historic Greenwood District.

> Unfortunately, the story [of Tulsa's Historic Greenwood District] is always told without understanding the circumstances that created this community and its wealth. What drew thousands of black immigrants from other states to the newly-created state of Oklahoma? This migration happened at a time when Jim Crow laws were at their harshest. My hope is that at some point one of the journalists who writes about Black Wall Street will thoughtfully consider this question.

> The story of the Greenwood District cannot be told completely without understanding the history of African chattel slavery by the Five Civilized Tribes in Indian Territory

and, specifically, in the context of the Muscogee (Creek) Nation. Citizens within these Indian Nations held people of African descent as property, freeing them after the Civil War through treaties in 1866 and making them tribal citizens with all the rights of Indian citizens. The Creek Freedmen land allotments are the foundation on which the wealth of the Greenwood District rests.[57] These allotments drew thousands of black seekers, particularly from the Deep South, to the area. These new migrants did business with the Creeks of African descent already present.

The map below shows the Creek Nation Territory domain. A clear one-third of the Creek Nation allotments, including mineral rights, went to its black citizens.

**Allotments of the Creek Nation 1899 thru 1906
According to Classifications of Creek Citizens**

It is my hope that journalists and others become more curious about the pre-history of Tulsa's Historic Greenwood
District.[58]

Buck Colbert Franklin, a prominent attorney in the early
Greenwood District and the father of eminent historian Dr. John
Hope Franklin, mused about the relationship of Tulsa to her red
and black pioneers:

> In the beginning, there was no segregation [in Tulsa] or ap-
> parently any thought of segregating the races. They lived
> together and were buried together. This was due, mostly, to
> the fact that the Indians and freedmen owned most, if not
> all, of the land. The federal government was in sole control
> of the titles to these lands, either directly or indirectly, and
> did not concern itself with the separation of races. In those
> days, I recall that Negro lawyers maintained their offices
> in downtown Tulsa and employed a white stenographer.
> There was at least one Negro barbershop, as well as a real
> estate office. At Archer and Cincinnati there was a [room-
> ing house] patronized by both races, and on the surface at
> least, no one thought anything about it.
>
> A few years before statehood [1907], however, there came
> to Tulsa two very rich Negroes, O.W. Gurley[59] and J.B.
> Stradford,[60] who immediately invested large sums in large
> acreages of real estate 'across the track.' Gurley bought
> some thirty or forty acres and had it surveyed, plotted into
> blocks, streets, and alleys, and put upon the market to be
> sold to Negroes only.[61] Then adjoining land was purchased
> by real estate men of other races, plotted and surveyed,
> streets and alleys laid out, and placed upon the market to
> be sold to Negroes only; and ever afterward the same pro-
> cess was repeated. In the end, Tulsa became one of the most
> sharply segregated cities in the country.

*   *   *   *

Following the great holocaust, there was a great letdown
in faith, ambition, hope, and trust. The immediate future
was blank. Two of the greatest leaders, O.W. Gurley and

J.B. Stradford, pulled up stakes and moved away, the former to California and the latter to Illinois.[62]

Sometime in the early nineteen-teens, legendary African American statesman and educator, Booker T. Washington, reportedly dubbed Greenwood Avenue, the nerve center of the community, "The Negro Wall Street," later updated to "Black Wall Street," for its now-famous bustling business climate.[63]

In 1913, seventeen-year-old Mabel B. Little arrived in the Greenwood District on a Frisco train from the all-black town of Boley, Oklahoma.[64] She had only $1.25. Much later in life, she reflected on what she saw upon arrival.

> Black businesses flourished. I remember Huff's Café on Cincinnati and Archer. It was a thriving meeting place in the black community. You could go there almost anytime, and just about everybody who was anybody would be there or be on their way.
>
> There were two popular barbeque spots, Tipton's and Uncle Steve's. J.D. Mann had a grocery store. His wife was a music teacher. We had funeral parlors, owned by morticians Sam Jackson and Hardel Ragston.
>
> Down on what went by the name of 'Deep Greenwood' was a clique of eateries, a panorama of lively dance halls, barber shops and theatres glittering in the night light, and a number of medical and dental offices.[65]

Similarly, young Mary Elizabeth Jones Parrish, who arrived in the Greenwood District in 1918, recalled:

> On leaving the Frisco station, going north on Archer Street one could see nothing but Negro business places. Going east on Archer Street for two or more blocks there you would behold Greenwood Avenue, the Negro's Wall Street, and an eyesore to some evil-minded real estate men who saw the advantage of making this street into a commercial district. This section of Tulsa was a city within a city, and some malicious newspapers take pride in referring to it [as] 'Little Africa.' On Greenwood one could find a variety

of business places which would be a credit to any section of the town. In the residential section there were homes of beauty and splendor which would please the most critical eye. The schools and many churches were well attended.[66]

The story of the Greenwood District in Tulsa, of Black Wall Street, is a story fundamentally about the human spirit—about the African American pioneers who built something magical, weathered its calamitous destruction, and shepherded its unlikely rebirth.

Tulsa, Oklahoma, "The Oil Capital of the World" shone brightly at the dawn of the twentieth century. Black gold oozed from Indian Territory soil, land once set aside for Native American resettlement.

J. Paul Getty. Thomas Gilcrease. Waite Phillips. They were among the men extracting fabulous fortunes from Oklahoma crude and living on Tulsa time.

As Tulsa's wealth and stature grew, so, too, did political, economic, and, particularly, race-based, tensions. The formative years of this segregated city coincided with a period of marked civil rights retrenchment and anti-black violence throughout the United States.

African Americans faced profound racial oppression in the United States during an era that ranks as a low-water mark in race relations. Suppression of civil rights, mass assaults on African American communities, and widespread violence, including lynchings, cast a pall over African American life and living.[67]

In 1919 alone, more than two dozen "race riots" erupted in towns and cities throughout the country. That same year, vigilantes lynched at least eighty-three African Americans across the nation.[68]

Despite this anti-black onslaught, the federal government failed to take decisive action to protect African Americans. When the House of Representatives passed a measure criminalizing lynching, the Senate rejected it.

The Greenwood District in Tulsa blossomed even amidst this "blacklash." African Americans in Tulsa engaged one another in commerce. In the process, they created a nationally-renowned hotbed of black entrepreneurial activity.

Legal segregation forced Tulsa's African Americans to do business with one another, diverting dollars away from the white community. This economic detour allowed the Greenwood District to prosper as dollars circulated repeatedly within the African American community. The community's insular service economy rested on a foundation of necessity. This necessity, in turn, molded the talented cadre of African American businesspersons and entrepreneurs that helped shape America's "Negro Wall Street."[69]

Greenwood Avenue, north of the Frisco Railroad tracks, became the hub of Tulsa's original African American community. Eclectic and electric, "people [began] to look upon Tulsa as the Negro Metropolis of the Southwest."[70]

The surrounding Greenwood District teemed with business and entrepreneurial activity. Nightclubs, hotels, cafes, newspapers, clothiers, movie theatres, doctors' and lawyers' offices, grocery stores, beauty salons, shoeshine shops, and more dotted the urban landscape.

This parallel black universe existed just beyond downtown Tulsa, separated from white Tulsa, physically, by the Frisco Railroad tracks, and, psychologically, by layers of social stratification. In it, African American businesspersons and professionals mingled with day laborers, musicians, and maids. African American educators molded young minds. African American clergy nurtured spirits and soothed souls.

Savvy entrepreneurs like Simon Berry developed their businesses around the needs of the community, niche marketing by today's standards. Berry created a nickel-a-ride jitney service with his topless Model-T Ford. He successfully operated a bus line that he ultimately sold to the City of Tulsa. He owned the Royal Hotel. He shuttled wealthy oil barons on a charter airline service he operated with his partner, James Lee Northington, Sr., a successful black building contractor. Simon Berry reportedly earned as much as $500 a day in the early 1920s.

Prominent professionals like Dr. A.C. Jackson transcended, if only temporarily, the color line. Dr. Jackson, christened the most accomplished Negro surgeon in America by the Mayo brothers (of

Mayo Clinic fame), treated patients of all races. Dr. Jackson died tragically in the 1921 catastrophe. By some accounts, Dr. Jackson, unceremoniously gunned down by a white teenager while surrendering at his residence and lacking medical attention, bled to death.[71]

Industrious families like the Williams found economic success in multiple ventures: a theatre, a confectionery, a rooming house, and a garage.

Business-savvy women like Mabel B. Little, a beautician, operated thriving enterprises. Women likewise added elegance and allure to storied Greenwood Avenue, especially on Thursday, the traditional "maid's day off." African American women, many of whom worked in the homes of affluent whites, took advantage of the day's opportunity to "gussie up" and stroll down Greenwood way.

Brilliant educators like E.W. Woods, principal of Booker T. Washington High School beginning in 1913 and for some thirty-five years thereafter, gained respect and renown throughout the city. Mr. Woods arrived in Tulsa by foot from Memphis in answer to a call for "colored" teachers. He became known as "the quintessential Tulsan" for his preeminent leadership in the realm of public education. The Tulsa Convention Hall—the only facility large enough to accommodate the throngs of mourners—hosted Mr. Woods' 1948 funeral.[72]

The Greenwood District pioneers parlayed Jim Crow into an economic advantage. They seized the opportunity to create a closed market system that defied Jim Crow's fundamental premise: African American incompetence and inferiority. From movie theatres to professional offices, from grocery stores to schools, from beauty salons to shoeshine shops, the Greenwood District seemingly had it all.

The economic success of the Greenwood District and its architects threatened the white power structure. As had been demonstrated in the countless racial assaults and lynchings throughout the United States in the early twentieth century, black economic prowess, as much as black political power, had to be held in check.

Perhaps the most compelling example of the trampling of the

black entrepreneurial inclination traces back to nineteenth century Memphis, Tennessee.

In 1892, People's Grocery, owned by three black businessmen, Thomas Moss, Calvin McDowell, and William Steward, competed, in the spirit of American capitalism, with a nearby white-owned store. Their small shop drew customers from this competitor.

A group of white men, animated in part by anger over the success of this black business, decided to eliminate the competition. They attacked People's Grocery. The owners fought back, shooting one of the attackers.

Law enforcement officers arrested the owners of People's Grocery. A lynch-mob broke into the jail, dragged them away from town, and murdered all three.

This horrific act of domestic terrorism reverberated throughout the nation and quelled the nascent entrepreneurial spirit within many African Americans.[73]

Journalist and anti-lynching crusader Ida B. Wells-Barnett penned an article condemning the barbarity and the henchmen who carried it out. She wrote in *The Free Speech and Headlight*: "The city of Memphis has demonstrated that neither character nor standing avails the Negro if he dares to protect himself against the white man or become his rival."[74]

Then, they came for her, destroying her office and her printing press. Visiting Philadelphia at the time of the mob visit, Wells escaped harm.[75]

Given this cultural milieu, and in light of the prevailing racial pecking order, the success of the Greenwood District, could scarcely be tolerated, let alone embraced, by the larger community. White hegemony had to be maintained.

The economic prowess of Tulsa's African American citizens, including home, business, and land ownership, caused increasing consternation and friction, propelled, in part, by the Ku Klux Klan and its sympathizers and media sensationalism. The notoriety and prosperity of Tulsa's African Americans and the ascendancy of their Greenwood District ran counter to the prevailing notion of black inferiority. Fear and jealously swelled over time and, finally, "the flames of hatred which had been brewing for years broke loose."[76]

Chapter Two

Remembering the "Riot"

*Racism is man's gravest threat to man--the maximum
of hatred for a minimum of reason.*

Abraham Joshua Heschel

By the early 1920s in Tulsa, African American success, including home, business, and land ownership, caused increasing consternation and friction. Black World War I veterans, having tasted true freedom only on foreign soil, came back to America with heightened expectations. Valor and sacrifice in battle earned them the basic respect and human dignity so long denied in America—or so they thought.[77] But the country had not yet changed, and Tulsa, Oklahoma, proved no exception.

The underlying climate of racial oppression for African Americans in the United States from colonization up to and during 1921 and the physical intimidation associated with it seems almost unfathomable today. It was open season on African Americans, as the dominant culture imposed all manner of legal and extralegal means to buoy white supremacy.

The United Confederate Veterans, founded in 1889, served as

the primary veterans' organization for former Confederate soldiers. Cities coveted the group's annual summer reunions, which
drew throngs of Confederate-aligned Americans to cities like Dal-
las, Little Rock, Amarillo, and, in 1918, Tulsa.[78]

Tulsa townsfolk treated the aging Rebels to free meals and trol-
ley rides, culminating in a lavish downtown parade. Tate Brady,
local businessman, onetime Ku Klux Klan member, and, later,
arguable role-player in the cataclysmic 1921 Tulsa Race Massacre, helped organize the September 24 - 26, 1918, assembly. Some
40,000 people, including 14,000 Confederate veterans, attended.

In 1919, there were more than two dozen notable race-relat-
ed events dubbed "race riots" in America. Black World War I veterans' increasing impatience with social, political, and economic
marginalization, coupled with white intransigence, exacerbated
the racial tumult.

In May 1919, Dr. George Edmund Haynes,[80] then an educator
employed as director of Negro Economics for the United States
Department of Labor, published his essay "Returning Soldiers,"
in which he noted:

> We return from the slavery of uniform which the world's
> madness demanded us to don to the freedom of civil garb.

> We stand again to look America squarely in the face and call a
> spade a spade.

> We sing: This country of ours, despite all its better souls have
> done and dreamed, is yet a shameful land . . .

> We return.

> We return from fighting.

> We return fighting.[81]

Race riot, both in terms of the 1919 "Red Summer" events and
the 1921 Tulsa disaster, is a term of art crafted by chroniclers of
news and history—powerful and privileged white men—to advance a narrative about African American status and stature in
this land.[82]

Red Summer, a term coined by James Weldon Johnson of the
National Association for the Advancement of Colored People, refers to a period in 1919 during which a series of race-based in-

cidents of civil unrest, routinely labeled race riots, occurred. Between May and October of that year, violent assaults on African American communities took place in more than two dozen American communities, including: Baltimore, Maryland; Chicago, Illinois; Elaine, Arkansas; Longview, Texas; Memphis, Tennessee; New York, New York; Omaha, Nebraska; and Washington, D.C.[83]

Several factors precipitated the racial tumult, including the systemic, institutional racism so prevalent in the era. Other triggers included three principal, related dynamics: (1) Labor shortages in northern and midwestern factories occasioned by white male enlistment in World War I at a time when European immigration had been curtailed; (2) The Great Migration of African Americans from the Deep South to northern and midwestern cities to fill job vacancies and, simultaneously, escape the social, economic, and political oppression characteristic of the Deep South; and (3) racial resentment, based on economic competition, on the part of working class white Americans in the northern and midwestern cities to which African Americans migrated.[84]

As previously noted, the "race riots" of the early twentieth century may be more accurately described as white riots, assaults, pogroms, massacres, holocausts, ethnic cleansings, and genocides. They generally involved invasions of black communities by death-and-destruction-focused white mobs. Use of the race riot label, which attaches to historical documents related to these events, should be accompanied by a robust discussion of: (1) Who created the term?; (2) Why was the term chosen?; (3) Is the term an accurate description of what transpired?; (4) What are some terms that might more accurately reflect what transpired; and (5) Should such an event transpire today, how might we insure that the process surrounding its naming is both procedurally and substantively sound?

Lynchings proliferated during this period, too. The May 25, 1911, lynchings of Laura Nelson and her son, Lawrence, in Okemah, Oklahoma, stand out even among the plethora of other such ghastly events throughout the country and over the decades.[85]

Lynchings in Oklahoma came in two waves:

In the first phase of lynching in Oklahoma, 1885 through 1907, most victims were whites, punished primarily as

THE SHAME OF AMERICA

Do you know that the United States is the Only Land on Earth where human beings are BURNED AT THE STAKE?

In Four Years, 1918-1921, Twenty-Eight People Were Publicly BURNED BY AMERICAN MOBS

3436 People Lynched 1889 to 1922

For What Crimes Have Mobs Nullified Government and Inflicted the Death Penalty?

The Alleged Crimes	The Victims	Why Some Mob Victims Died:
Murder	1288	Not turning out of road for white boy in auto
Rape	571	Being a relative of a person who was lynched
Crimes against the Person	615	Jumping a labor contract
Crimes against Property	332	Being a member of the Non-Partisan League
Miscellaneous Crimes	453	"Talking back" to a white man
Absence of Crime	175	"Insulting" white man.
	3436	

Is Rape the "Cause" of Lynching?

Of 3,436 people murdered by mobs in our country, only 571, or less than 17 per cent., were even accused of the crime of rape.

83 WOMEN HAVE BEEN LYNCHED IN THE UNITED STATES

Do lynchers maintain that they were lynched for "the usual crime"?

AND THE LYNCHERS GO UNPUNISHED

THE REMEDY

The Dyer Anti-Lynching Bill Is Now Before the United States Senate

The Dyer Anti-Lynching Bill was passed on January 26, 1922, by a vote of 230 to 119 in the House of Representatives.

The Dyer Anti-Lynching Bill Provides:
That culpable State officers and mobbists shall be tried in Federal Courts on failure of State courts to act, and that a county in which a lynching occurs shall be fined $10,000, recoverable in a Federal Court.

The Principal Question Raised Against the Bill is upon the Ground of Constitutionality.

The Constitutionality of the Dyer Bill Has Been Affirmed by—
The Judiciary Committee of the House of Representatives
The Judiciary Committee of the Senate
The United States Attorney General, legal adviser of Congress
Judge Guy D. Goff, of the Department of Justice

The Senate has been petitioned to pass the Dyer Bill by—
29 Lawyers and Jurists, including two former Attorneys General of the United States
19 State Supreme Court Justices
24 State Governors
3 Archbishops, 88 bishops and prominent churchmen
27 Mayors of large cities, north and south.

The American Bar Association at its meeting in San Francisco, August 9, 1922, adopted a resolution asking for further legislation by Congress to punish and prevent lynching and mob violence.

Fifteen State Conventions of 1922 (7 of them Democratic) have inserted in their party platforms a demand for national action to stamp out lynchings.

The Dyer Anti-Lynching Bill is not intended to protect the guilty, but to assure to every person accused of crime trial by due process of law.

THE DYER ANTI-LYNCHING BILL IS NOW BEFORE THE SENATE
TELEGRAPH YOUR SENATORS TODAY YOU WANT IT ENACTED

If you want to help the organization which has brought to light the facts about lynching, the organization which is fighting for 100 per cent. Americanism, not for some of the people some of the time, but for all of the people, white or black, all of the time

Send your check to J. E. SPINGARN, Treasurer of the

NATIONAL ASSOCIATION FOR THE ADVANCEMENT OF COLORED PEOPLE
70 FIFTH AVENUE, NEW YORK CITY

THIS ADVERTISEMENT IS PAID FOR IN PART BY THE ANTI-LYNCHING CRUSADERS.

NAACP flyer encouraging passage of the Dyer Anti-Lynching Bill[88]

NAACP flyer encouraging passage of the Dyer Anti-Lynching Bill.[88]

rustlers, 'highwaymen,' or robbers. In those years, 106 individuals were lynched for suspected criminal activities. Although 1892 was the peak year nationally, 1893–95 were the peak in the Twin Territories, with cattle/horse theft and robbery the main offenses. The 106 victims included 71 whites, 17 blacks, 14 Indians, one Chinese, and three of unknown race. After 1907 statehood, however, lynching entered a more racist phase. The numbers actually declined, but the victims were almost exclusively black. In this period lynching reinforced an existing social order that deprived blacks of political and economic rights and segregated them. The state constitution enshrined Jim Crow, and forty-one persons were lynched by 1930. Most of these incidents occurred from 1908 to 1916.[86]

These acts of domestic terrorism largely targeting African Americans reinforced white supremacy through acts of unspeakable cruelty and violence perpetrated by white vigilantes, aided, in many instances, by arms of the justice system. In 1921, at least 57 African Americans fell victim to lynchings. Despite these atrocities, the American government did little to protect her dark-skinned denizens. Indeed, the United States Senate thrice failed to pass measures making lynching a federal offense.[87]

The Roaring Twenties[89] augured in dramatic social and political change. A surging economy, mass consumerism, jazz-age flappers in an era of Prohibition, and the Harlem Renaissance of African American art and culture gave rise to this characterization of 1920s America.

The number of city-dwellers exceeded the number of farmers. America's wealth more than doubled in the decade. Consumerism spread as nationwide advertising and chain stores proliferated. For some, a common culture emerged: music, dance, and argot.

Many of the commonly accepted landmark events of the Roaring Twenties—Prohibition, rural to urban migration, immigration restrictions, the Sacco-Vanzetti and Scopes trials, the Lindbergh transatlantic flight and so much more—fail to indicate what a perilous time the 1920s were in America in terms of race relations. More than fifty years after the Civil War, America remained a house divided. Tulsa, too, split along racial fault lines.

Tulsa in the 1920s both mirrored and magnified some of the national trends. Oil fueled prosperity, at least for some. Wealth became concentrated. National connectedness increased. But Tulsa also became emblematic of America's unresolved and seemingly intractable racial discord.

Washington Irving, the American author, essayist, biographer, historian, and diplomat of the early nineteenth century, said: "History fades into fable; fact becomes clouded with doubt and controversy; the inscription molders from the tablet: the statue falls from the pedestal. Columns, arches, pyramids, what are they but heaps of sand; and their epitaphs, but characters written in the dust?"[90]

What Washington Irving said is only conditionally true. Those things happen only if we let them.

It is all too easy to gloss over the past. When we think of The Roaring Twenties we scarcely picture the prevalence of "race riots" and lynchings—of a fierce, unceasing anti-black animus playing out as domestic terrorism. We conveniently forget about the remarkable rise of the Ku Klux Klan, which boasted some 70,000 members in Oklahoma in 1921 and perpetrated more than two-hundred documented terroristic acts between 1921 and 1924.[91]

Tulsan James Leighton Avery, son of Cyrus Avery, often dubbed the "Father of Route 66," recalled the early days of the Klan in Tulsa:

> The Ku Klux Klan had become active in Tulsa a few years previously [*i.e.*, previous to the riot in 1921], about 1919, I think. Their BENO Hall [*i.e.*, the Klan's temple or 'Klavern'] had been constructed at Main and Easton Streets. 'Be No Catholic; Be No Nigger; Be No Jew!' was their propaganda. Father had no use for them, and, in his own way, did all he could to counteract their disruptive, cruel abuse of Tulsans.[92]

Though Cyrus Avery kept his distance, many white Tulsans roundly embraced the Klan. Tony Pringer, grandson of Herbert and Marie Eunice "Molly" Johnson, noted:

> My grandparents . . . lived near Sequoyah School in the

1,000 block of North Boston Avenue. Grandpa was a fire-fighter at the Denver Avenue station and he was a member of the Ku Klux Klan. It was just a common thing, a common practice, for white men in business and in government in Oklahoma during the early 1900s to belong to the Klan. It was more like a social organization, but then it could turn mean and violent if the occasion arose. Well the occasion arose with the race riot of 1921.[93]

Molly Johnson surreptitiously sheltered and fed black women in her basement during the massacre. Herbert Johnson, her Klansman husband, hunted down black refugees. Such was the schism in the Johnson household. Such was the schism in Tulsa.[94]

When we romanticize this tumultuous era, we sugarcoat the denial of basic political rights to a whole swath of American citizens.

On May 30, 1921, an elevator encounter between two teenagers, one black, the other white, in downtown Tulsa, lit the fuse that set Tulsa's African American community, the Greenwood District, alight. In terms of causality, the elevator incident might best be considered a trigger or catalyst for what followed. At the root of the massacre were systemic, structural problems (*e.g.*, institutional racism, jealousy, land lust) that produced a powder keg awaiting ignition.

Nab Negro for Attacking Girl In an Elevator

A negro delivery boy who gave his name to the public as 'Diamond Dick' but who has been identified as Dick Rowland, was arrested on South Greenwood avenue this morning by Officers Carmichael and Pack, charged with attempting to assault the 17-year-old white elevator girl in the Drexel building early yesterday. He will be tried in municipal court this afternoon on a state charge.

The girl said she noticed the negro a few minutes before the attempted assault looking up and down the hallway on the third floor of the Drexel building as if to see if there was anyone in sight but thought nothing of it at the time.

A few minutes later he entered the elevator she claimed, and attacked her, scratching her hands and face and tearing her clothes. Her screams brought a clerk from Renberg's store to her assistance and the negro fled. He was captured and identified this morning both by the girl and the clerk, police say.

Tenants of the Drexel building said the girl is an orphan who works as an elevator operator to pay her way through business college.[97]

Article in the *The Tulsa Tribune*, May 31, 1921.

Authorities arrested Dick Rowland. A white mob threatened to hang him. African American men, determined to protect the teen from the rumored lynching, marched to the courthouse that held young Rowland. Knowledge of the prevalence of lynchings of African Americans in America generally,[98] coupled with an acute awareness of a recent local, public lynching of a white teenager,[99] warranted their concern.

Law enforcement authorities asked them to retreat, assuring Rowland's safety. They left. The lynch-talk persisted.

A second group of African American men from the Greenwood District proceeded to the courthouse. The black men exchanged words with the swelling group of white men gathered on the courthouse lawn. A gun discharged. Soon, thousands of weapon-wielding white men chased the black men back to the Greenwood District.[100]

Law enforcement officers deputized some of the white assailants.[101] Mobs prevented firefighters from extinguishing the flames.[102]

In a span of fewer than twenty-four hours, people, property, hopes, and dreams vanished. Roving gangs burned the Greenwood District to the ground. Property damage ran into the millions, with both black and white Tulsans suffering staggering losses. Hundreds of people died. Scores lay injured. The vicious assault on the Greenwood District left many African Americans homeless and destitute. Some fled Tulsa, never to return.[103]

Many, including some white Tulsans, bemoaned the role of *The Tulsa Tribune* in stoking the flames of racial animus rising in the white community. One white survivor noted: *"The Tribune* practically invited the riot . . . I fear that *The Tribune* did more to incite the riot than to calm the passions of those involved."[104]

The Tulsa Tribune hardly stood alone in its willingness to sensationalize matters of race and galvanize anti-black animus. Prominent local presses throughout the country also exploited racial tensions and promoted white supremacy. For example, the *Omaha Daily Bee* fanned the flames of racial hostility to the point of incitement to violence at a time when the growth of the black population and competition for jobs caused racial friction in that Nebraska city.

The September 28, 1919, lynching of forty-year-old African American Will Brown, accused of raping a nineteen-year-old white girl, Agnes Lobeck, sprang in considerable measure from the reportage of the *Omaha Daily Bee*.[105] The paper's skewed coverage spawned a mob of some 250 men and women who seized Brown from the courthouse, nearly killing Mayor Edward P. Smith in the process. The Mayor, who attempted to dissuade the mob, was knocked unconscious and hanged from a lamppost, only to be cut down before succumbing. The vigilantes stripped, beat, hanged, shot, dragged, and burned Will Brown in the presence of a crowd that swelled to 20,000.[106] The lynch rope, cut into pieces, sold as souvenirs to those among the throngs whose appetites for vengeance were not satiated by the mere witnessing of such carnage. Legendary film star Henry Fonda, an Omaha native and fourteen at the time, observed the horror firsthand as a guest of his father.[107]

Similarly, just two years later in Tulsa, reportage of *The Tulsa Tribune* whipped up a frenzy. Dick Rowland's alleged assault on Sarah Page triggered unprecedented civil unrest. Fueled by sensational reporting, jealousy over black economic success, land lust, and a racially hostile climate in general, mob rule held sway.

> I can remember seeing a big open-bed truck and [on]the back end of that truck was a whole bunch of armed men standing up there with rifles. They had long guns, not pistols or anything. And they were just about to fill the back

end of that truck cruising around in this neighborhood. And, of course, the theory we all had, if they spotted any black person, there were going to let him have it, kill him.[108]

White men spilled across the Frisco tracks, looting, burning, and shooting as they penetrated deeper into the Greenwood District. "There were boys in the bunch from about 10 years upward, all armed with guns."[109] Black men "fought gamely and held back the enemy for hours . . . [until] the truth dawned . . . that [they] were fighting in vain to hold their dear Greenwood."[110]

According to eyewitnesses, overhead operations aided the ground assault. Prominent attorney Buck Colbert Franklin, in a recently discovered 1931 manuscript, recalled the strategic use of airplanes and their devasting impact.

> I could see planes circling in mid-air. They grew in number and hummed, darted and dipped low. I could hear something like hail falling upon the top of my office building. Down East Archer, I saw the old Mid-Way hotel on fire, burning from its top, and then another and another and another building began to burn from their top.

> Lurid flames roared and belched and licked their forked tongues into the air. Smoke ascended the sky in thick, black volumes and amid it all, the planes—now a dozen or more in number—still hummed and darted here and there with the agility of natural birds of the air.

> The side-walks were literally covered with burning turpentine balls. I knew all too well where they came from, and I knew all too well why every burning building first caught from the top. I paused and waited for an opportune time to escape. 'Where oh where is our splendid fire department with its half dozen stations?' I asked myself. 'Is the city in conspiracy with the mob?'

> •   •   •   •

> About mid-night [on May 31, 1921], I arose and went to the north porch on the second floor of my hotel and, looking in a north-westernly direction, I saw the top of stand-pipe hill literally lighted up by the blazes that came from the throats

of machine guns, and I could hear bullets whizzing and cutting the air. There was shooting now in every direction, and the sounds that came from the thousands and thousands of guns were deafening.[111]

Tulsa, Oklahoma: The Events of May 31 - June 1, 1921
An Abbreviated Timeline

Monday, May 30, 1921

- Early morning: Dick Rowland encountered Sarah Page in Drexel Building elevator. Somehow, Dick bumped into or brushed up against Sarah, who initially interpreted the incident as an assault, but later recanted her original claim.

Tuesday, May 31, 1921

- 3:00 p.m.: *The Tulsa Tribune* published a sensational (and largely fictitious) account of the Rowland-Page elevator incident.

- Late afternoon/early evening: A crowd of white Tulsans, initially numbering in the hundreds, but eventually swelling into the thousands, gathered at the courthouse where Rowland was being held in jail.

- 8:20 p.m.: Three white men entered the courthouse and unsuccessfully sought the turnover of Rowland.

- 9:00 p.m.: A group of about two dozen black men, some armed, drove to the courthouse to protect Rowland. After receiving assurances of his safety, they left.

- 9:00 p.m.: The arrival of the black men riled the burgeoning white mob, which now numbered more than one thousand. Members of the mob went home to retrieve guns and sought to steal guns, unsuccessfully, from the National Guard Armory.

- 9:15 p.m.: The white mob on the lawn of the courthouse, including men, women, and children, continued to grow and became increasingly agitated.

- 9:15 p.m.: Sheriff Willard M. McCullough tried to calm the crowd and send them home. They remained. He provided extra protection for Rowland.

- 10:00 p.m.: In response to unabating rumors of a lynch mob at the courthouse, a group of several dozen armed black men drove downtown and offered to help Sheriff McCullough protect Rowland, an offer the Sheriff rebuffed. During this same period, members of the black contingent and the ever-growing white mob exchanged words, a struggle over a black man's gun ensued, a shot rang out, and things spiraled out of control. The thousand-strong white mob, some of whose number had been deputized by local law enforcement, attacked. The group looted pawnshops and hardware stores, stealing guns and ammunition. A running gun battle ensued as the black men retreated toward the Greenwood District.

- 10:14 p.m.: Adjutant General Charles F. Barrett, commandant of the Oklahoma National Guard, received a long-distance telephone call from Major Byron Kirkpatrick, a Tulsa National Guard officer, advising him of the deteriorating conditions in Tulsa.

Wednesday, June 1, 1921

- Midnight - 1:30 a.m.: A gun battle raged along the Frisco tracks. The white mob conducted 'drive-by' shootings in the Greenwood District and began setting buildings on fire. A few dozen white members of the Tulsa National Guard intervened, first downtown, and later in the Greenwood District. The guardsmen began rounding up black civilians and turning them over to the police.

- 12:35 a.m.: Major Kirkpatrick phoned again, and was instructed by Governor J.B.A. Robertson, who was also on the line, to send a telegram signed by the police chief, the sheriff, and a judge, requesting that state troops be sent to Tulsa. The requisite signatures secured, Major Kirkpatrick transmitted the following telegram at 1:46 a.m.

WESTERN UNION TELEGRAM
Tulsa, Okla.
June 1, 1921

Governor J.B.A. Robertson Oklahoma City, Oklahoma. Race riot developed here. Several killed. Unable to handle situation. Request that National Guard forces be sent by special train. Situation serious.

Jno. A. Gustafson, Chief of Police
Wm. McCullough, Sheriff
V.M. Biddison, District Judge[112]

- 2:15 a.m.: Adjutant General Barrett informed Major Kirkpatrick that Governor Robertson had authorized state troops for Tulsa.

- 5:00 a.m. - 8:30 a.m.: A special train carrying one-hundred Oklahoma National Guard troops departed from Oklahoma City en route to Tulsa.

- 5:08 a.m.: A siren or whistle sounded and the invasion of the Greenwood District by the white mob proceeded in earnest. Looting, burning, and murder ensued. According to eyewitnesses, the invasion included planes circling overhead and dropping incendiary devices on the Greenwood District. Black Tulsans resisted.

- 8:00 - 9:00 a.m.: Chaos continued, with the Greenwood District overwhelmed.

- 9:15 - 11:30 a.m.: 'State Troops,' members of the Oklahoma National Guard from Oklahoma City, arrived, but they were not immediately dispatched to quell the remaining hostilities in the Greenwood District. More structures in the Greenwood District burned in the interim.

- 11:30 a.m. - 8:00 p.m.: Authorities declared martial law in Tulsa at 11:30 a.m. The final skirmish occurred at 12:30 p.m. State troops disarmed the remaining whites in the Greenwood District and sent them home. Reinforcement state troops arrived in Tulsa from other

Oklahoma communities to clear the streets. Tulsa May-
or T.D. Evans summoned the American Red Cross with
an urgent message: 'Please establish headquarters for
all relief work & bring all organizations who can assist you to your aid—The responsibility is placed in
your hands entirely.'[113] By all accounts, the Red Cross
performed admirably, earning the moniker 'Angels of
Mercy.'[114]

Mary Elizabeth Jones Parrish, an African American journalist
and contemporaneous chronicler of the Tulsa disaster, reflected on
the declaration of martial law in Tulsa:

One thing we noticed was that every one of our group that
we met was wearing a tag inscribed 'POLICE PROTEC-
TION.' On asking the meaning of this we were told that
the town was under Martial Law and all of our group had
to wear these badges in order to be permitted to come out
on the streets and that everyone had to be indoors before
seven o'clock. All places of business were also closed by
this hour.

*   *   *   *   *

[O]ne had to have some white person vouch for them regardless of their station in life before the trouble . . . . As I
have never worked for any white person in Tulsa I was at
a loss just what to do. It was plainly shown that a white
man's word was the only requirement to receive a card.
I pondered just what to do, then I thought of a business
firm and called them up. They came down and identified
me and that was sufficient. I received my card without any
trouble.[115]

High school teacher James T.A. West remembered the indignities of the internment round-up:

After lining up some 30 or 40 of us men they ran us through
the streets to Convention Hall, forcing us to keep our hands
in the air all the while. While we were running some of the
ruffians would shoot at our heels and swore at those who
had difficulty in keeping up. They actually drove a car into

the bunch and knocked down two or three men. When we reached Convention Hall we were searched again. There people were herded in like cattle. The sick and wounded were dumped out in front of the building and remained without attention for hours.[116]

Many African Americans spent days interned at Convention Hall, the Tulsa Fairgrounds, and McNulty Baseball Park.[117] By some accounts, the internment process had unintended consequences:

After all the men had been corralled, the women and children were told to go to the Public Parks where an armed guard would protect them and that a guard would protect their homes.

That ended the Riot so far as the Negro had anything to do with it.

Then came the great unthinkable, unspeakable climax. The White people went into those homes just vacated, carried away everything of value, opened safes, destroyed all legal papers and documents, then set fire to the buildings to hide their crime.[118]

Some white downtown churches (*e.g.,* First Presbyterian Church[119] and Holy Family Cathedral[120]) offered refuge, as did some white Tulsans.[121] Scores of black families spent weeks—even months—in makeshift tent cities set up by the American Red Cross.[122]

Tulsa's African American citizens heaped praise and gratitude upon the Red Cross:

Resolution of the East End Welfare Board

On the 31st night in May, 1921, the fiercest race war known to American history broke out, lasting until the next morning, June 1st, 1921. As a result of this regrettable occurrence, many human lives were lost and millions of dollars-worth of property were stolen and burned. Hundreds of innocent Negroes suffered as a result of this calamity—suffered in loss of lives, injury from gun-shot wounds and loss of property. Many of us were left helpless and almost hopeless. We sat amid the wreck and ruin of our former homes and peered listlessly into space.

It was at this time and under such conditions that the American Red Cross—that Angel of Love and Mercy came to our assistance. This great organization found us bruised and bleeding and, like the good Samaritan, she washed our wounds, and administered to us.

Constantly, in season and out, since the regrettable occurrence, this great organization, headed by that high class [C]hristian gentleman, Mr. [Maurice] Willows, has heard our ever cry in this our dark hour and has ever extended to us practical sympathy. As best she could, with food and raiment and shelter she has furnished us. And to this great [C]hristian organization our heartfelt gratitude is extended.

Therefore be it resolved that we, representing the entire colored citizenship of the city of Tulsa, Oklahoma, take this means of extending to the American Red Cross, thru Mr. Willows, our heart-felt thanks for the work it has done and is continuing to do for us in this our great hour of need.

Resolved further that a copy of these resolutions be sent to the American Red Cross Headquarters, a copy be mailed to Mr. Willows and his co-workers and that a copy be spread upon the minutes of the East End Welfare Board.

Respectfully submitted.

(SIGNED)

B.C. Franklin
E.F. Saddler
J.W. Hughes
I.N. Spears
P.A. Chappelle
Dimple L. Bush

Committee.[123]

In the end, Sarah Page refused to cooperate in the prosecution of Dick Rowland, the black teenager who allegedly assaulted her. Authorities spirited him out of town during the tumult in Tulsa. He wound up first in Kansas City, and then later in a Portland, Oregon shipyard where, it is believed, he died years later.[124]

A day-after account in the *Tulsa World* recounted the utter devastation and destitution faced by Tulsa's African American community in the wake of the riot.

> The heaviest fight took place between midnight and 6 o'clock Wednesday morning. Mobs of white men invaded Little Africa, intent upon killing every negro in sight. Several pitched battles ensued in which casualties occurred on both sides. It was shortly after midnight that whites apparently carrying kerosene or some other highly inflammable substance, entered the black district and started the fires that before daylight had reduced Little Africa to smoldering ruins. Greenwood Avenue, principal business street in the negro district, is a mass of broken bricks and debris. Only gas and water pipes [and some] bath fixtures remain to make the places where homes once stood. The negro residences remaining intact can almost be counted on one hand. There is not an undamaged business building owned by negroes in the entire district.

> *   *   *   *   *

> Personal belongings and house goods had been removed from most homes and piled in the streets. On the steps of the few houses that remained sat feeble and gray negro men and women and [the] occasional small child. The look in their eyes was one of dejection and supplication.

> Judging from their attitude it was not of material consequence to them whether they lived or died. Harmless themselves, they apparently could not conceive the brutality and fiendishness of men who would deliberately set fire to the homes of their friends and neighbors and as deliberately shoot them down in their tracks.[125]

Over about a sixteen-hour period, people, property, hopes,

and dreams all vanished. Black Wall Street, defiled, seemed, for the moment, defeated.

> [M]ore than one thousand homes were burned to the ground . . . . And as the homes burned, so did their contents, including furniture and family Bibles, rag dolls and hand-me-down quilts, cribs and photograph albums . . . .
>
> Gone, too, was the city's African American commercial district, a thriving area located along Greenwood Avenue which boasted some of the finest black-owned businesses in the entire Southwest. The Stradford Hotel, a modern fifty-four room brick establishment which housed a drug store, barber shop, restaurant and banquet hall, had been burned to the ground. So had the Gurley Hotel, the Red Wing Hotel, and the Midway Hotel. Literally dozens of family-run businesses—from cafes and mom-and-pop grocery stores, to the Dreamland Theater, the Y.M.C.A. Cleaners, the East End Feed Store, and Osborne Monroe's roller skating rink—had also gone up in flames, taking with them the livelihoods, and in many cases the life savings, of literally hundreds of people.
>
> The offices of two newspapers—the *Tulsa Star* and the *Oklahoma Sun*—had also been destroyed, as were the offices of more than a dozen doctors, dentists, lawyers, realtors, and other professionals. A United States Post Office substation was burned, as was the all-black Frissell Memorial Hospital. The brand-new Booker T. Washington High School building escaped the torches of the rioters, but Dunbar Elementary School did not. Neither did more than a half-dozen African American churches, including the newly constructed Mount Zion Baptist Church, an impressive brick tabernacle which had been dedicated only seven weeks earlier.[126]

In what seemed an instant, Tulsa descended first into chaos, then sheer madness.[127]

Jack Thomas, an elderly black Tulsan, recalled the horrors those fateful hours in his June 21, 1921, interview with Mary Elizabeth Jones Parrish:

> Roomers came in and told me that the White people were burning the Colored people's homes on Archer Street. Then I heard guns firing; this continued until early in the morning, when everyone ran away and left two other men and me. Later, the Guards came, told one of these men to come out, but he replied 'I am shot,' he then fell in my house, shot through the back. Then I came out of the house and tried to save something but failed.

> My greatest loss was my beautiful home and my family Bible. I am 92 years of age so they failed to bother me. I came up Easton to Frankfort Street [and] was nearly overcome by smoke but was rescued and carried to Convention Hall. Mrs. Johnson (White), of St. Louis, took me to the Catholic Church. I remained there until about 2 o'clock, then was carried to the Fair Grounds by the Red Cross, then brought back to the Methodist Church. A Colored lady told me to come to her house and live, but when we got there her home was in ashes. Mr. Williams (Colored) then took me in charge and I was afterwards taken over again by the Red Cross and kept out at the Park. Then I was recommended to some White man who would take care of me. There had been some Colored people to ask about me, one, a very dear friend of mine. As I have no children or relation, I had planned to will her my valuable property even before this happened for she has treated me as a father. They did not let her take me, but as they have let me out to go to the White man, I think I shall go her instead, as I would like for my property to fall to my own race. This is the worst scene that I have ever witnessed in my 92 years.[128]

Reporter Mary Elizabeth Jones Parrish recalled her own shock at the devastation of the Greenwood District: "Soon we reached the district which was so beautiful and prosperous when we left. This we found to be piles of bricks, ashes and twisted iron, representing years of toil and savings. We were horror stricken but strangely, we could not shed a tear."[129]

A.J. Smitherman, the editor and publisher of the *Tulsa Star*, a leading African American newspaper in Tulsa, lost his physical plant, valued at more than $40,000, and his home. He and his family managed to escape.

Smitherman penned a poignant blow-by-blow of the events of the Tulsa disaster. The following poem, likely published in 1922, appeared in Smitherman's NAACP extradition file.

The Tulsa Race Riot and Massacre

Whence those sounds in all directions
Firearms cracking everywhere;
Men and women all excited,
Cries of rioting fill the air.

Men with guns and ammunition,
Rushing madly to the fray,
Shooting, cursing, laughing, crying,
"Come on, boys, come on this way!"

"They are trying to lynch our comrade,
Without cause in law defi [sic];
Get your guns and help defend him;
Let's protect him, win or die.

'Twas the cry of Negro manhood,
Rallying to the cause of right,
Readying to suppress the lawless,
Anxious for a chance to fight.

So they marched against the mobbists
Gathered now about the jail,
While the sheriff stood there pleading,
Law and order to prevail.

Thus responding to their duty,
Like true soldiers that they were,
Black men face the lawless white men
Under duty's urgent spur.

Cries of "Let us have the nigger"
"Lynch him, kill him" came the shout,
And at once there came an answer
When a sharp report rang out.

"Stand back men, there'll be no lynching"
Black men cried, and not in fun
Bang! Bang! Bang! three quick shots followed,
And the battle had begun.

In the fusillade that followed,
Four white lynchers kissed the dust,
Many more fell badly wounded,
Victims of their hellish lust.

Quick they fled in all directions,
Panic stricken, filled with fear,
Leaving their intended victim,
As the news spread far and near.

Scattered now in great confusion
Filled with vengeance all anew
Leaders of the lynching party
Planned for something else to do.

"Blacks prevent a Negro's lynching"
Read a bold newspaper head,
In an extra night edition,
"Fifty Whites reported dead".

Rallied now with reinforcements
Brave (?) white men five thousand strong
Marched upon the Black defenders
With their usual battle song:

"Get the niggers" was their slogan,
"Kill them, burn them, set the pace.
Let them know that we are white men,
Teach them how to keep their place.

"Forward! March! command was given,
And the tread of feet was heard,
Marching on the Colored district,
In protest there came no word.

In the meantime rabid hoodlums
Now turned loose without restraint
Helped themselves to things of value

More than useless to complain.
Guns were taken by the hundreds,
Ammunition all in sight
Reign of murder, theft and plunder
Was the order of the night.

But our boys who learned the lesson
On the blood-stained soil of France,
How to fight on the defensive
Purposed not to take a chance.

Like a flash they came together,
Word was passed along the line:
"No white man must cross the border;
Shoot to kill and shoot in time!"

"Ready, Fire!" and then a volley
From the mob whose skins were white
"Give 'em hell, boys," cried the leader,
"Soon we'll put 'em all to flight."

But they got a warm reception
From black men who had no fear,
Who while fighting they were singing:
"Come on Boys, the Gang's all here."

Rapid firing guns were shooting,
Men were falling by the score,
'Till the white men quite defeated
Sent the word "We want no more."

Nine p.m. the trouble started,
Two a.m. the thing was done.
And the victory for the black men
Counted almost four to one.

Then the white went into council,
Hoping to reprise their loss,
Planned the massacre that followed,
Dared to win at any cost.

June the First, at five a.m.
Three long whistle blasts were heard,
Giving sign for concert action
To that cold blood-thirsty herd.

At the signal from the whistle
Aeroplanes were seen to fly,
Dropping bombs and high explosives,
Hell was falling from the sky.

On all sides the mob had gathered
Talking in excited tones
With machine guns, ready, mounted,
Trained upon a thousand homes.[130]

Black Tulsans were not without allies during the terror-filled hours of May 31 and June 1, 1921. As earlier noted, one such ally, First Presbyterian Church, sheltered African Americans fleeing the horrors of those dreadful days. Congregants, many of whom employed women of color as domestics, hid their employees from roving posses looking for unattached Negroes.[131]

The Church's pastor, Dr. Charles William Kerr, and his wife, Annie Elizabeth (Coe) Kerr, modeled leadership. Both had grown up and gone to school with African Americans in Pennsylvania, he in Slippery Rock, she in Parkers Landing. Together, they crafted and modeled cultural and spiritual life at First Presbyterian Church in what was, prior to Oklahoma statehood in 1907, Tulsey Town, Indian Territory.

Dr. Kerr, installed at First Presbyterian in 1900 and in his mid-forties at the time of the massacre, used his prominence to tamp down anger and promote peace. He challenged the menacing white mob hell-bent of exacting vigilante justice for an imagined sexual assault.

Dr. Kerr got wind of the lynch talk surrounding the black teen at the center of the controversy, Dick Rowland. When Kerr told his family that he was heading to the downtown courthouse to talk some sense into the burgeoning, angry white mob, his son, Hawley, insisted on going, too. Dr. Kerr allowed Hawley to serve as his driver, with strict instructions that he not exit the car, no matter what.

The pair drove up. The crowd obliged as Dr. Kerr alighted from the car dressed in his morning coat and hat, walked up the courthouse steps, and bellowed: "You may kill him, but you will have to kill me first."

Armed deputy sheriffs, shotgun sentries, stiff and masked, stood behind him. Silence prevailed.

After a few dramatic moments, Dr. Kerr descended the steps, strode through the now-parted crowd, and got into the car. Hawley dutifully drove off, a crisis averted, but only temporarily.

Dr. Kerr opened the First Presbyterian basement to African Americans seeking shelter from the storm, providing safe quarters, a place to sleep, and food. He ministered to those displaced, homeless persons encamped at the Tulsa fairgrounds. First Presbyterian offered them food, clothing, and toiletries.[132]

Mrs. Kerr became more directly involved. As the disaster unfolded, a frantic black man knocked on the screen door of the Kerr home at 1738 South Boston Avenue, ultimately damaging it and injuring himself. The man pleaded, "Help me! Hide me! They're going to kill me!" Mrs. Kerr ushered the man in and rushed him to the kitchen. She secreted him in a cabinet underneath the sink.

Not long thereafter, a garrulous contigent of agitated white men came calling. These vigilantes, canvassing white neighborhoods, seemed convinced they were on the trail of a Greenwood District refugee.

Mrs. Kerr, poised for the challenge, casually peeled potatoes as she engaged with the unwelcome visitors. She permitted them to search the entirety of the Kerr home. They found nothing, and soon exited.

The black man, aware of the departure of the marauders, came out from under the sink, wringing wet. Mrs. Kerr, surprised at his condition, exclaimed, "My, I didn't know my sink leaked so much," as she sat the man down and dressed his wounds with iodine. Flinching as the medicine penetrated his torn flesh, the man replied: "Lady, that ain't your sink. That was me! I thought for sure them Tulsa men would find me and string me up on a telephone pole like they said they was a-going to do!"[133]

Mrs. Kerr led the man upstairs for a bath and some clean, dry clothing belonging to Dr. Kerr. The man stayed on for dinner and spent the night. He returned in a few weeks to fix the screen door he damaged. He and Mrs. Kerr remained friends after the incident.[134]

Just months after the events of May 31 and June 1, 1921, First Presbyterian entertained the notion of assisting with the establishment of a "Colored" Presbyterian Church in Tulsa. They ultimately nixed the idea, concluding that "the colored people of this city have so many churches already."[135]

Dr. Kerr, deeply disturbed by the treatment of African American citizens, drafted a petition for a Congressional investigation into the Tulsa tragedy. He sought, unsuccessfully, to gain the backing of his congregants. The effort exposed deep fissures within First Presbyterian.

Lacking the backing of his congregation, Dr. Kerr filed the petition in his individual capacity. It fell on deaf ears.[136]

In the years following 1921, membership in the Ku Klux Klan ("KKK" or "Klan") swelled. Tulsa boasted a KKK women's auxiliary and, reportedly, a youth chapter, among the first such groups in the country.[137] Tulsa elites, including ministers, joined. Dr. Kerr declined. He even turned the tables, attempting to convert wayward Klansmen to Jesus. In the face of aggressive KKK recruiting efforts, he beseeched his congregants to avoid associating with the Klan.

Dr. Kerr's intelligence on the KKK came largely from black ministers. They knew who belonged to the Klan through information provided by their members who worked as maids or laundresses in white homes.

White KKK robes got soiled. Night-ridings, cross-burning, lashings, and miscellaneous extra-legal activities took their toll on the flowing, snow-colored garments. The black women who washed and ironed these pseudo-vestments provided owners' names—information valuable to themselves and members of Tulsa's African American community—to their pastors. The pastors, many of them friends of Dr. Kerr, reported out to him the names of Klansmen known to attend First Presbyterian.[138]

Two remarkable pieces of contemporaneous correspondence

offer revealing looks at Tulsa's racial and socio-cultural dynamics before, during, and immediately after the violence from the perspective of white Tulsans. They provide a lesser known, but equally critical, vantage and vital piece of the overall historical narrative still being constructed.[139]

The following letter dated June 2, 1921, (postmarked June 3, 1921) from Jessie Hannum in Tulsa, Oklahoma, to her sister in Tucson, Arizona, describes goings-on in Tulsa on May 31 - June 1, 1921, and immediately thereafter.

Dear Sister:

Tulsa has surely gone through a day of murder, bloodshed and fire yesterday. All night before last and all day yesterday a bloody race riot was going on full blast. I never dreamed of any thing [sic] so awful ever happening where I would have to witness it. You have undoubtedly read accounts of it in your papers before you get this letter.

There is a sharp line drawn here between the whites and the blacks.

The negroes all live in there [sic] own part of town here and it is called "Little Africa." The white people set fire to the town yesterday about day light and the whole thing went up in flames with a great loss of life. Mobs of white men stood with guns to keep the firemen from turning even a single stream of water on the blaze. All night we could hear the shots and they were coming thick and fast about five o'clock. We live about a mile or so from Little Africa but we could see the flames and big black clouds of smoke. There is a Curtis Airoplane [sic] field about three miles out from us and two or three big planes circled around in and out the smoke the whole time it was burning.

One of our neighbors who has two sons in the home guards told us that when the fighting was the worst about daylight the planes dropped bombs in the negro section.[141]

There was a fine church the colored people had just finished at a cost of $85,000 to $100,000 and it was simply grand. Today it is a total loss. Hays says just a pile of ruins.

They just had there [*sic*] opening services there not more than a month ago.

The hospitals are full of wounded, white and black, and as many more deaths are expected in the next few days among the wounded as have already occurred.

Hays worked all day in the negro district. He tore down many stable doors and let out horses and mules, hogs, and chickens. He helped colored women carry out part of their furniture. He wrapped up several cut and burnt hands and carried many little children out of burning houses. Some offered to help and some didn't. Those that didn't stood and looked on at all the suffering but those that wanted to help done so and no one offered to harm them. They let the blacks lay where they fell and Hays says he saw many. Down by the Frisco Depot a dead negro lay with his stomache [*sic*] cut open and his intestines laying on the ground and across his legs. He laid there several hours, the flies swarming thick over him.

Talk of war! This was sure war and a bloody one. This morning's paper estimated the negro dead at close to three hundred but it said that it may average a hundred more. They have no way yet of telling how many lost their lives in the fire. Hays wasn't there untill [*sic*] two or three hours after the fire started but they told him, men that were there, that the blacks run [*sic*] in their houses and the whites kept shooting and rather than be shot they stayed in untill [*sic*] the roof would fall and many burned alive.

They have all they could round up in Convention Hall and churches and about 2,000 out in the ball park. They are being fed and cared for but that seems such a pitiful little bit.

Families are separated wives and husbands, mothers and children, and many do not know if their loved ones are dead or wounded or if their houses were destroyed. They have started a relief fund this morning and the morning paper headed it with one thousand dollars, a judge gave $500 and another man gave $500. How I wish I had $500 to give them.

I have forgotten to tell you what started it all. A young colored boy assaulted a young girl that runs an elevator in a building down town [*sic*]. He assaulted her in the elevator. They were alone in it. The paper didn't say but from the account he must have stopped in between two floors.

She is a young orphan girl and is very well spoken of by all the people in this building and runs the elevator to pay for a course in business college.

They arrested the nigger and there was talk of lynching him. The blacks heard of it and over two hundred gathered at the courthouse well-armed at about ten o'clock and of course a large crowd of white people gathered too and the blacks opened fire on the unarmed whites. Calls for help and arms were sent out all over the city and in a little while the streets were full of dead and wounded. Some laid there till daylight.

White men broke into the hard-ware [*sic*] stores taking all the guns and ammunition. Some store owners came and opened willingly but those who didn't had their doors hammered down. Their loss is quite a lot.

Damage to the negro district is estimated at close to $2,000,000. Many white people owned property there and the insurance companies won't have to pay a cent as they are not liable in war or riot. Many negroes owned their own homes. Will send some clippings.[142]

This letter from Richard Lloyd Jones, publisher of *The Tulsa Tribune,* to Rev. Samuel A. Eliot, American Unitarian Association, Boston, Massachusetts, dated June 10, 1921, blamed black Tulsans for their own fate.

We surely have gone through exciting times here in Tulsa and we are all busy with reconstruction plans and with the tail ends of emergency relief. These things usually appear bigger elsewhere than the place they happen. The number of known dead is something under 35. But I am sure there are negro bodies that are lost in the ashes.

Our newspaper is on the edge of what was known as 'Nig-gertown.' The fire came within half a block of us. Our east wall was spattered with bullets. We observed the fight from our windows.

There is no question at all but that it was started by bad negroes. It is well established that they had been collecting guns and munitions and storing them for some time past. It has also been revealed that they had planned this attack for the 19th of this month and were then to be reinforced by gunned negroes from Muskogee and Kansas City. There was no plan for lynching the negro in jail. Some flannel[-] mouthed fool circulated such a story and the bad negroes of 'Niggertown' immediately came up town with their guns; our police and county officers acted like a lot of cow-ards and fled. Seeing negroes armed[,] the whites went for arms and the fight was on, and went from bad to worse.[143]

In the immediate wake of the death and destruction, two men exchanged letters. A man named Curtis from Detroit wrote to his friend, a man named Oliver in Tulsa. Oliver replied.

DEAR OLIVER:

I am, by our local newspaper, fully advised of the whole terrible tragedy there. Now that they have destroyed your homes, wrecked your schools, and reduced your business places to ashes, and killed your people, I am sure that you will rapidly give up the town and move North. Enclosed, please find draft for $40.00 to purchase your ticket to De-troit. Will be expecting you. CURTIS

DEAR CURTIS:

How kind of you to volunteer your sympathetic assistance. It is just like you to be helpful to others in times of stress like this.

True it is, we are facing a terrible situation. It is equally true that they have destroyed our homes; they have wrecked our schools; they have reduced our churches to ashes and they have murdered our people, Curtis, but they have not touched our spirit. And while I speak only for myself, let it be said that I came here and built my fortune with that SPIRIT, I shall reconstruct it here with that SPIRIT, and I expect to live on and die here with it. OLIVER.[144]

It is Oliver's unceasing optimist and indomitable human spirit that forms the core of the Greenwood District narrative.

The Booker T. Washington High School Class of 1921 adopted the motto ""By Repeated Blows the Oak is Felled," in Latin, *Multis Ictibus Dejicitur Quercus*.[145] On May 31 and June 1, 1921, repeated blows felled their community, the Greenwood District. Like the embedded roots system of that mighty oak, something significant survived. Despite the cruel cuts, the roots remained and the community regenerated.

The Black Dispatch, June 10, 1921.

Mount Zion Baptist Church on fire during the 1921 massacre.

Smoke billows in the Greenwood District during the1921 massacre.

The ruins of the 1921 massacre.

The Greenwood District alight during the 1921 massacre.

Body of slain massacre victim. Text on photograph reads: "Negro slain in Tulsa Riot, June 1, 1921."

Charred body of slain massacre victim. Text on photograph reads: "Charred Negro killed in Tulsa Riot, June 1, 1921."

Truck bears body of apparent massacre viction in downtown Tulsa in the midst of the massacre. Text on photograph reads: "Tulsa Race Riot, June 1st, 1921. Scene at Convention Hall."

Fire rages in and ravages the Greenwood District.

National Guard in Tulsa, during the 1921 massacre. Text on photograph reads: "National Guard machine gun crew during Tulsa Race Riot, June 1, 1921."

Black men being marched through Tulsa during the 1921 massacre.

The Greenwood District on fire, looking north, during the 1921 massacre.

The ruins of the Greenwood District, 1921.

The ruins of the Greenwood District, 1921.

Unidentified man looks upon massacre victim, 1921. Text on photograph reads: "A victim of Tulsa Race Riot, June 1, 1921."

The Black Dispatch, June 24, 1921

Chapter Three

Reclaiming the Regeneration

Earth knows no desolation. She smells regeneration
in the moist breath of decay.
George Meredith

Mother To Son
Langston Hughes

Well, son, I'll tell you:
Life for me ain't been no crystal stair.
It's had tacks in it,
And splinters,
And boards torn up,
And places with no carpet on the floor—
Bare.
But all the time
I'se been a-climbin' on,
And reachin' landin's,
And turnin' corners,
And sometimes goin' in the dark
Where there ain't been no light.
So, boy, don't you turn back.
Don't you set down on the steps.
'Cause you finds it's kinder hard.
Don't you fall now—
For I'se still goin', honey,
I'se still climbin',
And life for me ain't been no crystal stair.

Newspapers around the nation posted bold headlines about the terror in Tulsa.

The June 1, 1921, *Los Angeles Evening Express,* trumpeted: **175 Killed, Many Wounded, City Ablaze In Race War.**

The June 1, 1921, *Oklahoma Leader* declared: **9 Whites, 75 Blacks Die In Race War—8000 Tulsa Negroes Seek Protection.**

The June 2, 1921, *New York Times* headline blared: **85 WHITES AND NEGROES DIE IN TULSA RIOTS AS 3,000 ARMED MEN BATTLE IN STREETS; 30 BLOCKS BURNED, MILITARY RULE IN CITY.**[146]

The June 2, 1921, *Pittsburg Post* proclaimed: **Tulsa Race Riot Toll 80—Negro District Burned During Terrific Battle.**

The June 2, 1921, *Tulsa World* announced: **Dead Estimated At 100—City Is Quiet.**[147]

African American Tulsans faced long odds as they sought to rebuild what resembled a war zone and rebound from the man-made travesty that had befallen them. Oppositional forces emerged from multiple directions. Arguably, the City of Tulsa ranked chief among such adversarial powers.

The *Tulsa World*, decades later, editorialized about Tulsa's "badge of shame."[148]

Mayor T.D. Evans chaired the Tulsa City Commission and addressed that body on June 14, 1921, a mere two weeks after the hellish violence. His remarks bear recitation, in pertinent part:

MESSAGE—MAYOR TO COMMISSIONERS
(Tulsa Mayor T.D. Evans, June 14, 1921)

Gentlemen of the Commission: In connection with the negro uprising I desire to make some suggestions which may be helpful in arriving at a sound and correct solution of the various problems that now confront us. Since this trouble has happened, I know that you, as well as myself, have had all ordinary mortals could do to attend to the duties of the present without a thought of a permanent Policy to govern our future action as to the 'Burned District' and various needs connected with the same, but we must now look to the future because of the lease of power that the people have placed in our hands and seek to do things that are best suited to the needs of our great city.

*   *   *   *   *

Now, while I can't at this time cover all subjects that possibly should be covered and brought to your attention, yet a few points are suggested to mind.

First—Responsibility: Let the blame for this negro uprising lie rights where it belongs—on those armed negroes and their followers who started this trouble and who instigated it and any persons who seek to put half the blame on the white people are wrong and should be told so in no uncertain terms. We are told that twice before we assumed power as city officials that armed mobs of negroes visited the white section of the city and made certain demands under threats of force. They have come only Once in this administration. We are not Prophets, but we wager that trip number two will not take place soon.

Second—No Cause for this trouble: Even when these negroes were at the jail, there still was no reasons for their making any trouble. They were assured over and over again that the prisoner held by the sheriff was safe, that no one could get him. No organized mob was in the act of getting him, nor was there any danger apparent that they would get him. The occasion brought quickly around the Court House hundreds of men, women, and children as is usually the case when any rumor of this nature gets in the air. The great, great majority of white people who ran in were wholly unarmed. There was every reason to believe that when these negroes knew their prisoner was safe that the trouble would immediately stop because usually when a cause is removed, there will be no effect. A shot fired by a fool black person, evidently without cause, set the whole affair going and set the old fires of racial war and hatred going in all their fury.

Third—Officers: For the officers in the heart of the city and in the presence of hundreds of men, women and children to have pitched a battle by shooting would have meant the lives of many men, women and children who were in the crowd, and our list of killed and wounded might have been one or two hundred people. It is to the credit of these men who defended the city that night, being officers, National Guards, and Legion men, that they were wise enough to see this and to gradually work these disturbers back to the negro section. All this was done without a dollar's loss of property by fire in the heart of Tulsa and with very minimum of loss of life or personal injury.

Fourth—Place: It is the judgment of many wise heads in Tulsa, based upon observation of a number of years, that this uprising was inevitable. If that be true and this judgment had to come upon us, then I say it was good generalship to let the destruction come to that section where the trouble was hatched up, put in motion, and where it had its inception.

Fifth—Wrongs: All regret the wrongs that fell upon the innocent negroes and they should receive such help as we can give them if within our power. It, however, is true of any warfare that the fortunes of war fall upon the innocent along with the guilty. This is true of any conflict, invasion, or uprising. Think what would have happened had the Allies marched to Berlin.

Sixth—Firearms: We are told that in the colored section the negroes had guns in their homes and ammunition to use in such weapons. When, in the course of the last twenty-five years or more, has that not been true and where is the law by which anyone can prevent negroes having guns in their homes? We all know that law, both state and city, allows this and so far as I know, always has allowed it. In the past fourteen years I have often had occasion in dealing in lands and farm loans in the Creek Nation particularly, to be in negro homes. It has been much the exception to find any negro house or cabin where there was not one or two shotguns or revolvers and plenty of ammunition. I venture to say that this very day, within a radius of twenty-five miles of Tulsa, enough firearms can be obtained from negro homes alone to equip five-hundred men and prepare them for a pretty fair state of warfare.

Seventh: Nothing new—These uprisings are not by any means new or novel and they are no longer confined below the Mason and Dixon line. The cities are legion who have had more or less of riot trouble. Will law-abiding citizens cease business with the City of Tulsa or refrain from coming here on account of having had trouble of this kind? Have you heard of anybody staying out of Washington, D.C., because there was race trouble there? Chicago killed something like two thousand negroes not long ago and I believe the trouble lasted several days there, yet does any businessman stay out of Chicago or refuse to invest in property there on this account? The Court House was destroyed in a similar trouble in Omaha and the uprising was not put down there nearly so quickly as in this city, yet does anybody refrain from going to Omaha because of that affair? East St. Louis was visited by an outbreak far more serious than that in this city, yet none of us think of staying away from St. Louis. This list might be extended to cover many pages, and yet not exhaust all the illustrations. Let us immediately get to the outside the fact that everything is quiet in our city, that this menace has been fully conquered, and that we are going along in a normal condition and it will have a great influence to overcome the hundreds of wild rumors that have gone over the country. As the truth gradually reaches the outside, ninety-nine percent of the prejudices will be overcome.

Next, let us look to a few general ideas pertaining to reconstruction:

1. Let us not shirk the responsibility of doing that which is best for all, both black and white.

2. Let every transaction pertaining to the rights of all these property owners, both black and white, be characterized by the absolute honesty and see that each gets, in the parlance of the streets, a square deal.

3. A large portion of this district is well-suited for indus-

trial purposes; better adapted for these purposes than for residences. Once it is assured that it will be so used, there will be a decided rise in value, which will give the property owners more for the naked ground than his whole property was worth before the fire. Let the negro settlement be placed farther to the north and east.

4. We should immediately get in touch with all the railroads with a view to establishing a Union Station on the ground. The location is ideal and all the railroads convenient. From our acquaintances with all conditions after several days for settling back to a normal state, I believe a committee of citizens can now well be selected to constitute the legally-appointed committee for the city and to be known as a 'Reconstruction Committee' and I recommend such action.

It is well in the selection of this committee that we fully comprehend just the nature of the locality and the people with whom they must come in contact. Many well-known men in other lines could not handle this section to the best advantage. Persons who have lived there many years and helped blaze the way for greater Tulsa, who know every foot of the ground, and who are well-acquainted with these colored people, and who are honest and reliable, can best handle this proposition. I believe a committee consisting of the following men will be equal to the greater task of aiding and guiding us to a conclusion beneficial to all, *viz.,* Frank B. Long, Edward Short, C.G. Gump, J.W. Woodford, W.T. Brady, A.J. Biddison, S.R. Lewis, [and] J.W. Wilson.

Respectfully submitted,

T.D. Evans, Mayor

Dated June 14, 1921[149]

[NOTE: For clarity and ease of reading, the foregoing version of the Mayor T.D. Evan's remarks, taken from the June 14, 1921, minutes of the Tulsa City Commission, was edited to correct typographical and grammatical errors.]

Ruins of the 1921 massacre.[150]

The grand jury impaneled to investigate the calamity also blamed Tulsa's African American community for its own destruction, painting the murderous white mob as docile choir boys. That body's June 25, 1921, final report declared:

> We find the recent race riot was the direct result of an effort on the part of a certain group of colored men who appeared at the courthouse on the night of May 31, 1921, for the purpose of protecting one Dick Rowland then and now in the custody of the Sheriff of Tulsa Country for an alleged assault upon a young white woman. We have not been able to find any evidence either from white or colored citizens that any organized attempt was made or planned to take from the Sheriff's custody any prisoner; the crowd assembled about the courthouse being purely spectators and curiosity seekers resulting from rumor circulated about the city.[151]

Ever courageous, and despite the callous blame-shifting, African Americans rebuilt their community from the ashes. Official Tulsa leadership hindered the rebuilding and rebirth of Greenwood, blaming black citizens for their own plight, turning away charitable contributions for reconstruction, and creating various roadblocks. Some individuals and institutions in the greater Tulsa community stepped up, however, providing much needed assistance. The American Red Cross provided stellar care—medical care, food, shelter, and clothing—for victims.

By all accounts, the Red Cross contingent acted as post-Riot honest brokers. American Red Cross Director Maurice Willows, in his final report, noted: "[T]he Red Cross has had the unified support and good will of the whole population, all political factions and both newspapers." He continued, "the Red Cross is the only organization which could minister to both blacks and whites and maintain a strictly neutral position on all political and racial questions."[152]

Willows offered a scathing assessment of Tulsa's leadership in terms of the emergency and temporary relief efforts. He prefaced his report with a sobering reflection on the Tulsa terror:

> The story of the tragedy enacted in Tulsa, Oklahoma, on the night of May 31st, 1921, [and] the morning of June 1st, 1921, has been told and retold, with all sorts of variations, in the press of the country. Whatever people choose to call it, 'race riot,' 'massacre,' 'negro uprising,' or whatnot, the word has not yet been coined which can correctly describe the affair.

> This report attempts to picture the situation as representatives of the Red Cross found it, and to record the activities of the organization in bringing order out of chaos and in administering relief to the innocents.[153]

Willows' report characterized a situation in which political and economic forces and factors weighed heavily in how the relief effort for Tulsa's humanitarian crisis played out.

A seven-member Public Welfare Board drawn from the Chamber of Commerce and other Tulsa organizations on June 2 pledged financial support for the relief effort and appealed to national headquarters of the Red Cross to fund the cost of relief personnel. The Public Welfare Board swore off outside appeals for assistance, doubling down on its financial commitment: "Go ahead and take care of the relief as it should be done and we will finance all Red Cross needs."[154]

The Red Cross began execution of its relief plan. The Public Welfare Board began fundraising. That fundraising effort would be short-lived.

Mayor T.D. Evans declared the Public Welfare Board dissolved. He appointed a new seven-member body, the Reconstruction Committee, on June 14. Members of the defunct Public Welfare Board, having resigned office, nonetheless vowed individually and collectively to stand with the Red Cross in terms of financial backing.

Per Maurice Willows, "the [Reconstruction Committee] is politically constituted and is chiefly interested in maneuvering for the transfer of negro properties and the establishment of a new negro district." Moreover, "it became apparent that the Reconstruction Committee was powerless to raise funds, [so] the old committee members together with Chairman Fields of the Red Cross brought about a meeting of the County Commissioners and the Mayor."[155]

The County of Tulsa, the City of Tulsa, and private donors rallied to help fund continuation of the Red Cross relief effort.[156]

The Tulsa Tribune maligned the destroyed community, questioning aloud whether rebuilding should ever occur.

IT MUST NOT BE AGAIN

Such a district as the old 'Niggertown' must never be allowed in Tulsa again. It was a cesspool of iniquity and corruption. It was the cesspool which had been pointed out specifically to the Tulsa police and to Police Commissioner Adkison, and they could see nothing in it. Yet anybody could go down there and buy all the booze they wanted. Anybody could go into the most unspeakable dance halls and base joints of prostitution. All this had been called to the attention of our police department and all the police department could do under the Mayor of this city was to whitewash itself. The Mayor of Tulsa is a perfectly nice, honest man, we do not doubt, but he is guileless. He could have found out himself any time in one night what just one preacher found out.

In this old 'Niggertown' were a lot of bad niggers and a

bad nigger is about the lowest thing that walks on two feet. Give a bad nigger his booze and his dope and a gun and he thinks he can shoot up the world. And all these four things were to be found in 'Niggertown'—booze, dope, bad niggers and guns.[157]

The City of Tulsa also impeded rebuilding with its attempt to impose a stricter fire ordinance in the burned Greenwood District. Imposition of the extended fire limits, as proposed by the City, would have made rebuilding cost-prohibitive for many African Americans seeking to remain in their community. Under the ordinance, newly-erected structures would have to be constructed with fireproof materials.

The Tulsa City Commission passed the contentious fire ordinance, Ordinance No. 2156, on June 7, 1921. The Ordinance provided:

An Ordinance extending the fire limits of the City of Tulsa, Oklahoma, and amending Section 1 of Article 20 of Ordinance No. 1380, adopted April the 16th, 1915, and amending Section 1 of Ordinance No. 1486, adopted March the 24th, 1916, and amending Section 1 of Ordinance No. 1650, adopted March 3d [sic], 1917, and amending Section 1 of Ordinance No. 1658, adopted March 16th, 1917; and governing the construction, erection, alteration, repair, remodling [sic], re-building, moving, demolition, securing the inspection of building a structure and appurtenance thereto within and for the additional extension of the fire limits as herein provided; prescribing a penalty for violations of the same; repealing all ordinances or parts of ordinances in conflict with the provisions of this ordinance; and declaring an emergency.[158]

City leaders expressed a desire to convert the charred land into an industrial park, an idea whose appeal was strengthened by the proximity of the Greenwood District to the several railroad lines. Some among them took note of the fact that the proposed conversion of the area would also enhance the physical separation of the races.[159]

In the end, attorney B.C. Franklin fought successfully against the fire code measure. Explaining his rationale and strategy, Franklin noted:[160]

> We immediately filed an injunction action against the city to enjoin and prohibit it from enforcing the ordinance. Among other things, we alleged that the fire was not the fault of our client, Joe Lockard; that to enforce such an ordinance would be equivalent to confiscation of property without due process; and further, that for all practical purposes, it would make the city a party to a conspiracy against the plaintiff and other similarly situated to despoil them of their property; it would be using the city for the selfish purpose of arraying citizens against each other; and such acts were outside the legitimate police power of the city.

> We also instituted dozens of lawsuits against certain fire insurance companies who had insured properties of families and firms in the destroyed area, but in all cases where the policies did not insure against 'riots, civil commotion,' and the like, no recovery was possible—fully 95 percent of the cases.[161]

Calls for reparations fell on deaf ears. Such pleas came and went, none more eloquent than that of attorney and riot survivor, H.A. Guess:

> 'Tulsa Will' . . . The question is will Tulsa raise [sic] to the emergency and make good the losses which she visited upon her colored citizens in the upheavel [sic] of June 1st, better known as [the] Tulsa Race Riot? Will her broadminded, big-hearted leaders and town and empire builders surrender to the whim of a few political buccaneers and land schemers whose ulterior motive is self-aggrandizement at the expense of the public will, or, will they push aside some of the cob-webs of legal technicalities and face the issues of facts in a courageous [sic], generous and altruistic spirit that has so signally characterized the triumphal march at the head of modern civilization of the

proud Anglo-Saxton [sic] race, and proceed to get on foot plans for the rehabilitation of the burned district? . . . What are some of the things that should be foremost in such a program?

Reparation . . . will restore confidence of those whose faith has been seriously shaken; will give notice to the outside world that if Tulsa is big enough, strong enough, cosmopolitan enough to match the greatest race riot in American history, she is also generous enough, proud enough, rich enough and possessing enough respect for law and order and disdaining anything that savors of greed, graft and legal oppressions, to fail to do entire justice to a sorely tried people whose accumulations, in many instances, of a life-time, were swept away in a few hours and too, without any fault on their part. It may very well be said by Tulsa's legal advisors that there is no precedent for re-embursement [sic] in such cases; that a bond issue and election to make good the losses would be illegal. We answer that the race riot was also illegal and, since the damage wrought was also great, some way should be found to make good the loss. There is and should be an adequate remedy to adjust every great wrong.[162]

The law firm of Spears, Franklin & Chappelle provided legal assistance to victims. These African American lawyers lodged claims against the City of Tulsa and insurance companies for damage occasioned by the 1921 tragedy. Beyond that, they counseled and consoled their clients and made urgent appeals to African Americans nationwide for assistance. One of these men, B.C. Franklin, led the charge.

Mount Zion Baptist Church provides yet another example of the remarkable courage and determination of the people of post-Riot Greenwood. The $85,000 church, only six weeks old at the time of the massacre, had been built with the help of a $50,000 loan from a single, anonymous individual. Rumors during the unrest that preceded the event included a persistent story that Mount Zion housed a stash of arms for the looming racial conflict. The invading white mob torched Mount Zion, leaving nothing but a dirt floor basement.

Church members, still dazed by the devastation, made several key decisions. They elected to continue to meet, often in private homes. When presented with the option of extinguishing the $50,000 mortgage through bankruptcy, the church leadership balked. While the legal obligation could perhaps be eliminated, they felt a moral obligation to pay off the loan, even absent the building. Decades later, Mount Zion did just that. The church paid off the loan and raised enough money to build a new structure. Mount Zion remains a vital and vibrant part of Tulsa'a Historic Greenwood District.[163]

Mrs. Mary Elizabeth Jones Parrish, the young African American scribe from Rochester, New York, who came to Tulsa in 1918, offered yet another testimonial about the people of the Greenwood District. She noted that she came to Tulsa "not . . . lured by the dream of making money and bettering myself in the financial world, but because of the wonderful co-operation I observed among our people, and especially the harmony of spirit and action that existed between the business men and women." She saw something remarkable in Tulsa's Greenwood District.[164]

In short order, she and fellow denizens of the Greenwood District experienced the highest of highs and the lowest of lows: "After spending years of struggling and sacrifice, the people had begun to look upon Tulsa as the Negro Metropolis of the Southwest. Then the devastating Tulsa Disaster burst upon us, blowing to atoms ideas and ideals no less than mere material evidence of our civilization."[165]

Parrish reported on the devastation of the Greenwood District and in 1923 published a book entitled *Events of the Tulsa Disaster*.[166] The Parrish book includes an extensive business listing. Sample business advertisements included:

Telephone: Office, Cedar, 974; Residence, Osage 7090.
H. A. GUESS, Lawyer
Partee Building, Corner North Greenwood and East Archer St.
Civil and Probate Practice a Specialty

THE ROYAL HOTEL

This magnificent Hotel is a 30-room modern building. When in Tulsa you will do well to secure rooms at the Royal Hotel if you desire the convenience and comforts of home, combined with courteous treatment.

This Hotel is located on the corner of Greenwood and Archer Streets and is easily reached from all railroads running into Tulsa. It is in the heart of the Negro Business District and ten minutes' walk to town. L.W. THOMPSON, Proprietor

OLD LINE; STRAIGHT LIFE; LEGAL RESERVE

Are you satisfied with the amount of protection you are now carrying for your family and loved ones? If you cannot truthfully answer Yes to this vital question call and see J.M. TYLER, District Agent for Standard Life Insurance Co., Atlanta, Ga., 123½ North Greenwood, Tulsa, Oklahoma

RED WING HOTEL

The Red Wing Hotel is located on the corner of Greenwood and Cameron Streets and consists of 54 rooms. These rooms are all modern and homelike. The Red Wing Hotel is centrally located in the Colored District on the Sand Springs car line and the Greenwood jitney line. Our prices are reasonable. Our service is best. Mrs. Willie Ellis, Proprietress.

THE NOVELTY SHOP
5c, 10c and 25c Goods
210 East Archer Street
TULSA, OKLAHOMA

The Novelty Shop is one of Tulsa's busy places of business. This shop is owned by Mrs. E. Davis. Her pleasing personality and courteous treatment have won for her many friends and customers. During the Christmas holidays this splendid lady gave away many presents to children whose parents were not able to have Santa Claus visit them. She is, indeed, a credit to any community.

TRY US ONCE AND YOU WILL TRY US TWICE.

GRIER SHOE SHOP
J.L. Grier, Prop.
518 E. Archer
Tulsa, Okla.
Phone 7953

THE CREOLE SYSTEM OF GROWING HAIR
This Creole System will grow these ladies' hair in 18 months. It will grow yours. When all others have failed to cure your scalp of its disease and to grow your hair try the Creole System and be convinced. It has pleased the most fastidious. It will please you. You take no chance in giving it a trial. It is perfectly reliable. Mme. Hunt is the oldest and most skilled Hair Grower in this city. She is also a Manicurist and Manufacturer of Human Hair Goods.
MRS. GEO. W. HUNT, TULSA, OKLAHOMA

Henry Nails; J.H. Nails
Nails Borthers' Shoe Shop
We Carry a Complete Line of
black swan records
Phone, Cedar 1371
121 N. Greenwood
Tulsa, Okla.

IF YOU WANT LONG, BEAUTIFUL HAIR
Use the N.O.S. Hair Grower. A grower that has been in circulation for 10 years. A preparation prepared only by Mme. Nannie Ora Smith. Give it a trial and become a regular customer of the N.O.S. System. Use the
N.O.S. Hair Grower 75c
N.O.S. Pressing Oil 50c
N.O.S. Temple Oil 25c
Correspondence Lessons taught and Agents Wanted.
MME. NANNIE ORA SMITH
613 E. Archer St. Tulsa, Okla.

MADAM MABEL LITTLE

The Taylor System of Hair Dressing
Agents Wanted
Address 1301 N. Greenwood
Route 4, Box 47C

George W. Buckner, Special Representative of the National Urban League commented on the remarkable post-massacre rebuilding and the human spirt exhibited by the residents of the Greenwood District.

St. Louis Argus—April 21, 1922—Tulsa.

'Wonderful' is the spontaneous acclaim of anyone who visits Tulsa today after seeing the burned area immediately following the disaster there June 1st of last year. The former business section which consisted largely of Greenwood Avenue has been transformed from ragged, unsightly walls to modern structures where small, thriving businesses of every kind are meeting the needs of the people. The formed residential sections which resembled a camp of soldiers in war, having been covered with tents and impoverished shacks, are now being rapidly replaced by more substantial homes. But very few of the tents furnished by the Red Cross now remain. So much for a hasty material perspective.

What about the spirit now manifested by the Negroes? Let it be said unreservedly that the spirit exhibited from the beginning by the Tulsa Negroes, on the whole, should be the pride of the whole race. Under the most cruel and soul-crushing conditions they have simply put their backs against the wall determined to die, if needs be, in Tulsa.[167]

Remarkably, and in stunningly short order, the Greenwood District came alive once again, bigger and better than ever. Black and white Tulsans worked collaboratively to lure the annual conference of the National Negro Business League to Tulsa in 1925. Tulsa lawyer and community leader B.C. Franklin noted:

Mob violence and lawlessness have never done a community any good and never will. Tulsa had been given a black eye in 1921, and the entire city felt the aftermath of the riot. This was especially true of the colored section. Negroes from Tulsa traveling elsewhere or abroad were taunted and ridiculed about what had taken place. As is too often true, people everywhere of all races thought Tulsa was an unsafe place in which to locate and do business, and most of them thought there was not a good white person in the entire city.

To offset this widespread, entirely erroneous belief, there was a movement started early in 1925 to bring the National Negro Business League to the city . . . . The idea grew and became popular. The white section of the city, chagrined and still smarting under the almost nationwide misrepresentations of the good people of the city, thought the idea a good one and pledged their united support. Organizations were formed and committees appointed to carry forward the thought, and the national league accepted the invitation to hold its national gathering in Tulsa during August of that year.

Never before or since have the races in Tulsa been more determined to put forth a united front, and the undertaking succeeded to a degree hitherto unknown or since. The national meeting opened on the 19th day of the month and continued until the 21st. Negro business and professional men from all over the nation were present, including Dr. R.R. Moton, who had succeeded Booker T. Washington as principal at Tuskegee Institute, and who spoke at the meeting. Many other notables, among them Governor [Martin Edwin] Trapp [1923-1927], journeyed to Tulsa to welcome the visitors. The city was properly represented by its mayor, and many remained to attend and participate in the seminars.[168]

A year later, Dr. W.E.B. Du Bois visited Tulsa. Impressed at the recovery, he penned an article for the N.A.A.C.P.'s *Crisis* magazine, for which he served as founding editor, entitled, "Thank God for the Grit of Tulsa."

Black Tulsa is a happy city. It has new clothes. It is young
and gay and strong. Five little years ago, fire and blood
and robbery leveled it to the ground. Scars are there, but
the city is impudent and noisy. It believes in itself. Thank
God for the grit of Black Tulsa.[169]

That grit—that fortitude—the human spirt—defined the denizens of Tulsa's Historic Greenwood District as the smoke cleared
and the smoldering embers cooled. Survivor Henry C. Whitlow,
Jr., perhaps said it best: "If you have never known poverty, dejec-
tion, dissolution, vociferous denounciation [sic], hatred, and slan-
der directed toward you, you cannot appreciate the achievements
of the Negro during the 'Greenwood Era.'"

A Greenwood District business directory, *circa* 1935, evidenced
the community's stunning rebound.[170] By 1942, well over 200 businesses called the Greenwood District home.

In Tulsa's segregated Greenwood District, entrepreneurship
and relative affluence coexisted with deprivation and relative
squalor (*e.g.*, the lack of stable utility services, paved roads, and
running water in some places). The City of Tulsa shortchanged her
black citizens in myriad ways, including, notably, the allocation of
infrastructure projects.

Dr. Charles J. Bate came to Tulsa on April 28, 1940. He became one of about sixteen black doctors practicing in the city.[171]
He found in Tulsa a segregated medical establishment, but one in
which white doctors often treated black patients.

Tulsa's wealthy oil barons and elite businessmen insisted that
their black servants receive quality medical care. That meant treatment at white institutions like Morningside Hospital at 11th Street
and Utica Avenue (now, Hillcrest Medical Center) and St. John
Catholic Hospital at 21st Street and Utica Avenue (now, Ascension
St. John Medical Center). At Hillcrest, for example, black patients
received treatment on the first floor, recuperated briefly in "colored rooms" in the basement, and were then subjected to summa-
ry, sometimes premature, discharge. Dr. Bate recalled a particular incident that reinforced the second-class citizenship accorded
black patients in that era.

A very obese black woman showed up at Hillcrest in great distress. The attending physician examined her and determined that she needed an operation immediately for a large ovarian tumor; the 'tumor' turned out to be a healthy, black baby! The perplexed white doctor didn't know what to do with the baby; the mother was put in the 'colored ward' in the basement, but he couldn't put a screaming baby in there with recuperating adults. So the good doctor put the baby in a broom closet! That really bothered me and I did hold a grudge against that doctor. But one day when he and I were talking, he told me that the incident, as I had heard, was true. He said he was ashamed to be a part of a system that would treat another human being that way, but he said he had no choice. At that time, he simply could not have put that little black baby in the nursery with white babies in Oklahoma. I thought about it and I knew that he was telling the truth. So my grudge against him just dissolved and we became close friends.[172]

A graduate of Meharry Medical College in Nashville, Tennessee, Dr. Bate established his first office atop a rooming house at 350 North Greenwood. He practiced medicine and conducted surgery at Moton Hospital (603 East Pine Street) and Mercy Hospital (Eighth & Elgin Streets).

Dr. Bate found in the 1940s Greenwood District a stark contrast between place and people; between the physical environs and the people who inhabited them.

Tulsa was a city within a city. [T]here were about 20,000 blacks in an area . . . . less than four square miles. I had never seen living conditions in a city like they were in Tulsa. I'd never seen it. I saw houses—25-foot houses—I mean 25-foot lot—with 3 houses on one lot. And you'd have to go through the first two houses to get into the last house. There were outdoor privies everywhere. And none of the streets were paved in the Negro area of Tulsa . . . They didn't get paved up until the late 40s or 50s. Just mud streets everywhere. And very narrow. [I]t was interesting enough to see a church on almost every corner . . . . And another thing that was interesting was the railroad train went right up to Greenwood, which was the main thoroughfare. And when you do down on Greenwood, on a Thursday evening, that was maids' day off, and [people would] be so thick, you could hardly walk through there. The same thing on Saturday night . . . . [T]he spirit of the people in Tulsa was tremendous. They had very little, but I mean the people were spiritual.[173]

Black isolation just north of downtown Tulsa continued for decades, with some improvement after World War II. In the 1950s, residential segregation began to abate ever so slightly as the restrictive covenants that prevented home sales to black buyers fell to legal challenges and some Oklahoma City banks began offering home loans to African American customers in Tulsa. Changes in Tulsa leadership also helped loosen the foothold of segregation on the City.[174]

Another Tulsa lion, Reverend Benjamin S. ("B.S.") Roberts, spoke of the character of black Tulsans. Roberts, Tulsa's first elected black city councilor (1990), spent decades fighting for civil rights. With other ministers, he helped shepherd youth groups in the 1950s and 1960s, and facilitated sit-ins, wade-ins, try-ons (*i.e.*, protests designed to eliminate the proscription against African Americans trying on clothes in downtown stores), and park-ins (at Mohawk Park). Under the weight of moral, social, economic, and political pressure, African American access to public accommodations could no longer be denied. Reverend Roberts also led a voter registration drive that netted almost 10,000 new black voters.[175]

Reverend Roberts reflected on the civil rights struggles in an interview with Tulsa teacher, historian, and author Eddie Faye Gates:

> I am proud of what we did in the 1950s and 1960s. In a peaceful matter we showed the city the kinds of injustices that existed in Tulsa at the time and we helped to show them how to rise above that condition and make Tulsa a better place. But we can't rest of our laurels. We must be ever vigilant to recognize injustice, point it out,

and do something about correcting it. That's what vowed to do when I was just a boy in Georgia. I have been doing just that ever since![176]

Reverend Roberts looked fondly on his activist days, and on the people for and with whom he made his mark:

There were good days and bad days; there were days of danger, but there were also days of fun and frivolity. There were days of love, fellowship, and brotherhood so pure and tangible that it would move people to tears. The social and economic classes mingled in mutual cooperation to bring down the walls of racial segregation. The lowly walked along side the rich, famous, and powerful including popular comedian/activist Dick Gregory and the most powerful civil rights leader the nation has ever produced, Dr. Martin Luther King, Jr. It was a period unlike any other period in United States [h]istory."[177]

Dr. Bate and Reverend Roberts saw what so many others before and since witnessed: the incredible human spirit of Tulsa's African American community. The Greenwood story—the Black Wall Street experience—speaks to the triumph of the human spirit and to the timeless, universal virtues we all cherish: faith, determination, integrity, humility, and compassion.

As referenced by Reverend Roberts and noted earlier, on July 28, 1960, civil rights icon Dr. Martin Luther King, Jr., spoke at First Baptist Church North Tulsa. He extolled the virtues of nonviolence. He advocated for unity. He stressed the importance of exercising the franchise. He pressed the case for preparation and perseverance.[178]

Tulsa attorney James O. Goodwin, a college student at Notre Dame at the time, recalled the occasion, including a crowd of more than 1,000. "I was sitting right next to him," said Goodwin. "It was a light encounter, right after the event Dr. King came over to my dad's office." He described the venue as "packed," noting that Dr. King had by that time ascended to national prominence.

In 1968, Goodwin, his brother and father traveled to the funeral of the fallen civil rights icon. "We felt compelled to pay tribute to a man who meant so much to America."[179]

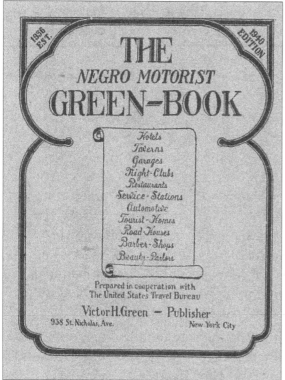

The Green Book (1940 Edition)[180]

Further evidence of the regeneration of the Greenwood District may be found in *The Negro Motorist Green Book*, later known as *The Negro Travelers' Green Book*, or simply, *The Green Book*.

The Green Book, the brainchild of Victor Hugo Green,[181] a Harlem postal worker, debuted in 1936 and continued publication until 1964. It aimed to assist African American travelers in Jim Crow America with public accommodations, services, and information they needed to venture out into the world unmolested, at a minimum, and, ideally, in relative comfort.

The 2018 Academy Award-winning film, *Green Book*, chronicled the relationship between a working-class Italian-American bouncer who became the driver of an African American classical pianist on a tour of venues through the 1960s Deep South. The film, told from the driver's perspective, tapped *The Green Book* as a backdrop for the men's adventures in the rigidly segregated South.

The introduction to the 1947 edition of *The Green Book* articulated its mission.

INTRODUCTION

The idea of 'The Green Book' is to give the Motorist and tourist a Guide not only of the Hotels and Tourist Homes in all of the large cities, but other classifications that will be found useful wherever he may be. Also facts and information that the Negro Motorist can use and depend upon.

There are thousands of places that the public doesn't know about and aren't listed. Perhaps you might know of some? If so, send in their names and addresses and the kind of business, so that we might pass it along to the rest of your fellow Motorists.

You will find it handy on your travels, whether at home or in some other state, and [it] is up to date. Each year we are compiling new lists as some of these places move, or go out of business and new business places are started giving added employment to members of our race.

When you are traveling mention 'The Green Book' so as to let these people know just how you found out about their place of business. If they haven't heard about This Guide, tell them to get in touch with us.

If this Guide is useful, let us know, if not tell us also, as we appreciate your criticisms.

If any errors are found, kindly notify the publishers so that they can be corrected in the next issue.[183]

Following are the Tulsa listings for 1939, 1947, and 1962 from the respective Green Books for those years:

1939
HOTELS
    Small—615 E. Archer Street
    Lincoln—E. Archer Street
    Red Wing—2016 N. Greenwood Avenue
    Royal—605 E. Archer Street
    Manard—922 E. Marshall Place
    McHunt—1121 N. Greenwood Avenue

TOURIST HOMES
    Mrs. R.C. Baughman—320 N. Greenwood Avenue
    Mrs. W.H. Smith—124½ N. Greenwood Avenue
    Mrs. Thomas Gentry—537 N. Detroit Avenue
    Mrs. C.L. Netherland—542 N. Elgin Street

RESTAURANTS
Plez's Chili Parlor—127 N. Greenwood Avenue
Barbeque—1111 N. Greenwood Avenue

BEAUTY PARLORS
Mrs. Smith's—524 E. Jasper Street
Cotton Blossom—106 N. Greenwood Avenue
Mrs. J. C. Mays'—523 N. Greenwood Avenue

BARBER SHOP
Leader—203 N. Greenwood Avenue

TAVERNS
Del Rio Bar—1448 N. Greenwood Avenue

SERVICE STATIONS
Mince—2nd & Elgin Streets[184]

1947
HOTELS
Small—615 E. Archer Street
Lincoln—E. Archer Street
Red Wing—2016 N. Greenwood Avenue
Royal—605 E. Archer Street
McHunt—1121 N. Greenwood Avenue
Warren Hotel—[no address listed]
Y.W.C.A.—621 E. Oklahoma Place

TOURIST HOMES
Mrs. W.H. Smith—124½ N. Greenwood Avenue
Gentry—537 N. Detroit Avenue
Mrs. C.L. Netherland—542 N. Elgin Street

RESTAURANTS
Barbeque—1111 N. Greenwood Avenue

BEAUTY PARLORS
Cotton Blossom—308 E. Haskell Street
May's—523 N. Greenwood Avenue

BARBER SHOP
Swindall's—203 N. Greenwood Avenue

SERVICE STATIONS
Mince—2nd & Elgin Streets

GARAGES
   Pine Street—906 E. Pine Street

DRUG STORES
   Meharry Drugs—101 Greenwood Avenue[185]

1962
   Avalon Motel—2411 East Apache Street
   C.L. Netherland Tourist Home—542 N. Elgin Street
   Del Rio Hotel—607½ N. Greenwood Avenue
   McHunt Hotel—1121 N. Greenwood Avenue
   Miller Hotel—124 N. Hartford Street
   Small Hotel—615 E. Archer Street
   W.H. Smith Tourist Home—124½ N. Greenwood Avenue
   Y.W.C.A.—1120 East Pine Street[186]

As political winds began to shift, so, too, did economic and social currents. Urban renewal signaled rough seas ahead for multiple properties, including those in Tulsa's Historic Greenwood District.

"Urban renewal" refers to a large-scale, comprehensive process of renovating or replacing housing and public works (*e.g.*, parks, public buildings, and roads) considered substandard or outdated. Urban renewal programs, though generally well-intentioned, often disproportionately impact the elderly, people of color, and the poor by forcibly removing persons in areas targeted for rehabilitation. These displaced residents typically cannot afford to live in the newly renovated areas because of higher taxes or rent. Wealthier individuals and enterprises fill the void via a process commonly known as "gentrification."

A key tool in the urban renewal arsenal is the power of "eminent domain,"[187] the power to take private property for public use by a state, municipality, or private person or corporation authorized to exercise functions of public character, following the payment of just compensation to the owner of that property.[188]

Tulsa was the first large Oklahoma city to form an urban renewal authority, which city commissioners approved in July 1959. Planning started in 1961 for the Seminole Hills Project, the state's first urban renewal project. Instead of bulldozing blocks of homes, the city pursued a program of clearing problem properties while rehabilitating others. In June 1968 the authority declared the ninety-one-acre project complete. Tulsa also initiated a downtown urban renewal program, declaring the heart of the district blighted. Dozens of properties were cleared and replaced with a new office complex anchored by the nine-square-block Williams Center.[189]

As noted, Tulsa's initial foray into the murky waters of urban renewal began in 1959. At a July 31, 1959, meeting of the Mayor and Board of Commissioners of the City of Tulsa, five individuals were appointed to the Urban Renewal Authority (renamed Tulsa Development Authority on May 2, 1986):[190] Leemon Nix, Chairman; Robert Laird, Vice Chairman; Murray McCune; Dr. Charles Christopher; and Roehm West.

The Board of Commissioners then passed the following resolution on November 17, 1959:

RESOLUTION 2339

A RESOLUTION DETERMINING THAT IT IS IN THE PUBLIC INTEREST THAT THE AUTHORITY OR POWERS PRESCRIBED BY HOUSE BILL 602 OF THE TEWENTY-SEVENTH LEGISLATURE OF THE STATE OF OKLAHOMA BE EXERCISED BY THE TULSA URBAN RENEWAL AUTHORITY, AND ELECTING TO HAVE SUCH AUTHORITY OR POWERS EXERCISED BY THE TULSA URBAN RENEWAL AUTHORITY; AND DECLARING AN EMERGENCY.

WHEREAS, it has been found and declared by the Board of Commissioners of the City of Tulsa, Oklahoma, by Resolution dated the 17th day of November, 1959, that one or more blighted areas exist within the corporate limits of the City of Tulsa, Oklahoma, and that the rehabilitation, conservation, redevelopment, or a combination thereof, of such area or areas is necessary in the interest of the public health, safety, morals and welfare of the residents of such area; and

WHEREAS, the Legislature of the State of Oklahoma has passed and approved House Bill #602 of the Twenty-seventh Legislature, Title 11 Okl. St. Section 1601 *et seq.*, authorizing the appointment of an Urban Renewal Authority to exercise certain powers set out in said House Bill 602 necessary to perform the rehabilitation, conservation or redevelopment of blighted areas; and

WHEREAS, the Mayor of the City of Tulsa did appoint, on the 7th day of July, 1959 [*sic,* the actual date was July 31, 1959], Commissioners of the Tulsa Urban Renewal Authority which appointments were approved by the Board of Commissioners of the City of Tulsa on the 7th day of July, 1959 [*sic,* the actual date was July 31, 1959]; and

WHEREAS, it has been found to be in the public interest to have the authority or powers prescribed by said House Bill 602 of the Twenty-seventh Legislature of the State of Oklahoma to be exercised by the Tulsa Urban Renewal Authority.

NOW, THEREFORE, BE IT RESOLVED BY THE BOARD OF COMMISSIONERS OF THE CITY OF TULSA, OKLAHOMA:

Section 1. That the exercise of the authority or powers prescribed by House Bill #602 of the Twenty-seventh Legislature of the State of Oklahoma by the Tulsa Urban Renewal Authority is in the public interest and for public uses and purposes and is necessary for the rehabilitation, conservation, redevelopment or a combination thereof, of blighted areas within which exist within the corporate limits of the City of Tulsa, Oklahoma.

Section 2. That the Board of Commissioners of the City of Tulsa, Oklahoma, hereby elect to have the Tulsa Urban Renewal Authority exercise the authority or powers prescribed by House Bill #602 of the Twenty-seventh Legislature of the State of Oklahoma to the extent that the same may be exercised by the Tulsa Urban Renewal Authority under the provisions of said House Bill #602.

Section 3. That an emergency exists for the preservation of the public peace, health and safety, by reason whereof this Resolution shall take effect immediately upon its adoption and approval.

PASSED, and the emergency clause ruled upon separately and approved this 17th day of November, 1959.

APPROVED, this 17th day of November, 1959.

James Maxwell, Mayor[191]

Superimposed on the 1951 aerial view of the Greenwood District[192] that follows is the route of Interstate 244, a product of urban renewal. The roadway tore through the heart of the teeming community, striking a near-fatal blow.

This ostensibly unintended consequence of highway location became all too common throughout the nation, so much so that intentionality remains, at best, an open question.

[The] intertwined history of infrastructure and racial inequality extended into the 1950s and 1960s with the creation of the Interstate highway system. The federal government shouldered nine-tenths of the cost of new Interstate highways, but local officials often had a say in selecting the path . . . . [I]n most American cities in the decades after the Second World War, the new highways . . . . were steered along routes that bulldozed 'blighted' neighborhoods that housed its poorest residents, almost always racial minorities.

*   *   *   *

[I]nterstates were regularly used to destroy black neighborhoods [and] keep black and white neighborhoods apart.[193]

Beyond the ravages wrought by urban renewal ("urban removal" in the eyes of many locals),[194] integration undermined the financial foundation of the Greenwood District as a business enclave. Forced segregation created an economic detour--a somewhat insular economy in the African American sector. When integration opened economic channels, dollars flowed outside the

Illustration showing how Interstate 244 bisects the famed Black Wall Street community.

community without a commensurate inflow of white dollars.

In Tulsa as elsewhere, integration swung open the doors of once-off-limits white establishments to African American customers accustomed to patronizing black-owned merchants. Widespread integration, begun in earnest in the 1960s, likewise dangled the corporate ladder (at least its lower rungs) in front of educated and motivated African Americans seeking greener pastures. This outflow of talent undermined the economic foundation of the Greenwood District.

New opportunities—a wider selection of goods and an expanded array of job opportunities—ironically eroded black entrepreneurial communities.

As African American incomes rose, so, too, did the yearning for the trappings of the American Dream. With these bigger bankrolls came increased purchasing power and the capacity to exit from traditional black communities and move into available integrated and suburban neighborhoods.

Integration thus left black shopkeepers with fewer customers. Those customers who remained often lacked significant buying capacity because of financial challenges. Some black merchants, particularly in core urban communities, fell prey to shoplifting, burglary, and robbery.[195]

As Tulsa grew, so, too, did its need for connectivity. With the automobile as king, the demand for new highways soared. One such road, Interstate 244, now bisects what was once the heart of the Greenwood District. Crews completed the final section of that thoroughfare, the north leg of the "Inner Dispersal Loop" (the freeways system encircling downtown Tulsa), in December 1975.[196]

Add to the foregoing factors a new business climate less favorable to sole proprietorships. Many African American shops, because of their small scale, charged higher prices than larger chain stores. This pricing differential proved frustrating and alienating, especially for a black clientele with other options.

One final factor merits mention: the aging of the early Greenwood District pioneers without a systematic succession process to fill the void. Mom-and-pop-type operations often do not survive beyond the lives of the original mom and pop. Death, disability, retirement, relocation or other changes in life circumstances often spelled doom for the enterprise.

Succession planning for small businesses might consist of: (1) Determining priorities in terms of personal transition desires and business/customer needs; (2) Reviewing current structure and future business needs to determine the appropriate successor; (3) Building a transition plan grounded in financial and personnel needs; and (4) Executing the plan. The Greenwood District businesses generally lacked this kind of strategic, sustainable succession planning for what might have been more accurately called "Black Main Street."[197]

Given this complicated mix of factors integral to business

health, one begins to understand why the Greenwood District declined beginning in the 1960s, and continuing throughout the 1970s and early 1980s.

Now experiencing a renaissance, the ghosts of Greenwood District past loom large on the horizon. Is the Greenwood District poised for a new wave of innovation and commerce? Is another black entrepreneurial mecca possible? How might the Greenwood District address concerns around revitalization without gentrification (at least in the pejorative sense of the word)?

Chapter Four

Reflecting on the Renaissance

*Every renaissance comes to the world with a
cry, the cry of the human spirit to be free.*

Ann Sullivan Macy

"Deep Greenwood," the intersection of Greenwood Avenue and Archer
Street.[198]

Healing History

Hannibal B. Johnson

Unfortunate history,
Unpardonable sin,
Wretched deeds,
Where to begin?

Riots and lynchings,
And dastardly deeds,
Here in America,
Sowing the seeds.

Hate and violence,
Darkness and despair,
Moments in time,
Lacking in care.

Untold stories,
Of privation and pain,
Unheralded heroes,
Insoluble stain.

Lies and deceptions,
Some great, some small,
Diminish our standing,
Not one, but all.

Cuts and bruises,
Scrapes and scars,
Pages of history,
Legacy of wars.

Festering wounds,
Unhealed by time,
Regret and remembrance,
Of actors and crimes.

History remains,
Inconvenient, perhaps,
Our ignorance, though,
Sets its own traps.

Healing our history,
Knowing the truth,
Binds us together,
Elder and youth.[199]

As noted, in the immediate wake of the Tulsa disaster, the City's elected leader, Mayor T.D. Evans, urged collective amnesia. In an address to the Tulsa City Commission on June 14, 1921, Mayor Evans called the massacre "inevitable" and beseeched Tulsans to aid its victims, whom he noted "should receive such help as we can give them."

Mayor Evans did not stop there. He implored Tulsans to keep it all close to the vest: "Let us immediately get to the outside the fact that everything is quiet in our city, that this menace has been fully conquered, and that we are going on in a normal condition." Unapologetic and ever the Tulsa booster, Mayor Evans sentiments could be summed up in two words: move on.[200]

Dwain Midget, Director of the Working in Neighborhoods Department for the City of Tulsa, expressed a different, hopeful vision for moving on as relates to the Greenwood District:

> Black Wall Street is a concept. [The Greenwood District] will never be Greenwood of the 1920s, 1930s or 1940s. For me, as an African American, I'm looking for a new Black Wall Street. Where in my community can I resurrect a new Black Wall Street? Maybe on Peoria (Avenue) from Archer (Street) all the way down to 66th Street North. There are black people there, and there is ample opportunity to build. Black Wall Street doesn't have to be on Greenwood [Avenue].[201]

Two seminal events heightened awareness of and attention to the remarkable Greenwood District history, and thereby helped catalyze a renaissance—not a renaissance of black entrepreneurship, but rather a renaissance of spirit; a rejuvenated interest in history and heritage that stoked modest development and major publicity; an unshackling of the mind.

First, Scott Ellsworth, a doctoral student under the tutelage of Dr. John Hope Franklin, published a book from his Duke University doctoral dissertation in history in 1982. That book, *Death in a Promised Land*,[202] sparked immense interest and spawned a slew of further research and writing.

Second, the Oklahoma Legislature formed the Oklahoma Commission to Study the Tulsa Race Riot of 1921 in 1997 (the "Riot Commission").[203] That deliberative body studied the massacre, drew conclusions, and made recommendations. Its final report attracted worldwide attention.

In addition to the Elsworth book and the Riot Commission report, prominent Tulsans began giving voice to this largely unspoken chapter of Tulsa history. Chief among them was lifelong Tulsan and the city's first female mayor, Susan Savage.

A Mayor's Apology

Former Tulsa Mayor M. Susan Savage, who served from July 13, 1992 - April 1, 2002, issued what is likely the first public apology for the Tulsa travesty by a prominent public official. She later noted: "I did know a little about Tulsa's 1921 Race Riot while growing up, however, it was not until early in my first term as Mayor that I was confronted with the generational trauma and the pervasive impact of this tragedy."[204]

Mayor Savage, on the occasion of the 75th anniversary of the Riot in 1996, noted that although she grew up in a prominent family in Tulsa, she had reached adulthood by the time she learned about the Tulsa terror in some detail. "It just wasn't something that people discussed," she said.[205]

At reconciliation services hosted by Rev. G. Calvin McCutcheon, Sr., on June 4, 2000, Mayor Savage remarked:

> Dr. McCutcheon, thank you for hosting this service.
>
> Welcome to the honored guests this evening—survivors of Tulsa's worst moment; and to the pastors of those churches that were destroyed.
>
> Welcome to their families and friends. Welcome to Dr. John Hope Franklin whose intelligence and insight are an inspiration—it is always a pleasure to have you come home.
>
> Welcome to distinguished guests and all Tulsans.
>
> Racism remains the most insidious of challenges in our community raising the fundamental question of how we work to resolve it in a way that promotes unity rather than division and hostility.
>
> In my view, we begin as we have begun for several years—to seek to openly confront that which has divided us—through relentless effort—'relentless, moral effort' to use the words of author Shelby Steele. We begin with words of sorrow, regret and renewal.
>
> I am deeply sorry for the indignity, the hurt, the atrocities that our citizens endured in 1921. I am sorry for the hatred that drove people to kill, to injure, to destroy the lives of so many. I am sorry for the lack of action and response that our officials took and I am sorry for the ease with which people justified their inhumanity towards their fellow Tulsans. To the victims, I say Tulsa is sorry for what happened to you and we reach out to you for

your wisdom, strength and forgiveness.

Often we learn that following every tragedy, an opportunity arises.

Through the exceptionally important work of the Race Riot Commission, Tulsans have been focused on what happened during those dark days in our history. It has not been an easy or comfortable discussion nor something that many people have wanted to hear. However, if we are to repair the damage that was done, if we are to repair and restore relationships, if we are to emerge stronger and more determined to build one Tulsa, then we must stand together. To quote the June 2, 1921, *Tulsa World*, 'There is but one way in which Tulsa can rehabilitate itself...by rebuilding that which has been destroyed. Tulsa must restore that which has been taken. The sins of a comparative few are thus visited upon the whole community.'

As a lifelong Tulsan, and as Mayor of Tulsa, I embrace the vision and the obligation that we can do better. We can and will learn from our past and continue to build Tulsa into a community where fairness, tolerance and respect are the guiding principles among our citizens.[206]

The Riot Commission report, previously referenced, merits fuller attention. Following are key details from that comprehensive analysis.

The Report of the Oklahoma Commission to Study the Tulsa Race Riot of 1921

The Riot Commission included the following individuals:

Chairman
T.D. "Pete" Churchwell, *Tulsa*

Commissioners
Currie Ballard, *Coyle*
Dr. Bob Blackburn, *Oklahoma City*
Joe Burns, *Tulsa*
Dr. Vivian Clark, *Tulsa*

Representative Abe Deutschendorf, *Lawton*
Eddie Faye Gates, *Tulsa*
Jim Lloyd, *Tulsa*
Senator Robert Milacek, *Waukomis*
Jimmie L. White, Jr., *Checotah*

Advisors
Dr. John Hope Franklin, *Durham, NC*
Dr. Scott Ellsworth, *Portland, OR*

Sponsors
Senator Maxine Horner, *Tulsa*
Representative Don Ross, *Tulsa*

The Riot Commission's February 2001 final report chronicled the facts surrounding those fateful hours in Tulsa history. The preamble to that document called for reparations:

> This Commission fully understands that it is neither judge nor jury. We have no binding legal authority to assign culpability, to determine damages, to establish a remedy, or to order either restitution or reparations. However, in our interim report in February 2000 the majority of Commissioners declared that reparations to the historic Greenwood community in real and tangible form would be good public policy and do much to repair the emotional and physical scars of this terrible incident in our shared past. We listed several recommended courses of action including direct payments to riot survivors and descendants; a scholarship fund available to students affected by the riot; establishment of an economic development enterprise zone in the historic Greenwood district; a memorial for the riot victims.
>
> In the final report issued today, the majority of Commissioners continue to support these recommendations. While each Commissioner has their own opinion about the type of reparations that they would advocate, the majority has no question about the appropriateness of reparations. The recommendations are not intended to be all inclusive, but rather to give policy makers a sense of the

Commission's feelings about reparations and a starting place for the creation of their own ideas.[207]

The core findings of the Riot Commission included:

- Black Tulsans had every reason to believe that Dick Rowland would be lynched after his arrest on charges later dismissed and highly suspect from the start.

- They had cause to believe that his personal safety, like the defense of themselves and their community, depended on them alone.

- As hostile groups gathered and their confrontation worsened, municipal and county authorities failed to take actions to calm or contain the situation.

- At the eruption of violence, civil officials selected many men, all of them white and some of them participants in that violence, and made those men their agents as deputies.

- In that capacity, deputies did not stem the violence but added to it, often through overt acts themselves illegal.

- Public officials provided firearms and ammunition to individuals, again all of them white.

- Units of the Oklahoma National Guard participated in the mass arrests of all or nearly all of Greenwood's residents, removed them to other parts of the city, and detained them in holding centers.

- Entering the Greenwood district, people stole, damaged or destroyed personal property left behind in homes and businesses.

- People, some of them agents of government, also deliberately burned or otherwise destroyed homes credibly estimated to have numbered 1,256, along with virtually every other structure—including churches, schools, businesses, even a hospital and library—in the Greenwood [D]istrict.

- Despite duties to preserve order and to protect property, no government at any level offered adequate resistance, if any at all, to what amounted to the destruction of the neighborhood referred to commonly as 'Little Africa' and politely as the 'Negro quarter.'

- Although the exact total can never be determined, credible evidence makes it probable that many people, likely numbering between one and three hundred, were killed during the riot.

- Not one of these criminal acts was then or ever has been prosecuted or punished by government at any level, municipal, county, state, or national.

- Even after the restoration of order, it was official policy to release a black detainee only upon the application of a white person, and then only if that white agreed to accept responsibility for that detainee's subsequent behavior.

- As private citizens, many whites in Tulsa and neighboring communities did extend invaluable assistance to the riot's victims, and the relief efforts of the American Red Cross in particular provided a model of human behavior at its best.

- Although city and county government bore much of the cost for Red Cross relief, neither contributed substantially to Greenwood's rebuilding; in fact, municipal authorities acted initially to impede rebuilding.

- In the end, the restoration of Greenwood after its systematic destruction was left to the victims of that destruction.[208]

In addition to these findings, the Riot Commission made five specific, prioritized recommendations more generally described earlier:

1. Cash reparations payments to Riot survivors;
2. Cash reparations payments to heirs of survivors who lost property in the riot;
3. The establishment of a scholarship fund for Riot survivor heirs;
4. Business development incentives for the Greenwood District; and
5. A memorial museum.[209]

Several organizations and entities echoed their support for

reparations of various types, including the Tulsa Reparations Coalition and the National Coalition of Blacks for Reparations in
America ("N'COBRA").[210]

When it comes to the question of reparations, we are left with
a question of morality and justice: As a civilized society, what actions must we take to salve the wounds of our own making? If
we are as civilized as we profess to be, then we are responsible,
collectively, for the actions of those in whom we have, over time,
invested political power. We accept the benefits that accrue across
generations. We must likewise accept the burdens. As such, if
amends are to be made, if injustices are to be remedied, if wrongs
are to be righted, the ultimate responsibility rests upon each of our
shoulders.

Many Tulsans seem to agree that some sort of reparations,
broadly defined, are essential if we are to triumph over our tragic
past.[211] Indeed, we have begun making amends. Striking the appropriate balance—creating the right mix of measures that will
help us attend to our historical baggage—remains a challenge. So,
too, does following through on our good intentions.

Reflections on the Oklahoma Commission to
Study the Tulsa Race Riot of 1921 (1997 - 2001)

Two members of the Oklahoma Commission to Study the Tulsa
Race Riot of 1921, T.D. "Pete" Churchwell and Vivian Clark-Adams, Ph.D., agreed to respond to the author's questions about the
Riot Commission's work, their personal experiences, and the legacy of that chapter in their lives.

T.D. "Pete" Churchwell, Commission Chairman

T. D. "Pete" Churchwell, former CEO of American Electric Power, Public Service Company of Oklahoma ("AEP-PSO")
chaired the Riot Commission. He reflected on that life-altering experience.

> First a bit of history. I met Don Ross in the late sixties at
> the Tulsa Urban League. I quickly learned that we shared
> an interest in the 1921 riot. I was one of the few white
> Tulsans of my generation that even knew about the riot.
> How I knew is a whole other story, but I knew.

In 1971, I read the groundbreaking account of the riot by Ed Wheeler in *Impact* magazine. It also contained an interview by Don with his former history teacher, Mr. W.D. Williams, a riot survivor. These articles generated a controversy across the community at the time and raised a subject no one was ready to talk about.

Don's and my careers went separate directions. By the time I returned to Tulsa in 1996 as President of PSO, Don was a fixture in the State Legislature and had guided legislation establishing the Oklahoma Commission to Study the Tulsa Race Riot of 1921. I met Don at a dinner in Oklahoma City and told him I wanted to be involved. That involvement took up the next two and a-half years of my life.

My point in telling you this is my firm belief that without Don's leadership, his ability to work across political and racial lines, the riot would still be in the shadows. Much of the credit for whatever positive progress, awareness, and change has taken place in Tulsa and Oklahoma is due to the life and work of Don Ross.

1. What is your most vivid memory of the Riot Commission?

I would say my most vivid memories of the Riot Commission were meeting and listening to survivors and their eye-witness testimony about what happened to them and their families. It is a shame that more of these accounts were not captured and recorded, while more of the survivors were alive, younger and in good health. Eddie Fates Gates should be commended for her tireless efforts to track down and record the living survivors' stories.

My most cherished memory is meeting John Hope Franklin. Getting to meet him, getting to know him ever so slightly, getting to visit with him in his home and getting a personal tour of his beloved greenhouse. He was such a gentleman, scholar, and so critical to our final product.

2. What was the mission of the Riot Commission?

Our statutory mandate was to write a true, accurate, and scholarly report of the riot. A State report had never been prepared. The only official state documents were the 'After Action' reports from the National Guard. While many stories about the riot had been written over the years, there was no official state report as would have normally been prepared after an event of that magnitude.

3. How would you describe the functioning of the Riot Commission, including the relationships between and among the its members?

The Riot Commission was made up of outstanding and diverse citizens, some of whom I am sad to say are no longer with us. Our members had different political and ethnic backgrounds and held strong beliefs and opinions.

We knew on day one that there would be issues we would have difficulty dealing with. However, I cannot recall a single incident where members were discourteous or disrespectful of one another even when significant differences were on the table. We did not line up along racial, political or geographic lines. We made every effort to move forward by consensus, not by voting. When I compare our day-to-day interactions to what we have seen on television and read about today, we were the picture of civility and decorum. I am proud of that and the report speaks for itself. At the end of the day, we remained respected individuals and friends.

4. Did the Riot Commission fulfill its mission?

I believe it did. But time and history, and people like yourself may be in a better position to judge. I am extremely proud of the final product, but time will tell.

5. What was the Riot Commission's greatest challenge?

I think [our greatest challenge was] in coming to terms with information, analysis, and facts that didn't agree with our personal opinions or what we thought we knew;

issues like mass graves, bodies being dumped in the river, who fired the first shot, or the use of aircraft. However, I would say the greatest challenge was the whole issue of reparations, and what our role should be in that regard.

6. In terms of the challenge previously described, how did the Riot Commission respond to or address it?

In the final report I can't think of a situation where we did not accept the findings of resource consultants, all of who were experts in their fields. For example, we adopted the findings of Dr. Clyde Snow, Dr. Allen Witten, and Dr. Robert Brooks with regards to possible burial locations and actual identification of those known killed both black and white. As you know, Dr. Brooks is revisiting the burial site using new technology. This may bring new light to this question. The point is our findings stood the test of time to this point.

With regards to reparations, the members were in unanimous agreement that reparations were appropriate. Nothing at the state or local level had ever been done to recognize the loss of life and property as result of the event. The difficult challenge was agreeing on what specifically should be done. The challenge was met by agreeing that it was not our responsibility to dictate to the Legislature and Governor, but rather to report that the Riot Commission agreed that reparations were indeed appropriate and to recommend a range of possible approaches for the legislature to consider.

I must add at this point while there was consensus on the report, there were discussions about the possibilities for a 'Minority Report.' This idea was acceptable to the Riot Commission if those suggesting it had the data, facts, and evidence to support their positions. Some of this discussion was quite passionate and emotional. At the end of the day, no minority report was issued.

7. What was the Riot Commission's greatest accomplishment and what is the Riot Commission's

legacy?

The principal accomplishment and legacy of the Riot Commission are interrelated. We put this horrific event squarely in the eye of the public in a clear, professional, historical, and undisputable report—a document available to any citizen. While the Legislature never took any meaningful action, I would like to think that the report has played a role, however small, in all the positive efforts at reconciliation in the Tulsa community, in making the riot a part of our public awareness and education, in the long overdue re-development of the north end of downtown Tulsa, including the Greenwood area, and in making Tulsa a more progressive and livable city for all its citizens.

My disappointment is that I don't think the report has gotten the recognition and attribution it deserved. To me the report is a fundamental research document for anyone studying the riot for whatever purpose. The books, movies, and television shows that I am aware of give no attribution to the report, and in some cases don't tell the story accurately. It makes me sad to think that this exceptional body of work is not being studied and used to it fullest.

8. What, if anything, would you have done differently in connection with the Riot Commission's work?

I wish the effort could have started years earlier, and the Riot Commission could have had more time and budget. It is good to see that others are continuing to look at the context, detail, and emotional and cultural setting that existed at the time of the riot. I don't know if I would change anything about our process. It worked because of the wonderful and dedicated people involved.

9. What work remains after the Riot Commission's efforts?

Hatred, discrimination, and oppression are as old as mankind and recorded history. The work of the Riot Commission and efforts like it all over the world will never be done. The best hope for all of us is to continue to shine the bright light of truth on such atrocities wherever and whenever they occur. Our hope for mankind is the hearts of mankind, not in governments, kings or rulers. We are all part of an endless process of learning to live together and to love our neighbors as ourselves.[212]

Commissioner Vivian Clark-Adams, Ph.D.

Dr. Vivian Clark-Adams, a retired African American college professor, also agreed to share her thoughts on the work of the Riot Commission and her role as a member of that body.

1. What is your most vivid memory of the Riot Commission?

On the positive side, the most vivid memories were of the race riot survivors when they would come and share their experiences—their strength, their courage, their faith. On the negative side, one of the sessions with Beryl Ford actually made me angry. Mr. Ford, an amateur historian and I believe a physicist by trade, tried to disprove the eyewitness accounts about the bombing of Greenwood. His thesis was that non-military incendiary devices were not developed well enough in that day and time for them to be thrown from a plane without blowing up the plane. Commission member Jim Lloyd countered that phosphorus was a substance that was readily available and could be used because it would explode only upon impact. Mr. Ford acknowledged that possibility. However, the assigned reporter from the *Tulsa World* wrote his column as if Ford's argument was supported. This incident and others made me realize that certain 'powers that be' were trying to minimize the destruction, and impact of the 1921 Tulsa Race Riot.

2. What was the mission of the Riot Commission?

The main responsibilities of the Riot Commission were to identify and certify survivors and their losses, to develop an accurate, thorough historical record of the 1921 Tulsa Race Riot, and to take the opportunity to make recommendations, specifically regarding reparations.

3. How would you describe the functioning of the Riot Commission, including the relationships between and among its members?

Overall, the Riot Commission functioned reasonably well. Riot Commission members were selected to include a diversity of ethnicities, political views, and expertise. Thus, divisions were inevitable. At the end, however, I believe all members, except one, made some compromises.

4. Did the Riot Commission fulfill its mission?

I believe it did. We had good leadership in [Dr. Bob] Blackburn and [Pete] Churchwell, both making sure we addressed each responsibility as thoroughly as possible.

5. What was the Riot Commission's greatest challenge?

I believe the greatest challenge was maintaining interest, motivation, direction, and production and minimizing conflicts, despite strong internal and external pressures.

6. In terms of the challenge previously described, how did the Riot Commission respond to or address it?

Again, the leadership kept us on task and the Commission members were dedicated to this effort and intent on completion of the work.

7. What was the Riot Commission's greatest accomplishment?

I believe the Riot Commission's greatest accomplishments were the identification of the survivors and its official report. Dr. Danney Goble did an excellent job of bringing it all together in written form.

8. What is the Riot Commission's legacy?

After the Riot Commission ended its work, I received a number of invitations from Tulsa Global Alliance to address visiting foreign groups who requested information about the Riot Commission. I began to realize that one of the main legacies was the precedent and blueprint we set for addressing a politically explosive historical racial injustice. Although we were not completely successful, there were other countries who were interested in our process and whatever measure of success or accomplishment we achieved.

9. What, if anything, would you have done differently in connection with the Riot Commission's work?

I had been 'stewing' over the riot for a number of years before I was selected for the Riot Commission. Therefore, I entered with a certain mindset and determination, like most of the other members. If I had to do it over, I probably would have been a little more open to the opposing opinions. However, as I mentioned earlier, I made some compromises, as did most of the other members.

10. What work remains after the Riot Commission's efforts?

Since the Riot Commission did recommend reparations, this issue needs to be addressed before we can consider our work done. It is imperative that the State of Oklahoma and the City of Tulsa sincerely acknowledge their complicity in the 1921 Tulsa Race Riot and pay the survivors and/or their descendants for their undeserved losses. The money to build [John Hope Franklin] Reconciliation Park would have been better spent on paying reparations to the survivors and their families.[213]

The Response of the Oklahoma Legislature to the Riot Commission Report

The Oklahoma Legislature created several vehicles and entities to address the Riot Commission's recommendations and move toward reconciliation and healing. The Legislature passed the 1921 Riot Reconciliation Act, signed into law by Governor Frank Keating, a Tulsan, on June 1, 2001.

The Act gave a full-throated endorsement to the work of the Riot Commission:

> The documentation assembled by The 1921 Riot Commission provides strong evidence that some local municipal and county officials failed to take actions to calm or

contain the situation once violence erupted and, in some cases, became participants in the subsequent violence which took place on May 31 and June 1, 1921, and even deputized and armed many whites who were part of the mob that killed, looted, and burned down the Greenwood area.

The staggering cost of the Riot included the deaths of an estimated 100 to 300 persons, the vast majority of whom were African-Americans, the destruction of 1,256 homes, virtually every school, church and business, and a library and hospital in the Greenwood area, and the loss of personal property caused by rampant looting by white rioters. The Riot Commission estimates that the property costs in the Greenwood district was approximately $2 million in 1921 dollars or $16,752,600 in 1999 dollars. Nevertheless, there were no convictions for any of the violent acts against African-Americans or any insurance payments to African-American property owners who lost their homes or personal property as a result of the Riot. Moreover, local officials attempted to block the rebuilding of the Greenwood community by amending the Tulsa building code to require the use of fire-proof material in rebuilding thereby making the costs prohibitively expensive.

The 48th Oklahoma Legislature in enacting the 1921 Riot Reconciliation Act of 2001 concurs with the conclusion of the 1921 Riot Commission . . . . [T]his response recognizes that there were moral responsibilities at the time of the [R]iot which were ignored and [have] been ignored ever since rather than confront the realities of an Oklahoma history of race relations that allowed one race to 'put down' another race. Therefore, it is the intention of the Oklahoma Legislature in enacting the 1921 Riot Reconciliation Act of 2001 to freely acknowledge its moral responsibility on behalf of the state of Oklahoma and its citizens that no race of citizens in Oklahoma has the right or power to subordinate another race today or ever again.[214]

The 1921 Riot Reconciliation Act provided a governance structure and seed money for a memorial/museum, established an education and scholarship program, and created an entity to study long-term economic redevelopment for the Greenwood District.

1. The 1921 Tulsa Race Riot Memorial of Reconciliation Design Committee & John Hope Franklin Reconciliation Park

The Oklahoma Legislature also established The 1921 Tulsa Race Riot Memorial of Reconciliation Design Committee and appropriated $3.7 million dollars of a $5 million pledge for the initial planning phases of a memorial/museum. The monies funded a public park that commemorates the history of Tulsa's Greenwood District, including the tragic circumstances surrounding the massacre.

Supporters of the public park concept acquired land, and in October 2008, the Tulsa City Council approved $500,000 in funding that, when added to private and state funds on hand, allowed for the scheduling of groundbreaking ceremonies. Backers turned soil for the three-acre park on November 17, 2008, at 415 North Detroit Avenue, between North Elgin and Detroit Avenues at the junction of the Brady District (now, the "Tulsa Arts District") and the Greenwood District.

Historian John Hope Franklin, son of Tulsa lawyer B.C. Franklin, attended. This would be the last public appearance for this scholar and humanitarian before his death on March 25, 2009, in Durham, North Carolina, prior to the October 27, 2010, dedication of the park that bears his name: John Hope Franklin Reconciliation Park. The park fosters Franklin's approach to history: acknowledge the past, learn from it, and look to the future.

The park's opening brought to fruition nearly a decade of discussion, planning, and development. Attractions include two large works by noted sculptor Ed Dwight and a dozen bronze informational plaques, ideal for education and reflection.

Originally funded by the State of Oklahoma, City of Tulsa and private donors, John Hope Franklin Reconciliation Park is now owned by the city and managed by the non-profit corporation, John Hope Franklin Center for Reconciliation, formed in 2007.[215]

The Center's mission is to transform the bitterness and mistrust caused by years of racial division, even violence, into a hopeful future of reconciliation and cooperation for Tulsa and the nation.[216] The Center's long-term plans include the addition of a research library and conference center that will facilitate the hosting of local, state, and national events focused on community understanding.[217]

2. The Greenwood Area Redevelopment Authority

The Oklahoma Legislature further fashioned The Greenwood Area Redevelopment Authority to explore ways to revitalize the business district in the Greenwood community, roughly bounded by Detroit Avenue to the west, the Midland Valley Tracks to the east, Archer Street to the south, and Pine Street to the north. The Legislature appointed members of the Authority, but did not fund it. The authorizing statute provides, in pertinent part:

A. There is hereby created the Greenwood Area Redevelopment Authority. The Authority shall be an instrumentality of the state.

B. The Authority is created in order to provide a method to facilitate the redevelopment of the Greenwood Area.

C. In addition to other responsibilities imposed pursuant to the Greenwood Area Redevelopment Authority Act, the mission of the Authority shall be to assist in finding methods for other entities, both in the private sector and public sector, to promote the investment, reinvestment, development and revitalization of qualified metropolitan areas.

D. The Authority shall be governed by a board of trustees which shall consist of twenty (20) members to be appointed or who shall serve on the board of trustees for the Authority . . . .

Added by Laws 2001, c. 315, § 10. Amended by Laws 2002, c. 395, § 3, eff. Nov. 1, 2002.[218]

3. The Tulsa Reconciliation Education and Scholarship Program

The Oklahoma Legislature also put in place The Tulsa Reconciliation Education and Scholarship Program and appropriated $20,000 to fund it. Authorizing language for the Program provided:

(a) The Tulsa Reconciliation Education and Scholarship Program was established by HB 1178, the '1921 Tulsa Race Riot Reconciliation Act of 2001,' which was signed into law on June 1st 2001. The Act was amended by HB 2238 of the 2002 legislative session.

(b) The purpose of the program is to make available a maximum of 300 scholarships to residents of the Tulsa School District, which was greatly impacted both socially and economically by the civil unrest that occurred in the city during 1921. The program is to begin with the 2002-03 school year or as soon thereafter as practicable, subject to the availability of funds.

(c) The further purpose of the program is to establish and maintain a variety of educational support services whereby residents who qualify for the program will be prepared for success in postsecondary endeavors. [70 O.S. §2621][219]

The Oklahoma State Regents for Higher Education set aside $30,000 in a trust fund for future scholarships. The program initially funded one-time $1,000 scholarships for two qualifying high school seniors from each of Tulsa's nine public high schools and one charter school. To be eligible to receive the Tulsa Reconciliation Scholarship, a student had to be enrolled in the Tulsa public high school that nominated him/her and his/her family income could not exceed $70,000. Guidelines provided that the scholarships could be used for courses at any public or private institution in Oklahoma, as well as any career technology center.[220]

Some Tulsa Community Responses to the Commission Report

Tulsa responded to the Commission report in a variety of ways. Following are synopses of some of the more prominent, substantial initiatives that ensued after that seminal 2001 document issued.

1. Tulsa Say No To Hate Coalition

Formation of the Tulsa Say No To Hate Coalition preceded the

Riot Commission report by more than a decade, but the group nonetheless took note of the release of the report and considered how it might better engage with the community with a view toward reconciliation.

The Tulsa Say No To Hate Coalition is, first and foremost, an open-ended volunteer network of community-based and civic organizations established as a forum in which to share trends and development, best practices, and calendar events and activities related generally to diversity, equity, and inclusion, more specifically, to hate-based activity in the Tulsa area.

Members of the Tulsa Say No To Hate Coalition include: City of Tulsa Human Rights Department; City of Tulsa Police Department; Community Service Council of Greater Tulsa; Coalition of Hispanic Organizations; Islamic Society of Tulsa; Jewish Federation of Tulsa; Oklahoma Center for Community and Justice; Oklahomans for Equality; Tulsa PFLAG; Tulsa City-County Library; Tulsa County Sheriff's Office; Tulsa Interfaith Alliance; Tulsa Metropolitan Ministry; Tulsa Public Schools; Union Public Schools; and YWCA Tulsa.

The Tulsa Say No To Hate Coalition works to: eliminate hate-based bigotry and violence in the community; incorporate the needs and issues of the diverse community in planning and strategic processes throughout the community; increase understanding of the identities and experiences of all members of the diverse community through curricular and other educational initiatives; and provide positive leadership in the realm of diversity.[221]

2. NCCJ Racial Reconciliation Project

In 2001, The National Conference for Community and Justice (formerly, the National Conference of Christians and Jews, "NCCJ"), now OCCJ, the Oklahoma Center for Community and Justice, received principal cash grants from Williams and Bank of Oklahoma, and contributions from other individuals and groups, to sponsor a series of diverse focus groups, coordinate public forums, and generate other activities aimed at addressing the issue of racial reconciliation. The specific goals of the Racial Reconciliation Project included: promoting constructive dialogue among diverse audiences about race relations and racial reconciliation (*i.e.,* closing real and perceived gaps in opportunity based on race and building transracial relationships beyond the superficial); promoting awareness about race relations; gathering pertinent data; inspiring individuals and groups to work on race relations projects with a view toward systemic enhancement; and providing key decision-makers with reliable information upon which sound decisions about our diverse community may be made.

The City of Tulsa provided an in-kind grant of administrative support. NCCJ worked closely with Williams, Bank of Oklahoma, the City of Tulsa, the Greenwood Cultural Center, and a host of community groups to bring together a broad, diverse spectrum of the community in search of viable strategies for promoting unity and harmony. The Riot Commission's 2001 report provided the springboard for these dialogues, activities, and events. The two-year process provided information and ideas for systemic action within the community and beyond.

Then-NCCJ Chair Dr. Mouzon Biggs, Jr., appointed a task force to continue the work of the Racial Reconciliation Project, its primary charges including identifying and clarifying specific racial issues that need to be addressed in Tulsa and generating creative, long-term solutions tailored to the dynamics of the Tulsa community.[222]

3. Riot Survivors Awarded Medals of Distinction

Twenty riot survivors received the Oklahoma Medal of Distinction at the fourteenth biennial A.C. Hamlin Banquet at the Cowboy Hall of Fame in Oklahoma City on April 25, 2001.[223] More than 1,000 people attended the special ceremony sponsored by the Oklahoma Legislative Black Caucus. Celebrated screen actor and Tulsa native Alfre Woodard delivered the keynote address. Just prior to the event, she expressed her optimism for her home state: "I am really excited about the notion that Oklahoma is [poised] to set a precedent in terms of looking at its past and therefore paving the way to a remarkable future."[224]

4. Community Reparations Fund for Riot Survivors

Tulsa Metropolitan Ministry ("TMM") and other groups created a reparations fund for riot survivors ("The Tulsa Metropolitan Ministry Reparations Gift Fund"), ultimately raising nearly $50,000. Each of the more than 100 identified survivors received payments totaling about $400 in a symbolic healing gesture.[225] Supporters of TMM included: Unitarian Universalists, members of the Jewish community, the Church of Jesus Christ of Latter-day Saints, the African Methodist Episcopal Church, the Islamic Society of North America, the Roman Catholic Church, and the Orthodox Church in America.[226]

At the time of the last distribution from The Tulsa Metropolitan Ministry Reparations Gift Fund in 2003, TMM Executive Director Steve Cranford emphasized the symbolism: "This was a gift from the religious community that was given to recognize a debt that remains outstanding."[227]

Survivors appreciated the gesture. TMM received a note signed by three survivors, Olivia Hooker, Samuel D. Hooker, and Naomi Hooker Chamberlain that read: "Greetings from three survivors of the 1921 Tulsa Race Riot. The interfaith community, by your message and gifts, has created a well of healing that will go down in history. Yours was the first sign of a caring community and we feel its effect deeply. We shall always keep you in our thoughts and prayers."[228]

5. The Survivor Project

The Greenwood Cultural Center, then under the leadership of Executive Director Fai Walker, brought together a group of Riot survivor allies to fashion The Survivor Project. The initiative sought to cater to the needs of the aging survivors. Coverage of that work included a reporting session from a meeting Ms. Walker attended:

> Fai Walker reported that her group of volunteers and Community Partners met with 30 survivors in May [2002]. Life Senior Services is assessing the needs of the survivors and all but one is participating. The Tulsa Area United Way is considering funding for a position at Life Senior Services to do the on-going assessment. Thirty young women have been trained as companions.[229]

6. The Tulsa Metropolitan Chamber of Commerce Race Riot Task Force

The Tulsa Metropolitan Chamber of Commerce (now, the Tulsa Regional Chamber), then led by Chairman John Gaberino, received and reviewed the 2001 final report of the Riot Commission. In response, the group formed the Tulsa Metro Chamber of Commerce Race Riot Task Force to examine ways to heed its recommendations. The Chamber Task force "met several times to formulate a recommendation to present to the Chamber Board in addressing the Race Riot Commission's report."[230] The Chamber Task Force met with African American leaders to explore possible recommendations.

Invitees to the outreach meeting included—

Tulsa Metro Chamber Group: John A. Gaberino, James D. Dunn, Ron King, Paula Marshall-Chapman, Ed Keller, Mayor Susan Savage, Derek Gates, Robert B. Watson, Jr., Chuck Patterson, Robert E. Lorton, Steve Turnbo, Hans Helmerich, Ruth Ann Fate, David Sawyer, Gary Trennepohl, Jay Clemens, Nancy Day, Hannibal B. Johnson, and Gary Clark; and

North Tulsa Group: State Representative Don Ross, Senator Maxine Horner, Tulsa City Councilor Joe Williams, Tulsa City Councilor Roscoe Turner, Wilbert Collins, Julius Pegues, Judy Eason-McIntyre, Reuben Gant, Michael Pierce, Michael Johnson, Rev. Melvin Easiley, Lena Bennett, Fai Walker, Melvin Gilliam, Rev. M.C. Potter, and Rev. W.R. Casey.[231]

Specifically, the Chamber Race Riot Task Force explored the role the Tulsa business community might play in fostering reconciliation in a way "that is beneficial to the business community and also helps the North Tulsa community."[232] Chairman Gaberino noted: "I have learned so much this past year, not only about that horrific event but about the current state of race relations in Tulsa," adding that reparations are a way to try to make up for what happened "the same as private foundations and the government are making payments to the survivors and families of those killed in the 9/11 tragedy." At the time, some expressed interest in a private fundraising effort to generate a pool of money from which to pay riot reparations.[233] Attendees expressed broad support for Chamber involvement with the construction of a riot memorial, the impaneling of a Greenwood District redevelopment authority, and the creation of a scholarship fund memorializing the riot.[234]

Chamber chair Gaberino, a Tulsa attorney, assisted with a fundraising effort led by the Riot Commission that generated close to a half-million dollars for college scholarships for the descendants of riot survivors. Several higher education institutions agreed to match these monies. Scholarships were awarded to Tulsa high school students, but the scholarships were made generally available—open to students with no direct connection to the riot.

The Riot Commission, disappointed that their original intent to fund scholarships *for descendants of riot survivors* had not been carried out, elected to redirect the remaining monies to the Oklahoma Historical Society, led by Dr. Bob Blackburn. The Oklahoma Legislature had authorized the Oklahoma Historical Society to serve as stakeholder for funds it had pledged to help build John Hope Franklin Reconciliation Park, "owned" by the Oklahoma Historical Society and situated on land donated by the City of Tulsa. The funding allocation from the Oklahoma Legislature came up short of the originally-announced five million dollars. With the assistance of Dr. Bob Blackburn, the Riot Commission's redirected funds went toward the park-building effort.

7. The University of Tulsa Buck Colbert Franklin Memorial Civil Rights Lecture

The Buck Colbert Franklin Memorial Civil Rights Lecture honors one of Oklahoma's pioneering African American attorneys. In the aftermath of the massacre, B.C. Franklin served his community and his profession by assisting its victims. Working from a tent because his office and home were destroyed during the melee, he represented clients, filed briefs, and fought back against the violent injustice and the city's assault on Tulsa's African American community.

In addition to honoring B.C. Franklin, the Buck Colbert Franklin Memorial Civil Rights Lecture pays tribute to the legacy of his son, the late eminent historian Dr. John Hope Franklin, who delivered the first lecture in the series circa 2001.[236]

The Case for Judicially-Mandated Reparations

On February 24, 2003, several massacre survivors, represented by a legal team that included famed O.J. Simpson defense counsel Johnnie Cochran, Harvard Law School Professor Charles Ogletree, Randall Robinson of TransAfrica, Florida personal injury attorney Willie Gary, University of Alabama Law Professor Suzette Malveaux, and other notables, sued the City of Tulsa and the State of Oklahoma, based largely on the 2001 Riot Commission report.[237]

Professor Ogletree said the state and city should compensate the victims and their families "to honor their admitted obligations as detailed in the commission's report."[238] The plaintiffs eschewed pursuit of cash reparations, instead seeking systemic relief: the establishment of educational and health-care resources for current residents of Greenwood District.[239]

In 2004, United States District Court Judge James O. Ellison in Tulsa dismissed the lawsuit and the Tenth Circuit Court of Appeals in Denver subsequently affirmed that decision, both citing the running of the statute of limitations on the then-80-year-old case.[240] The Supreme Court of the United States declined, without comment, to hear the appeal in May of 2005.[241]

The sustainability of the case turned on the applicability of the standard two-year statute of limitations applied to the bringing of damage claims like those of the survivors. The legal team argued that the statute of limitations should not apply to these claims because government officials withheld critical information at the time, and, furthermore, the pervasiveness of racism in Oklahoma courts of the day would otherwise have prevented a full and fair hearing of the matter.

In November 2005, Professor Ogletree also filed a petition with the Organization of American States' Inter-American Commission on Human Rights for assistance.[242] The petition included many of the arguments made in connection with the dismissed Oklahoma federal court lawsuit, including arguments about the effect of the statute of limitations. It also alleged a violation of the Organization of American States Declaration of the Rights and Duties of Man. As a practical matter, the United States would not be bound by any decision rendered, and does not recognize the jurisdiction of the Inter-American Court.[243]

The Organization of American States filing shined a spotlight on the matter and attracted additional, albeit fleeting, scrutiny for the City of Tulsa and the State of Oklahoma. Still, no reparations ensued.

In April 2007, Professor Ogletree appealed to the United States Congress to pass a bill extending the statute of limitations for the case, given the long suppression of material about it.[244]

In response, United States Representative John Conyers (D-Michigan), chairman of the House Judiciary Committee, introduced H.R. 1995—110th Congress: *Tulsa Greenwood Riot Accountability Act of 2007* on April 23, 2007,[245] a bill that would extend the statute of limitation on civil claims by these survivors.

In their "Dear Colleague" letter seeking co-sponsors for the legislation, Representative Conyers and Representative Jerrold Nadler of New York noted: "The 1921 Tulsa Race Riot was one of the most destructive and costly attacks upon an American community in our nation's history." Conyers added: "Tulsa's Black community was a tremendous example of self-sufficiency during segregation and Jim Crow, only to be destroyed in race riots. These families deserve the ability to seek justice in our court system and my bill would allow them to do that."[246]

The bill received a hearing, but not a floor vote. Witnesses testifying at the hearing included Dr. John Hope Franklin and survivor Dr. Olivia J. Hooker.[247]

On April 1, 2009, Representative Conyers once again tried his hand at getting Congressional relief for the survivors. He introduced a follow-up bill. The next day, the bill lapsed for lack of a quorum of the subcommittee of the House Judiciary Committee.[248] The bill, H.R. 1843—111th Congress: *John Hope Franklin Tulsa-Greenwood Race Riot Claims Accountability Act of 2009,"*[249] would have extended to five years the statute of limitations for federal claimants whose claims were previously filed in court and dismissed without reaching the merits.

Had they been successful, the 2007 and 2009 bills would have provided a mechanism for a determination on the merits of the claims brought by survivors and descendants of the victims of the massacre, such claimants being denied determinations on the merits because of the applicable statute of limitations.

Undeterred, Representative Conyers introduced *H.R. 5593—112th Congress: John Hope Franklin Tulsa-Greenwood Race Riot Claims Accountability Act of 2012* on May 8, 2012.[250] This measure would have allowed the claims previously deemed time-barred by the courts to proceed. It, too, languished in committee.

Representative Conyers explained the moral underpinnings of his persistence:

> The case of the Tulsa-Greenwood Riot victims is worthy of Congressional attention because substantial evidence suggests that governmental officials deputized and armed the mob and that the National Guard joined in the destruction. The report commissioned by the Oklahoma State Legislature in 1997, and published in 2001, uncovered new information and detailed, for the first time, the extent of the involvement by the State and city government in prosecuting and erasing evidence of the riot. This new evidence was crucial for the formulation of a substantial case, but its timeliness raised issues at law, and resulted in a dismissal on statute of limitation grounds. In dismissing the survivor's claims, however, the Court found that extraordinary circumstances might support extending the statute of limitations, but that Congress did not establish rules applicable to the case at bar. With this legislation, we have the opportunity to provide closure for a group of claimants—many over 100 years old—and the ability to close the book on a tragic chapter in history.[251]

Still resolute, Representative Conyers persisted. He introduced *H.R. 98—113th Congress: John Hope Franklin Tulsa-Greenwood Race Riot Claims Accountability Act of 2013* on January 3, 2013. Like its 2012 predecessor, the 2013 incarnation declared that any person (including the state of Oklahoma) who, in connection with the massacre, acted under color of any statute, ordinance, regulation, custom, or usage of the state of Oklahoma to subject, or cause to be subjected, any person to the deprivation, on account of race, of any right secured at the time of the deprivation by Oklahoma law, shall be liable to the party injured in a civil action for redress.

The measure thus would have allowed claims for damages notwithstanding the federal court decision in *Alexander v. State of Oklahoma*, 391 F.3d 1155 (10th Cir. 2004), which found such claims were time-barred and not to be determined on the merits. By its terms, the measure prescribed that any civil action lodged under its provisions must be filed within five years of its enactment.[252]

Despite Representative Conyers' valiant efforts, no legislative fix to the judicial time bar on massacre-related claims would be forthcoming. No such remedy appears likely any time soon.

In June 2019, Congress held a hearing on a bill that would create a commission to study slavery and subsequent race-based discrimination. The measure would also empower the commission to make recommendations on reparations--measures to repair the damage occasioned by decades of racial injustices. Such recommendations would address the role of public and private bodies, including institutions of higher education, corporations, and religious and associational institutions, as direct beneficiaries of the systemic oppression of African Americans.[253]

Eric J. Miller, a law professor at Loyola Marymount University and one of the lawyers involved in the 2003 lawsuit seeking reparations for Tulsa rmassacre survivors, testified, making the connection between reparations for slavery and reparations for other historical traumas, including the massacre. Professor Miller noted: "The Tulsa experience is emblematic of many African American communities around this country. While monetary payment was [seen as] a beginning for economic justice, it [would not be] enough without racial justice to repair the specific race-based wrongs of the Tulsa massacre and its aftermath."[254]

The John Hope Franklin Center for Reconciliation

The John Hope Franklin Center for Reconciliation, a nonprofit organization formed in 2007 ("JHF Center"), sought to build its reputation through its programs and projects before acquiring a physical home. As previously noted, the 2008 groundbreaking for John Hope Franklin Reconciliation Park ("JHF Park") was Dr. John Hope Franklin's last public appearance.

JHF Park emerged from the findings and recommendations of the Riot Commission. That body urged that a substantial monument or memorial be constructed to commemorate the tragic events of 1921. The Oklahoma Legislature created a group denominated the "1921 Tulsa Race Riot Memorial of Reconciliation Design Committee." The preamble to its mission statement fairly summarizes the gravity of the task with which it was charged:

> One of the great failures of our society is man's inhumanity toward his fellow man. The Tulsa Race Riot of 1921 stands as a stark reminder of this horrible ethos that belies us all as human beings. The Tulsa Race Riot Report, issued in 2000 [*sic*], chronicles for the first time officially, the horrors that occurred over those two days of infamy in 1921. Now, Oklahomans are challenged with the opportunity and the responsibility to begin to heal some of the wounds that still remain. While we understand that no amount of money, no monument regardless of size and scope, and no other offerings of remuneration and expression of sorrow can ever restore what was lost nor compensate for the human horror that took place, we still must try. And by trying to do what is right, perhaps we enhance that healing process and, at the same time, educate our young people about what can happen when people allow hate and prejudice to invade their souls. The Race Riot Memorial of Reconciliation Design Committee has an incredible opportunity and an awesome responsibility. The journey in the coming months and years will be enlightening, painful, educational, and crucial for the future welfare of our City. We approach this project with humility and passion.[255]

Dr. John Hope Franklin noted in *The Color Line*:[256] "We need to do everything possible to emphasize the positive qualities that all of us have, qualities which we have never utilized to the fullest, but which we must utilize if we are to solve the problem of the color line in the twenty-first century."

The JHF Center seeks to transform society's divisions into social harmony through the serious study and work of reconciliation. The JHF Center focuses on: (1) Education—Increasing public knowledge and understanding; (2) Scholarship—Creating new knowledge through scholarly work; (3) Community Outreach—Opening conversations to bring communities together; and (4) Archives—Laying a foundation for scholarship by gathering materials for research.

In 2010, the JHF Center launched an annual "Reconciliation in America" national symposium series. The symposia explore current academic research and community projects that address the general theme of reconciliation in America. Consistent with that mission, the symposia highlight the study of historic events around which reconciliation is needed and offer insights into best practices that foster hope and healing. By convening scholars and practitioners, the JHF Center hopes to promote a dialogue among those who work to bridge societal divides. The efforts of the JHF Center and others, have heightened awareness of and attention to the massacre and its legacy.[257]

In 2011, the John Hope Franklin Center began an ambitious project to survey Tulsa residents on race relations. This baseline race relations survey measured Tulsa-area attitudes about current racial issues and knowledge of racial history and was developed by a collaborative research team from the John Hope Franklin Center for Reconciliation and the Center of Applied Research for Nonprofit Organizations at the University of Oklahoma—Tulsa.

In all, 2,063 respondents completed surveys. Results from the survey were presented by focusing on comparisons of attitudes and perspectives among the four largest racial/ethnic groups (White, Hispanic/Latino, Black/African American and American Indian). The research process consisted of anonymous web-based and paper-and-pencil instruments that included qualitative and quantitative questions.

JHF Center board chair Julius Pegues said at the time, "This survey helps guide our work at the Center. If we understand where we are and where we have been, we can provide a better future for our children."

Key findings from all groups converged on certain propositions:

> *Race Relations Generally:* (1) Race relations are poor in Tulsa; (2) Discussions about race are necessary to improve

intergroup relations; (3) Racial and ethnic discrimination still exists.; and (4) Tulsa would benefit from increasing racial diversity in neighborhoods.

The 1921 Tulsa Race Riot: (1) The riot negatively impacted Tulsa's economic and social landscape; (2) Knowledge about the riot is relevant to improving race relations in Tulsa; (3) Information about the riot has not been adequately shared with younger generations; and (4) The riot should be taught in public schools.

Racial Reconciliation: (1) If racial reconciliation were achieved, we would have improved diversity across neighborhoods, quality education for all, opportunity and fairness in employment, and social relationships and interactions among all Tulsans; (2) For racial reconciliation to occur, we need better communication, education, and engagement on the part of government and community institutions (*e.g.,* city government, religious institutions, and schools); and (3) There is great hope for improved race relations for the future.

Complete survey results are available on the JHF Center website, www.jhfcenter.org.

The Undoing of Massacre-Related Indictments of African American Men

On December 11, 2007, Tulsa County District Attorney Tim Harris sought and received from Tulsa County District Judge Jesse Harris the dismissal of the remaining 1921 indictments against black men for alleged offenses tied to the massacre, most prominently, the charge of "inciting a riot."

District Attorney Harris sought the dismissal of all remaining indictments, dozens in number, after Barbara A. Seals Nevergold, Ph.D., a biographer of A.J. Smitherman, publisher of the *Tulsa Star,* a prominent black Tulsa newspaper of that era, urged the dismissal of the Smitherman indictment. Prosecutor Harris cited a breakdown in the rule of law after the massacre and a pursuit of the interests of justice in seeking the dismissals. Smitherman fled Tulsa following the massacre. He became an outspoken civil rights advocate in Buffalo, New York, where he published the *Buffalo Star*, later, the *Empire Star*.

Judge Harris had previously dismissed the indictment against J.B. Stradford, a prominent attorney and businessman, in 1996.[258] Stradford left town after the indictment and established a successful law practice in Chicago. His family became a quintessential Chicago success. His granddaughter, Jewel C. Stradford Lafontant, graduated from Oberlin College and the University of Chicago Law School. A Republican, she served as United States Deputy Solicitor General, the highest-ranking woman in the administration of President Richard M. Nixon.[259]

Oklahoma Governor Frank Keating joined a host of Stradford relatives and community members at the indictment dismissal ceremony, where he awarded J.B. Stradford an honorary executive pardon.[260]

Greenwood District Rising; "North Tulsa" Emerging

Tulsa's Historic Greenwood District, located in the quadrant Tulsans refer to as North Tulsa, continues to transform. In the decades after the massacre, African Americans moved farther north and still hold a significant presence in that section of town. For some, North Tulsa has become synonymous with "black Tulsa," a designation once associated only with the Greenwood District.

Myriad developments have directly or indirectly affected the trajectory of "black Tulsa." This section chronicles some of them.

Before cataloguing the many initiatives begun and ongoing in the Greenwood District, a gentle reminder of what was, what is, and what might be is in order.

The Greenwood Cultural Center honored Tulsa native and celebrated actor, director, and playwright Tim Blake Nelson with its Legacy Award on April 15, 2010. Excerpts from Nelson's spellbinding remarks that evening follow:

A Community's Pluck, Pride and Persistence
By Tim Blake Nelson

When O.W. Gurley purchased 40 acres of land around what would come to be known as Greenwood Avenue, he could not have imagined what would be accomplished by African Americans in Tulsa, Oklahoma, in but a decade.

By 1921 no fewer than 10,000 former slaves and their descendants had joined him north of the rail yards in an area the whites of south Tulsa called 'Little Africa,' but more progressive minds labeled 'the Negro Wall Street.'

The red brick buildings along Greenwood house doctors, lawyers and entrepreneurs of every stripe. Millionaires pepper the community, and there stood more churches in Greenwood than in all the rest of Tulsa.

Across town a barely nascent Jewish community was taking shape, led in part by a gentleman from central Europe named Sam Miller who one day would sponsor the immigration of my mother and her parents.

My mother, Ruth Nelson—whom I never tire of crediting with my own accomplishments for having raised my siblings and me with such love, diligence and care—taught us to appreciate the advantages we had. These were considerable. I attended private school. I lived in a fine south Tulsa neighborhood where my siblings and I ate gourmet meals nightly at family dinners during which formal discussion involving literature, philosophy, and politics were proctored by two extremely well-educated and attentive parents.

Like many south Tulsa families, we also had a maid, and she is here tonight. Her name is Geneva Walker, and I don't think my mother would take umbrage if I credit her with partially having raised my siblings and me.

She hails from the community that honors me here tonight, and just as I credit my mother with instilling in me the values and work ethic to accomplish what I have, I credit Geneva Walker as well.

Indisputably, she was, and will forever continue to be, a member of our family.

While I imagine she was paid well, and I know she was treated well by my parents, Geneva Walker's color-blind generosity in loving, disciplining, washing, picking up after and selflessly nurturing children not her own as if they were he own, for literally decades of her life, is its own luminous and far-reaching beacon.

Your choosing to honor me tonight is another, because it shows an almost absurdly generous indifference to a history that should divide us.

On May 31 and June 1, 1921, much of what surrounds us was in flames.

White marauders crossed into north Tulsa and destroyed an African American community unrivaled at the time for the pluck, ingenuity, pride, and dignity with which it had accomplished so much, so visibly in so little time. Some 7,000 were left homeless, hundreds were killed, truckloads of African American corpses rumbled past eyewitnesses, including one crested by the remains of a little boy who'd been shot in the back as he ran.

In the aftermath of what remains the most egregious race riot in American history, *The Tulsa Tribune* urged that Greenwood, much of which was razed, never be rebuilt.

Within a decade north Tulsa was back; wounded deeply but rebuilt. Its inhabitants would persist through the Depression, send children off to three wars in Europe, Korea and Vietnam, participate passionately in the civil rights movement and see an African American born in Hawaii and raised in Kansas become president.

Because my mother, taught in Tulsa's Jewish community to give back more than she is given, works with many of you, and spends hours of every day in oblique and sometimes direct support of your mission, I know of your persistence, your dedication and your indefatigable confidence in what can be.

The warm spirit with which you reach across cultures to honor a son from the very part of our city that would have denied you, makes what I have done seem insignificant by comparison.

I am immensely proud therefore to stand before you tonight not because of what I have accomplished, but rather as a reflection of what you have accomplished.

Your expansive view of the world and its future allows us all, without shame, pity, anger or reservation to call ourselves proud and forward-looking Tulsans together.[261]

As Tim Blake Nelson suggested, Tulsa's African American community boasts a considerable legacy of achievement. Efforts to burnish and sustain that legacy continue. Noteworthy initiatives in or affecting the traditional African American community include those focused on five critical dimensions: (1) Education; (2) Entrepreneurship & Business Development; (3) History, Arts & Culture; (4) Public Spaces; and (5) Community-Building.

Education

1. The Push for Inclusive Curriculum

May 31, 2021, marks the centennial of the Tulsa's darkest hour, a defining moment in Tulsa and American history. Despite its significance as the worst so-called race riot in American history, even some Tulsans remain oblivious to this tragic event. Still more claim only a superficial familiarity with it.

Teaching and learning are vital, particularly in terms of lessons around our shared humanity. The carnage and chaos Tulsa witnessed in the spring of 1921—continued evidence of our capacity for inhumanity, one toward another—must never be allowed to happen again. Through teaching and learning, we may: (1) begin the process of reconciliation in earnest; (2) recapture our too-often unacknowledged sense of shared humanity; and (3) create for posterity a community more open, inclusive, and loving than the one in which we live today. Healing the still-festering wounds left by the Tulsa tragedy is possible if we incorporate this potent, painful, poignant legacy into school curricula in deliberate, systematic, and sustainable ways. Curriculum counts.

Dr. Martin Luther King, Jr. once observed: "The function of education is to teach one to think intensively and to think critically."

Absent attention to substantive detail—to curricula—education fails in its core mission. When we sanitize our past, we stifle our ability to analyze it intensively and critically. We limit our capacity to learn and grow from our mistakes and missteps. We burden the future with our unresolved past.

The history surrounding the Tulsa of 1921 is but one case in point. Some believe a conspiracy of silence enveloped the community in the wake of the catastrophe and muzzled it for decades thereafter. Tulsans scarcely spoke of this traumatic event privately, let alone publicly. As previously noted, a host of psychological factors including shame, blame, fear, guilt, and post-traumatic stress disorder engulfed the community, stifling constructive dialogue and engagement. Few dared to address it through education— pedagogically. Textbooks omitted references to this ugly chapter in our history.

Rick L. Oglesby, an Oklahoma history teacher in Tulsa, noted:

> Having been a secondary teacher of Oklahoma History from 1966 through 1971, I can testify that at that time the saga of Black Wall Street appeared nowhere in the Tulsa Public Schools curriculum. If those events were at all addressed beyond my own classroom, it was also done as an individual teacher's 'enrichment' of the standard teaching materials. [I wish that] back then I had access to the wealth of detailed information and testimonials that are at hand today. I am grateful for and proud of those Tulsa citizens and elected officials who have continued to work so diligently to bring the full story of the Massacre to light.[262]

The full dimensions of this epic tragedy, buried layers-deep in the Tulsa's community consciousness, have only been recently realized. Arguably, that years-long obfuscation stunted Tulsa's growth, both physically and spiritually. The failure to come clean about Tulsa's dirty little secret undermined the ability of the community to: understand Tulsa's role in the twentieth century American race drama; build trust across the great chasm of race; and use history as a catalyst for strategic, transformational change.

Things began to change with the 1997 convening of the eleven-member, legislatively-created Riot Commission. That body changed the trajectory of massacre coverage and prompted a groundswell of public interest in how Tulsa has dealt with its past.

The Riot Commission's endorsement of cash reparations drew intense attention. Questions loomed: "Who owes what to whom and why?"; and "Assuming there is a debt to be paid, will that debt ever be fully discharged?" Indeed, early media focus on money payments dwarfed coverage of the other items and, more importantly, drowned out discussion of broader philosophical questions centering on the definition of and rationale for reparations. Those foundational questions about reparations merit additional consideration.

Reparations make amends for injustices. The idea behind reparations is to reconcile, repair, and restore that which has been damaged. Properly conceived, reparations help us bridge divides, bolster trust, and build community. By design, reparations move us toward hope, health, and healing.

How is it possible to satisfy the core definitional criteria for reparations—to make amends—and the fundamental rationale underlying reparations—reconciliation—without a viable effort to educate the community on the cause for which reparations are to be made? Surely, a baseline of knowledge about the event for which reparations are offered is the *sine qua non* of meaningful reparations. Broad-based support for reparations hinges on community awareness about our history—the events that transpired before, during, and after the fateful event initially documented as the 1921 Tulsa Race Riot.

The Riot Commission did not explicitly call for curriculum reform, arguably the most meaningful, enduring form of reparations imaginable. This stunning omission undercut its other recommendations. No matter what else we may do, we will not be whole unless and until we own our past, process it, and integrate its lessons into our present and our vision for the future. Teaching and learning are essential to this process. As such, curriculum counts.

After years of deafening silence, the ghosts of Greenwood past emerged in full force as the Riot Commission went about its business. Prominent newspapers, domestic and foreign, covered Tulsa's monumental, historic tragedy. *The New York Times,* the *Wall Street Journal,* the *Los Angeles Times, The San Francisco Examiner, Le Monde,* and *The Times of London* all featured stories about Tulsa's tragic past. So, too, did broadcast media. The History Channel, Showtime, and all the major networks produced massacre-related features. Our past has a way of haunting us despite our vigorous attempts to escape it.

As the media discovered, the devastation itself is only part of the fascinating Greenwood District story. Indeed, one cannot fully appreciate the devastation wrought by the mob action in 1921 without first understanding something of what was destroyed. Prior to the massacre, Greenwood District founders built a bustling black entrepreneurial Mecca: Black Wall Street. That many of those same trailblazers rebounded and rebuilt is a testament to human spirit. Like the massacre itself, these heroic, visionary men and women merit resurrection. That we have squandered the opportunity, time and time again, to learn about and from this rich past is an injustice unto itself.

There has been a growing recognition of the centrality of curriculum in addressing the massacre and Tulsa's Historic Greenwood District. On October 12, 2008, the Tulsa City Council passed a massacre-inspired resolution supporting, among other things, the teaching of an appropriate curriculum to ensure the massacre is adequately covered in Oklahoma's educational institutions as an historical event. It was a call for reparations. It was a call to action. It was a moment of hope.

Other substantial advances have been made. Teaching about this history is part of the State of Oklahoma's "Priority Academic Student Skills" proficiency expectations for various subjects and grade levels. Some ninth-grade Oklahoma history textbooks now include a discussion of the massacre. Creative teachers have supplemented regular curricula with massacre-related materials and experiential activities. The John Hope Franklin Center for Reconciliation compiled supplementary curricular materials on the massacre,[263] worked with Tulsa Public Schools to make them widely available to educators, and participated in teacher training sessions. The African American Resource Center at Tulsa's Rudisill

Regional Library maintains available-to-the-public kits of materials on Greenwood District history. The annual Reconciliation in America symposium, sponsored by the John Hope Franklin Center for Reconciliation, brings together scholars and practitioners to spur racial reconciliation efforts. The 1921 Tulsa Race Massacre Centennial Commision champions massacre-related education and curriculum enhancement in a variety of ways.

Curriculum reform is a core piece of the puzzle. While these are encouraging developments, much work remains to be done.

Several questions come to mind for those who might oppose an inclusive curriculum that tackles weighty matters like the 1921 massacre in Tulsa: Why not be honest and transparent? Why not infuse interdisciplinary teachings about this history into our curricula? Why not ask the provocative questions that expose the present manifestations of past horrors? These questions need answers.

In March of 2012, the Oklahoma Senate passed a bill that would have mandated the teaching of the massacre history in Oklahoma public schools. Senate Bill 1381 by Senator Judy Eason McIntyre, D-Tulsa, and Representative Jabar Shumate, D-Tulsa, passed by a vote of 33-6, and then headed to the Oklahoma House of Representatives. The bill noted: "School districts shall ensure that information concerning the Tulsa Race Riot of 1921 is presented in high school courses in United States history or Oklahoma history." There would have been no cost to implement the legislation.[264]

In the end, the bill was not heard. The bill's authors were told that this history was already being taught.[265]

At least in Tulsa Public Schools, textbooks provide a broad, if superficial, overview of the topic—a substantial improvement over total omission. Both the Oklahoma and the United States History Standards established by the State of Oklahoma encourage attention to the massacre and related topics:

OKLAHOMA HISTORY STANDARD: 'Examine multiple points of view regarding the historic evolution of race relations in Oklahoma including Senate Bill 1 establishing Jim Crow laws, the growth of all-Black towns, the Tulsa Race Riot and the resurgence of the Ku Klux Klan.'

Content Standard 4.2 (1920s through 1940s)

U.S. HISTORY STANDARD: 'Describe the rising racial tension in American society, including the resurgence of the Ku Klux Klan, increased lynchings, race riots as typified by the Tulsa Race Riot, and the use of poll taxes and literacy tests to disenfranchise blacks and poor whites.'[266]

At the national level, coverage of the massacre seems to be spotty at best. Textbooks tend toward broad overviews instead of in-depth coverage of events. For example, major textbook publisher McGraw-Hill addressed the Red Summer riots of 1919 as a single phenomenon and synthesized the racial and labor tumult that defined the post-World War I era in the early 1920s. McGraw-Hill does not cover the massacre as a singular event.[267]

The author has used his book, *Black Wall Street: From Riot to Renaissance in Tulsa's Historic Greenwood District*, as the basis for university and continuing adult education courses about the massacre and the entrepreneurial history of the Greenwood District. See Appendix B for a curriculum guide based on the book.

Karlos K. Hill, Ph.D., Interim Director and Associate Professor, African and African American Studies and Faculty Fellow, Dunham College, University of Oklahoma, launched a pilot teacher institute in the summer of 2018 aimed at educating teachers about Greenwood District history and curriculum development and enrichment around that rich narrative. The initial session targeted Tulsa teachers, but the program will expand statewide under the umbrella of the 1921 Tulsa Race Massacre Centennial Commission.

Danielle Neves, Deputy Chief of Teaching and Learning at Tulsa Public Schools, explained the aims of the school district in terms of teaching about Tulsa's Historic Greenwood District.

> In Tulsa, we have a significant opportunity to share and celebrate the history of Black Wall Street and the historic Greenwood District. We also are charged with a tremendous responsibility to provide our students and community members a deep understanding of the tragic events of the Tulsa Race Massacre in 1921. As we continue to expand our students' study of the history of Tulsa

across grade levels, [Hannibal B. Johnson's] *Black Wall Street* serves as a central text for students' and teachers' learning about the history of the Greenwood District. This phenomenal text is a must-read for all educators and community members who seek to support city-wide reconciliation.

In the summer of 2018, we launched the first Tulsa Race Massacre Institute, bringing together teachers, leaders, and community members to learn collaboratively with the goal of equipping teachers with the resources and support they need to teach the Tulsa Race Massacre in ways that promote diversity, cross-cultural understanding, and racial healing. During the first Institute, as participants grappled with the events of the deadliest race massacre in American history and the worst civil disturbance since the Civil War, a collective and intentional shift in our shared language was made as we committed to reframing the narrative from 'riot' to the more appropriate descriptor of 'massacre.' We will continue to develop our shared and multi-perspective understanding as well as practices for teaching difficult history through summer institutes and ongoing learning opportunities for teachers as we expand the number of teachers who are poised to share this history with students. Mr. Hannibal B. Johnson continues to be a key partner for the district as we work together to educate our community and build the road to reconciliation and healing.[268]

On May 8, 2018, House Bill 3221, co-written by Senator Kevin Matthews, became law. That measure added study of the Emancipation Proclamation and Juneteenth to the social studies curriculum for Oklahoma schools.[269] Previously, Senate Joint Resolution 21, passed in 1994, and championed by Senator Maxine Horner and Representative Don Ross, declared the third Saturday in June a state holiday in celebration of Juneteenth.[270]

2. North Tulsa Leadership Programs

In recent years, a spate of African American leadership organizations emerged to tackle issues within North Tulsa,[271] foremost among them, economic development. Such organizations include:

North Tulsa Economic Development Initiative, Inc.

The North Tulsa Economic Development Initiative, Inc. ("NTEDi") is a nonprofit organization that provides economic development leadership for North Tulsa in terms of social enterprises and works to improve the well-being and quality of life for people in low-resource communities. The group concentrates on rebuilding North Tulsa, one project at a time.

NTEDi supports initiatives related to economic development, education, workforce, and housing. It markets the positive attributes of North Tulsa, primarily through community engagement and partnerships with other entities. Tolerance and inclusion rank as core values. Among other projects, the group holds an annual education forum designed to spur interest in revitalization and business development efforts for current and future residents of North Tulsa.

The organization also sponsors an annual book scholarship awards celebration that encourages the continued education of senior high school students who have promising college futures, but may lack the additional resources necessary to obtain books or supplies required to support their college educational goals.

Dr. Lana Turner-Addison, President of NTEDi, noted: "We are striving to do more to support students through multiple avenues. By providing additional supplemental funds toward the cost of books and supplies, we are able to help relieve some of the burden of college expenses for some students. For many students, a book scholarship is an excellent way to aid them while earning a college education."[272]

LEAD North

LEAD North started as the North Tulsa Development

Council ("NTDC"). Former Tulsa mayor, Kathy Taylor created NTDC as a four-month pilot leadership program in 2007. Following the inaugural academy, six leadership participants, as part of their class project, pledged to continue the leadership development program. NTDC classes met regularly to cover topics including economic development, education, city government, health and human services, business ethics and culture – all specifically geared to the growth of North Tulsa. In 2013, the NTDC underwent a significant transformation, morphing into LEAD North, and shifting focus on equipping participants with the skills and tools to lead, explore, and develop. This change emphasized the initial focus of providing participants with the knowledge, skills, connections, and coaching necessary to cultivate leadership within the context of North Tulsa.[273]

NorthTulsa100

Donna Jackson, M.Div., founded NorthTulsa100 in 2013 to commemorate the 100th Anniversary of the massacre with 100 newly-established brick-and-mortar businesses/companies by May 31-June 1, 2021, the 100th anniversary. The group also advocates for general economic development and opportunity in North Tulsa.[274]

The goals of NorthTulsa100 include: (1) promoting a positive image of North Tulsa; (2) advocating, creating and supporting economic development and business enterprise; (3) commemorating the 100th anniversary of the fall of Black Wall Street; and (4) using the entrepreneurial history of Deep Greenwood Tulsa/Black Wall Street to fuel the economic future of all North Tulsa, showcase the economic strength of the past, and give future generations of entrepreneurs reasons to build businesses.[275]

3. Langston-Tulsa

Langston University, the oldest historically black college/university west of the Mississippi, opened a satellite Tulsa campus in the Greenwood District during the 2008-2009 academic year. Langston University is a public university headquartered in Langston, Oklahoma—the only such historically-black college or university in the State of Oklahoma. Founded March 12, 1897, the school's namesake is John Mercer Langston, a Virginia legislator.[276]

The Langston-Tulsa campus sits on 17.9 acres surrounding the intersection of Greenwood Avenue and King Streets. It is an independent branch campus of Langston University, offering academic and community development programs for traditional and nontraditional students. The school offers upper division courses in twelve programs at the baccalaureate level and master's degree programs in Urban Education, Entrepreneurial Studies, and Rehabilitation Counseling.[277]

4. Tulsa Public Schools Racial Disparities in Education Resolution

In 2019, the Tulsa school board discussed a proposed resolution acknowledging that the City, not unlike many American cities, has a long history of racism and the primacy of race as a predictor of not just academic futures, but of overall success in America.

Part and parcel of the history of racism in the context of Tulsa schools is school segregation. A 1977 report by the United States Commission on Civil Rights, Oklahoma Advisory Committee, examined Tulsa's slog through the desegregation years.

> Up until 1954 all Tulsa schools were totally segregated by race. In the fall of 1955, school attendance zones in Tulsa were redrawn, utilizing the neighborhood school concept, but without regard to race, color, religion, or national origin. The new zones placed some black children in previously all white schools, and some white children in previously all black schools. This realigning of attendance zones, however, was negated by the school board's policy of allowing any student to transfer from a school in which his or her race was minority to a school where his or her race was a majority upon the request of the parents. In May of 1965 the Tulsa public schools' plan for desegregation was submitted to the U.S. Commissioner of Education. Since then, although this school district has made progress in bringing about school desegregation,

much remains to be done. School enrollment statistics for the 1975-76 school year indicate that many schools are still segregated. By choosing to define an integrated school as one having not more than 90% enrollment of a single race, the Tulsa district has not presented an accurate picture on the status of school desegregation. White flight from this district to surrounding suburban districts is a major problem. The affirmative [action] program instituted by the school district has not been carried through. Furthermore, the burden of busing has fallen on the black community. On the positive side, the magnet school plan has been extremely successful.[278]

This history, coupled with numerous social, economic, and political factors, helps explain some of the seemingly intractable racial disparities that persist in the educational arena.

The resolution embraced the power of educational systems to chip away at structural, systemic racism, and noted the "school system can be a powerful institutional driver of systemic change," and pledged to correct "pervasive racial disparities" that "exist across key indicators of student success throughout Tulsa Public Schools, including discipline, reading proficiency, achievement, attendance, advanced course participation and graduation rates."

Jamie Lomax, Director of Organizational Learning and Equity at TPS, emphasized "it's not just Tulsa Public Schools . . . [what] we are trying to call out here is that there are systemic and structural inequities that don't require any individual person to do anything directly that is biased. It is that our systems in our country are built in such a way that we see persistent racial disparities."[279]

Tulsa Public Schools' plans for an equity resolution followed on the heels of the release of the City of Tulsa Equality Indicators report. That document highlighted glaring racial disparities in housing, economic opportunity, health, criminal justice, education and other areas across the city. In the academic arena, the report noted, among other things, that poor students achieved less than their wealthier counterparts and black students were three times more likely to be suspended than whites.

"Acknowledging that you have an issue is the first step," said

Deputy Superintendent Paula Shannon. "We know that we have challenges. We are still asking questions to figure out how students are experiencing the system, how we continue to change implementation of disciplinary practices or the way we provide certain supports to white students versus black students versus Latino students. We're still working to understand what's happening to our different student communities."

Equity ranks among Tulsa Public Schools' core values.[280] As previously referenced, in 2018, Tulsa Public Schools renamed four schools after a lengthy, deliberative process that determined these schools' namesakes misaligned with the system's values and, as such, should not be retained. The school board, on recommendation of a community task force, concluded that the names, because of a close association with slavery and/or other acts of inhumanity, communicated off-putting and offensive messages to swaths of the student population and community about their relative worth to and welcome in Tulsa Public Schools.

Tulsa Public Schools also hosted a series of "Exploring Equity" community conversations beginning in 2016 addressing a wide range of issues in education, including immigration, trauma, Native American educational equity, Tulsa history, and LGBTQ inclusion.[281]

5. African American Community-Based Educational Options

A. Greenwood Leadership Academy

The Greenwood Leadership Academy ("GLA") is one of the several community-based educational options serving, principally, Tulsa's African American community. GLA recounts its history as follows:

> During the meetings, two things became apparent: 1) African-American children in Tulsa lag behind their peers academically with too many stuck in failing schools with little chance of changing their circumstance, and 2) there is a real desire from African-American leaders to change this trajectory through a community-based effort. The group determined that if the community could positively impact one seven-school feeder pattern in North Tulsa,

then the 4,800 Black students currently attending failing schools would have access to significantly improved educational opportunities.

With this vision in mind, the group decided to act, and the Tulsa C.A.R.E. (Creating Action to Reform Education) Alliance, now Met Cares Foundation ("MCF"), was born. MCF, a secular not-for-profit organization, is made up of some of the most prominent African American leaders in Tulsa. They are an impressive group of individuals from a broad range of backgrounds and professions who are determined to rebuild North Tulsa into a thriving community and reclaim its stature of Black excellence.

In December 2016, MCF entered into a formal partnership with the Tulsa Public Schools to establish the first ever 'partnership school' in the state of Oklahoma – with that, Greenwood Leadership Academy was born.[282]

B. Tulsa Legacy Charter School

Tulsa Legacy Charter School ("TLCS"), sponsored by Tulsa Public Schools, is another such community-based educational option. Its mission is to create a culture of excellence by providing a rigorous, arts-infused curriculum that prepares students for college and the world beyond.

It aims for its students to achieve the highest level of academic success, be responsible citizens and view learning as a life-long journey. Through it all, TLCS hopes to fundamentally change the trajectory of public education through its work.[283]

C. Langston Hughes Academy for Arts and Technology

Another option, Langston Hughes Academy for Arts and Technology ("LHAAT"), billed itself as "a powerhouse charter school in the heart of North Tulsa." LHAAT, a charter school sponsored by Langston University, struggled with personnel and governance issues.[284] It acquired new leadership to continue serving the north Tulsa community, but closed in 2019.

D. KIPP

The Knowledge is Power Program ("KIPP") is a nationwide

network of free open-enrollment college-preparatory schools located in low-income communities. KIPP ranks as America's largest network of charter schools.

KIPP seeks to empower all students with the academic, character, and life skills necessary to succeed in high school, college,
and the competitive world beyond by providing outstanding educators and more time in school learning. It is a public, tuition-free,
open-enrollment, college-preparatory, charter middle school committed to enabling North Tulsa students to reach and complete
college.

KIPP Tulsa College Preparatory serves under-served students
in the fifth through eighth grades, building partnerships among
parents, students, and teachers that puts learning first.

KIPP students across the nation demonstrate that demog-
raphy does not define destiny. Over 85% of KIPP students hail
from low-income families and are eligible for the federal free or
reduced-price meals program. Among Kipp students, 95% are African American or Latino. Nationally, more than 95% of KIPP middle school students have graduated high school, and more than
85% of KIPP alumni have gone on to college.[285]

These specialty charter schools operate as independently run
public schools, with greater flexibility in its operations accorded
in exchange for greater performance accountability (at least theo-
retically). The "charter" establishing each school is a performance
contract detailing the school's mission, program, students served,
performance goals, and methods of assessment.

Charter schools are public schools of choice. Families choose
them for their children.. They must demonstrate performance in
the areas of academic achievement, financial management, and organizational stability or face closure.[286]

Entrepreneurship & Business Development

1. Development in the Greenwood District

In a June 2008 announcement, Tulsa Mayor Kathy Taylor revealed that a stadium for the local AA baseball team, the Tulsa
Drillers, would be built in the Greenwood District. The 6,200-seat
venue would be nestled up against Interstate 244, and be bounded
by Elgin Avenue and Archer Street, abutting the businesses that

line the 100 block of North Greenwood Avenue.[287] The stadium would serve as a connector for the Greenwood, Brady (now, Tulsa Arts), and Blue Dome Districts, and talk of further development in the area included a hotel near the stadium and a proposed light rail system to shuttle people from the area of the stadium to other points, including the west bank of the Arkansas River. Several new developments, including a mixed-use residential and commercial property called GreenArch,[288] emerged soon thereafter.

That stadium, ONEOK Field, is named for ONEOK, a natural gas utility. It sits on the southern edge of the historic Greenwood District adjacent to downtown, hosts the Tulsa Drillers AA baseball team and FC Tulsa of the United Soccer League. The Tulsa Drillers played their first game before a sellout crowd at ONEOK Field on April 8, 2010. Country music star Tim McGraw threw the first pitch.[289]

ONEOK Field did not come without controversy. Reuben Gant, former president of the Greenwood Chamber of Commerce, said in 2013 interview with the *Richmond Times-Dispatch*:

> Building the ballpark was very contentious. We were faced with a decision of: What do we do with this land? Our history as a people was being ignored and not being given its just due. And so, how do we affect that in a positive way? And knowing it would be controversial to build a ballpark, we also knew we needed exposure, without compromising our history and our legacy.
>
> *   *   *   *   *
>
> There are people who live here today who have no idea or knowledge of the historical perspective of Greenwood. So what we wanted to do was expose the district to residents and businesses who didn't know anything about the district.
>
> *   *   *   *   *
>
> [Some saw the ballpark as] an attempt to bury the history and the legacy of the Greenwood District. But what we did as a group is, we met with city officials and the leaders of the development group to stress the importance of

the preservation. We negotiated what we consider to be a permanent stamp on the development.[290]

Division over the wisdom of locating ONEOK Field in the heart of Tulsa's Historic Greenwood District remains.

Mechelle Brown, Program Coordinator for the Greenwood Cultural Center, echoed the voices of those who remain skeptical, at best: "What we were told years ago is that the ballpark would bring jobs. However, when you go to the ballpark, you rarely see a lot of African Americans working there and definitely not in administrative positions. It did not bring jobs to our community, and it has not had a huge impact economically."[291]

Former City Councilor Jack Henderson continues to believe in the correctness of his early support for the project, maintaining that ONEOK Field has helped revitalize the Greenwood District and spurred commercial development. Henderson noted:

> A lot of people don't see that as a positive because a lot of people didn't want the stadium to come. They thought they lost so much with the Greenwood District experience. I don't see it like that. I see it as a positive. It is going to take time, but I think we are going in the right direction now with other things being added to Greenwood.[292]

GreenArch, located at 10 North Greenwood Avenue, is one of the "things added" Henderson predicted. Debuting in 2014, the $9.5 million project combined 70 affordable apartments with nearly 9,500 square feet of retail space on the southwest corner of Archer Street and Greenwood Avenue, across the street from ONEOK Field. GreenArch LLC, the development entity behind the privately funded project, includes the Hille Foundation and Greenwood Community Development Corporation.[293]

Tulsa Mayor G.T. Bynum announced on August 5, 2017, that the City of Tulsa and USA BMX had identified an industrial site on the east end of the Greenwood District, Evans-Fintube (the former location of Oklahoma Iron Works), as the preferred site for USA BMX's national arena and headquarters. The Mayor noted: "We are bringing an Olympic sport and its national audience to the Greenwood District. Much as the BOK Center was a public project that spurred private investment in downtown, we believe this partnership with USA BMX is the first step in drawing significant private investment to this area of North Tulsa." Mayor Bynum emphasized the new site location will allow for economic growth north of downtown and in the historic Greenwood District.[294]

While the proposed USA BMX facility has not been controversial *per se*, some members of the African American community have expressed concerns over the level of community engagement in the project and participation in the economic opportunities it portends.[295]

In 2019, a new addition to the Greenwood District emerged in the form of the executive offices of Vast Bank (formerly, Valley National Bank), located at 110 North Elgin Avenue. The six-story structure also houses In The Raw (a sushi bar), BKD CPAs & Advisors, and Summit Financial Group.[296]

On June 28, 2019, WPX Energy, an exploration and production company, unveiled plans to build a new headquarters in Tulsa's Historic Greenwood District, with a total investment of more than $100 million. The building will be located on the square block bounded by Detroit Avenue and Martin Luther King, Jr. Boulevard to the east and west and Cameron Street and Reconciliation Way to the north and south.

Tulsa Chamber President and CEO Mike Neal noted: "WPX has operations across the United States and could have built elsewhere, so the very intentional decision to locate a new corporate headquarters in the Greenwood District shows a deep commitment to Tulsa and the company's 450 are employees. This investment in one of Tulsa's most historic neighborhoods will have a positive economic impact on our community for decades to come."[297]

The WPX headquarters, an expanse of 245,000 square feet slated to open in 2022, will feature a 15,000-square-foot section dedicated to commercial retail space. The company and some Greenwood District advocates see the space as an opportunity to attract black entrepreneurs. Plans for the WPX facility also include a public pathway connecting nearby park Guthrie Green and John Hope Franklin Reconciliation Park. WPX CEO Rick Muncrief noted, "We're also being very thoughtful about the role we can play in honoring Greenwood and helping bring people together." WPX spent months meeting with community stakeholders as the project evolved.[298]

2. Black Wall Street 2.0

Black Wall Street 2.0 seeks to revitalize and enhance the Black Wall Street community. Its educational focus centers on youth, with an emphasis on finance, business, and general resource management. Its goal is to create a new generation of entrepreneurship grounded in the rich history of the Black Wall Street pioneers.

Black Wall Street 2.0 maintains a community reinvestment fund, a collection of pooled capital, intended to support burgeoning businesses and a resource hub for up-and-coming entrepreneurs.

Tyrance Billingsley, a Black Wall Street 2.0 leader, sums it up thusly:

> I am involved in Black Wall Street 2.0 because I feel that it is destiny. This is my calling. As an ambitious young black male born in the heart of one of the wealthiest black communities ever to exist in America, I will rise up and build up as many people as I possibly can in order to push the boundaries of what was previously thought to be financially and economically possible. I have pushed for the creation of a community reinvestment fund, a pool of resources for community development, for well over a year. To link up with a group that sees merit in this idea is a life-giving experience. In short, Black Wall Street 2.0 wants to rebuild, revive, and transcend historic Black Wall Street and move it into the future. We hope to build a wealthy and thriving community, not just in the Greenwood District, but in all Tulsa, such that the nation will view us a the 'shining city on a hill' in terms of both entrepreneurship and race relations.[299]

3. Dream Tulsa

Dream Tulsa, an initiative of the George Kaiser Family Foundation in Tulsa, invited black entrepreneurs and professionals from around the country for a weekend-long event (May 17 - 20, 2018) that explored growth and leadership opportunities in Tulsa.

Participants learned more about the city, its history, and its culture. Tulsa ranked #1 on a recent *Forbes* magazine "Ten Best Cities for Young Entrepreneurs" list[300] and ranked well on various other lists related to affordability, business climate, and tourism opportunities.

Dream Tulsa attracted individuals who self-identified as being: (1) open to new adventures in a thriving city; (2) passionate about networking with local leaders; (3) excited about exploring a diverse array of opportunities in Tulsa; and (4) energized by the idea of spending a weekend with thirty other like-minded, ambitious, and curious black leaders.

Dream Tulsa participants took in: (1) guided tours of Tulsa's neighborhoods; (2) discussions with Tulsa's top philanthropists; (3) visits to local restaurants, bars, fitness outlet, and cultural offerings; (4) "meet-and-greet" opportunities with diverse heads of industry; (v) the history of Black Wall Street and aspirations for the future. In short, they discovered firsthand what it means to Dream Tulsa.[301]

Dream Tulsa is but one of several entrepreneurial-based initiatives of the George Kaiser Family Foundation, whose central mission is to ensure that every child receives an equal opportunity to succeed. Fulfilling that mission requires keen emphasis on opportunity and equity.[302]

4. Resilient Innovative Social Entrepreneurs

Resilient Innovative Social Entrepreneurs ("R.I.S.E") empowers, educates, and unifies urban professionals as transformative change agents through community, business and leadership development.

In 2017, R.I.S.E. formed out of a need to see real change in the community and to provide a platform for individuals, who have been historically silent, to rise up and be heard.

R.I.S.E. serves as the Professional Network of Coalescent Community Development Corporation, a non-profit organization established to improve the quality of life and remove systemic inequality for the residents of low-to-moderate-income neighborhoods, specifically in North Tulsa.[303]

5. The Black upStart

In July 2019, a national initiative aimed at training black entrepreneurs came to Tulsa. The Washington, D.C.-based pop-up school, The Black upStart, branded its Tulsa version "Black Wall Street: Tulsa Edition."

On three consecutive weekend sessions in July 2019, just over a dozen black entrepreneurs assembled in an inaugural cohort to learn business skills from experienced black faculty members. Class members learned about starting a business, manufacturing products, creating a business plan, and securing capital.

The tuition-free program sponsored jointly by the Tulsa Economic Development Corporation and the George Kaiser Family Foundation provided access to funding to its graduates.

Prior to the launch of the initiative, Brandon Oldham, a program associate with the George Kaiser Family Foundation, reflected on the rich history of entrepreneurship in Tulsa: "One of the things that history shows us is that Tulsa is a place where entrepreneurs, and specifically black entrepreneurs, can thrive and grow."[304]

6. Girls Coding Summer Camp

Google/YouTube's 2017 Codebreaker of the Year, Robinne Burrell, conducted a week-long, free STEM (*i.e.*, science, technology, engineering, and math) summer camp for Tulsa girls from June 18-22, 2018, at the University of Tulsa. She repeated the program in 2019. Burrell, a creative at the forefront of technology and emerging media, brought to the camp her extensive background working with brands spanning digital, interactive, mobile, and social experiences. As a hands-on product developer, Burrell brokered key digital partnerships for Amazon/IMDb and Myspace. She built digital products for NBC's *The Voice*, Comedy Central, Steven Spielberg's The VR Company, and Google through Redflight Innovation, where she serves as Principal of that company's award-winning team.

The camp, filled with coding, robotics, 3D printing, the science of augmented reality, and entrepreneurship in a fun-filled atmosphere, sought to (re)ignite a vibrant entrepreneurial ecosystem in Tulsa that starts with secondary and post-secondary students and prepares them to be the entrepreneurial leaders of tomorrow.

The initiative targeted some four dozen girls from schools throughout the Tulsa area, including Booker T. Washington High School, Jenks High School, Central High School, Edison Preparatory School, Carver Middle School, Owasso High School, and Collegiate Hall Charter School.

Los Angeles-based RedFlight Mobile, represented by Robinne Burrell, the Tulsa Regional STEM Alliance, TD Williamson, Inc., and the University of Tulsa sponsored the camp, a repeat of an experience Burrell facilitated for the Mandela family in South Africa during the summer of 2017.[305]

7. USA BMX and the Evans-Fintube Site in the Greenwood District

Construction is now underway in Tulsa's Historic Greenwood District at the Evans-Fintube site on the national arena and headquarters for USA BMX, previously referenced. BMX is an abbreviation for bicycle motocross or bike motocross, a cycle sport performed on BMX bikes, either in competitive BMX racing, freestyle BMX, or general on- or off-road. BMX is an Olympic sport and USA BMX is its sanctioning body. The City of Tulsa worked diligently with USA BMX and local and state economic development professionals to secure a prime Tulsa location for the arena and headquarters.

For two decades, Tulsa has hosted the American Bicycle Association's Grand Nationals at Expo Square, the Tulsa County Fairgrounds, which features one of the nation's largest clearspan buildings for large indoor events. The event has morphed into the "largest race on earth," with 3,000 competitors and more than 6,000 family members who travel to Tulsa from across the U.S., Canada, and as far away as Australia. Each year, the Grand Nationals provides a $12 million economic impact to the Tulsa community during Thanksgiving weekend.

The City-of-Tulsa-owned Evans-Fintube site, the former location of Oklahoma Iron Works, ranked among the key areas included in a Brownfields Area-Wide Planning Pilot Grant from the Environmental Protection Agency because of the presence of asbestos, lead-based paint, and other contaminants. The grant facilitated redevelopment through specific strategic initiatives that addressed both environmental and development issues at important sites in North Tulsa.

Rose Washington, Executive Director of the Tulsa Economic Development Corporation ("TEDC"), noted: "Because of TEDC's partnership with the City of Tulsa, I've spent countless hours with City and community leaders discussing Brownfield issues as well as evaluating redevelopment proposals. When I heard about the BMX prospect and the potential it brings to the area, for the first time I was ecstatic because this project has the opportunity to draw visitors from across the globe that will get acquainted with Historic Greenwood."

In 2016, Tulsans approved Vision Tulsa, an $884 million sales tax renewal package that makes substantial investments in economic development, education, public safety, streets, and transportation needs citywide.

Vision Tulsa facilitated the push to make Tulsa the world headquarters for an Olympic sport: BMX racing. With a $15 million investment from Vision Tulsa, the City is expected to see more than 100,000 visitors attending more than 100 local, state, and national events in the first five years. The BMX events could generate some $11 million in economic impact for Tulsa over this five-year time span.

The Evans-Fintube site, developed in 1911, covers approximately 22.3 acres along the 100 block of North Lansing Avenue. Formerly a steel manufacturing facility that contained a foundry, it once claimed the title of the largest manufacturing facility in Tulsa. Evans-Fintube lies just north of downtown Tulsa separated only by I-244. Its location in Tulsa's Historic Greenwood District places it proximate to OSU-Tulsa, ONEOK Field, Langston-Tulsa, the Oklahoma Educational Television Authority, historic African American churches, and a host of residential and commercial properties. It is also proximate to the flourishing Tulsa Arts District.[307]

8. Urban Coders Guild

Tulsan Mikeal Vaughn launched the Urban Coders Guild in the fall of 2018. The Urban Coders Guild is a free, after-school initiative designed to provide disadvantaged Tulsa high school students with training in mobile app development, entrepreneurship, and project management.

Vaughn, M.B.A., P.M.P., is a Project Manager at Tulsa Public Schools and an experienced project management professional with experience across multiple IT disciplines and technologies, including telecommunications, network/server infrastructure, and web and application development. His work history and experience attest to his success at building cohesive, high-performing teams laser focused on strong relationships and positive project outcomes.[308] Vaughn sought opportunities to leverage his leadership expertise as IT project manager. Founding the Urban Coders Guild accomplished just that.

Vaughn, a graduate of Booker T. Washington High School in Tulsa, the University of Maryland, and Temple University—Japan, noted:

> In a much larger and civic sense, I imagined building in
> Tulsa a cadre of coders who could take on whatever proj-

Flyer for Urban Coders Guild (2018)[310]

ects employers might have. I wanted to make sure that if someone came up with some brilliant idea, like the next Uber or the next Airbnb or a billionaire idea, that we have people here that would be able to support that.

I [also] want to give (the students) some real, soft skills. In the coding industry, there are lots of people who are great at coding and developing applications but are not that good at soft skills . . . . Even if they don't want to be coders, you would have those additional skills so they can explore other avenues.[309]

9. Black Wall Street Market & Greenwood Farmers Market

Black Wall Street Market, formerly known as Afrika Hotep Market, a combination farmers market, flea market, and grocery store in North Tulsa, seeks to leverage existing community resources to build up North Tulsa.

The food aspect of the market helps fill a gaping hole. The United States Department of Agriculture has long deemed much of the North Tulsa, including downtown and most neighborhoods north of Interstate 244—areas with significant concentrations of African Americans—as a food desert. "Food desert" describes an area without access to affordable, healthy food options within an easily traveled distance. A significant number of low-income Tulsans reside in North Tulsa.

"So even if you popped (a grocery store) right in the middle of that, you'd still have a good 3-mile radius all the way around," said Katie Plohocky, co-founder of the Healthy Community Store Initiative, which reaches food deserts in the Tulsa area with a mobile grocery store.[311]

In addition to the Black Wall Street Market, the Greenwood Cultural Center began the Greenwood Farmers Market on September 1, 2018. Initially running weekly in late summer/early fall, that gathering provided another option for community member access to fruits, vegetables, and other nutritious foodstuffs. The market includes food trucks and artisans as a means by which to promote black entrepreneurship. The Greenwood Farmers Market, located at 322 North Greenwood Avenue, complemented the Black Wall Street Market, which is located farther north at 5616

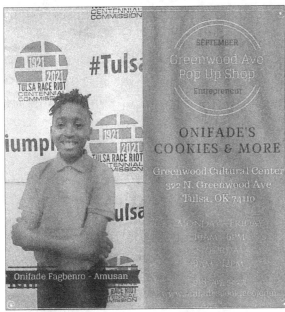

Young entrepreneur Onifade Fagbenro-Amusan at the Greenwood Avenue Pop-Up Shop.[314]

North Osage Drive.[312]

The Greenwood Avenue Pop-up Shop opened concurrent with the debut of the Greenwood Farmers Market. The Pop-Up Shop afforded entrepreneurs the opportunity to test the commercial waters in a temporary space inside the offices of the 1921 Tulsa Race Massacre Centennial Commission, then located within the Greenwood Cultural Center.

The initial September 2018 tenant, Onifade Fagbenro-Amusan, an eleven-year-old baker, sold cookies, cakes, and pies, including gluten-free and vegan options. Proceeds from his sales helped fund his trip to Africa.

Young Onifade, assisted by his mother, sold out on his first day. Customers left in the lurch went online to place orders for his sweet treats.[313]

10. Tulsa's Young Professionals ("TYPROS")

Founded in 2005, "TYPROS" provides local young professionals with opportunities unavailable elsewhere. TYPROS attracts and retains young talent in the Tulsa metro region and helps craft Tulsa's next generation of business and community leaders.

Since its inception, TYPROS has embraced diversity and inclusion as mission-centric, including programming and leadership cultivation. Its Diversity Crew (*i.e.,* committee) fosters openness and celebrates differences through education and conversation.

TYPROS often works collaboratively. When seeking out new partners, it pays special attention to minority-owned, women-owned, veteran-owned, and LGBTQ-owned businesses.[315]

11. Peoria-Mohawk Business Park

Sharing the wealth—extending economic prosperity to North Tulsa—remains a stated priority of community leaders and citizens alike. Residents of North Tulsa, a significant number of whom (a majority, in some sectors) are African Americans, have long complained of lack of investment and disparities in economic opportunities.

The long-articulated goal of boosting prosperity in North Tulsa perhaps came one step closer to fruition in 2019. Muncie Power Products Inc. announced plans to invest $50 million in the Peoria-Mohawk Business Park, located at Peoria Avenue and 36th Street North, for a 300,000-square-foot plant that will employ well over 200 people. City leaders hope the investment by Muncie, the business park's first resident, spurs additional, substantial economic revitalization in the area.

The Peoria-Mohawk Business Park resulted from a collaboration among Tulsa citizens, the George Kaiser Family Foundation, and the City of Tulsa. Tulsa citizens approved a 2016 Vision Tulsa sales tax renewal to develop the site. The George Kaiser Family Foundation donated the land. The City of Tulsa plans to create at Tax Increment Finance District to assist with additional investment and redevelopment.[316]

History, Arts & Culture

1. Leadership Tulsa Focus on Greenwood History

Leadership Tulsa identifies, develops, and connects diverse leaders who impact the community through service. The flagship Leadership Tulsa program helps individuals enhance personal, professional, and community leadership skills. Through a series of monthly meetings, participants explore the systems and needs of Tulsa, discuss issues facing the city, develop the skills and techniques to lead effectively, and build a network to make a difference in the community.

The nine-month program includes: orientation and an overnight retreat; monthly class days covering geographic regions of the city as well as topics including education, healthcare, business, the arts, social services, and community history; and a hands-on board internship with a choice of nearly 100 area nonprofit organizations.

Leadership Tulsa class members experience Greenwood District history as part of their tour of Tulsa. After a lecture about the historic African American community, they are encouraged to engage around the lessons of history and its implications for present-day Tulsa.

Wendy Thomas, Executive Director of Leadership Tulsa, explained the rationale for the group's emphasis on history:

> Leadership Tulsa is committed to training Tulsa's next generation of leadership to be thoughtful, community-connected, and resilient. Sharing the history of the Greenwood District helps us do all three. The story of Tulsa is in large measure the story of the individual people who made their lives here, took risks to build families and businesses, and the leaders who made good decisions and bad decisions. From the entrepreneurial spirit that helped build the Greenwood community to the resilience of those who rebuilt after the terrible race riot, we are the students of their struggles and learn from their example. As we examine the unique circumstances that led to the race riot as well as the larger context of what was happening in the United States, we are asked to examine the role of leaders in their time and in ours. As we hear the unedited words from personal letters as well as newspaper articles, the events of the race riot are brought to harsh light in a way that draws us in and helps us walk a mile in other shoes. As a result, our participants are more informed about our community history and also more understanding of its continuing impact today. We believe that you can't lead a city you don't love and you can't love a city you don't know. Knowing our unique history is an essential part of the Leadership Tulsa journey.[317]

2. Massacre Survivors Documentary and Other Documentation

On October 19, 2008, the documentary film *Before They Die!*[318]

premiered in Tulsa. It chronicled the survivors of the massacre. Producers pledged some proceeds from showings of the film would benefit the survivors. At the event, Tulsa Mayor Kathy Taylor declared the day "Journey to Healing Day" and offered a formal apology to the two-dozen massacre survivors in attendance. (Tulsa's thirty-sixth mayor and its first female mayor, Susan Savage, and Oklahoma's twenty-fifth governor, Frank Keating, a Tulsan, had both offered apologies in the past.)[319] Numerous other documentaries and treatments of the history surrounding the massacre had been previously made, including *In Search of History: The Night Tulsa Burned* (1999) featured on the History Channel.[320]

Lonnie G. Bunch III, Founding Director of the Smithsonian National Museum of African American History and Culture, which opened in September 2016, said: "The African American experience is the lens through which we understand what it is to be an American."[321] Tulsa history plays a significant role in our understanding of what it means to be American. The city's history figures prominently among the Museum's offerings.

A hint of the vibrancy of Black Wall Street in the post-massacre era may be found in moving footage from Reverend Harold Mose Anderson, who used his home movie camera to capture Black Wall Street from 1948-1952. Patricia Sanders donated the film to the National Museum of American History Archives Center in 2010.[322]

3. Race Riot Suite

In 2011, Tulsa-based Jacob Fred Jazz Odyssey, a jazz fusion combo, recorded *Race Riot Suite*, a seven-movement extended suite inspired by the massacre. The work, written, arranged, and orchestrated by band member Chris Combs, explores its subject matter through music with a Tulsa connection: bluegrass, Western swing, ragtime, Dixieland jazz, free jazz, and blues. The recording took place in legendary Church Studio, less than a mile from the epicenter of the riot.[323]

The ambitious piece drew favorable critical reviews:

> 'A beautifully orchestrated, melodically rich piece that celebrates Greenwood as much as it laments the wanton violence that destroyed the neighborhood.'—*Boston Globe*

Tulsa's Jacob Fred Jazz Odyssey features a core quartet of Brian Haas on piano, Chris Combs on lap steel, Jeff Harshbarger on bass, and drummer Josh Raymer. These musicians regularly tap into the roots of their musically rich region to inform their forward-thinking sound. Their tour-de-force *Race Riot Suite* has garnered critical raves for the savvy way it draws from the traditions of the great Territory jazz bands of the 1920s and 1930s while focusing on the infamous 1921 Tulsa race riot that resulted in the deaths of hundreds of black Tulsans and the destruction of an entire city district, the prosperous Greenwood community, then known as the Black Wall Street.

Written, arranged, and orchestrated by Chris Combs, the suite (which was released on CD) is performed here by JFJO joined by guest tenor sax player Mark Southerland and a horn section from Ohio State's School of Music.

Here are excerpts from two more raves for *The Race Riot Suite*.

'The 12-part suite pinballs between majestic melodies, free improv, and ragged New Orleans rhythms, sometimes all within the same song . . . . Expect a heavy dose of history, but an even heavier dose of forward-looking, down-home jazz.'—*Time Out New York*

'Rather than simply evoking Greenwood's destruction, however, the suite encompasses the region's creative ferment . . . . The score captures the energy of Greenwood's fervent churchgoers and the rollicking territory dance bands that crisscrossed the Southwest.'—*Los Angeles Times*[324]

4. *Cherokee Nation v. Nash:*[325] *A Successful Challenge to Black Disenfranchisement*

"Exclusion is never the way forward on our shared paths to freedom and justice." —Bishop Desmond Tutu

Tulsa's Historic Greenwood District sits on what were once Cherokee Nation allotments and Muscogee (Creek) Nation Tulsa townsite set-asides. Today, descendants of the Cherokee and Muscogee (Creek) Freedmen dot the Greenwood District and North Tulsa region, where African Americans constitute a demographic majority in several sectors. These Freedmen descendants continue to fight for their citizenship rights in the context of their historical tribal communities.[326]

The Cherokee Freedmen recently won a major legal victory in their continuing quest for recognition within the Cherokee Nation. Who are the Freedmen and what did they win?

In the 1830s and 1840s, the United States government forcibly removed the Five Civilized Tribes (Choctaw, Chickasaw, Muscogee (Creek), Cherokee, and Seminole) from their homelands in the Southeast to Indian Territory, present-day Oklahoma. Persons of African descent, some free, some enslaved, accompanied the tribes; they often intermixed with Indians socially, culturally, and intimately.

At the end of the Civil War, the federal government negotiated treaties (collectively the Treaty of 1866) under which the Muscogee (Creek), Cherokee, and Seminole Nations adopted persons of African ancestry in their midst and their descendants (collectively the "Freedmen") as tribal members. The Choctaw and Chickasaw Nations jointly negotiated similar treaties, which included optional Freedmen adoption provisions. The Choctaws grudgingly adopted their Freedmen in 1883. The Chickasaws never did.

At the turn of the twentieth century, the federal government dissolved tribal nations and terminated their communal land ownership system. The Dawes Commission facilitated this process by dividing Indian lands and allotting them to individual tribe members. As the first step, Commission agents compiled registration rolls (the Dawes Rolls) for the tribes.

In each case, federal emissaries drew up a Dawes Blood Roll and a Dawes Freedmen Roll. The Blood Roll documented the enrollee's Indian blood. Commission agents listed virtually all persons who showed evidence of African ancestry (meaning those who looked black) on the Freedmen Roll.

Given the longstanding ties between Native Americans and African descendants and the prevalence of cross-cultural relationships, this binary configuration—*either African or Indian*—obscured the fact that some Freedmen possessed Indian blood. Thus, some Freedmen were denied their "Indianness."

The federal government began conditioning some tribal benefits on an applicant's ability to demonstrate possession of Indian blood via ties to an ancestor on the Dawes Commission "Blood Rolls." The Freedmen, lacking the requisite evidence, were not qualified for various tribal benefits, which adversely impacted their status and relative economic posture.

Some tribes, including the Cherokees, instituted measures requiring Indian blood not just for specified benefits, but for tribal membership. These tribes typically relied upon the Dawes Rolls as the single source of proof. One would have to trace an ancestor back to the Blood Rolls to evidence one's entitlement to such benefits and, for Cherokees, to tribal membership.

Issues of Indian blood aside, the Treaty of 1866 offered the strongest argument for Freedmen citizenship within the Five Civilized Tribes. It sets forth what the Freedmen and others consider unassailable evidence of the Tribes' intent to accord the Freedmen the same rights granted to other tribal members.

In recent years, the Freedmen debate raged most noticeably in the Cherokee Nation. In *Lucy Allen v. Cherokee Nation Tribal Council* (2006), the Cherokee Nation Supreme Court declared unconstitutional legislation designed to limit Cherokee tribal membership to those who could demonstrate their Cherokee-by-blood status.

The Court's decision rested upon Article III of the 1975 Cherokee Nation Constitution. The Court held that the law impermissibly prescribed tribal membership criteria more restrictive than that set forth in the Constitution. After the *Allen* decision, the Cherokee Nation began accepting and processing Freedmen citizenship applications, enrolling more than one thousand.

Then-Cherokee Nation Principal Chief Chadwick Smith led the opposition to Freedmen citizenship, culminating in a successful 2007 referendum petition that amended the Cherokee Nation Constitution. The measure limited Cherokee citizenship to those of Indian ancestry listed in the Blood Rolls.

Following this setback, Freedmen advocate Marilyn Vann, attorney John Velie, and many Freedmen and their allies rallied the troops. Political and legal maneuvering, including court challenges and Congressional lobbying, kicked into high gear. A court granted provisional citizenship for Freedmen already enrolled as the battle languished in federal court.[327]

The legal landscape changed on August 30, 2017. Thomas F. Hogan, a federal judge in Washington, D.C., upheld the citizenship rights of the Cherokee Freedmen in *Cherokee Nation v. Nash*.

Judge Hogan held that the Treaty of 1866 guaranteed citizenship for persons previously enslaved and their progeny. He opined: "The history, negotiations, and practical construction of the [Treaty of 1866] suggest no other result . . . Consequently, the Cherokee Freedmen's right to citizenship in the Cherokee Nation is directly proportional to native Cherokees' right to citizenship."

The Cherokee Nation, under the leadership of Principal Chief Bill John Baker,[328] accepted the *Nash* decision and began the process of reincorporating its Freedmen back into the tribal fold. This conciliatory gesture settled the matter and ended a contentious and divisive chapter in Cherokee history.

Nash provided powerful, positive precedent for inclusion of the Freedmen of the other members of the Five Civilized Tribes. Litigation may be inevitable in the other tribes in the absence of proactive, conciliatory efforts around Freedmen inclusion.

The Greenwood Cultural Center ("GCC"), located in the heart of Tulsa's Historic Greenwood District and situated on a former Cherokee allotment, selected three recipients for its 2019 fundraiser, the Legacy Award Dinner, which honors individuals and/or entities whose work on behalf of African American causes merits recognition and elevation.[329]

On April 18, 2019, GCC saluted: Chief Bill John Baker and the Cherokee Nation; Marilyn Vann, president of the Freedmen Association of the Five Tribes; and David Cornsilk, a key Freedmen ally and advocate within the Cherokee Nation. Together, the Cherokee Nation, Ms. Vann, and Mr. Cornsilk offered a vivid example of reconciliation in action.

GCC honored the Cherokee Nation for its warm and welcoming reception of the Freedmen descendants after the *Nash* decision. GCC honored Marilyn Vann for her diligent pursuit of the rights of the Freedmen descendants, most notably as leader of the Freedmen Association of the Five Tribes and a lead plaintiff in the *Nash* case. GCC honored David Cornsilk for his years-long work on behalf of Cherokee Nation citizens of Freedmen descent.

In July of 2018, the Freedmen of the Muscogee (Creek) Nation filed a federal lawsuit against the Muscogee (Creek) Nation and the United States Department of the Interior.

The Creek Freedmen lawsuit sought full tribal citizenship. In addition, the legal challenge beseeched the court to declare the tribe's constitution in violation of the Treaty of 1866, which guaranteed tribal citizenship to the tribe's freed slaves (*i.e.*, the Freedmen) and their descendants, as well as other black Creeks. In 1979, the Department of the Interior approved a law in the tribe's constitution that restricted citizenship eligibility to those with proof of Creek lineage (*i.e.*, Creek blood).[330]

On May 6, 2019, a federal court dismissed the case without prejudice (*i.e.*, plaintiffs may refile) for failure on the part of the plaintiffs to exhaust their tribal remedies. That is, the plaintiffs did not allege that they ever applied for citizenship in and were denied citizenship by the Muscogee Creek Nation.[331]

Presumably, plaintiffs will heed the exhaustion of remedies edict and refile the case. Plaintiffs' attorney Damario Solomon Simmons commented: "We know the law is on our side, the facts are on our side, and history is on our side. This is just another obstacle we have to overcome."[332]

5. Black Wall Street Airport Exhibit

In 2015, Bill White, then Business Development Manager with the Tulsa Regional Chamber, had a vision. That vision fast became a reality. White knew the Black Wall Street story remained unknown to many. His vision represented one small step toward recapturing history.

White's simple idea: Create an exhibit, housed at Tulsa International Airport ("TIA"), designed to inform and inspire the residents of Tulsa and travelers from all stations in life: The Black Wall Street/Greenwood District Airport Exhibit. The eight-feet-tall-by-fifteen-feet-long exhibit, consisting of two, two-sided polycarbonate panels with LED lights, opened on June 14, 2016.

The exhibit gave Tulsans and travelers alike the opportunity to learn a great deal about Tulsa's rich history and celebrate the City's entrepreneurial spirit. It also helped spur cultural (or "heritage") tourism, a growing area of economic activity, by encouraging those who view the exhibit at TIA to tour Tulsa's Historic Greenwood District.

Exhibit themes included: Roots, Riot, Regeneration & Renaissance. The exhibit reflected a first-of-its-kind and a unique showcase featuring strong pictorial and rich textual history. It explored the roots of the Greenwood District—the lives and times of the individuals who came to Tulsa to lay claim to the American Dream. The exhibit examined the infamous massacre using photos, newspaper headlines, and eyewitness accounts. It considered the post-massacre regeneration—how, despite numerous obstacles, the Greenwood District came back to life stronger and better with little outside assistance. It looked at the renaissance—how the Greenwood District is making a comeback with the help of major developments in and around the area.

The exhibit created a context that addressed the relationship between Tulsa and its African American community, not just for the benefit of Tulsans, but for all who visit the city.

This remarkable visual narrative offered a provocative look at the impact the Greenwood District has had, and continues to have, on Tulsa, and became an inspirational vehicle. It carried forth the legacy of African American entrepreneurship through the sharing of the Black Wall Street story.[333]

6. Black Wall Street Mural

On June 1, 2018, Tulsa dignitaries helped unveil a Black Wall Street mural outside the Greenwood Cultural Center. Set against a black backdrop, the north-facing wall of Interstate 244 cutting across the Greenwood District says "Black Wall St." in large, white-framed block letters, each of which illustrates a part of Tulsa's black history.

The "K" includes imagery of Black Wall Street set alight during the massacre, with flames and smoke trailing up to the concrete barrier of the highway. The first "L" contains an eagle in a nod to *The Oklahoma Eagle*, Tulsa's black-owned newspaper, while the

"T" shows off Booker T. Washington High School's hornet mascot.

The Tulsa Race Massacre Centennial Commission, TYPROS (Tulsa's Young Professionals) Foundation, and Fowler Ford sponsored the installation of the mural, which sprung out of a partnership between the Greenwood Cultural Center and Tulsa artist Chris "Sker" Rogers, who worked with Tulsan Bill White and Kansas City-based graffiti artist Donald "Scribe" Ross to complete the project.

Ross, who has also installed murals in the Kendall-Whittier and Tulsa Arts Districts, said he hoped the Black Wall Street illustration "plants some seeds in the community" so it can be unified.

"We expect this new Black Wall Street mural will increase tourism to the community, will foster new conversation about our shared past and our shared future, and will bring people together," Rogers noted. White echoed that view, noting that he has received a variety of comments about the interpretation of the mural.[334]

7. Greenwood Avenue: A Virtual Reality Experience

Greenwood Avenue: A Virtual Reality Experience, shot in Tulsa in the summer of 2018, premiered on YouTubeVR in October 2018. Created by Ayana Baraka and partially funded by a grant from Google and funding from Women Make Movies, a nonprofit organization promoting women in filmmaking, the five-part series revolves around a fourteen-year-old African American girl named Agnes living in Tulsa's Historic Greenwood District at the time of the massacre.[335]

Through Agnes' eyes, spectators bear witness to a young love and life cut short; a community burned to the ground, and Agnes with it. Agnes reflects an amalgam of stories from survivors, witnesses, newspaper clippings, and books.

Project creators tapped virtual reality technology to place viewers in Agnes' shoes, bringing the history of Black Wall Street back to life. "A lot of people think it's a tall tale," director Talibah Newman said. She continued, "The violence that destroyed Greenwood—and the conditions that led to it—are things many would rather forget, but our job as filmmakers is to create awareness and make sure the history doesn't become lost."

Agnes' tale gives viewers a sense of what an economic and

cultural oasis Tulsa's Greenwood District once provided for African Americans and of the terror of the hours between late May 31, 1921, and mid-day June 1, 1921, when it was razed.

The crew for the project, mostly from California, spent a week filming in the Greenwood District, with a view toward recreating a 1921 atmosphere on a tight budget of under $200,000.

Producers considered filming in Los Angeles, but ultimately creator Ayana Baraka decided that the project had to happen, if at all, in the Greenwood District. "It was definitely a magical place, and that's what we're trying to capture," Baraka said.

Baraka began developing the project three years prior to the start of filming while at the University of Southern California, shortly after learning about Greenwood District history for the first time.

"It's been almost 100 years, and people still don't know about this. It hasn't been dissected . . . or even really accepted," she said. "How can we get over something that hasn't even been recognized?"

The project is ultimately about educating. As such, the creators sought to make clear that racism, in this case and most others, is no simple thing. "It's about stuff, it's about money, it's about things," project writer Spade Robinson said. "It's about a group of people feeling like they inherently deserve these things. I want the community of Tulsa, the descendants of people who died, descendants of people who survived, to feel seen and heard," Robinson noted. "That's the most important thing to me."[336]

8. Tulsa '21: Black Wall Street

Tulsa '21: Black Wall Street, a play by Tulsa native Tara Brooke Watkins about the events surrounding the massacre and its legacy, debuted in June 2018.

Watkins spent two years researching and writing the play, which chronicles the events leading up to the Tulsa tragedy. She delved into archives in preparation for drafting the script for the play. She also conducted story circles in which individuals from throughout the city discussed the social issues associated with the massacre and told personal stories.[337]

Public Spaces

1. Gathering Place

The largest privately-funded public park in America opened to rave reviews in Tulsa on September 8, 2018. The *Tulsa World* heralded the transformative project:

> For years, Tulsans have wondered what a half billion bucks looks like.
>
> Saturday, they witnessed it firsthand with the public opening of Gathering Place, the $465 million, riverfront park that was the vision of George Kaiser and a slew of philanthropists who followed his lead.
>
> As thousands filtered through meticulously crafted 66.5 acres, it was hard to find anyone who wasn't impressed.[338]

Place-making played a significant part of the vision for Tulsa's Gathering Place. So, too, did finding common ground, literally and figuratively, on which Tulsans may come together in shared celebration of that which unites them.[339]

> Our story began with the George Kaiser Family Foundation and an extraordinary dream to transform nearly 100 acres of Tulsa's iconic waterfront along the scenic Arkansas River into a dynamic, interactive environment. Tulsans needed a welcoming, natural space where members of our diverse communities could come together to explore, learn and play.
>
> After years of planning, generous donations and input from the community, Tulsa's dream became reality. In 2014, Gathering Place broke ground on Tulsa's world-class park. The dream of a space to celebrate and gather along the river was becoming reality.
>
> The next chapter is filled with excitement as we welcome our first guests in 2018. The children, families and friends of Tulsa will write the narrative from there, an ongoing adventure sure to inspire wonderful moments for generations to come. We look forward to witnessing memories made and celebrating the collective growth experienced

through Gathering Place, where your adventures will only be limited by your own imagination.

We are Gathering Place. We are Tulsa. We are diverse, passionate and true to our beliefs. We remain consistent in our mission, as a project led by George Kaiser Family Foundation, that we all become united in our love for our community. Relatives, close friends, neighbors, we are all family. We are united from every zip code, from the city to the suburbs, from the river to the hills, from the north to the south, from the west to the east. Gathering Place is the ultimate expression of Tulsa's spirit of unity. A place for everyone.[340]

The man behind Gathering Place and so many of the ongoing Tulsa beautification and betterment efforts is billionaire Tulsa-booster George Kaiser. Tulsa's leading philanthropist uses his vast wealth and considerable network to identify, research, and evaluate projects and initiatives that have the potential of making Tulsa a more beautiful, economically vibrant, equitable, and inclusive city.

Three Tulsans captured Kaiser's impulses and impact:

What I've come to appreciate in working with George Kaiser is that he's one of the smartest people you will ever meet. The financial success is an after effect of that remarkable intelligence. Similarly, the work that he does in the community carries the same intellectual heft. Take Gathering Place. To many, it is a really nice park. To him, it is a vehicle for reversing the increasing isolation and polarization we see in society. All the individual elements of the park are thoughtfully considered tools to that end. All of us in Tulsa are fortunate to call someone with his combination of intellect, resources and altruism our neighbor. *Tulsa Mayor G.T. Bynum*[341]

George Kaiser has helped turn a group of underutilized properties into an international showcase for the arts—Tulsa Arts District. Starting with the anchors of Cain's Ballroom and Brady Theater [renamed the "Tulsa Theater"], George, through the George Kaiser Family Foundation, has expanded the district's ability to host visual arts in several venues, as well as performances. The Guthrie Green and its variety of programming has become a great magnet for diversity and fun. With his vision for the district, others have been encouraged to invest in the community where all Tulsans can live, work and play. Many local entrepreneurs have launched their dreams alongside of George's, with a result of all ships rising with the tide. The speed and intensity of development in the district is a direct result of GKFF [George Kaiser Family Foundation] involvement and long-term commitment. *Bob Fleischman, president of the Tulsa Arts District Business Association*[342]

George Kaiser is the gold standard for a philanthropist willing to tackle even the toughest community challenges. While most Tulsans know how he rallied the community to bring us an amazing Gathering Place, many don't know that behind the scenes, he has been a key funder for an organized effort to reduce teen and unintended pregnancy in Tulsa. And the collaborative efforts are paying off. Since 2009, teen births in Tulsa County have dropped by 53.3 percent. That's great news for our community and far outpaces other teen birth-rate reductions in our region. Kaiser and his outstanding team don't spend much time talking about or celebrating successes such as this because they know there is yet much work to be done since we still have other significant social challenges looming. *Alison Anthony, president and CEO of the Tulsa Area United Way*[343]

On January 18, 2019, Tony Moore, executive director of Tulsa's Gathering Place, announced that the park had been voted the best new attraction in the United States in USA Today's 10 Best Readers' Choice contest, besting attractions in major cities like Chicago and New York. Since its September 2018 opening, Gathering Place has hosted thousands of visitors, well over a half-million in its first few months of operation.[344]

2. Osage Prairie Trail

The Osage Prairie Trail is a "rails to trails" project that follows the corridor of the old Midland Valley Railroad. The trail links Oklahoma State University-Tulsa with the town of Skiatook to the north. The trail is lighted in places for night use and passes through both urban and rural landscapes. The southern end is mostly suburban, while around Skiatook and Sperry the trail takes on a more countryside atmosphere.

The ten-feet-wide paved trail includes eight pedestrian bridges, one of which was a renovated historical highway bridge. The trail passes through a variety of woodland and grassland habitats. A planned, future expansion will extend the trail to Birch Lake in Osage County.[345]

3. Tulsa's Historic Greenwood District on Display

A. National Museum of African American History and Culture

Tucked away on the third floor of the Smithsonian's National Museum of African American History and Culture, which opened in September 2016 on the National Mall in Washington, D.C., is the typewriter of Buck Colbert Franklin, an attorney who moved to Tulsa's Historic Greenwood District just prior to its cataclysmic destruction in 1921. B.C. Franklin is the father of the late eminent historian John Hope Franklin and the grandfather of John W. Franklin, a former senior manager at the Smithsonian.

B.C. Franklin lost his law office in the disaster. Undeterred, he set up shop in an American Red Cross tent. His typewriter tapped out legal documents used on behalf of clients as he sought redress for the unprecedented mob violence that fleetingly gripped Tulsa, leaving Black Wall Street and surrounding areas in tatters.

That typewriter, together with other artifacts, offers a window into Tulsa's prominent and prosperous black entrepreneurial community, its demise at the hand of white mobsters, and its phoenix-like rise after the decimation. John W. Franklin and his colleagues gathered all manner of treasures—photos, film, newspaper articles, personal letters, pennies that melted in the fires—from several sources, including the Greenwood Cultural Center, the University of Oklahoma, and survivors and their families.

Months before the exhibit debuted, United States Senator James Lankford, R-Oklahoma City, spoke on the Senate floor to draw attention to the 95th anniversary of the Tulsa's signature disaster. The Senator reminded listeners that the 100th anniversary of the event looms, and the question of the moment then will be: What has changed since 1921?[346]

Senator Lankford toured the massacre exhibit with John W. Franklin in December of 2016, seeing for the first time some of the photos and artifacts from the era. He expressed his belief that the exhibit will help educate people about a bleak chapter in Oklahoma history that many would rather forget. For Senator Lankford, though, the complete story of the Greenwood District, including the rise of black entrepreneurship evident in the success of Black Wall Street, must be told, not just the horrors of the 1921 massacre.[347]

B. Tulsa Historical Society & Museum

Locally, the Tulsa Historical Society & Museum maintains a virtual exhibit on the 1921 calamity that presents all the relevant material in its collection. Through interactive software at an iPad kiosk located inside the facility, visitors may browse through digital reproductions of photographs, newspaper clippings, and other archival materials. In addition, a free version of the virtual exhibit (Internet accessible) is available for teaching purposes.[348]

C. University of Tulsa McFarlin Library Special Collections

The University of Tulsa Department of Special Collections and University Archives maintains a compilation of digital images from numerous sources, including several uncredited photograph collections (*i.e.*, from donors who sought anonymity). Among these are the Maxine Wiandt photographs (courtesy of Al Brophy), the Sarah Blackwood donation, and a set extracted from the Francis Schmidt scrapbooks. These images and documents provide a basic grounding in Tulsa's tumultuous racial history, *circa* 1921.

Some materials refer to the various racial and cultural groups, including the African American community concentrated in the Greenwood District and various Native American demographics.

Such items include an unidentified family scrap book from the Greenwood District and a trove of historical photographs. Also included is a copy of the 1924 Booker T. Washington yearbook and a copy of the Mary Elizabeth Jones Parrish book, *Events of the Tulsa Disaster*.

Collected photos include:

- Postcards—Prints that were made into postcards (once a common practice);
- Photographic prints—Photos printed from the original negatives; and
- Photographic reproductions—Second or later generation photographs, frequently made by scanning in a photograph or photographing another image, resulting in the creation of a new negative (derivative works that lack the detail of photographic prints).

The University of Tulsa houses a massacre archive as well.[349]

D. Greenwood Cultural Center

The Greenwood Cultural Center maintains photographs of the Greenwood District before, during, and after the 1921 disaster and a number of documentary treatments Tulsa's Historic Greenwood District. It also houses a collection of survivor photographs and biographies, as well as various newspaper and magazine articles.[350]

4. Booker T. Washington High School Monument

Community members erected a monument to the original Booker T. Washington High School in the Greenwood District in 2003. The monument sits on the campus of Oklahoma State University-Tulsa, which now effectively controls the land on which Booker T. once sat.

Location
Tulsa: On the Oklahoma State University-Tulsa campus, south of Administrative Hall, 36°9'50 N 95°59'18 W

Inscription
Booker T. Washington High School Tulsa, OK 1913-1950

Constructed on this site in 1913, Booker T. Washington

served as the separate school for Black students in Tulsa. The first building was a four-room wooden frame structure. A sixteen-room brick facility with a basement replaced the original building in 1919. BTW High School was one of the few structures to survive the Tulsa Race Riot of 1921. The American Red Cross administered disaster relief from the school, which served as a safe haven for the victims of the riot. Under the leadership of principal Ellis Walker Woods (1913-1948), the school flourished. BTW High School has produced a significant number of scholars and citizens, who have made contributions to the state, the nation and the world. The North Central Association accredited the school in 1925-1926. BTW High School moved to its current location, 1631 East Woodrow Place, in 1950. The quest for educational excellence, enlightenment, and advancement continues on this historic site, now OSU-Tulsa.[351]

Today's Booker T. Washington High School, located at 1514 East Zion Street, arguably Oklahoma's finest public high school,[352] serves as a magnet school option for a multiracial student population. Its new, broader mission is "to provide an academically rigorous education within an environment of multicultural diversity and to develop all students' critical thinking skills which are necessary for success in a global society."[353]

5. Standpipe Hill Marker

On June 12, 2014, The University Center at Tulsa Authority and Oklahoma State University-Tulsa jointly dedicated a historical marker in recognition of Standpipe Hill. The University Center at Tulsa, a consortium of higher education institutions including Oklahoma State University ("OSU"), was established on land adjacent to Standpipe Hill in the 1980s. The campus became OSU-Tulsa on January 1, 1999.

OSU-Tulsa President Howard Barnett noted in a news release: "Standpipe Hill played a role in the tragic unfolding of the Tulsa Race Riot, which had a lasting impact on this area of our city. The ceremony will remember the lasting impact of that event and other historical events that happened at Standpipe Hill and look at the role it continues to play in Tulsa as part of OSU-Tulsa."

Located south of John Hope Franklin Boulevard between Detroit Avenue and Martin Luther King Jr. Boulevard, the marker tells the story of Standpipe Hill, including its importance during the massacre, its significance as home to higher education offerings in Tulsa, and the grand aspirations it could inspire in terms of the community's future development.

Glenda Love, chair of the Standpipe Hill Historical Marker Committee and a former OSU-Tulsa trustee, noted: "The dedication is a time for our community to come together and remember the tragic history of this area and its influence on Tulsa. Remembering the past will help us move forward in a spirit of reconciliation to create a more prosperous future for all of Tulsa." Ms. Love's committee examined historical documents and researched legends associated with Standpipe Hill to compile text for the marker.

The City of Tulsa constructed its first water tower in 1904. Standpipe Hill derives its name from that stovepipe-shaped tower. The City demolished the tall, cylindrical unit in 1924, constructing a new water storage unit on Reservoir Hill just a few miles north.

The text on the Standpipe Hill marker plaque reads as follows:

> In 1904 the City of Tulsa built a water tower in the shape of a stove pipe. Thus, Standpipe Hill was named.
>
> To the east, the Greenwood community would grow and prosper, providing the success of 'Black Wall Street.'
>
> The Race Riot of 1921 resulted in the death of many African American people, the destruction of hundreds of homes and the burning of churches and businesses in Greenwood. All of this could be seen from atop Standpipe Hill.
>
> From the seeds of overwhelming destruction, African-Americans moved back and rebuilt. But this rebirth of Greenwood would give way to suburban flight and urban renewal.
>
> In the 1980s a new vision was conceived. Land east and north of the hill was dedicated to public higher education for all Tulsans and the region.

More to come . . . .

History Remembered and a Future to be Embraced

Dedicated June 2014

To what has been and what will be . . .[354]

Community-Building

1. March Toward CommUNITY

On October 5, 2008, the Oklahoma Center for Community and Justice ("OCCJ") sponsored "March Toward CommUNITY" designed to promote inclusiveness and community cohesion. Some 1,400 people took part in the march.

OCCJ is a human relations organization working to ensure respect and understanding for all people through education, advocacy, and dialogue. OCCJ works to eliminate bias, bigotry, and racism.[355]

2. Tulsa City Council Riot Resolution

On October 9, 2008, the Tulsa City Council passed a massacre-inspired resolution that supported: (1) the completion of the John Hope Franklin Reconciliation Park and the establishment of the John Hope Franklin Center for Reconciliation; (2) efforts to seek federal designation of the John Hope Franklin Center for Reconciliation as a National Park Service memorial site, alongside its other sites that preserve and memorialize places of historical and cultural significance and highlight the diversity of the American people; (3) the establishment of the Tulsa Reconciliation Education program and the teaching of an appropriate curriculum to ensure the massacre is adequately covered in Oklahoma's educational institutions as an historical event; and (4) the creation of the Mayor's Community Race Relations Committee to follow up on the implementation of the foregoing items. Mayor Kathy Taylor approved the resolution on October 13, 2008.[357]

The "Whereas" clauses to that Resolution explain the motivation for and impetus behind it:

WHEREAS, the 1921 Tulsa Race Riot stands among the most tragic and violent events in Tulsa and the nation's history; and,

WHEREAS, the survivors and their descendants have waited for more than eighty-six years for reconciliation between the races and for healing of the lasting psychological and emotional effects of the 1921 Tulsa Race Riot; and,

WHEREAS, the Mayor of the City of Tulsa and the Tulsa City Council recognize that acknowledging the victims of this tragic event in a real and tangible way is good public policy because it will promote reconciliation and help heal the emotional and physical scars left in the wake of the 1921 Tulsa Race Riot; and,

WHEREAS, the Mayor of the City of Tulsa and the Tulsa City Council, by passage of this Resolution, intend to send a clear message to the world that the citizens of City of Tulsa, Oklahoma, embrace tolerance, reconciliation and justice for all people; and,

WHEREAS, commemoration of the 1921 Tulsa Race Riot is appropriate for the goals and objectives of the National Park Service to preserve and memorialize the diversity of the American people and sites of historical and cultural significance[....][358]

3. The Charter for Compassion

At its June 25, 2015, meeting, the Tulsa City Council approved the Tulsa Interfaith Alliance-led resolution to recognize Tulsa as a "Compassionate Community" and authorized the Human Rights Commission to continue working to raise awareness about compassion and highlight opportunities for individuals and groups to engage in compassionate action. The action affirmed the message of the International Charter for Compassion:

The Charter for Compassion

The principle of compassion lies at the heart of all religious, ethical and spiritual traditions, calling us always to treat all others as we wish to be treated ourselves. Compassion impels us to work tirelessly to alleviate the suffering of our fellow creatures, to dethrone ourselves from the centre of our world and put another there, and to honour the inviolable sanctity of every single human being, treating everybody, without exception, with absolute justice, equity and respect.

It is also necessary in both public and private life to refrain consistently and empathically from inflicting pain. To act or speak violently out of spite, chauvinism, or self-interest, to impoverish, exploit or deny basic rights to anybody, and to incite hatred by denigrating others—even our enemies—is a denial of our common humanity. We acknowledge that we have failed to live compassionately and that some have even increased the sum of human misery in the name of religion.

We therefore call upon all men and women to restore compassion to the [center] of morality and religion[,] to return to the ancient principle that any interpretation of scripture that breeds violence, hatred or disdain is illegitimate[,] to ensure that youth are given accurate and respectful information about other traditions, religions and cultures[,] to encourage a positive appreciation of cultural and religious diversity[,] to cultivate an informed empathy with the suffering of all human beings—even those regarded as enemies.

We urgently need to make compassion a clear, luminous and dynamic force in our polarized world. Rooted in a principled determination to transcend selfishness, compassion can break down political, dogmatic, ideological and religious boundaries. Born of our deep interdependence, compassion is essential to human relationships and to a fulfilled humanity. It is the path to enlightenment, and indispensable to the creation of a just economy and a peaceful global community.[359]

4. Still She Rises

Women are the fastest-growing segment of the prison population in the United States. At twice the national rate, Oklahoma leads the way. Still She Rises,[360] tapping the holistic defense model pioneered by The Bronx Defenders, brings hope to the women of North Tulsa, many of whom are people of color. In Tulsa, a grant from the George Kaiser Family Foundation and funding from other generous individuals makes Still She Rises possible.

Still She Rises aims to:

- **Reduce** jail time and increase the number of non-incarceration sentences that women with children serve to minimize the harmful long-term effects of incarceration on women and families.

- **Defend** mothers involved in the criminal justice system against the painful and unnecessary removal of their children and the potential dissolution of their families.

- **Preserve** women's hard-earned jobs, maintain stable housing and public benefits, defend against the forfeiture of property, correct criminal record errors, preserve rights challenging police misconduct, and educate judges and prosecutors about the debilitating consequences of arrest and incarceration.

- **Provide** individualized social support to families, in addition to connecting them to vital services like substance abuse treatment, counseling, and parenting classes.

- **Assist** families in negotiating court fee reductions and creating payment plans for these fees to ensure that they do not become trapped in debt, resulting in the further destabilization of their lives.

- **Serve** as a clearinghouse and backup center for public defenders nationwide seeking to develop better ways to represent women and preserve families.[361]

5. *The Black Wall Street Times*

The Black Wall Street Times' Mission
A Letter from the Editor-in-Chief

March 26, 2017

Dear Friends,

I started *The Black Wall Street Times*, a new media company, with the hope that it will serve as a crucial addition to traditional news outlets by elevating stories directly impacting our community.

Hegemony controls most of the media, which causes the issues that impact marginalized communities to be chronically underreported and presents an imbalanced image of minorities in mass media.

We fight to document and highlight minority reporting and stories that are too often overshadowed by the continuing power of America's hegemonic media.

Our goal is to inspire a digital renaissance of the original Black Wall Street in Tulsa, Oklahoma, by focusing on issues that promote the betterment of our community and elevate minority issues within society at large. Many of the staff, writers, and editors at the Times stand on the shoulders of the giants from the peak of the Black Wall Street era.

Yours truly,

Nehemiah D. Frank
Founder & Editor-in-Chief[362]

The Black Wall Street Times is a wholly-online publication, a media project that lacks the legacy costs and overhead associated with conventional print publications. It is nimble in terms of its ability to cover breaking and time-sensitive news.

6. 100 Resilient Cities

100 Resilient Cities—("100RC") Pioneered by The Rockefeller Foundation helps cities around the world become more resilient in terms of their reactions to the physical, social, and economic challenges that define twenty-first century life. 100RC funds a Chief Resilience Officer in each member city who leads the resilience efforts, offers resources for drafting a resilience strategy, provides access to private sector, public sector, academic, and NGO (non-governmental organization) resilience tools, and grants membership in a global network of peer cities to share best practices and challenges.

On June 5, 2018, Tulsa Mayor G.T. Bynum unveiled Tulsa's first resilience strategy. Resilient Tulsa, a holistic citywide plan developed in partnership with 100RC, is an action-oriented roadmap for an inclusive and equitable Tulsa.

Resilient Tulsa represents a new approach to address the City's most pressing and interconnected challenges. The result of extensive consultation with stakeholders from across the City and developed with financial and technical backing from 100RC, Resilient Tulsa sets forth a framework for a Tulsa rife with opportunity and access for all.

"Tulsa has made great strides in the last few years in acknowledging the disparities that exist in our community, but acknowledgment is not enough," Tulsa Mayor G.T. Bynum said. "The Resilient Tulsa strategy is a plan of action for building a city where every person has an equal shot at a great life. To follow through on the implementation of this plan, I am also establishing the Mayor's Office of Resilience & Equity. Now begins the long and difficult work which is necessary to build a better city for future generations of Tulsans."

With racial equity at its core, Resilient Tulsa addresses critical resilience challenges: economic inequality; disaster preparedness; civic services; and improved health outcomes. The Mayor's Office of Resilience and Equity, led initially by Chief Resilience Officer DeVon Douglass, spearheads implementation of Resilient Tulsa. Douglass lent to the initiative a personal philosophy and work ethic centered on community empowerment:

> The profession you choose should be the place where your deep gladness and the world's deep hunger meet. That is advocacy at its core. When advocating for people in need, I am at my best. I use my experience, education, and expertise to eliminate policies that harm marginalized people in our communities.[363]

Local Resilient Tulsa partners include the Tulsa Police Department, 1921 Tulsa Race Massacre Centennial Commission, Workforce Tulsa, the Zarrow Family Foundations, and other philanthropic outlets. Those partners and others support Resilient Tulsa in achieving its forty-one tangible actions.

"This strategy is a direct result of the community feedback we received from Tulsans, City Leadership, the Resilient Tulsa Steering Committee, Racial Equity Advisory Committee and dozens of community partners," Douglass said. "This roadmap came from the hearts, minds and efforts of Tulsans who sought to make advancements in our community by collaborating together."

The plan includes an actionable set of visions, goals, and measures that address the City's most pressing stresses and seeks to build capacity among residents and City systems alike to better withstand future shocks.

Resilient Tulsa is organized into four overarching visions which, taken together, strive to produce long-term solutions to challenges ranging from extreme weather events to significant racial, economic, and health inequities. Each action also outlines success metrics the City will use to track progress. Visions include:

1. **Create an Inclusive Future That Honors All Tulsans:** To grow as a unified, strong community, Tulsa will reconcile its past and form a future that celebrates cultural heritage and eliminates systemic discrimination.

2. **Equip All Tulsans To Overcome Barriers and Thrive:** By eliminating existing disparities, Tulsa can build a more equitable foundation in which all residents can flourish, regardless of their race, ethnicity, residence, health, income, gender, or criminal history.

3. **Advance Economic Opportunity for All Tulsans:** Changes in labor demand, although disruptive to traditional industry, present a new opportunity for Tulsa to equip all residents with the necessary tools to achieve long-term financial stability and prosperity.

4. **Transform City and Regional Systems to Improve Outcomes for All Tulsans:** Tulsa will model and advocate for local and regional systems that accurately identify and effectively address community needs on a day-to-day basis.

"We congratulate Mayor Bynum, Chief Resilience Officer Douglass, and the City of Tulsa for taking this historic step toward creating a lasting resilient future," said Otis Rolley, Managing Director of North America at 100 Resilient Cities. "Resilient Tulsa is a blueprint for overcoming long-standing racial and ethnic disparities, and for ensuring that the city's prosperity equally benefits all Tulsans. We are excited to continue the next stage of our partnership with the City of Tulsa, and to collaborate around implementation of this aspirational strategy."

Resilient Tulsa builds off a wealth of existing City plans dedicated to further shaping Tulsa into a world-class city. Recent campaigns include the City's largest economic development capital improvements program, Vision Tulsa; the first immigrant community inclusion plan,[364] the New Tulsans Initiative; and the Office of Performance Strategy and Innovation, a City department that aims to deliver better services and drive transparent decision-making. Tulsa's Equality Indicators framework and report served as an influential contribution to Resilient Tulsa, evident in the strategy's focus on racial equity.[365]

Krystal Reyes became Chief Resilience Officer for the City of Tulsa, effective May 6, 2019, succeeding DeVon Douglass. Reyes, who came to Tulsa from New York City, previously worked as the Director of Community Engagement for the Division of Family and Child Health at the New York City Health Department. Prior to that, she served stints as Executive Director of the Hunts Point Alliance for Children, a community-based organization located in the South Bronx, and as Senior Advisor for Children and Family Services in the Office of the Deputy Mayor for Health and Human Services.[366]

7. Mosaic

Mosaic, formed in 2012, is the Tulsa Regional Chamber's diversity business council. Mosaic seeks to create awareness about the competitive business advantage of maintaining a diverse and inclusive climate and aiming for equity throughout workplaces in the Tulsa region.

Mosaic leverages the region's diversity to improve perceptions of the Tulsa community and grow the economy. Ultimately, Mosaic wishes to catapult the Tulsa region into the forefront of diversity, equity, and inclusion through talent recruitment initiatives and business retention and expansion efforts.

Mosaic's five key metrics, or five "pillars," mirror best practices adopted by programs across the country. These pillars provide the foundation for Mosaic's work: CEO commitment; diverse suppliers; people; internal policy; and community outreach.

Mosaic's programs include:

1. **Economic Inclusion Forum:** Annual symposium on creating inclusive workplace cultures;

2. **Diversity Awareness Month:** Annual celebration of Northeast Oklahoma's diverse cultural assets;

3. **New member orientation:** Quarterly introduction to Mosaic's values and programming;

4. **Lunch & Learn:** Informative sessions covering a range of diversity and inclusion-related topics;

5. **Executive Roundtable:** "Safe space" for senior executives to work through corporate diversity strategies;

6. **Quarterly networking events:** Opportunities for Mosaic members to interact after hours;

7. **D&I Peer-to-Peer:** Networking opportunities specifically for diversity and inclusion professionals; and

8. **Crucial Conversations:** Honest discussions about current affairs and their impact on regional inclusivity.[367]

8. Greater Tulsa Area African-American Affairs Commission

In 2017, Tulsa Mayor G.T. Bynum and District 1 Councilor Vanessa Hall-Harper announced plans to create the Greater Tulsa Area African-American Affairs Commission. That body, consisting of twenty-one leaders focused on addressing racial disparities in Tulsa and enhancing opportunities for black Tulsans, held its orientation meeting in December 2017.

The Commission, which meets monthly, seeks to address ten areas of need detailed in *The Covenant with Black America*, a 2006 anthology consisting of essays by a variety of analysts, activists, and academics. Each chapter outlines one key issue and provides a list of resources, suggestions for action, and a checklist for what concerned citizens can do to keep their communities progressing socially, politically, and economically. Topics include: securing health care; improving public education; equal justice under the law; community-centered policing; affordable housing; claiming democracy; strengthening rural roots; providing access to good jobs; environmental justice; and closing the racial divide.[368]

9. Black Wall Street Arts

The brainchild of Ricco Wright, Ed.D., Black Wall Street Arts ("BWSA") emerged in 2018 as a full service arts' organization, housing a theatre company, a visual arts agency, a creative arts agency, an art gallery, and an education initiative.

The Black Wall Street Art Gallery debuted on September 7, 2018, taking advantage of the proximate First Friday Art Crawl, a popular Tulsa arts experience, in the neighboring Tulsa Arts District.

The Art Crawl, established in 2007 as a year-round monthly event, features galleries, studios, museums, and pop-up galleries in various shops in the Tulsa Arts District. Local artists display and sell their works. The monthly event routinely draws thousands.[369]

Some 2,000 persons attended the opening of the Black Wall Street Art Gallery—a large, diverse group of patrons. By design, the Gallery creates platforms for local artists, with a focus on conciliation. Shown works typically juxtapose black and white artists and stimulate thinking about racial history, its present legacy, and opportunities to make reparation—to heal historical wounds.

Other elements of BWSA remain in various stages of implementation.[370]

10. *All Souls Unitarian Church*

Seekers who came to Tulsa intent on seizing the opportunities appurtenant to a booming oil town started All Souls Unitarian Church ("All Souls") as a liberal religious voice for community development. They envisioned a congregation coming together for the worship of God and the service of humankind and built a Church of the Free Spirit. Today, All Souls, the largest Unitarian congregation in the United States, boasts members from all walks of life and from a broad ideological spectrum.

The All Souls Statement of Purpose, 1957, noted:

> Our church is an embodiment and celebration of the world as we hope it will one day become. A climate of profound hospitality, love and acceptance radiates from our campus and our members. Our sanctuary is bursting with people from a diversity of theologies, philosophies, ethnicities, cultures, colors, classes, abilities, generations, sexual orientations and political persuasions, all dwelling together in peace, seeking the truth in love and helping one another. Our compassion is reflected in our actions to care for one another, our neighbors and the environment. Our religious education involves all ages and aims at connecting heads, hearts, and hands.[371]

All Souls launched a capital campaign for a new sanctuary in 2018, with the goal of celebrating its centennial there in 2021, coinciding with the 100th anniversary of the massacre. Congregants see symbolism in the synchrony.

In 2021, a new All Souls designed, funded, led, and attended by black and white Tulsans, together, along with many persons reflecting various other races and ethnicities, will rise in downtown Tulsa on Sixth Street, the street on which the 1921 eruption began. The church will face the historic Greenwood District. A bell perched on the roof of the church overlooking a reconciliation garden will sound annually, once every hour, during the hours over which the massacre took place.[372]

The All Souls Unitarian Church Centennial Vision, 2021, declared:

All Souls Unitarian Church in Tulsa is dedicated to religion but not to a creed. Neither upon itself nor upon its members does it impose a test of doctrinal formulas. It regards love of God and humankind, and the perfecting of our spiritual natures to be the unchanging substance of religion and the essential gospel of Jesus. Consecrating itself to these principles it aims at cultivating reverence for truth, moral character and insight, helpfulness to humanity, and the spirit of communion with the infinite. It welcomes into its worship and fellowship all who are in sympathy with a religion thus simple and free.[373]

This vision is aligned with the teachings and spirit of the Reverend Dr. Martin Luther King, Jr., who proclaimed: "The church must be reminded that it is not the master or the servant of the state, but rather the conscience of the state. It must be the guide and the critic of the state, and never its tool. If the church does not recapture its prophetic zeal, it will become an irrelevant social club without moral or spiritual authority."[374]

11. The Tale of Two Zip Codes: Life Expectancy by the Numbers

Where you live in Tulsa can determine how long you live. Babies born a few miles apart might have lifespans that differ by 10 years or more. How can two babies with seemingly similar beginnings experience such a drastic difference in how long they may live? More importantly, how can the community come together to improve health and demonstrate change is possible?[375]

The Tulsa Health Department and several community partners conducted a retrospective study of life expectancy between a South Tulsa zip code (low poverty; high income) and a North Tulsa zip code (high poverty; low income). Researchers uncovered a 13.8-year disparity between the two zip codes for the 2000 – 2002 period.

In 2006, public health officials, community partners, city leaders, philanthropists, and universities deemed the health disparities between these two zip codes unacceptable and set out to make improvements. Community organizers engaged residents of North Tulsa to glean input and buy-in for change.

Community leaders initiated several health initiatives, including the construction of the Tulsa Health Department's North Regional Health and Wellness Center, the University of Oklahoma Wayman Tisdale Specialty Health Care facility, Morton Comprehensive Health Services clinic, and the stabilization of the Oklahoma State University teaching hospital in downtown Tulsa. These measures contributed to increasing access to health care for the vulnerable North Tulsa population.

The life expectancy gap narrowed from 13.8 during the 2000 - 2002 period to 10 years during the 2011 - 2013 period. This marked improvement in outcomes illustrated the power of collective impact when partners' initiatives and investments align with community need.

Significant disparities still exist, but the challenge has been identified, targeted, and attacked.[376]

12. Vision 2025

On September 9, 2003, Tulsa County voters approved a one-penny, thirteen-year increase in the Tulsa County sales tax for regional economic development and capital improvements. The package, dubbed "Vision 2025: Foresight 4 Greater Tulsa," represented the culmination of herculean efforts to grow economic and community infrastructure for future generations.

Select Vision 2025 projects affecting the Greenwood District include:

1. **OSU-Tulsa:** Vision 2025 funds constructed the community's first Advanced Technology Research Center, a 123,000-square-foot facility that focuses on the development of next-generation composites and materials in demand for cutting-edge applications within the aerospace, biotechnology, telecommunications, and manufacturing industries.

2. **Langston-Tulsa:** Vision 2025 funds constructed a new classroom building that includes space for administration, academic, and community outreach programs, fueling an expected doubling of enrollment and graduates.

3. **Morton Comprehensive Health Services:** Vision 2025 funds constructed a new health center and training facility that represents a $14 million infrastructure investment in North Tulsa. The new structure sits in Lansing Business Park, an approximately 100-acre plot just north and east of the heart of the Greenwood District, catering to small-to-medium-sized sites for office, warehouse, distribution, research and development, light assembly, manufacturing, and service uses. Planners conceived Lansing Business Park, proximate to downtown, as a tool with which to broaden the job base in inner-city Tulsa.[377] In addition to Morton Comprehensive Health Services, Lansing Business Park houses Emergency Medical Services Authority and Northeast Oklahoma Food Bank.

4. **Midland Valley Downtown Trail Extension:** Vision 2025 funds constructed a portion of a multi-use trail that provided the previously missing stretch linking the Midland Valley Trail at 15th Street to the 4th Street/Archer bike route. This trail serves as part of a revitalization strategy to enhance and improve the connections between Downtown Tulsa and adjacent neighborhoods. The trail extends to suburban communities as well.

5. **Oklahoma Jazz Hall of Fame:** Tulsa County Commissioners approved on January 12, 2004, the purchase of the Tulsa Union Depot, the historic Tulsa train station, for use by the Oklahoma Jazz Hall of Fame to be developed with Vision 2025 funds.[378]

13. A Street Fit For A King

Effective October 15, 2012, and pursuant to Tulsa City Council approval in June, the City of Tulsa renamed a portion of North Cincinnati Avenue between East Archer Street and East 65th Place North. The span became Martin Luther King, Jr., Boulevard. The Boulevard cuts through the heart of Tulsa's traditional African American community.

"Changing the name to Martin Luther King Jr. Blvd. is a positive step for Tulsa," said then District 1 City Councilor Jack Henderson. "As I've traveled across the country, I've noticed that most cities have a Martin Luther King Jr. street. I believe it is time for Tulsa to honor Martin Luther King Jr.'s legacy. I also hope re-naming the street will spark economic development opportunities in the area. I am excited about the completion date nearing, as this honor is long overdue."[379]

14. Emerson Montessori School

Tulsa Public Schools converted Emerson Elementary School, a neighborhood school located at 910 North Martin Luther King, Jr, Boulevard, to Oklahoma's only public Montessori school beginning in the 2018-2019 school year.

The Montessori method builds student independence by incorporating individualized instruction plans and student-led projects that encourage children to learn at their own pace. It also emphasizes social development by encouraging students to help one another learn and treat each other with compassion, empathy, and tolerance.

Teachers serve as facilitators and guides in an open learning environment. The Emerson campus features a food forest and community garden, among other innovative concepts.

A portion of the 2015 Tulsa Public Schools bond issue covered the expansion and redevelopment of Emerson.

Tulsa Superintendent Deborah Gist emphasized at a 2017 school board meeting that Montessori is an innovative approach not used by any other public school in Oklahoma. She also pointed out that Montessori is a deeply researched, time-tested approach to education that relies heavily on data to track educational outcomes.[380]

15. The Greenwood Art Project: 2018 Bloomberg Philanthropies Public Art Challenge Winner

At a January 17, 2019, press conference at the Greenwood Cultural Center, former New York City Mayor Michael Bloomberg, Tulsa Mayor G.T. Bynum, nationally-renowned artist and Macarthur Fellow Rick Lowe, members of the 1921 Tulsa Race Massacre Centennial Commission, and a host of local dignitaries and community members celebrated the announcement of a $1 million grant to the City of Tulsa, one of five cities to win the Bloomberg Public Art Challenge, to fund a grand public art project in Tulsa's Historic Greenwood District.

The Greenwood Art Project will commemorate the massacre and celebrate the resilience of the Tulsa's Historic Greenwood District—Black Wall Street. The Centennial Commission plays a lead role in project administration and implementation.

Mayor Bloomberg noted that "public art . . . has the unique ability to reach people and change the way they think about the world around us." He continued, "Public art adds a new energy to city life, it connects people and it provokes conversation and debate, and it can inspire action."

Rick Lowe later added, "What we want to create is a kind of energy around [the riot] centennial where everybody is thinking outside the box." Lowe spoke of involving a wide array of people in the project, including artists, developers, and community leaders.

Lowe considers his work "social sculpture," which aims to "take the whole environment of a neighborhood and . . . try to use creativity at its best in every aspect of that neighborhood, whether it's through real estate development, through architecture, through history, [or] social networks."[381]

16. Rev. Dr. Martin Luther King, Jr. Parade

The nation first observed the Rev. Dr. Martin Luther King, Jr., holiday on January 20, 1986. The federal holiday honoring the civil rights icon happens annually on the third Monday of January.

Tulsa Public Schools, to the consternation of many, remained open on January 20, 1986, the largest public-school system in the country to deny official recognition to the holiday. Protests at City Hall and the Education Service Center signaled swelling community outrage at the slight.

More than 9,000 students skipped classes that day to attend the smallish (about 400 participants) King Parade. More than 25% of the students in the school district, and almost 100% of students in predominately-black North Tulsa schools, missed the whole day or attended school just long enough to stage walkouts. Musician and community activist Leon Rollerson noted: "There were a lot of people who didn't want to accept that Martin Luther King, Jr. was being recognized. But there were a lot of people, black and white, who were determined to do it anyway."[382]

Today, Tulsa's hosts one of the largest King Parades in the country. Tulsa Public Schools participates in a variety of King-themed events and activities. Whatever hesitation may have existed initially seems to have fully abated.

Chapter Five

A New Day in Tulsa

You may have a fresh start any moment you choose, for this thing we call 'failure' is not the falling down, but the staying down.

Mary Pickford

A Chief's Apology

On September 21, 2013, Tulsa Police Chief Chuck Jordan apologized[383] on behalf of the Tulsa Police Department for law enforcement's dereliction of duty during the events of May 31 and June 1, 1921.[384] His remarks came at the outset of "Literacy, Legacy and Movement Day," an event meant to promote cultural awareness, literacy, health, and entrepreneurship. Starting at the park named after Dr. John Hope Franklin, participants walked to various significant spots in the Greenwood District.

Chief Jordan's remarks bear full recitation:

> Good morning ladies and gentlemen. I would like to start by reading you the Tulsa Police Department Oath of Office. Every police officer takes this oath before going into the police service.

> Having been duly appointed a police officer of the City of Tulsa and peace officer of the State of Oklahoma, I do solemnly swear that I will defend, enforce, and obey the Constitution and laws of the United States, the State of Oklahoma, and the Charter and Ordinances of the City of Tulsa.

> That I will obey the lawful orders of my superior officers and the regulations of the Tulsa Police Department.

> That I will protect the rights, lives, and property of all citizens and uphold the honor of the police profession with my life if need be.

> This I solemnly swear.

> On May 31st and June 1st of 1921 the officers of the Tulsa

Police Department did not live up to the oath that they took.

I cannot apologize for the actions, inaction and dereliction that those individual officers and their Chief exhibited during that dark time, but as your Chief today, I can apologize for our police department. I am sorry and distressed that the Tulsa Police Department did not protect its citizens during those tragic days in 1921.

I have heard things said like 'well that was a different time.' That excuse does not hold water with me. I have been a Tulsa Police Officer since 1969 and I have witnessed scores of 'different times.' Not once did I ever consider that those changing times somehow relieved me of my obligation to uphold my oath of office and to protect my fellow Tulsans.

I will also tell you that this is not the same Tulsa Police Department as 1921. I hope that the dedication and commitment that your officers demonstrated in the wake of the Good Friday killings[385] shows our community that hate-motivated crimes or any other evil visited on our citizens will not be tolerated and the perpetrators will be brought to justice.

The men and women that work for you today are committed to upholding every sentence of their oath of office. That includes putting their lives on the line to protect the citizens they serve if need be.

While we should never forget the crimes and injustices that were committed in 1921, you can rest assured that your police department today will never allow such an atrocity to occur. We will be in the front lines to protect your lives, your families and your property.

We took an oath to do so. And your police department today will honor that oath.[386]

Authorities removed Tulsa's massacre-era police chief partly because of his handling of the event. Chief John Gustafson[387] came under fire for ineptitude in office. A Tulsa grand jury deemed him culpable for the massacre, essentially on a dereliction of duty theory, forcing him from office. Gustafson faced trial for misfeasance and malfeasance: for failing to take proper precautions to protect life and property during the massacre, and for conspiring to free automobile thieves and collect rewards.[388] Though convicted by a jury in July of 1921,[389] Chief Gustafson never did time in prison.[390] He worked as a private detective. Other than Chief Gustafson, no other white official was convicted on massacre-related charges of any magnitude whatsoever.[391]

Tulsa City Councilor Jack Henderson characterized Chief Jordan's remarks as a "big statement." "I know this chief and I know that he means it," Henderson said, further noting that "history is there" and that addressing it is part of moving forward. Tulsa State Representative Kevin Matthews, who later became a State Senator and Chair of the 1921 Tulsa Race Massacre Centennial Commission, described the Chief's statement as a "great symbolic gesture to start the healing process."[392]

The apology caused a stir nationally. A San Francisco paper noted: "There are times when an apology actually has meaning and impact. That was the case on Saturday, Sept. [21], 2013, in Tulsa, Oklahoma, when Chief Chuck Jordan of the Tulsa Police Department apologized to the Black people of the city for the 1921 attack on 'Black Wall Street.'"[393]

Chief Jordan's public display of contrition captured the attention of the *Tulsa World*, too:

Chief Jordan's apology is a symbolic and meaningful gesture

No one would think less of Tulsa Police Chief Chuck Jordan if he'd decided against apologizing for his department's failure 92 years ago to protect citizens during the 1921 Race Riot. But a lot of people will think more of him because he did.

Jordan was not born when the deadly riot claimed dozens of lives and destroyed the Greenwood commercial district and surrounding neighborhood. Several officers reportedly joined in the mayhem, setting fire to buildings and failing to quell the violence. John Gustafson, police chief at the time, later was removed from office partly because of his handling of the riot.

Jordan said that he was 'distressed' that the department had not stepped in and that 'officers of the TPD did not live up to the oath that they took.'

'I have heard things said like "well, that was a different time." That excuse does not hold water with me. I have been a Tulsa police officer since 1969, and I have witnessed scores of 'different times.' Not once did I ever consider that those changing times somehow relieved me of my obligation to uphold my oath of office and to protect my fellow Tulsans.'

Jordan delivered his remarks Saturday at an appropriate forum, the 'Literacy, Legacy and Movement Day,' an event meant to promote cultural awareness, literacy, health and entrepreneurship. The event started at the park named for the late John Hope Franklin, a historian, author and Presidential Medal of Freedom recipient.

Jordan's gesture doesn't change the past, but it nevertheless is meaningful and sets the tone for the future. It reinforces his determination that his department's relationship with the African-American community be open and honest. In apologizing, Jordan did what none of his predecessors had done. His action sends an important message: This is not the same police department as those in the past. This is a 'new day.'[394]

On May 31, 2016, the 95th anniversary of the massacre, Chief Jordan donated a framed image of Tulsa's first African American police officer, Barney S. Cleaver, to the Greenwood Cultural Center.

Cleaver, born in Newbern, Virginia, in 1865, attended public school there through age fifteen. He then moved to Charleston, West Virginia, working on a steamer and later in the coal mines. As an Oklahoma & Gulf Coal Company employee, he served as an immigrant agent, bringing more than four thousand employees from West Virginia to Oklahoma.

While living in Coalgate, Oklahoma, Cleaver was appointed Special Deputy United States Marshal under Captain Grady. He moved to Tulsa, *circa* 1907, signing on as a Tulsa Police Department patrolman. He later became Tulsa County Deputy Sheriff under Sheriff William ("Bill") McCullough.

Deputy Sheriff Cleaver and his wife, Vernon Wren, lived at 508 North Greenwood in 1914. He owned an interest in the building across the street from the Cleaver home, the Cleaver-Cherry building.[395]

Those on hand for the unveiling of the Cleaver portrait included Mayor Dewey Bartlett, City Councilor Jack Henderson, members of the Tulsa Police Department Black Officers Coalition, and members of the Greenwood Cultural Center board of directors.

The Protocol of Policing

The Tulsa Police Department sees itself differently than it did in 1921—indeed, differently than it did just a decade ago. In a fall 2018 editorial, the *Tulsa World* lauded what is widely perceived to be a new era in policing.

Tulsa Police On Right Track With Training Changes

Tulsa Police Department training isn't what it used to be, and that's a good thing.

All professions—including law enforcement—evolve as changes occur in technology, culture and expectations. Transformations in training and professional development are required to stay relevant.

As reported by *Tulsa World* reporter Corey Jones, TPD is ahead of the curve by revamping its training philosophy.

The force has moved from a warrior-like perspective to a model incorporating community involvement and social skills.

That doesn't mean officers won't be proficient with a gun or able to chase down criminals. Those traditional defense standards of survival remain and are critical to police work.

What has changed is the military mindset and approach to the job.

Law enforcement training has been criticized nationally and locally for lacking cultural awareness and de-escalation techniques. The public is demanding more nonlethal options and relationship building from officers.

In response, three years ago, TPD dropped its boot camp-like new recruit academy to reflect more realistic scenarios and education.

This shift includes more role-playing exercises where an officer is dealing with difficult people, those who may be yelling and cursing. Previously, every scene involved a criminal trying to kill the officer.

Officers attend classes to understand Muslim and LGBTQ culture and the 1921 Tulsa race massacre. They are helped in their understanding of other cultures through a new competency program to include implicit bias.

Being an active part of the community—whether through mentoring or spur-of-the-moment pickup basketball games—goes hand-in-hand with this model.

This update adds more tools for officers to use in tense situations and builds trust within neighborhoods.

We commend TPD for its work in improving training. It is a more effective and thorough way to keep our community safe.[396]

In addition, the Tulsa Police Department continues its community outreach and engagement efforts through initiatives like the Mayor's Police and Community Coalition ("MPACC") and the Community and Police Leadership Collaborative ("CAPLC").

MPACC, a city of Tulsa-based, bi-monthly forum, brings together city and police leadership with representatives of a wide range of community constituencies. The aim is, first and foremost, to build the personal relationships on which trust turns. Secondarily, MPACC provides an ongoing opportunity for information-sharing and reciprocal education, police-to-community, and community-to-police.

CAPLC, a joint venture between the Tulsa Police Department and Leadership Tulsa, brings together about a dozen police officers and an equal number of community members for a shared leadership experience over about a six-month period. Each police officer is paired with a community member for the duration of the program. In those dyads, each person guides the other through a personal experience illustrative of his/her world. For example, the police office might take his/her community member partner on a ride-along. The community member might take his/her police officer partner to an area of the community that is culturally distinct (*e.g.*, a mosque; a LatinX market; a noteworthy venue like the Greenwood Cultural Center). Other highlights include a day-long retreat, regular class sessions, and a group project.

Creation of the Tulsa Police Activities League ("TPAL") represented another milestone in community/police relations. TPAL fosters positive community/police relations and builds trust through the intentional engagement of, primarily, children and youth, and works collaboratively with SKYWAY Leadership Institute ("SKYWAY") to provide structure to the newly repurposed Tulsa Public Schools ("TPS") HelmZar Challenge Course.

TPS closed HelmZar Challenge Course in 2016. SKYWAY began operating in October 2018, taking inventory, assessing the facility and course elements, and making substantial repairs and replacements.

SKYWAY strives to break down barriers and create authentic relationships within the schools and community, and most especially between youth (particularly, youth of color) and the Tulsa Police Department. The program emphasizes trust and hope, both of which are subject to measurement.

SKYWAY initially trained more than twenty facilitators and developed programming and supplementary training for them, including everything from modules on trauma-informed responses to the science of hope. A partnership with the University of Oklahoma-Tulsa aids in the research and analysis of data derived from these efforts.

SKYWAY hosted its first group on January 21, 2019, and has since served countless Oklahoma students, first responders, community groups, and at-risk youth (including children from the Tulsa Boys Home, Youth Services of Tulsa, and first offenders programs), and a host of other community and corporate groups.

In the summer of 2019, the Oklahoma Office of Juvenile Affairs noted its interest in working with SKYWAY to assess, address, and positively impact the disproportionate contact of minority youth ("DMC") with police at key contact points. SKYWAY intends to intervene at the primary point of contact—schools—to reduce the DMC. Using its Effective Police Interaction with Youth ("EPIY") training and the HelmZar Challenge Course, SKYWAY will track changes both in its youth participants and its TPAL police officer cohort.[397]

Addressing Race in Law Enforcement and Criminal Justice

Events in recent criminal justice matters suggest hope for Tulsa's historically deep racial fissures. Both matters illustrate that race need not always overwhelm interpersonal dynamics and dictate outcomes.

On Good Friday, April 6, 2012, a string of shootings in North Tulsa left three African Americans dead and two injured. Law enforcement quickly apprehended the suspects.

Alvin Lee Watts and Jacob Carl England, both listed as white in court documents, accepted plea agreements on December 16, 2012. They pleaded guilty to three counts of first-degree murder, two counts of shooting with intent to kill, and five counts of malicious intimidation or harassment on account of race, color, ancestry or national origin (*i.e.*, hate crimes under Oklahoma law). The plea agreements called for life-without-parole sentences. Prosecutors dropped requests for death sentences for both defendants. Had they gone to trial, both defendants would have faced the death penalty.[398]

The run-up to the capture of these perpetrators proved noteworthy. Law enforcement and leaders in the African American community came together in a remarkable display of cooperation, presenting a unified front that identified and captured the culprits. That same spirit of cooperation, collaboration, and reciprocal trust would be called upon once again just a few years later.[399]

On April 27, 2016, a Tulsa County jury deliberated less than three hours, finding Robert Bates criminally negligent for shooting and killing an unarmed suspect while on duty as a Tulsa County Sheriff's Office reserve deputy in 2015. Jurors recommended the maximum sentence of four years in prison after finding Bates guilty of second-degree manslaughter for mistaking his revolver for his Taser and shooting Eric Harris.

That the jury, with not one African American panelist, convicted a well-heeled white businessman for the shooting death of an African American man with a checkered past surprised many.[400]

On the heels of the Bates shooting and conviction, another high-profile shooting involving a black victim and a white law enforcement officer inflamed community tensions. Tulsa Police Officer Betty Shelby mortally wounded Terence Crutcher as he approached a still-running vehicle in the middle of a North Tulsa street. The following *Tulsa World* timeline captured the critical elements of the Friday, September 16, 2016, encounter:

- **7:34 p.m.:** Dispatchers send Officer Betty Shelby and another officer to a domestic violence-related call.

- **7:36 p.m.:** Police receive a call that a man had left his vehicle running in the middle of the road with doors open near 36th Street North and Lewis Avenue. That caller indicated that a man ran from the vehicle saying, 'It's going to blow.'

- **7:41 p.m.:** On her way to a domestic-related call, Officer Shelby came upon the scene with the abandoned vehicle that had not yet been dispatched to an officer. She related to a dispatcher that the man at the scene was uncooperative. Another officer joined Officer Shelby at the scene.

- **7:43 p.m.:** Helicopter footage began, showing Terence Crutcher slowly walking with arms up toward his vehicle while being followed at a close distance by two uniformed officers. One of the men in the helicopter noted that it appeared a Taser was about to be deployed, and the other commented that Crutcher 'looks like a bad dude, maybe on something.' When Crutcher reached the closed driver's door of his vehicle, Taser sights can be seen on his back. A gunshot rang out, at which point the two officers shuffle backward and two other officers cluster around. Crutcher's right arm dropped to his side. The angle of the video shifted, making it difficult to see the position of Crutcher's limbs, but it appeared Crutcher's left arm also came down, and about twelve seconds after the shot his body fell to the ground next to the driver's side door.

- **7:44 p.m.:** A female officer's voice can be heard crying out, 'Shots fired!' A dispatcher exclaimed: 'We need EMSA here.'

- **7:46 p.m.:** A uniformed officer approached Crutcher, who was unresponsive.

- **7:47 p.m.:** Multiple officers appeared to more thoroughly examine the body.[401]

The following Monday, September 19, 2016, Tulsa Police Chief Chuck Jordan joined Tulsa Mayor Dewey Bartlett, Tulsa County District Attorney Steve Kunzweiler, and United States Attorney for the Northern District of Oklahoma Danny Williams for a press conference. All expressed a desire for transparency, expediency, and, ultimately, justice, amidst community clamor for institutional changes in law enforcement aimed at eliminating perceived race-based disparities, particularly disparities in the use of lethal force.[402]

On September 22, 2016, Tulsa County District Attorney Stephen Kunzweiler announced that Officer Betty Shelby had been charged with first-degree manslaughter for the death of forty-year-old Terence Crutcher, and a warrant had been issued for her arrest. The incident, captured on widely-broadcast police videos, became a flashpoint in the national debate over racial bias in policing and among law enforcement agencies.[403]

The swift and definitive law enforcement response to the Crutcher tragedy may have marginally strengthened the bonds of trust between the community—particularly black residents—and Tulsa's leadership, including the leadership of the Tulsa Police Department. That said, the shooting itself reinforced the widely-held perception in the African American community that law enforcement agents disproportionately and unfairly target African American males, particularly in use-of-force situations.

Some African American clergy heaped praise upon City officials for their initial handling of the Crutcher shooting while also calling out race-based disparities in policing:

A joint statement issued by key north Tulsa pastors on Friday praised city leaders' handling of the fatal shooting of a black man by a white police officer and said the culture in law enforcement fosters violence against blacks.

Surrounded by some two dozen black ministers, the Rev. M.C. Potter, pastor of Antioch Baptist Church, the senior clergyman in the group, read the statement during a morning press conference at the historic First Baptist Church North Tulsa.

'We are hopeful that justice will prevail, particularly in light of the way the city leaders have acted expeditiously and in an attempt for transparency,' Potter said.

'We believe their actions have helped us to minimize the negative impact that an already tragic event has caused.'

The statement continues: 'We are deeply concerned about the culture of policing the community of color.'

'We are convinced that the current culture of policing fosters violence against black people, and black males in particular.'

Police Chief Chuck Jordan, who has been praised by President Barack Obama and the local black community for his handling of the case, declined to comment on the pastors' statement.[404]

Tulsa's daily newspaper, the *Tulsa World*, echoed widely expressed sentiments about the city's remarkable composure in the wake of the Crutcher shooting. *Tulsa World Magazine* even named six key African American clergy—the Revs. Rodney Goss, Ray Owens, Anthony Scott, M.C. Potter, Warren Blakney, and Weldon Tisdale—as joint "Tulsans of the Year" for their roles in articulating community concerns and tamping down potential violent outbursts from frustrated and, in some cases, outraged, black Tulsans.

Ashley Parrish, *Tulsa World Magazine* Editor, noted:

> When we sat down to name the Tulsans of the Year, we knew it wouldn't be easy. Whatever else you say about 2016, it's been a memorable year. A mayor's race. Business mergers and nonmergers. Development in all areas of town and the suburbs. Then there was the gut punch of Terence Crutcher. No matter anyone's opinion about the case and the subsequent charges against a police officer, the community's response said a lot about Tulsa. About its resilience. Its faith. And its leadership. We decided one Tulsan of the Year just wasn't enough. One face on the cover couldn't do justice to 2016. So we put six faces on the cover. The six north Tulsa pastors who many credit with providing comfort and leadership when the city needed it most.[405]

Not all Tulsans praised the Tulsa Police Department for its handling of the fatal shooting of Terrence Crutcher, though few, if any, advocated the kind of contentious protests sometimes seen in such situations. Marq Lewis, leader of the community advocacy group "We The People Oklahoma," called for more accountability and transparency.[406]

On May 17, 2017, the jury in the Crutcher shooting reached its verdict after nine hours of deliberation, acquitting Officer Betty Shelby of a first-degree manslaughter charge in the case. The decision sparked small-scale protests, all peaceful.[407]

Tulsa Mayor G.T. Bynum and Police Chief Chuck Jordan held a press conference the day after the verdict. The Mayor echoed what many people of color see as the City's greatest challenge: racial disparities. He also addressed persistent concerns about violence in the wake of the verdict: "I would remind Tulsans that our history shows us African Americans in Tulsa have not been the instigators of lawlessness and violence. They have been the victims of them."

The Mayor stressed that the City has begun efforts to improve community/police dynamics, and that those efforts would not be derailed by the verdict.

"It does not change our work to institute community policing measures that empower citizens to work side by side with police officers in making our community safer," Mayor Bynum said. "And no one has been calling for the resources to implement community policing more actively over a longer period of time than the men and women of our Tulsa Police Department."

The Mayor also noted the City's efforts to improve the relationship between the community and law enforcement by enhancing community policing efforts, facilitated by a large-scale addition of police officers and the deployment of officer body cameras by the end of 2017.[408]

Several months prior, on December 15, 2016, Bynum announced the creation of a twenty-six-member Tulsa Commission on Community Policing, charged with recommending policing strategies.[409] The Mayor gave the group ninety days to deliberate, with recommendations due by March 15, 2017, the Mayor's 100th day in office.

Tulsa voters funded the community policing approach in a Vision Tulsa tax package earlier in 2016, providing for the permanent funding of 160 additional Tulsa police officers. The Tulsa Commission on Community Policing examined best practices and nationwide strategies as part of its due diligence in the establishment of community-wide consensus on how the additional officers might be put to their highest and best use. Its meetings were open to the public.

Members of the Tulsa Commission on Community Policing includ the Mayor, Tulsa City Councilors, Tulsa Police Department leadership, and diverse members of the Tulsa community.[410]

The Commission's recommendations[411] included a broad range of items that track the pillars of the President's Task Force on 21st Century Policing prduced during the administration of President Barack Obama.[412]

The Equality Indicators Report, a fact-finding project of the

Resilient Tulsa initiative previously discussed, revealed troubling race-based disparities at virtually all stages of engagement with law enforcement. The Tulsa City Council held hearings on the matter.[413]

Mayor Bynum also proposed the creation of an Office of the Independent Monitor ("OIM") based on a similar concept in Denver, Colorado. The OIM would help oversee Tulsa's community policing initiative and review and make recommendations about use-of-force incidents, which disproportionately involve African Americans.

Reputable studies revealed low levels of trust in the African American community for law enforcement. As envisioned, the OIM, by virtue of its independence, would help build bonds of trust, particularly between the police and the African American community.[414]

In memory of her twin brother, Tiffany Crutcher celebrated their birthday on August 16, 2017, with the launch of the Terence Crutcher Foundation, dedicated to creating and sustaining programs that prevent, identify and address issues of inequity toward minority communities. The group defined its ambitious purpose thusly:

> The mission of the Terence Crutcher Foundation is to engage the community, law enforcement, and policymakers in creating and sustaining an approach to prevent, identify and address issues of inequity pertaining to minority communities in Tulsa, Oklahoma, and around the country. The Terence Crutcher Foundation is committed to empowering, developing programs, and raising awareness regarding issues that impact at-risk, disenfranchised people of color with an emphasis on African-American males. It is our desire to change the narrative that perceive black men as **BAD DUDES** and pipeline them into a 'community of achievers' through personal growth, education, and attainable resources.[415]

The Crutcher family, with deep roots in Tulsa, pledged to channel lingering grief over their loved one's death into efforts aimed at improving the lives of young black men.

The vision of the Terence Crutcher Foundation—Belief, Attitude and Determination—derives from the acronym BAD, a take on the provocative declaration, "Looks like a bad dude," made by a helicopter-based Tulsa police officer just moments before the Terence Crutcher slaying.

Terence Crutcher Foundation initiatives focus on education and anti-violence programs. One such effort seeks to "inspire at-risk, disenfranchised African American males to tap into their God-given potential through educational sessions including: personal growth and development, financial literacy, labor market etiquette, and understanding the political process, thus empowering them to become model citizens and affording them the opportunity to live their absolute best life."[416]

Among other initiatives, the Terence Crutcher Foundation offers educational scholarships to high school seniors in Tulsa who face adversity and barriers to accessing higher education.[417]

On June 13, 2018, Terence Crutcher's father, Reverend Joey Crutcher, appeared before the Tulsa City Council to urge the implementation of policing reforms recommended by the Crutcher family and members of the community,[418] imploring: "Please be advised that tragedies like this will continue to happen if you don't make some major changes."[419] The proposed reforms included updating use-of-force policies and conducting external, independent investigations of in-custody deaths and police use of force resulting in death of injury.[420]

Disturbing comments left on a website chronicling Reverend Crutcher's plea may be indicative of the community's remaining work around issues of race:

- "Whatever. They should have taught YOU how to raise your kid. Now we gotta teach you how to keep your mouth shut."

- "Yep always cops fault your POS thug son was high on drugs."

- "[B]eing high is not necessarily a death sentence, if it had been a blonde haired blue eyed female High on drugs Betty Shelby wouldn't have shot her, there's not too many people that are willing to say Betty Shelby would've took the same actions."

- "His son could have prevented his OWN death."[421]

After her acquittal on first-degree manslaughter charges, Betty Shelby returned to duty at the Tulsa Police Department. A few months thereafter, she left to join the Rogers County Sheriff's Office as a deputy.

In August of 2018, Rogers County Sheriff's Deputy Betty Shelby offered a class titled "Surviving the Aftermath of a Critical Incident" at the Tulsa County Sheriff's Office. The free, four-hour class, accredited by the Council on Law Enforcement Education and Training ("CLEET"), counted toward two hours of mental-health training. Typical attendees for such courses include local, state and federal officers, as well as district attorneys and other prosecutors.

According to a course synopsis on a state government website, the class aimed to inform participants about "many of the legal, financial, physical, and emotional challenges" that may arise after an officer shoots someone:

Surviving the Aftermath of a Critical Incident

Description: This course will describe some of the challenges in dealing with the aftermath of a critical incident such as an officer involved shooting. Participants will be exposed to many of the legal, financial, physical, and emotional challenges which may result from a critical incident in an effort to prepare LEO's for the aftermath.

Instructor: Deputy Betty Shelby of the Rogers County Sheriff's Office.[422]

That session drew sharp criticism on social media and from Marq Lewis, leader of We the People Oklahoma. Lewis and others questioned the decision by the Tulsa County Sheriff's Office to allow Rogers County Deputy Sheriff Shelby to instruct the class, citing statements from jurors in her first-degree manslaughter trial that challenged her fitness for duty and judgment. Lewis urged the Sheriff's Office to replace the course with de-escalation training.

Tulsa County Sheriff Vic Regalado defended the class, noting that Shelby routinely taught such classes, no one involved in the class was paid, and the Tulsa County Sheriff's Office often hosted CLEET-certified courses because the agency had a large training space.[423]

Another high-profile case captured the community's attention in 2016 and 2017. A jury convicted former Tulsa Police Officer Shannon Kepler, 57, of first-degree manslaughter on October 18, 2017. The same jury recommended that he serve 15 years in prison and pay a $10,000 fine.

The conviction came in Kepler's almost-unprecedented fourth trial on a first-degree murder charge in the death of 19-year-old Jeremey Lake. Kepler, a white, off-duty office who claims Muscogee (Creek) heritage, shot Lake, a biracial teen who identified as black.

Kepler's previous first-degree murder trials, in November 2016, February 2017 and July 2017, ended in mistrials when the juries could not reach verdicts. As was the case in the July 2017 trial, Tulsa County District Judge Sharon Holmes, an African American, allowed jurors to consider first-degree manslaughter as an alternative to first-degree murder.

Lake began a romantic relationship with Kepler's daughter, Lisa, shortly before Kepler fatally shot Lake on August 5, 2014. Kepler learned of the relationship through Lisa's Facebook profile. Lisa met Lake at a homeless shelter near Lake's home around July 28, 2014.

Kepler told the jury he went to the residence where Lake lived with his aunt to give his daughter information about Lake that he obtained using Tulsa Police Department investigative tools. He professed concern for his daughter's safety.

Kepler admitted that using his work-related apparatus to investigate Lake violated Tulsa Police Department policy. He nonetheless asserted that he had a right to self-defense when he interacted with Lake around 9:15 p.m. on the day of the fatal shooting because Lake pointed a gun at him. Only Kepler claimed to have seen a gun anywhere near Lake.

Kepler testified that he went from his job at the Tulsa Police

Academy to his east Tulsa home. He remained there for a couple of hours, and then drove the family's black Chevrolet Suburban, which had his old service revolver in it, to Lake's house.

Homicide Detective Mark Kennedy testified that investigators recovered a copy of a police report from a contact Lake had with police when he was a minor, which had Lake's Maybelle Avenue address and his presumed race—which District Attorney Steve Kunzweiler noted was black—written on the back.[424]

The Matter of Mass Graves

On October 2, 2018, Tulsa Mayor G.T. Bynum publicly announced his intention to investigate the prospect of mass graves long rumored to hold the bodies of, primarily, black riot victims.[425] Accounts of mass graves include that of eyewitnesses like Tulsan Clyde Eddy, who, as a boy at the time of the massacre, saw white laborers at Oaklawn Cemetery digging what he described as a trench and, nearby, several wooden crates housing black bodies.[426] In addition, the reportage of Walter White, the NAACP executive and investigative journalist who visited Tulsa in the immediate wake of the massacre, suggested mass burial sites:

> O.T. Johnson, commandant of the Tulsa Citadel of the Salvation Army, stated that on Wednesday and Thursday the Salvation Army fed thirty-seven Negroes employed as grave diggers and twenty on Friday and Saturday. During the first two days these men dug 120 graves in each of which a dead Negro was buried. No coffins were used. The bodies were dumped into the holes and covered over with dirt.[427]

Mayor Bynum cast the search as a homicide investigation: "If you get murdered in Tulsa, we have a basic contract with you that we will do everything we can to find out what happened to you and render justice for your family. That's why we are treating this as a homicide investigation for Tulsans who we believe were murdered in 1921."[428]

The official count of massacre deaths remains at 37, though virtually no one who has studied the matter believes that figure to be accurate. Indeed, the Oklahoma Commission to Study the Tulsa

Race Riot of 1921, in its 2001 final report, left open the possibility that mass graves may exist in Tulsa, mostly likely at or near Newblock Park, 1710 Charles Page Boulevard; Rolling Oaks Memorial Gardens (formerly, Booker T. Washington Cemetery), at 4300 East 91st Street; and Oaklawn Cemetery, at the corner of 11th Street and Peoria Avenue.[429]

Then-City Councilor Bynum and former Tulsa City Councilor Jack Henderson met with former state archaeologist Bob Brooks in 2012 to discuss the matter. Brooks worked with the Riot Commission more than a decade earlier to explore, through excavation and other means, the prospect of mass grave sites. Mayor Bynum reached out to Brooks after assuming the top spot in City government.

At the outset, Mayor Bynum explained a three-phase process:

> What we are looking at doing is really three phases. First, identifying if there are mass graves at all. And if there are, identifying what kind of mass grave it is. Is it a pauper's grave, or is it a true mass grave from the massacre? And third, if it is a mass grave from the massacre, then we want to do forensic examination on the bodies that are there to hopefully identify them and their causes of death. I think all of that will help inform a greater understanding around what happened in 1921.[430]

Mayor Bynum's public announcement of this investigatory process came in a Facebook post:

> In 2012, I read a news story about the potential of mass graves from the 1921 Tulsa Race Massacre. As a city councilor, I felt a responsibility to look into it and worked with my City Council colleague Jack Henderson to interview a number of people who had worked on the issue over the years.
>
> There are three main potential sites in question. The first is Newblock Park. Crews doing testing on the ground there encountered difficulty because of piping and underground infrastructure throughout the park. The second is Booker T. Washington Cemetery, where previ-

ously marked graves were found in a disturbed state by researchers in the late 1990s. The third is Oaklawn Cemetery. On the western boundary of the cemetery, there is a grassy field with no marked graves. Yet an abnormality was detected underground in that area that would be consistent with a mass grave. Researchers cautioned that it could be a so-called 'pauper's grave' (in which Tulsans too poor to afford the cost of burial might have been buried in the early 20th Century) or it might be from 1921. An older gentleman recounted for the Race Riot Commission that he saw, as a young boy, bodies being dumped there during the Massacre.

Councilor Henderson and I turned our findings over to the City Administration, but nothing ever came of it. I promised myself that if I ever became mayor and had the authority to direct further examination I would.

Now I am. In recent months my staff and I have discussed a path forward with archaeological experts. We are meeting with Councilor Vanessa Hall-Harper and others in the weeks ahead to solidify the plan and timelines.

I did not intend to make this public until we had that plan in place. But at a North Tulsa community meeting today, I was asked by a pastor if I would be willing to initiate this investigation of the alleged unmarked graves. I felt the need to be up front with him about the work we have done and are doing.

Our path forward will follow three main lines:

1. Use modern technology in a minimally invasive way to determine if there are unmarked graves at each of the three sites in question.

2. If there are unmarked graves, determine their nature —are the bodies victims of violence consistent with the massacre or do they appear to be the remains of people who died from natural causes?

3. If there are bodies that appear to be 1921 Race Massacre

victims, do whatever forensic examination is possible to determine their identities and causes of death.

We do not begin this process with a certain outcome. We may not find any mass graves. Or we may. Tulsans are compassionate and supportive toward victims of violent crime—and that standard should apply whether they are victims in 2018 or 1921. All Tulsans deserve to know what happened in 1921—especially the descendants of victims. This is a matter of basic human decency.

While we are doing this work, I am incredibly thankful for all the volunteers whose research and commitment over decades have put us in a position to finally act. The only way to move forward in our work to bring about reconciliation in Tulsa is by seeking the truth honestly.[431]

The Oklahoma Archaeological Survey, which participated in similar work under the auspices of the Oklahoma Commission to Study the Tulsa Race Riot of 1921 (1997-2001), and the Oklahoma Medical Examiner's Office will lead the effort. Site excavations will occur if new technology detects ground anomalies consistent with the existence of a mass grave.

If human remains are uncovered, the Medical Examiner's Office will work to identify them through a DNA matching process. Given the time since burial, the process is likely to be both laborious and protracted.[432]

In addition to persistent tales of mass graves from both black and white Tulsans, other as-yet-unverified accounts detail unmarked individual graves in undisclosed locations, including on parts of then-active coal mines and pits. Still other accounts suggested that unknown individuals cremated bodies and propelled the narrative that men tossed bodies into the Arkansas River. According to most tellings, the unknown dead are presumed to be African American, but some believe the number of white Tulsans killed in the massacre to be underreported as well.[433]

On a related note, *Mapping Historical Trauma in Tulsa, 1921 to*

2021, is a research project stemming from a partnership between Dr. Alicia Odewale, an assistant professor of anthropology at the University of Tulsa, specializing in the archaeology of Afro-Caribbean enslavement and freedom in the Danish West Indies, and Dr. Parker VanValkenburgh, an assistant professor of anthropology at Brown University, specializing in the archaeology of Colonial Peru. Both are Tulsa-born archaeologists committed to collaborative research that brings together students and a diverse group of community partners in Tulsa to recover and critically evaluate new material evidence from the 1921 massacre.

Their multi-year project seeks to unite digital mapping, collaborative archaeological excavation, and the curation and public presentation of research results, with a view toward creating new, critical sites of memory for Tulsans. Ideally, such sites would connect to the Tulsa disaster, force contemplation around its legacy, and stimulate critical thought around ways to leverage this history, both in the present and for the future.

The effort expands upon the work of the Riot Commission, employing archaeology to document the impact of the 1921 tragedy on the fabric of the Greenwood District and Tulsa.

Project work includes two stages:

1. The development of the Greenwood District WebGIS, a public website centered on a map-based interface, which will provide users with access to images, oral histories, and other archival documentation of the Greenwood District before and after 1921 and allow them to visualize its effects; and
2. Collaborative archaeological excavations with locations targeted based on historical data, involving the participation of both community members and student researchers, and yielding artifacts and data that can in turn be incorporated and presented in the Greenwood District WebGIS.[434]

The Matter of the Brady District/Tulsa Arts District

Tulsa's former Brady District, a now-thriving, near-downtown center of arts and culinary variety, came under scrutiny in 2013 when revelations about its namesake, Wyatt Tate Brady, surfaced.

The Brady name also affixed to the Brady Theater, so named because of its location on what was once Brady Street and its proximity to the a residential area that bore his name[435] and includes
former Brady land holdings. Tate Brady had for decades been remembered as a wealthy, prominent Tulsa founding father.

> Five years after his arrival in Tulsa, on April 18, 1895,
> Brady married Rachel Cassandra Davis, who came from
> a prominent Claremore family. She was 1/64th Cherokee,
> which gave her new husband special privileges among
> the Cherokee tribe. Together, the Bradys had four chil-
> dren. On January 18, 1898, Brady and other prominent
> businessmen signed the charter that established Tulsa
> as an officially incorporated city. Tate Brady was now a
> founding father of Tulsa.[436]

Revelations about Brady's lesser-known ties to the Ku Klux
Klan and his possible role in the massacre sparked fierce debate
over changing the name of the district which bore his surname.[437]

For some, the answer seemed crystal clear:—the name must
change given Tate Brady's card-carrying affiliation with this vicious, racist organization. For others, though, the core question
loomed beyond the clear emotional choice: Will the re-naming of
The Brady District advance race relations and promote racial reconciliation in Tulsa?

The latter group argued that the naming of the Brady District
amounted to but a symptom of larger, more important, issues—
concerns about power, privilege, and the writing of historical narratives. Addressing those issues would require ensuring: (i) the
teaching of inclusive, unvarnished history; curricula reflecting the
people, places, and events, good and bad, that shaped who and
what Tulsa is as a community; and (ii) the seating of a multiplicity
of voices and perspectives at the decision-making table when it
comes to community issues—in short, diversity, equity, and inclusion.

Others argued in favor of using that name, the Brady District,
as an opportunity to work on the core issues—as a teachable moment—rather than getting bogged down in a divisive, destructive

battle over a name change that may do little to move the needle on race relations and racial reconciliation.

The Brady District (now, the Tulsa Arts District) is a private collective, not an officially designated city enclave. That said, the city has used the Brady District moniker in connection with governmental affairs. For example, in 1993, the city created a Brady District tax increment financing district or "TIF." By the time the TIF ended in 2017, it had generated millions of development dollars that changed the trajectory of the area with enhancements such as improved lighting, sidewalks, trees, park benches, trash cans, and landscaping.[438]

The City of Tulsa chose to act on what it deemed to be the only aspect of the debate within its purview: the name of Brady Street within the Brady District. Ultimately, the Tulsa City Council chose to rename it M.B. Brady Street in honor of Civil War photographer Matthew Brady,[439] who had no apparent connction to Tulsa. The street also bears the honorific title, "Reconciliation Way." That resolution arguably satisfied few and accomplished little.

Years later, at its October 24, 2018, meeting, the Tulsa City Council discussed a proposed ordinance, effective February 1, 2019, that would rename M.B. Brady Street to "Reconciliation Way," which was already the vanity name attached to the segment of the street within the downtown Inner Dispersal Loop.

Outgoing Councilor Blake Ewing proposed the change, citing regret over the then five-year-old compromise that resulted in changing the street name from Brady Street to M.B. Brady Street. As previously noted, the renaming came amidst a public outcry over the links of the street's namesake, city founder Tate Brady, to the Ku Klux Klan and his possible role in the destruction of Tulsa's African American community in 1921.

Councilor Ewing, having had years to ponder the matter and engage with community members, noted: "I have kind of lamented that outcome for years and years, and I just feel like in a lot of ways, things have changed. The council makeup's a little bit different than it was then, and the Brady District has become the (Tulsa) Arts District. I just think the community is in a better place to go back and correct that decision. The timing is right for a lot of different reasons."

Explaining why "Reconciliation Way" should be the new street moniker, Councilor Ewing noted: "I believe that reconciliation is happening every day, that it has happened in a lot of ways and that there's still more of it to happen. I like the story that it tells and that it has the potential to tell. To me, it's just more meaning-ful."[440]

At the November 28, 2018, meeting of the Tulsa City Council, Councilors approved, 8-to-1, the change from M.B. Brady Street to Reconciliation Way, effective July 1, 2019. Anonymous donors agreed to cover part of the costs of changing street markers and other public signage. Councilor Ewing, tasting victory at his final meeting, noted:

> I believe our community's story should be that five years later, we are capable of changing the name from Brady to something else. Not because we have healed, or because race relations in Tulsa are where they should be, but be-cause we are one step better, and I like it that we're one step [better].

We cannot change our history. We cannot erase the fact that Tate Brady, not unlike many of his contemporaries here and else-where, lived multi-dimensional lives; that they thrived as business and civic leaders at a time when white supremacy held sway. That in no way excuses their lack of moral courage, but it does remind us of how far we have come.[441]

The ultimate irony is that the erstwhile Brady District has be-come precisely what Tate Brady would never have envisioned, and likely never embraced: A diverse, inclusive community filled with shops, museums, eateries, and parks that reject his narrow world view and believe in one Tulsa. That is something to celebrate.

Business owners renamed the Brady District in the fall of 2017. The new moniker, the "Tulsa Arts District," is objectionable to few, if not wholly satisfactory to all.

On December 6, 2018, Peter Mayo, owner of the historic Brady Theater, formerly, Tulsa Convention Hall, announced a planned name change for the popular venue. In 2019, the new name be-came the "Tulsa Theater." The move, several years in the making, began when the City of Tulsa opted to remove Tate Brady's name from the street from which the building took its name. Mayo decided to act: "When the City Council made that decision, we took that as the incentive to make the change."

Mayo purchased the theater from the city of Tulsa in 1978, after the Tulsa Performing Arts Center opened to serve as the City's principal performance venue. He first called it the "Old Lady on Brady," shortening that two years later to the Brady Theater.

The Kansas City, Kansas, architectural firm Rose and Peterson originally designed the 1914 structure as a municipal auditorium and convention hall. Promoters billed "Convention Hall," as it was known for the first forty years of its life, as the largest hall between Kansas City and Houston.

In 1921, Convention Hall housed interned African Americans detained by the National Guard during the decimation of Tulsa's African American community.

In 1930, world-renowned architect Bruce Goff spearheaded a thirty-two-day interior remodel of the building, during which the barn-like interior morphed into an elegant showplace. Goff's Art Deco makeover included draperies and seats, vertical wall panels of white plaster decorated with thin gold dividers, gilded air conditioning grilles, and acoustic ceiling tiles painted green, blue, white, and gold, together with five massive green-and-white, centrally-installed pendant light fixtures.

Front and rear additions to the original 1914 structure came in 1952, including upper and lower lobbies, to what became the "Tulsa Municipal Theater." The building garnered a listing on the National Register of Historic Places in 1979. Its architectural design was then known as Western Classic Revival.

Legions of greats graced the facility through the years, including: Tony Bennett, Al Green, Ed Sullivan, B.B. King, Robin Williams, Rosemary Clooney, Will Rogers, David Copperfield, Glen Campbell, Bill Cosby, Enrico Caruso, Victor Borge, touring Broadway musicals, and performances by Tulsa Ballet, Tulsa Opera, and the Tulsa Philharmonic.[442]

Another location within the City of Tulsa that once sported the Brady surname, Brady Heights, changed its name to "The Heights."[443] This north Tulsa neighborhood that has been listed on the National Register of Historic Places since 1980.

Tulsa Regional Chamber:
Acknowledgement, Apology, and Atonement

At a May 28, 2019, press conference, the Tulsa Regional Chamber donated relevant portions of its 1921 minutes to the Greenwood Cultural Center in response to a call for archives related to the massacre. The Chamber saw an opportunity, through the contribution of archival material, to lay bare its role in life-altering Tulsa events. Though one simple act in the present cannot undo damage occasioned in the past, the Chamber viewed the gesture as but one small step toward atonement.

By its own admission, the Chamber has too long remained silent about its role, through acts of omission and commission, in the Tulsa tragedy of 1921. The presser offered the Chamber an opportunity to acknowledge this lapse in judgment, apologize for the harm it caused, and highlight ways in which it is working to atone for the historical trauma still evident after almost 100 years.

The minutes from pertinent 1921 Chamber meetings, while mostly routine, revealed a troubling mindset and an unmistakable leadership vacuum. References to the 1921 destruction of the Greenwood District are often cavalier and callous. A blame-the-victims attitude prevails. Condescension looms in calls to seize the burned lands and repurpose them for railroad and corporate uses. White supremacy reigns.

> Shortly after a white mob brought death and destruction to Greenwood's thriving segregated business district, the chamber put out a press release that said, in part, 'Tulsa feels intensely humiliated and, standing in the shadow of this great tragedy, pledges its every effort to wiping out the stain at the earliest possible moment and punishing those guilty of bringing the disgrace and disaster to this city.'
>
> Those were brave words, but empty ones.
>
> Within weeks, the records show, the chamber had disbanded its executive welfare committee amid a dispute with the city and with little accomplished;[444] little mean-

ingful help was given to those who had been left destitute and homeless. The city's business leadership never
said another word about 'punishing those guilty,' and
no white man ever faced criminal sanctions. Meanwhile,
Tulsa was looking at Greenwood as a good place for a
railroad station and helping those who kept the massacre
out of the history classes.

The promise to wipe out the stain of the race massacre became a conspiracy to erase it from the world's memory.[445]

Chamber CEO Mike Neal reminded attendees that while the
Chamber cannot undo the past, it can assure Tulsans that the twenty-first century Chamber leadership looks different than its early
twentieth-century predecessors and, more importantly, thinks differently. The new Chamber celebrates diversity, equity, and inclusion, and serves one Tulsa.[446]

The 1921 Tulsa Race Massacre Centennial Commission

The 1921 Tulsa Race Massacre Centennial Commission (the
"Centennial Commission"), organized by Oklahoma Senator Kevin Matthews in 2015, works to leverage the rich history surrounding the massacre by facilitating actions, activities, and events that
commemorate and educate all citizens. The Centennial Commission sponsors some events and activities independently, but mostly collaborates with and/or sanctions the mission-related events
and activities of other organizations.

The Centennial Commission launched publicly on October 31,
2016, with a press conference at the State Capitol in Oklahoma
City. Numerous state dignitaries attended the kick-off, including:
Oklahoma Senator Kevin Matthews, U.S. Senator James Lankford,
and Oklahoma Secretary of State Chris Benge. *See Appendix C for
additional information.*

Critical to the success of the Centennial Commission was the
establishment of collaborative and sustainable relationships between and among key organizations in the Greenwood District,
including the Greenwood Cultural Center, the John Hope Franklin
Center for Reconciliation, and the Greenwood Chamber of Commerce.[447] While the latter entity struggled with a host of financial,

governance, and personnel challenges, the other two forged a working relationship that supported the work of the Centennial Commission. The following letter summarizes that agreement.[448]

Mayor G. T. Bynum, in a summer 2018 letter, encouraged all Tulsans to rally behind the Centennial Commission.

July 6, 2018

The 1921 Tulsa Race Riot Centennial Commission
P.O. Box 702683
Tulsa, OK 74170

Greetings Commissioners:

On Friday, June 29, 2018, members of the Board of Directors of both John Hope Franklin Center of Reconciliation (JHFCR) and the Greenwood Cultural Center (GCC) met to discuss closer collaborations between the two entities. We realize the focus of each organization is distinct and separate, and both organizations seek to preserve and sustain their individual missions. And, we also acknowledge our missions are similar enough that the potential of working together opens doors of opportunity that otherwise would not be available.

With the goal of building a collaborative partnership as the backdrop of our discussion, members of Board of Directors of both JHFCR and GCC agreed to move forward with creating a legally binding document that will strengthen and sustain both organizations. Anticipating success, this collaborative relationship will be transformational. Generations to come will enjoy and benefit from the opportunity to know the rich and thriving history of the Greenwood District and its people. Further, this relationship will help elevate and advance the national discussion on race relations.

Therefore, we are requesting that the Commission, provide whatever assistance you can to help move us forward. We are open to any recommendations and/or guidance in employing a consultant and/or individual to help develop a legally binding document formalizing the collaborative relationship.

Please, know that the respective boards of JHFCR and Greenwood Cultural Center are ready to engage and welcome your participation and assistance.

Sincerely,

Dwain E. Midget, Interim Chair
Greenwood Cultural Center

Julius Pegues, Chairman
John Hope Franklin Center for Reconciliation

cc. Board of Directors, John Hope Franklin
Center for Reconciliation
Board of Directors, Greenwood Cultural Center
Frances Jordan-Rakestraw, Executive Director
Reuben Gant, Executive Director

July 30, 2018

Dear _____ :

Almost a century ago, Tulsa was home to one of the most vibrant business centers in the nation: the Historic Green-wood District - an area also known as Black Wall Street. On the evening of May 31 through the afternoon of June 1, 1921, Greenwood was decimated by a white mob. African-American Tulsans lost their lives, their homes, and their business-es. This event marks one of the darkest moments in our na-tion's history.

While the district rebuilt after the massacre, years of set-backs left it in ruins, severely limiting the entrepreneurial potential of this once flourishing Tulsa community. The 1921 Tulsa Race Massacre Centennial Commission has sum-moned leaders from throughout our city to engage wide-spread community support for the momentous centennial in 2021. As the 100th anniversary of the Tulsa Race Massacre approaches, Tulsa and Tulsans must own our history, work together and continue to build trust within our community - showing that we have come a long way from the division that ushered in this heinous act.

As Mayor of Tulsa, I am writing to ask you to consider the unique role you might play in commemorating this event. Every Tulsan has a unique contribution to make. Perhaps it is through the arts or education. Perhaps it is through busi-ness expertise or non-profit experience. Faith leaders and elected officials alike have a part to play in this historic mo-ment in our city's history. Let's ensure that when all eyes are on Tulsa in 2021, our city stands out as a national model of reconciliation. Should you have specific questions about the work of the 1921 Tulsa Race [Massacre] Centennial Com-mission, please don't hesitate to visit its website at https://www.tulsa2021.org/ or contact its project manager, Jamaal Dyer, at j.dyer@tulsa2021.org.

Thank you for giving this thoughtful consideration. I hope you will take part in this pivotal opportunity for Tulsa.

Best regards,

G.T. Bynum Mayor City of Tulsa[449]

"Black Wall Street" Groups

Several "Black Wall Street" groups have formed across the country to celebrate and highlight Black entrepreneurs and Black-owned businesses. One such group describes itself as follows:

> Official Black Wall Street is a digital platform and directory of over 1,400 verified Black-owned businesses around the world.

> Studies show that out of our $1.1 trillion buying power only 2% is invested in black-owned businesses. This platform was created out of a need to support businesses that are owned and operated by black entrepreneurs to funnel more of that money back into our communities. The most common challenge however is discovering black companies and verifying that older businesses are still black-owned. That is where Official Black Wall Street comes in.[450]

In the Capitol Rotunda

The State Capitol in Oklahoma City, Oklahoma, boasts a magnificent display of portraits of Oklahoma historical figures, among them, numerous African American icons. Though not explicitly tied to Greenwood District history, the prominent display of these individuals nonetheless says something about the State's willingness to at least acknowledge its tortuous past—a past that many of these men and women bumped up against and held firm. These luminaries helped us see ourselves more clearly, something we can do only if we choose to look at the past. These portraits offer an educational opportunity that may help the State paint a more inclusive mosaic moving forward.

Among those African Americans honored with Capitol Rotunda portraits[451] is Dr. John Hope Franklin,[452] the son of Tulsa attorney B.C. Franklin and a 1931 graduate of Booker T. Washington High School in Tulsa. Artist Everett Raymond Kinstler honored the iconic scholar and historian.[453] A Simmie Knox portrait of another prominent Tulsan, Benjamin Harrison Hill (1904 - 1971), also adorns the walls of the Capitol Rotunda. Voters elected Hill to the Oklahoma House of Representatives in 1968, the first African

American elected by Tulsans to the Oklahoma Legislature.[454]

At the Smithsonian National Museum of African American History and Culture

Buck Colbert Franklin, a prominent Tulsa lawyer who represented black victims of the riot, recalled the horrors of that seemingly-never-ending moment in time in a 1931 manuscript housed at the Smithsonian. "On they rushed, whooping to the top of their voices like so many cowboys and firing their guns every step they took," he wrote. Those painful recollections are part of "The Power of Place" exhibition at the Smithsonian National Museum of African American History and Culture. The exhibited opened on September 24, 2016, in Washington, D.C.

Franklin's unpublished document, discovered in 2015, joined several other pieces in a collection that tells the story of the obliteration of Tulsa's "Black Wall Street" in an orgy of white violence against African Americans. The unmistakable core message of the narrative, however, is the remarkable ascendance of the human spirit, as evidenced by the rebuilding of the Greenwood District even in the face of long odds and open hostility.[455]

The National Museum of African American History and Culture embraces a bold vision:

> In many ways, there are few things as powerful and as important as a people, as a nation that is steeped in its history. Often America is celebrated as a place that forgets. This museum seeks to help all Americans remember, and by remembering, this institution will stimulate a dialogue about race and help to foster a spirit of reconciliation and healing.
>
> There are four legs upon which this museum will stand:
>
> 1. The first is to create an opportunity for those that care about African American culture to explore and revel in this history.
>
> 2. Equally important is the opportunity to help all Americans see just how central African American history is for all of us. The museum will use African American history and culture as a lens into what it means to be

an American.

3. Additionally, the museum will use African American culture as a means to help all Americans see how their stories, their histories, and their cultures are shaped and informed by international considerations and how the struggle of African Americans has impacted freedom struggles around the world.

4. Finally, as a 21st-century institution, the museum must be a place of collaboration. We must be a truly national museum that reaches beyond Washington to engage new audiences and to collaborate with the myriad of museums and educational institutions, both nationally and internationally.

Ultimately, the National Museum of African American History and Culture should be a place of meaning, of memory, of reflection, of laughter, and of hope. It should be a beacon that reminds us of what we were; what challenges we still face; and point us towards what we can become.[456]

Conclusion

Amplify, clarify, and punctuate, and let
the [reader] draw his or her own conclusion.
Keith Jackson

One of the largely unspoken, but just-beneath-the-surface questions on the minds, if not the tongues, of uncertain white Americans during the tumultuous Civil Rights Era was: "What do those people really want?" In retrospect, the obvious, if not intuitive, answer is: Those people want the same things you people want—the same things most sentient beings want: to be free; to be treated fairly; to lead lives not constricted by irrational and unjust policy and practice.

The massacre survivors wanted those things, too. In the end, most wanted the chance to tell their stories so the world might be aware; so no other individuals might have to endure the physical and emotional pain associated with others' failure to acknowledge their full humanity; so history would be repeated.

1921 Tulsa Race Massacre
Selected Survivor Recollections

J.B. Bates
(June 13, 1916 - December 17, 2008)

I was only five years old, too young to know the significance of a riot, but I do remember that my mother was so frightened that I knew that something was terribly wrong. The militia took dad and my uncles to detention. While the militia was busy taking the men in the family away, my mother slipped away with my sister Roxanna and me and ran to hide in a chicken house. With us was an old man on a walking stick. While we were running, an airplane flew over real low and someone in the plane shot and killed that old man! My mother often talked about the riot, but my dad NEVER talked about it!

Kinney I. Booker
(March 21, 1913 - March 1, 2006)

At the time of the Tulsa Race Riot of 1921, my parents and the five of us children lived at 320 North Hartford Avenue. We had a lovely home, filled with beautiful furniture, including a grand piano. All our clothes and personal belongings—just everything—were burned up during the riot. Early on the morning of June 1, 1921, my parents were awakened by the sounds of shooting and the smell of fire, and the noise of fleeing blacks running past our house. My dad awakened us children and sent us to the attic with our mother. We could hear what was going on below. We heard the white men ordering dad to come with them; he was being taken to detention. We could hear dad pleading with the mobsters. He was begging them 'please don't set my house on fire. But, of course, that is exactly what they did just before they left with dad. Though dad went outside the house with the mobsters, he slipped away from them when they got pre-occupied splashing gasoline or kerosene on the outside of the house to speed up the burning. He rushed to the attic and rescued us. We slipped into the crowd of fleeing black refugees. Thank God we did not burn up in that attic!

Otis Grandville Clark
(February 13, 1903 - May 21, 2012)

I got caught right in the middle of that riot! Some white mobsters were holed up in the upper floor of the Ray Rhee Flour Mill on East Archer and they were just gunning down black people, just picking them off like they were swatting flies. Well, I had a friend who worked for Jackson's funeral home and he was trying to get to that new ambulance so he could drive it to safety. I went with him. He had the keys in his hand, ready for the takeoff. But one of the mobsters in the Rhee building zoomed in on him and shot him in the hand. The keys flew to the ground and blood shot out of his hand and some of it sprayed on me. We both immediately abandoned plans to save that ambulance! We ran for our lives. We never saw my stepfather again, nor our little pet bulldog, Bob. I just know they perished in that riot. My stepfather was a strong family man. I know he did not desert us. I just wish I knew where he was buried.

Ernestine Gibbs
(December 15, 1902 - July 23, 2003)

A family friend came from a hotel on Greenwood where he worked, and knocked on our door. He was so scared he could not sit still, nor lie down. He just paced up and down the floor talking about the 'mess' going on downtown and on Greenwood. When daylight came, black people were moving down the train tracks like ants. We joined the fleeing people. During this fleeing frenzy, we made it to Golden Gate Park near 36th Street North. We had to run from there because someone warned us that whites were shooting down blacks who were fleeing along railroad tracks. Some of them were shot by whites firing from airplanes. On June 1, 1921, we were found by the Guards and taken to the fairgrounds. A white man who mother knew came and took us home. Going back to Greenwood was like entering a war zone. Everything was gone! People were moaning and weeping when they looked at where their homes and businesses once stood. I'll never forget it. No, not ever!

Leroy Leon Hatcher
(May 23, 1921 - January 31, 2004)

My parents, Augustus and Lois Muster Hatcher, were living in the Greenwood area at the time of the riot, somewhere over by Brady Street. My mother said that the riot commotion reached our house early the morning of June 1, 1921, while we were all sound asleep. The mobsters kicked in the door, threw a Molotov cocktail, or something or other, which set things on fire in the house. My dad told her to run, to join the crowd. He said he would be coming right behind us. But he never did. I don't know if the mobsters grabbed him and killed him right there in the house or what. All I know is that he was missing. My mother never forgot that day as long as she lived. She said she ran nine miles with me, a nine-day-old baby, in her arms, dodging bullets that were falling near her. After the riot was over, my mother looked and looked for my father, but she never found him. His loss haunted her the rest of her life, and it ruined my life, too. I believe my father was killed in that riot. I just wish I knew where he is buried. I would just like to pay my respects to him.

Wilhelmina Guess Howell
(April 25, 1907 – December 18, 2003)

I have had a lifelong connection with the Greenwood District. My father, H.A. Guess, had a law office on Greenwood Avenue, and my mother's brother was the famous Mayo Clinic-trained surgeon Dr. A.C. Jackson, who was so brutally murdered by mobsters during the Tulsa riot. The fact that the riot destroyed my father's office and led to the death of my uncle seemed very ironic to me. My relatives had come to Oklahoma to get away from racism, violence, and death in Tennessee. In fact, Grand-father Guess just barely made it out of Tennessee alive. A Ku Klux Klan lynch mob had come for him. But Grandpa couldn't be kept down. Neither could my father, H.A. Guess, be kept down. After the riot, he rebuilt and reopened his law practice. Before he died, Dad said that one of the things he was proudest of was that he represented black riot victims when they filed claims for riot damages. Some of his records were used by the Oklahoma Commission to Study the Tulsa Race Riot of 1921 when they were searching for documentation to prove culpabil-ity for riot damages. I never got over the death of my beloved uncle, Dr. A.C. Jackson. He was my hero.

Simon R. Richardson
(January 2, 1914 – November 28, 2003)

On June 1, 1921, when things got so bad, my grandparents sent me on with the neighbors, the Butlers. The Butlers hooked up two mules to a wagon and we headed for Mohawk Park to get away from the fast-approaching mobsters. My grandmother and my cousin were picked up by the Guards and taken to the Red Cross. Men and boys were taken by the militia to the Con-vention Center. In all this commotion, my grandmother didn't know where I was. I was missing from her for two days and she was so worried. She was just sick with grief. She thought I had been killed. A few days after the riot, blacks were released from detention and most were reunited with their families. But some people were not reunited. Some were never heard of again, like the Butlers who took me to safety in their wagon pulled by the two mules. My grandparents tried and tried to locate them after the riot, and when I grew older, I tried to locate them, but they were never heard of again. I wonder if they are buried in some secret place.

Veneice Dunn Sims

(January 21, 1905 - December 10, 2006)[457]

There had been rumblings on the night of May 31, 1921, that there was going to be trouble in Little Africa. But we hadn't paid much attention to the rumors. In fact, my siblings and I were out in the front yard. We were just looking around to see if we could find out what all the commotion was about. All at once, bullets began dropping into our yard. I was just terrified. When bullets are falling all around a person, you just don't know what to do. I didn't know whether to drop down on the ground, or whether I should run. For a while, I just stood rooted to the ground. I was just paralyzed. My father had heard bullets hitting the roof and sides of our house and he ran out to find us children. He called us into the house. Then he decided we had better run to safety. The mobsters were getting too close. We could see cars full of white men going down Greenwood Avenue, guns blazing and bullets flying at running black people.

Wess H. Young, Sr.

(February 20, 1917 – September 30, 2014)

On the day of the riot, black men, women, and children who were running from white mobsters were picked up by guardsmen. The women and children in our group were taken to Booker T. Washington High School on the corner of Elgin and Frankfort Avenue. The men were marched to the fairgrounds in the area of 15th Street and Harvard Avenue. The captured blacks were given vaccines and food. They stayed until some white person came and vouched for them. Some stayed three to four days; others stayed two to three weeks before some white person came and claimed them. The troops put up tents for homeless black people. Most all the wonderful buildings, commercial and residential, had been looted and burned down during the riot. It was an exception for a building to have remained untouched, though a few did.

Excerpts from interviews by Eddie Faye Gates
Member, Oklahoma Commission to Study the Tulsa Race Riot of 1921[458]

Tulsa's shame, the slaughter and human suffering inflicted on Tulsans by Tulsans, is both symptomatic and emblematic of the arc of African American oppression. Pain and progress define the journey.

How should we deal with our historical racial trauma, in Tulsa and elsewhere?

At the outset, the process requires truth-telling—acknowledging our tortuous past without adornment and excuse—and honest conversation about the power, privilege, and pain borne of that history.[459] That truth-telling—that acknowledgement—is necessary, but not sufficient. Apology and atonement must follow.

The Winter Institute in Mississippi strikes an appropriate balance in its vision statement:

> The Winter Institute envisions a world where people honestly engage in their history in order to live more truthfully in the present; where the inequities of the past no longer dictate the possibilities of the future. We envision a world where people of all identities are treated equally; where equality of and access to opportunity are available and valued by all; where healing and reconciliation are commonplace and social justice is upheld and honored. We acknowledge and recognize that it is not enough for us to be intentional, but we must be purposeful in making this vision a reality . . . .[460]

The year 2021 marks the centennial of a seminal moment, not just in history of Tulsa, but in the history of Oklahoma and America, too. The occasion calls for solemnity, to be sure, but for thoughtful reflection, too.

Tulsa's 1921 massacre, arguably the worst of many "race riots" in the twentieth century American history as measured by lives lost and property destroyed, temporarily stilled Tulsa's famed and frenzied black business sector in the Greenwood District, laying waste to much of the black community. In addition to decimating persons and property, the riot left psycological scars miles wide and oceans deep—wounds as yet not fully healed.

In a November 8, 2008, editorial, the *Tulsa World* described the massacre as "a badge of shame that Tulsa will never fully live down." The decades-long silence that shrouded the event in secrecy—for some, a "conspiracy of silence"—only compounded that ignominy.

Like an irremovable scarlet letter, the massacre is a shame never fully erased. Our inability to live down this dreadful part of our past suggests that we ought to focus our energies on ways to *live up* to our potential. Now is the time to pause to ponder our past, its present legacy, and our shared future as a community; to remember, reclaim, and reconcile our history.

As we round the bend toward the centenary of this milestone, it behooves us to rededicate ourselves to healing our history, engaging in an appreciative inquiry into our past, and reaffirming our too-often-spotty commitment to diversity, equity, and inclusion.

Healing our history—addressing historical racial trauma—entails acknowledging past misdeeds and missteps, embracing the past, not selectively, but holistically; offering sincere, genuine apology for the needless suffering of others; and fashioning appropriate reparations measures—atoning—making amends—repairing, as best we can, the damage.

To do this—any of this—requires that we engage, constructively, with one another in way-forward dialogue. It is about working through shared trauma and pain toward common understanding and shared space.

Few cities match Richmond, Virginia, in terms of the breadth and depth of racial reconciliation work. For decades, Richmond leaders have tackled the issue of race so many other cities simply avoid.

Begun in 1993 as a flagship program of Initiatives of Change USA, Richmond, Virginia-based Hope in the Cities ("HIC") uses honesty, empathy, intentional conversation, responsibility and truth-telling to challenge white privilege, structural racism, and embedded histories of inequality.

HIC seeks to create in Richmond and elsewhere environments in which deep listening, accountability, and just histories transcend competing identities and interests. Richmond, the former seat of the Confederacy and the second largest city in the country to profit from capitalist economies in domestic enslavement and trading, actively grapples with the legacies of its past.

In 1993, The Unity Walk conference brought hundreds of global leaders to Richmond for a fuller walk and work through Virginia's history, centering on the contributions of First Nations and peoples of African descent to the state and country's developments. This event marked Richmond as the first city in the United States to publicly and formally recognize its racial history and embrace the long-marginalized narratives of its people of color.

Over two decades of evidence-based work, HIC has built trusted collaborative relationships with a wide range of leaders including community-based activists and organizations, educational institutions, business and corporations, media, nonprofits, civic groups, elected officials, expert practitioners, and faith-based centers.

HIC methodologies include workshops, capacity-building interventions, facilitated dialogues, and experiential learnings. Its focus is on: (1) acts of acknowledgement and reconciliation; (2) honest conversation; and (3) personal responsibility.

Both domestic and international communities have embraced HIC's innovative change processes.[461]

Richmond, a trailblazer in this work, is not alone. Chicago offered a more recent example of what is possible. In 2019, that city launched an initiative to promote constructive engagement and healing.

Chicago 1919: Confronting the Race Riots, a year-long initiative that heightened the Chicago Race Riot of 1919 in the city's collective memory, engaged Chicagoans in public conversations about the legacy of Chicago's past racial tumult.

Racial tensions related to policing, migration, and housing peaked in 1919. *Chicago 1919* used this history as a lens through which to understand modern Chicago. Law and policy created, solidified, and reinforced segregation and inequality over the past 100 years.

Chicago 1919 programs highlighted specific expressions of institutionalized racism, from policing and education to housing and the media. People across the City shared in a collective reckoning with a little-known, but pivotal, historical epoch, with a view toward recognition, reconciliation, the reimagining of a shared future.[462]

We are committed to similar, sustained initiatives in Tulsa.

Like healing our history, an appreciative inquiry requires a searching look in the rearview mirror. It counsels us to look back for inspiration and example—for past positives that captivate and catalyze us in the present to fashion a more favorable future. The circumstances surrounding the Tulsa disaster offer just such an opportunity.

Tulsa's calamity leveled a storied enclave of black business-persons—independent, intelligent, and inspired—who gained renown for their entrepreneurial pluck. Greenwood District pioneers envisioned lives beyond the imagination of many African Americans of the time. They saved money and built economic enterprises, many not just not once, but twice. They thrived amidst deep-seated, race-based hostility from virtually all quarters, raising the social, political, and economic bars during a period characterized by bleak race relations.

The lessons and legacy of the Black Wall Street architects offer a springboard from which to empower young men and women, promote self-development and self-sufficiency, and launch a new corps of black business owners. Historical role models matter, not as replacements for such paragons in the here-and-now, but as supplements to them.

"Black Wall Street" is as much about a mindset—a construct built on promise and possibility—as it is about place. We are less limited by the rigors of race and the rigidities of residence.

The ancestors, by precept and example, showed us what could be. Thus empowered, we, in tribute to them, should seize upon all our relative advantages to make it so.

Successful twenty-first century entrepreneurs cannot be bound by the binary racial equation of the past. At the community, state, national, and global levels, racial and ethnic diversity abounds. Our challenge is figuring out ways to leverage that diversity in ways that support equity and inclusion, all to our mutual advantage.

Diversity, equity, and inclusion rest on the fundamental proposition that our shared humanity trumps all that might otherwise separate and divide us. Our community is defined by how we treat the least among us. The hours spanning May 31 and June 1, 1921, in Tulsa provided a tragic, but illustrative, case study of our capacity for inhumanity.

We suffer trauma when events disturb our fantasy of a fair and just world. Sometimes, such events extend over time and generations. Such is the case in Tulsa's Historic Greenwood District, whose founders traced their lineage back to enslavement, sharecropping, and Jim Crow-style second-class citizenship in the Deep South. Escaping that racial crucible, they discovered a seeming Promised Land in Indian Territory, only to be formally subjected to mirror-image Jim Crow segregation at Oklahoma statehood in 1907. Nonetheless, they built a flourishing entrepreneurial community against all imaginable odds.

The Greenwood District emerged as a national symbol of prosperity, celebrated as America's Negro Wall Street—later, Black Wall Street.[464] Its denizens suffered through the 1921 massacre, their community obliterated in a fit of unchecked jealousy and rage perpetrated by fellow Tulsans—by their white neigbors.

These indomitable men and women began rebuilding even as the ashes smoldered, facing institutional resistance and now more keenly aware that the fantasy of a fair and just world was no longer theirs to entertain.

Without doubt, there have been economic openings for some, better education for some, and, at least marginally, enhanced social capital in the decades since those existential challenges. While not ubiquitous, open, honest dialogue, particularly around race, no longer occurs in mere whispers.

Still, persistent disparities in virtually every realm offer overwhelming of evidence of foundational fissures in the Tulsa community. Caused and sustained by intergenerational traumas, the inequities require much more in the way of repair, much more investment by each of us.

Recovery from trauma presupposes an end to traumatic events, a protective cocoon of resilience, security, protections, and, finally, hope that a different narrative for the future may be installed and maintained.

The return of hope—of a widespread belief in fairness and justice—depends on the elimination of trauma, often researched in literature today as Adverse Childhood Experiences, for our children.

As community stewards, we must marshal the resources necessary to heal the wounds of trauma that continue to shorten lives, disable otherwise healthy people, foster addictions, and, too often, create narratives of despair. When our dream becomes the shared narrative of brotherhood and sisterhood, of shared humanity, then we will have moved closer to the "one Tulsa" many have so long awaited.[463]

As the five-score anniversary of the Tulsa tragedy approaches, let us exhale, and then let us breathe freely, oxygenating our efforts on three fronts: (1) healing our history; (2) making an appreciative inquiry into our past; and (3) recommitting to diversity, equity, and inclusion. If we do this, we will have honored the memory of one of our darkest days by illuminating it with a bright new light.

The operative question in 2021 will be: "What has Tulsa become in the interim between the 1921 disaster and the present?" This book set out to address that inquiry.

Similarly, the salient inquiry one hundred years from now, in 2121, will be: "What has Tulsa become in the interim between the 100th anniversary of the 1921 disaster and the present?"

Perfection—a utopia—is not possible. We will always be judged on the work we have done between some historical baseline and the here and now.

Let us always ask: What must we do to ensure that the future is an improvement over the past and present?

As if

As if shackles never bound.
As if lashes never welted.
As if rape never traumatized.
As if slip knots never hanged.
As if knives never pierced.

As if fire never charred.
As if bullets never silenced.

As if you see right past me.
As if I have no soul.
As if I too were not human.
As if my blackness should be cured.

As if freedom were free.
As if justice meant "just us."
As if separate were equal.
As if Jim never crowed.
As if we moved with all deliberate speed.
As if our rights came civilly.
As if the action were affirmative.
As if opportunity were equal.

As if time heals all wounds.
As if bygones could be bygones.
As if regret remedied.
As if acknowledgment atoned.
As if forgiveness were reflexive.
As if reconciliation came without sacrifice.

As if race no longer mattered.
As if meritocracy were universal.
As if privilege ceased to exist.
As if power were diffuse.

As if roots were extracted.
As if history no longer hobbled us.
As if psychic scars ever vanished.
As if we could start over.

As if words were solutions.
As if listening were hearing.
As if it were so simple.
As if we would just go along.
As if we could just get along.

As if you really know me.
As if you really care.

As if you see the future.
As if you see me there.
As if we share a destiny.

As if what is must be.
As if it were inevitable.
As if destiny were predetermined.
As if God were finished.

As if time stood still.
As if power came from without.
As if we were but pawns.
As if we should simply surrender.

As if we could all rise up.
As if we could wrest control.
As if we could all come together.
As if we could see the forest through its trees.

As if . . . .
As if . . . .
As if . . . .
As if a change is gonna come.

Appendix A

Tulsa's Historic Greenwood District, Past and Present

A Photographic Exposition

Greenwood Past

Williams Dreamland Theatre, an early landmark in Tulsa's Historic Greenwood District, *circa* 1920.

The Regal Theater, the second coming of Tulsa's Historic Greenwood District.

The Stradford Building, early days, Tulsa's Historic Greenwood District.

The Gurley Building, early days, Tulsa's Historic Greenwood District.

Tulsa's Historic Greenwood District prior to the 1921 massacre.

Ramsey Drug Store in Tulsa's Historic Greenwood District, *circa* 1950s.

The rebuilt Williams Dreamland Theatre, *circa* 1940s.

Meharry Pharmacy, owned by pharmacist Lloyd Reed Rollerson, in Tulsa's Historic Greenwood District, *circa* 1950s.

Greenwood Present

Tulsa Theater, formerly, "Brady Theater," once Tulsa Convention Hall.

Black Wall Street Memorial on the grounds of the Greenwood Cultural Center.

GreenArch, a multiuse development on the corner of Greenwood and Archer in Tulsa's Historic Greenwood District.

The Greenwood Cultural Center, 322 North Greenwood Avenue.

Entry to John Hope Franklin Reconciliation Park in Tulsa's Historic Greenwood District.

Langston University-Tulsa, a satellite campus of Langston University, the farthest west of the Historically Black Colleges and Universities.

ONEOK Field, home of the minor league baseball team Tulsa Drillers and FC Tulsa, a professional soccer team.

Vernon A.M.E. Church, whose basement survived the 1921 massacre, 311 N. Greenwood Ave.

Mt. Zion Baptist Church, targeted for destruction by the riotous mob in 1921, 419 N. Elgin Ave.

An aerial view of present-day Tulsa, looking west.

Tulsa's Historic Greenwood District looking north on Greenwood Avenue from Archer Street, *circa* 2015.

A view of the Greenwood Cultural Center and downtown Tulsa from the north.

Unidentified man views the 1921 Black Wall Street Memorial at the Greenwood Cultural Center.

Appendix B

Righting the Wrongs of History
Thoughts on Reparations and the 1921 Tulsa Race Massacre

By Hannibal B. Johnson

The arc of the moral universe is long, but it bends toward justice.
Dr. Martin Luther King, Jr.
(adapted from Theodore Parker, *circa* 1850)

Tulsa, "The Oil Capital of the World," glistened at the dawn of the twentieth century. Black gold made many a millionaire.

The growth of Tulsa's wealth and stature coincided with a raw anti-blackness in America.

Still, Tulsa's African American community, the Greenwood District, thrived. Black Wall Street, an entreprenurial hub, buzzed with economic activity.

Cognitive dissonance set in. The success of the Greenwood District could scarcely be tolerated, let alone embraced, by the larger white community, engulfed as it was in white supermacist propaganda. African American success increased consternation and friction.

The breadth and depth of anti-blackness in early twentieth century America seems almost unfathomable today. Brazen acts of violence and unspeakable cruelty went unpunished. In 1919 alone, more than two dozen major race-based disturbances, labeled "race riots," flared across America. In 1921, the year of the massacre, white vigilantes lynched some 57 African Americans in various locations throughout the country. Despite these atrocities, the United States Senate thrice failed to pass measures to make lynching a federal offense.

Tulsa would prove emblematic of America's racial tumult and, as noted earlier, a case study on the legacy of slavery and the need for a conversation about reparations for African Amricans.

In Tulsa, a seemingly random encounter between two teenagers, one white, the other black, catalyzed the massacre. The *alleged* assault on seventeen-year-old Sarah Page by nineteen-year-old Dick Rowland triggered unprecedented civil unrest. Page ultimately recanted her initial claims and refused to press charges against Rowland. By then, news of the incident had taken on a life of its own. Fueled by sensational reporting by *The Tulsa Tribune* and a racially hostile climate, mob rule held sway.

Authorities arrested Rowland. A white mob threatened to lynch him. A small group of black men, determined to protect the teen, marched to the courthouse where Sheriff McCullough held Rowland. Asked to retreat and assured of the young man's safety, Rowland's would-be protectors left the premises. But lynch talk persisted. Still concerned about Rowland, a second group of black men, a few score in number, proceeded to the courthouse. They exchanged words with the swelling group of white men gathered outside the courthouse. A gun discharged, the opening salvo in Tula's tragedy loosed.

Soon, throngs of weapon-wielding white men crossed over the Frisco tracks, invading the Greenwood District, intent upon wreaking havoc. Some law enforcement officers stood idly by. Others deputized white hoodlums, in effect, giving them license to plunder and pillage "Little Africa," the City's "Negro quarter." Despite pockets of resistance from black men, chaos, carnage, and catastrophe ensued.

Some sixteen hours of volcanic violence left little unscathed. Roving gangs set fire to homes and businesses, reducing them to charred rubble, and threatened Tulsa firefighters with their lives if they attempted to extinguish the flames. They killed and maimed—scores of men, women, and children, mostly black, lay dead, dying, and wounded in what looked like a theatre of war. The unmitigated violence forced thousands of black Tulsans into homelessness, destitution, and despair. The breadth and brutality took an emotional toll palpable even today.

Some brave souls in Tulsa's white community showed remarkable compassion. Individuals and churches (notably, First Presbyterian Church and Holy Family Cathedral) offered shelter and comfort. The American Red Cross earned the moniker "Angels of

Mercy" by providing food, shelter, and clothing and, just as importantly, reaffirming the humanity of Tulsa's marginalized black citizens.

Many soldiered on after the massacre, even in the face of overt hostility from some local media and relative indifference from Tulsa leadership. A rapidly resurgent Greenwood District quickly emerged. The community peaked in the 1940s.

In the end, though, America's black entrepreneurial mecca, could not survive. Integration, urban renewal, changing economic conditions (including the dawn of a mass production, and a mass audience retail economy), and the aging of its pioneers led to decline in the 1960s.

Decades later, a renaissance transformed the area into an eclectic mix of entities, including the Greenwood Cultural Center, Oklahoma State University-Tulsa, Langston University-Tulsa, ONEOK Field, John Hope Franklin Reconciliation Park, and Oklahoma Educational Television Authority ("OETA"). A smattering of small businesses housed in properties owed by the Greenwood Chamber of Commerce, residences, and massacre-era black churches are reminders of bygone days.

The Silent Divide

Despite its significance, some Tulsans, even more Oklahomans, and most Americans remain oblivious to this watershed event. For decades, Tulsa's massacre, the worst incident of civil unrest of its kind in American history, remained shrouded in mystery, cloaked in secrecy, and draped in conjecture. Few spoke openly of the Riot's horrors. Why?

Some blame a "conspiracy of silence." Something far less sinister may have been at work. White Tulsans felt some mix of embarrassment, shame, and guilt. Some black Tulsans feared additional violence; others refused to burden their children with information that might limit their aspirations. Still others likely suffered post-traumatic stress, rendering them unwilling or unable to relive the massacre through its retelling.

One clear and lasting effect of that decades-long silence has been a persistent gulf of distrust between Tulsa's black and white communities. Not talking about the massacre allowed unhealed wounds to fester. The chasm still lingers, marginally diminished, but no less real.

Arguably, the first significant breach in this silence occurred in 1971, the fiftieth anniversary of the massacre, with the publication of an article by Ed Wheeler entitled 'Profile of a Race Riot" in *Impact Magazine*.[465] Later, in 1982, Scott Ellsworth's groundbreaking book, *Death in a Promised Land: The Tulsa Race Riot of 1921*,[466] set tongues a-wagging. In 1997, the Oklahoma Commission to Study the Tulsa Race Riot of 1921 convened, drawing international attention. Local media, including the *Tulsa World*, soon began regular coverage of this history and its legacy. National media offered intermittent coverage. Books, including this author's 1998 work, *Black Wall Street: From Riot to Renaissance in Tulsa's Historic Greenwood District*,[467] appeared in rapid succession. John Hope Franklin Reconciliation Park[468] opened in 2010, providing a permanent, experiential opportunity to engage with this history.

In recent years, Tulsans have begun to grapple with this terrible human tragedy.

Almost a century removed, the specter of the massacre looms large. How do we heal our haunting history? How do we atone for the damage inflicted so long ago? How do we restore trust and move toward reconciliation? Our answers to these critical questions will determine whether we narrow existing racial gaps or allow the great abyss of color-based distrust to span future generations.

The Case for Reparations

Providing reparations—making amends—is essential to reconciliation. Reparations serve specific objectives, namely: to acknowledge an injustice; to apologize and make retribution (atone); to educate the community; to deter future occurrence of the injustice; and to clarify human rights. Proponents understand that restorative justice, the "make whole" aspiration behind reparations, cannot be literally realized. Lives, once lost, cannot be resuscitated. Minds, once traumatized, cannot be eased. Economic momentum, once blunted, cannot be fully recaptured.

Some fear that debating reparations, let alone offering them, opens a Pandora's Box best left buried and forgotten. *Where will it end?* some ask. Nonetheless, absent reparations, grievances magnify and multiply; present-day healing cannot occur.

To address the issue of reparations, in 1997 the Oklahoma Legislature authorized the Oklahoma Commission to Study the Tulsa Race Riot of 1921 to investigate and evaluate the massacre and make recommendations. The Riot Commission's sometimes-contentious deliberations drew worldwide media attention and prompted a groundswell of public interest in Tulsa's community dynamics—how the city has dealt with its past, and the impact of that past on Tulsa's present and future.

In 2001, the Riot Commission issued its final report. Among its recommendations were various types of reparations, in priority order: payments to living survivors and to descendants of those who suffered property damage during the massacre; a scholarship fund; business tax incentives for the Greenwood District; and a memorial.

The case for reparations outlined in the Riot Commission report rested on specific criteria: compelling, documented evidence of government complicity at the city and, arguably, the state level; identifiable victims and their heirs; a defined geographic community adversely affected (*i.e.,* Greenwood District); measurable or estimable economic losses attributable to the incident; and a thorough record of the people, places, and events associated with the massacre.

Money Myopia

Talk of reparations drew swift and vocal opposition, at least initially, attributable, in part, to lack of knowledge about the massacre and an unnecessarily narrow construction of the word "reparations."

Though fairly broad in scope, the Riot Commission's recommendations elevated monetary payments to first-priority status. Cash reparations, the most contentious of its list of five, drew wide attention. The Riot Commission's embrace of cash reparations emboldened organizations like the National Coalition of Blacks for Reparations in America, which saw it as precedent for broader monetary reparations for slavery.[469] Sensing controversy, early media coverage of the debate dwarfed coverage of alternative modes of atonement. This near-exclusive focus drowned out discussion of broader philosophical definitions of and rationale for reparations.

Critics failed to acknowledge the scope of damage wrought by the massacre (and its lasting effects) and discounted the need for reparations. Proponents unwittingly fueled resistance by focusing on cash payments as *the* essential, if not quintessential, form of reparations.

A high-profile lawsuit further coalesced media attention. In February 2003, galvanized by the Riot Commission report, a coterie of national, star-caliber attorneys joined forces with local legal talent in filing *Alexander v. Governor of State of Oklahoma*, a money damages lawsuit on behalf of massacre survivors and their descendants against the City of Tulsa and the State of Oklahoma. On March 22, 2004, a Tulsa federal district court dismissed the case, holding that the two-year statute of limitations barred all claims. A federal court of appeals sustained the dismissal, and the United States Supreme Court declined to review the case, thus ending the push for court-mandated monetary massacre reparations.

Some argued the lawsuit deepened racial fissures in the city and state, if only temporarily. Critics perceived the litigation as having been instigated by outside rabble-rousers and claimed it stymied organic, community-based initiatives to memorialize the massacre and promote reconciliation. The experience raised two compelling questions: Is litigation, as opposed to, say, legislation or conciliation, a viable approach to securing reparations? Are cash payments the only acceptable form of reparations?

Litigation was, arguably, counterproductive, particularly if the aim was community reconciliation. Litigation, by its very nature, leads to adversarial relations, not the rational dialogue needed for reconciliation. Moreover, securing monetary damages in courts of law for events like the massacre (and there were many such events in the early twentieth century) would require a sort of national reckoning. Courts would have to open our history to examine the effects of racism, then acknowledge injustices and prescribe remedies. Decisions in such cases would affect not just individuals, but cities, counties, states, and even the federal government. Is the judiciary equipped to carry out this kind of re-examination of our past and, assuming it is, how likely is it to do so?

Expanding The Conversation

In recent years, the conversation has broadened. Data gathered and compiled by Chad V. Johnson, Ph.D., his University of Oklahoma colleagues, and community partners in 2011 suggested broad support for reparations of some sort.[470] The ambitious community-wide survey investigated knowledge of the massacre and attitudes about race relations in Tulsa. Two thousand respondents engaged in the process. By substantial margins, respondents agreed: the massacre adversely affected social and economic dynamics in Tulsa; the massacre story has not been adequately shared; all Tulsans should know about the massacre; the massacre should be taught as part of public school curriculum; and race relations in Tulsa rank only as poor to fair, and amelioration will require dialogue and other programs or actions. Locally, most citizens support a variety of reparation measures. Monetary reparations, however, appear to be less important and more contentious.[471]

Other approaches to making amends exist, forms more likely to be accepted and implemented by broad community consensus—for example, the Riot Commission's recommendation for a memorial. Both the City of Tulsa and the State of Oklahoma have embraced a passel of non-monetary reparations without labeling them as such and without formally admitting culpability for massacre-related offenses.

Mayor G.T. Bynum and former Tulsa Mayors M. Susan Savage and Kathy Taylor offered public apologies for the massacre during their respective tenures. The Oklahoma Legislature created several vehicles to address the Riot Commission's recommendations: the Tulsa Race Riot Memorial Reconciliation Design Committee (out of which emerged the John Hope Franklin Center for Reconciliation, charged with creating a massacre-related memorial); the Greenwood Area Redevelopment Authority (charged with reinvigorating businesses in the Greenwood District); and the Tulsa Reconciliation Education and Scholarship Program (charged with creating education scholarships tied to massacre remembrance). The Oklahoma Legislature also awarded medals of distinction to several massacre survivors in a 2001 State Capitol ceremony.

The Riot Commission's recommendations did not include perhaps the single most powerful and enduring mode of reparations imaginable: curriculum reform. The generation-spanning potential of education to transform race relations in Tulsa and beyond is enormous. Like Holocaust curricula, the idea behind massacre curricula is straightforward—it is imperative to examine our past so that we may learn from it. To paraphrase Maya Angelou: Our history, despite its wrenching pain, cannot be unlived; but, if faced with courage, it need not be lived again.

No matter what else we may do, we will not be whole unless and until we own our past, process it, and integrate its lessons into our present and our vision for the future. Teaching and learning are essential to this process.

Educational reparations have been pursued. The Tulsa City Council passed a massacre-related resolution in 2008 supporting curriculum to ensure the massacre is adequately covered as an historical event. Similarly, as noted previously, the John Hope Franklin Center for Reconciliation works with Tulsa Public Schools to make curricular materials on the massacre widely available to educators. The Centennial Commission continues to push for curriculum enhancement. Progress is being made.

Despite these advances, the need for curriculum reform remains urgent. The massacre appears on a list of the State's Priority Academic Student Skills (PASS) topics about which students *should* know something. But these measures are aspirational, with no effective means for evaluation. The inclusion of massacre history in textbooks remains scattershot and shallow. Moreover, textbook inclusion alone does not guarantee the teaching of that material. Infusing massacre history, systematically, in the core curriculum so that Oklahoma students will, not *may*, be exposed to it is a necessary step forward.

Taking Responsibility

A thoughtful, vigorous, and productive dialogue on reparations requires an understanding of the promise, possibilities, and parameters of these ameliorative measures. Most Tulsans agree that reparations are essential if we are to triumph over our tragic past. Indeed, we have begun making amends. Striking the appropriate balance—creating the right mix of measures that will help us heal our history—remains a challenge. So, too, does following through on our good intentions.

When considering reparations, we are left with a question of morality and justice: As a civilized society, what actions must we take to salve the wounds of our own making? We accept the benefits that accrue across generations. We must likewise accept the burdens. If amends are to be made, if injustices are to be remedied, if wrongs are to be righted, the ultimate responsibility rests upon each of our shoulders.

That responsibility, though more widely acknowledged than ever, maintains its perch on our collective shoulders.

Appendix C
1921 Tulsa Race Massacre Centennial Commission
An Overview

The 1921 Tulsa Race Massacre Centennial Commission will leverage the rich history surrounding the massacre by facilitating actions, activities, and events that commemorate and educate all citizens. The Centennial Commission, an Oklahoma State Senate-created body, has begun the work of commemorating the anniversary of the massacre, with an emphasis on recapturing the entrepreneurial spirit of the famed "Black Wall Street," Tulsa's African American cultural and economic hub. Obliterated in the massacre, Black Wall Street rose from the ashes in a display of resilience and self-sufficiency rarely rivaled.

The Centennial Commission is organized into five standing committees: Arts & Culture, Economic Development, Education, Reconciliation, and Tourism. A Steering Committee oversees the work of these groups.

The Tulsa Community Foundation acts as the Centennial Commission's fiscal agent. As such, contributions to the Centennial Commission are tax-deductible.

The Centennial Commission will both sponsor its own initiatives and sanction community projects consistent with its mission. Its vision includes a star-studded, nationally prominent series of culminating activities and events leading up to the 100th anniversary of the massacre, May 31 - June 1, 2021.

The Centennial Commission sees the fast-approaching centenary as yet another opportunity to turn tragedy into triumph—a chance to show the world how far Tulsa has come since those dark days in 1921. We own our history; it cannot be changed. Our opportunity lies in using our agency to use that history as a call to moral arms; as a springboard for collective engagement focused on a strong, safe, prosperous community for all of us.

Centennial Commission Key Points

- In October 2015, Oklahoma Senator Kevin Matthews led an effort to create a state commission to leverage the upcoming centennial of the 1921 Tulsa Race Massacre.

- The 1921 Tulsa Race Massacre Centennial Commission works to educate Oklahomans and others about the 1921 Tulsa Race Massacre and its impact on the city, state and nation, and to do so in an experiential, sustainable way that builds community cohesion.

- The Centennial Commission's work extends beyond the massacre to education and social justice now and for the foreseeable future.

- The Centennial Commission's sub-committees include: Arts and Culture, Education, Tourism, Reconciliation, Marketing and Public Relations, and Economic Development.

- The Centennial Commission invited three Greenwood District organizations to join in its work: the Greenwood Cultural Center, John Hope Franklin Center for Reconciliation, and the Greenwood Chamber of Commerce.

- Functionally, the Centennial Commission's principal decision-making body is its Steering Committee, a group composed of sub-committee heads, members from the Greenwood District organizations, donors, City of Tulsa representatives and Tulsa Regional Chamber representatives.

- The Centennial Commission seeks to make Tulsa's Historic Greenwood District a sought-after tourist destination and a vibrant center of commerce that fosters sustainable entrepreneurship.

- The Centennial Commission's main projects include capital improvements to the Greenwood Cultural Center and the creation of a world-class, museum-quality center dedicated to the Greenwood District narrative.

• The Greenwood Cultural Center and John Hope Franklin Center for Reconciliation signed a collaboration agreement. A leadership committee composed of board members and executive directors from these two nonprofits, as well as two Commission members, met regularly to execute capital plans and provide the necessary leadership for Greenwood District enhancements envisioned by the Centennial Commission.

• Centennial Commemoration activities in 2021 will take place over the 100 days immediately preceding the 100th anniversary on May 31, 2021.

• The community's input and participation will be vital in planning 100 experiences, including such diverse offerings as documentary screenings, speakers and book readings.

• The Centennial Commission's capital campaign began with a target of $16 million. It has since been increased to $30 million.

• The Centennial Commission will receive $5.3 million from a City of Tulsa bond package and $1.5 million from the State of Oklahoma.

• The Centennial Commission and the City of Tulsa applied for the Bloomberg Art Prize and won. Houston-based artist Rick Lowe serves as the lead artist on the project. Jerica Wortham serves as the Greenwood Arts Project Manager.

HEALING HISTORY

A BLACK WALL STREET CURRICULUM GUIDE
(Recommended for grades 8 – 12+)

Hannibal B. Johnson

If you don't know history, then you don't know anything.
You are a leaf that doesn't know it is part of a tree.
Michael Crichton

HEALING HISTORY

A BLACK WALL STREET CURRICULUM GUIDE

Hannibal B. Johnson

Hannibal B. Johnson's *Black Wall Street: From Riot to Renaissance in Tulsa's Historic Greenwood District* traces the history of Tulsa's African American community, renowned nationally in the early twentieth century for its preeminent African American entrepreneurship. *Black Wall Street* is a testament to the human spirit.

In the spring of 1921, America's worst "race riot" took place in Tulsa, Oklahoma, home to a bustling African American entrepreneurial center known as "Black Wall Street." Alternatively labeled, among other things, a white assault, a massacre, a burning, a genocide, an ethnic cleansing, a holocaust, a pogrom, a calamity, a catastrophe, and a disaster, the event officially known as the 1921 Tulsa Race Riot, but commonly referred to today as the 1921 Tulsa Race Massacre, claimed as many as 300 lives, most of them African American. Property damage, confined to the African American community, exceeded $1.5 million dollars in 1921 currency, some $25 million dollars today.

African American Tulsans overcame, rebuilding their community, the Greenwood District, from its smoldering embers in the face of opposition and obstructionism. By 1942, the area boasted more than 200 black-owned, black-operated business establishments.

All Americans should know this history—the heights of economic activity and the depths of social despair visited upon the

Greenwood District. *Black Wall Street* resurrects this too-long-marginalized narrative.

Black Wall Street exposes and illuminates diversity and inclusion-related themes still relevant today. It provides the basis for fruitful learning opportunities in a variety of contexts and subject matter areas, including history, economics, sociology, journalism, civics, human relations, and music.

This Curriculum Guide distills the core lessons of *Black Wall Street*. It offers tools and approaches that bring this history to life in the twenty-first century.

"We cannot blaze the trails to our future unless
we first retrace the footsteps of our past."

Hannibal B. Johnson

1921 Tulsa Race Massacre Survivor Stories

In Their Own Words

Clarence Bruner
(born July 28, 1904)

*When the riot broke out, I was a teenager working as a bellhop at
the Mills Hotel in downtown Tulsa. We made good money. Tulsa
was a booming oil town and people were always coming to Tulsa.
Hotels, restaurants, entertainment places, taxis, shoe shine parlors, department stores, banks, churches (so many on Boulder Avenue that it was called Cathedral Row) - all profited in the booming oil town. And then came the riot!*

DeLois Vaden Ramsey
(born March 5, 1919)

*My father, Hosea Oscar Vaden, owned one of the most popular
pool halls in Tulsa at the time of the Tulsa riot. Vaden's Pool Hall
was located on Greenwood Avenue next to Art's Chili Parlor.
Across the street was another popular pool hall, Spann's Pool*

Hall. *Younger people went to Spann's and older people came to dad's pool hall. Famous people were always coming to play pool at Vaden's Pool Hall. Boxer Joe Louis always came by my dad's pool hall to buy newspapers. Dad sold 'Black Dispatch' newspapers and also white Tulsa newspapers. My parents also owned a home on Elgin Street, which burned to the ground in the riot. I was too young to personally remember details of the riot, but I heard my parents talk about the riot - how bad it was, how it destroyed so much property that blacks had worked so hard to acquire.*

Kinney I. Booker

(born March 21, 1913)

At the time of the Tulsa Race Riot of 1921, my parents and the five of us children lived at 320 North Hartford Avenue. We had a lovely home, filled with beautiful furniture, including a grand piano. All our clothes and personal belongings - just everything - were burned up during the riot. Early on the morning of June 1, 1921, my parents were awakened by the sounds of shooting and the smell of fire, and the noise of fleeing blacks running past our house. My dad awakened us children and sent us to the attic with our mother. We could hear what was going on below. We heard the white men ordering dad to come with them; he was being taken to detention. We could hear dad pleading with the mobsters. He was begging them, 'Please don't set my house on fire.' But, of course, that is exactly what they did just before they left with dad. Though dad went outside the house with the mobsters, he slipped away from them when they got preoccupied splashing gasoline or kerosene on the outside of the house to speed up the burning. He rushed to the attic and rescued us. We slipped into the crowd of fleeing black refugees. Thank God we did not burn up in that attic!

The foregoing passages are excerpts from interviews by educator and author Eddie Faye Gates, member of the Oklahoma Commission to Study the Tulsa Race Riot of 1921. These reflections are part of a photographic survivor exhibit housed at the Greenwood Cultural Center and funded by the Maxine and Jack Zarrow Foundation.

Healing History
A *Black Wall Street* Curriculum Guide
Hannibal B. Johnson

Including Chapter-By Chapter Highlights From . . .

Ground Rules

Ground rules form the foundation upon which constructive dialogue about *Black Wall Street* may be built. These are particularly important when discussing race, racism, and racial violence, all key elements of the *Black Wall Street* saga.

Four agreements for courageous conversations will encourage forthright, robust dialogue. These four agreements will serve as our ground rules.

1. **Stay engaged:** Listen actively; share generously; and think critically.

2. **Speak your truth:** Own your experiences, observations, and perceptions; let others own theirs. Use "I" messages. Your truth is the only truth to which you can authoritatively speak.

3. **Expect discomfort:** You may not always feel comfortable, but you should always feel safe. Temporary discomfort borne of inconvenient truths and a painful past is a necessary stepping stone to progress.

4. **Expect and accept non-closure:** Our work, like the difficult issues around which we will dialogue, is ongoing. We will not solve all the world's problems, but we will acknowledge, articulate, and attack some of them.

Individuals evaluate difficult subject matter in four primary ways: emotionally (heart), intellectually (mind), morally (soul), and socially (hands and feet). Most people lean toward one of these four principal processing filters. Self-awareness is important. Ask: "How do I process information?" "Am I cognizant of others' processing modes—the fact that others may process things differently?"

Adapted from: Glenn E. Singleton and Curtis Linton, *Courageous Conversations About Race: A Field Guide for Achieving Equity in Schools* (Thousand Oaks, CA: Sage Publications, Inc., 2005)

Cardinal Conversations

The *Black Wall Street* story, from triumph to tragedy and back again, reveals much about Tulsa's African American community. It is in many ways emblematic of American racial dynamics.

The following four questions will stimulate cardinal conversations about *Black Wall Street*. These exchanges will tie things together and help students understand the power of our past and the peril of ignoring it.

1. What happened?

2. Why did it happen?

3. How does what happened affect us today?

4. Given what happened, what is our role in reclaiming the past as we shape our present and future?

Learning Objectives

- Understanding local history of national and international significance through the prism of *Black Wall Street*.

- Appreciating lessons in leadership, diversity, equity, and inclusion, and community demonstrated in the historical setting of *Black Wall Street*.

- Applying lessons in leadership, diversity, equity, and inclusion, and community derived from *Black Wall Street* on a personal level.

- Using *Black Wall Street* history as a springboard and catalyst for strategic, transformational work in the areas of leadership, diversity and inclusion, and community.

Introduction: About the Human Spirit
Curtis/Oliver Letters

In the immediate wake of the massacre, two friends exchanged letters. A man named Curtis from Detroit initiated the correspondence, writing to his friend, Oliver, in Tulsa.

DEAR OLIVER:

> I am, by our local newspaper, fully advised of the whole terrible tragedy there. Now that they have destroyed your homes, wrecked your schools, and reduced your business places to ashes, and killed your people, I am sure that you will rapidly give up the town and move North. Enclosed, please find draft for $40.00 to purchase your ticket to Detroit. Will be expecting you. CURTIS

DEAR CURTIS:

> How kind of you to volunteer your sympathetic assistance. It is just like you to be helpful to others in times of stress like this.

> True it is, we are facing a terrible situation. It is equally true that they have destroyed our homes; they have wrecked our schools; they have reduced our churches to ashes and they have murdered our people, Curtis, but they have not touched our spirit. And while I speak only for myself, let it be said that I came here and built my fortune with that SPIRIT, I shall reconstruct it here with that SPIRIT, and I expect to live on and die here with it. OLIVER

Chapter One
Roots

One can never consent to creep when one feels an impulse to soar.
Helen Keller

Chapter One: Key Points

- 1830s/1840s—Trail of Tears.

- African Americans among the Five Civilized Tribes.

- The "Exodusters": Black migration to Oklahoma and the proliferation of all-black towns.

- Late 1800s—Boosterism movement (E.P. McCabe, booster extraordanaire).

- Wilhelmenia Guess Howell story—escape from the South.

- Tulsa as "The Magic City" and "The City with a Personality."

- A Tale of Two Cites: Segregation in Tulsa.

- O.W. Gurley opens a business in the Greenwood District in 1906. Mabel B. Little arrives in Tulsa as a teen in 1913.

- E.W. Woods: "The Quintessential Tulsan"; Booker T. Washington High School's first principal; his walk from Memphis to Sapulpa, then on to Tulsa.

- Exemplary entrepreneurs and professionals: Simon Berry (business/entrepreneurship); A.J. Smitherman (editing/publishing); J.B. Stradford (law/entrepreneurship); Dr. A.C. Jackson (medicine); B.C. Franklin (law); and the Williams family (business/entrepreneurship).

Chapter One: Talking Points

- *What do the words "the human spirit" mean to you?*
- *Is "the human spirit" something that can be taught?*
- *What person, living or dead, embodies "the human spirit"?*
- *What were race relations like in the late nineteenth and early twentieth century? To what extent are race relations different*

today?

- *Are there still places in America from which certain groups seek to escape? If so, where and why?*

- *"Black Wall Street" is a reference to the entrepreneurial character of the Greenwood District. What factors made the Greenwood District successful as an entrepreneurial hub? Are those factors present or lacking today?*

- *What was the role of women in the late nineteenth and early twentieth century?*

- *How might life have been different during the early twentieth century if women had played a greater role in civil society?*

- *How is it possible to flourish in an oppressive environment?*

On Your Own: Chapter One Activities

1. Research significant events and people connected with your family's roots from 1900-1921. Compare them with the people and events in the early Greenwood District. Discuss the value of knowing one's personal and community roots.

2. Explore Oklahoma's all-black towns, past and present. Consider, at a minimum, the reasons for their formation, definitional criteria, and the existential challenges they have faced through the years. How are these towns like the Greenwood District?

3. Test your knowledge of Oklahoma's all-black towns by taking a quick quiz. Match the numbered items on the left with the appropriate lettered items on the right.

4. Examine Oklahoma demographics, particularly those based on race/ethnicity, from the massacre era. Compare your findings with current demographics. Consider how demographics may influence social tensions and factors that may lessen the likelihood of discord and/or violence.

5. Segregation made a community like the Greenwood District—Black Wall Street—not only possible, but neces-

1. Dr. Ernest Holloway	a. Movement in Clearview (1914) to repatriate African Americans
2. "Chief Sam"	b. Coach of the "Great Debaters"; Langston University professor
3. Pretty Boy Floyd Gang	c. Adopted Boley in the 1970s
4. "Back to Africa"	d. Adopted Taft in the 1970s
5. Redd Foxx	e. One possible meaning of the name of an Oklahoma all-black town
6. Rodeo	f. First black-owned bank in the United States
7. James Lilley Correction Center	g. Founder of successful Boley business
8. John Mercer Langston	h. Movie made in Boley *circa* 1920
9. Ada Lois Sipuel Fisher	i. Event in Boley that draws thousands on Memorial Day weekend
10. Smokaroma	j. Farthest west of America's HBCUs
11. Farmers & Merchants Bank	k. Langston graduate who integrated OU Law School
12. "I excel"	l. IXL
13. Booker T. Washington	m. The most well-known all-black town
14. Langston University	n. Facility housing more than half of the population of one all-black town
15. *The Crimson Skull*	o. Congressman and diplomat
16. Boley	p. Prominent early 20th century visitor to Boley who praised the town
17. Flip Wilson	q. Long-serving Langston University president
18. Maurice Lee	r. Robbed Farmers & Merchants Bank in 1932
19. Melvin Beaunorus Tolson	s. Led a "Back to Africa" movement in Clearview
20. Year of incorporation: 2000	t. International enterprise located in Boley

KEY: 1. (q.); 2. (s.); 3. (r.); 4. (a.); 5. (d.); 6. (i.); 7. (n.); 8. (o.); 9. (k.); 10. (t.); 11. (f.); 12. (e.); 13. (p.); 14. (j.); 15. (h.); 16. (m.); 17. (c.); 18. (g.); 19. (b.); 20. (l.)

Ottowa ("O.W.") Gurley
Black Wall Street Founding Father[472]

Yours Fraternally,
Dr. A. C. Jackson,
Consulting Physician & Surgeon
Chronic diseases and diseases of Women a Specialty.
Calls made in the country.   Phone 2573   In office at Night:
Corner Greenwood and Archer   Tulsa, Okla.

Dr. A.C. Jackson
Preeminent Physician & Surgeon

Chapter Two
"Riot"

He conquers who endures.

Persius

Chapter One: Key Points

- James Weldon Johnson of the NAACP dubbed 1919 "Red Summer." More than twenty-five "race riots" dotted the American landscape.

- Massacre contributory factors—racism, jealosy, land lust, the KKK, *The Tulsa Tribune.*

- Trigger event: Elevator incident involving teenagers Dick Rowland and Sarah Page.

- Foundational causes: Systemic oppression; land lust; and media propaganda.

- *The Tulsa Tribune* editorial reportedly entitled "To Lynch a Negro Tonight" remains missing.

- Massacre Accounts: LaVerne Cooksey Davis and Alice Andrews.

- Fate of Dr. Arthur Jackson, nationally-renowned surgeon.

- Martial law declared in Tulsa.

- Internment of Tulsa's African Americans (recall the later, United States Supreme Court-sanctioned internment of Americans of Japanese ancestry during World War II); green cards co-signed by employers required to exit camps.

- 100-300 dead, hundreds wounded, over $1.5 million in property loss (in 1921 dollars, conservatively estimated); the worst "race riot" in American history.

- Role of shame in the white community.

Chapter Two: Talking Points

- *What role did "mob psychology" (i.e., group influences) play in the* massacre?

- *Does "mob psychology" still impact the way some people deal with diversity and inclusion issues such as discrimination and hate crimes?*

- *To what extent is "race riot" a misnomer? What would be a more accurate descriptor? Who names historical events, including historical traumas?*

- *Some eyewitnesses reported seeing planes bomb the Greenwood District as the violence raged. Assuming this to be true, what is the significance of the act of citizens bombing other citizens? Are there other occasions on which such a domestic bombing has occurred? If so, identify the occasion(s) and explain the circumstances.*

- *One editorial in The Tulsa Tribune, reportedly an incitement to riot, remains missing. What factors might explain the mysterious disappearance of this piece of history?*

- *Authorities interned African Americans during the massacre, ostensibly for their own protection. What is the significance of this extraordinary measure, internment, and on what other occasions in modern history has it been used?*

- *What was the role of the Ku Klux Klan nationally and in the Riot?*

- *How influential are hate groups today?*

- *How do we counteract the messages and actions of hate groups?*

- *Could the massacre have been avoided and how might we prevent something like the massacre from happening again?*

- *Of what value is talking about tragedies?*

- *Discuss the phenomenon of historical trauma and its consequences/legacy.*

- *What can we learn from the past?*

On Your Own: Chapter Two Activities

1. Research significant racial conflicts and race-based violence in the United States (1915-1925). Examples of relevant research avenues include lynchings, the activities of the Ku Klux Klan, "sundown towns," and the many "race riots" that occurred during that era. Consider how racial conflict and race-based violence affected communities then and how such conduct affects communities now.

2. Examine the role of the media in the instances of racial hostility and violence referenced above. Choose one compelling example to synopsize and share with classmates/colleagues.

3. Consider how the criminal justice system and other organs of government responded to the racial violence in Tulsa. How might these governmental entities respond to such a crisis today?

4. List five things you can do to improve race relations and intercultural understanding in your community. For each item listed, note a timeline and the resources/assistance you will need to be successful.

5. The massacre was a moral failing of monumental proportion. Take some time to reflect on you own "moral compass." List the principles and values you look to for guidance as you face life's moral challenges and ethical dilemmas. Next to each principle or value, list its source.

6. Textual and video first person accounts of the early Greenwood District and the massacre exist. Review some of these survivor stories, and then consider the following questions:

   • What emotions did you detect in these survivor accounts?

   • How did you feel listening to or reading these survivor accounts?

   • Based on the survivor accounts you examined, what

do the survivors want (*i.e.*, what they would like to do or have done on their behalf because of their status as survivors)? Please explain.

- Do the survivor stories you reviewed have anything in common with the survivor stories associated with other crimes against humanity (*e.g.*, Holocaust survivors, victims of South African apartheid, those who escaped Rwandan genocide)? Please explain.

- Are human tragedies on the scale of the massacre preventable? If so, how and by whom?

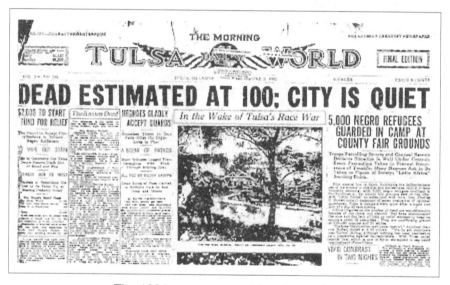

The 1921 massacre and its aftermath.

Chapter Three
Regeneration

Keep your face to the sunshine and you cannot see the shadow.
Helen Keller

Chapter Three: Key Points

- Mount Zion Baptist Church story.

- Greenwood District resilience.

- First Baptist Church of North Tulsa spared because it was mistaken for a white church.

- City's efforts to impede rebuilding—attempts to amend the fire code and rezoned parts of the burned area.

- Business and railroad "land lust;" efforts to seize the Greenwood District for commercial purposes.

- Role of B.C. Franklin in challenging Greenwood District removal and remaking by City, business, and railroad interests.

- A post-massacre editorial in *The Tulsa Tribune* on the prospect of rebuilding the decimated Greenwood District: "It Must Not Be Again."

- The Greenwood District rises from the ashes, peaking circa 1942 with more than 200 black-owned, black-operated businesses.

- Ms. Mabel B. Little, Greenwood District original, speaks to the rebuilding in her book *Fire on Mount Zion: My Life and History as a Black Woman in America*.

- Life went on in Tulsa post-massacre—Nancy Feldman stories (Bar Association and Philbrook Museum); life's little indignities.

- The Greenwood District deteriorated beginning in the 1960s—prominent factors included: integration, urban renewal, changing economic conditions, and the aging of the architects of its success.

Chapter Three: Talking Points

- *White Tulsa leadership erected numerous obstacles to the rebuilding of the Greenwood District after the massacre. Nonetheless, African Americans pressed on. Why might people stay put even in the face of extreme hostility from their own community?*

- *What barriers impeded the rebuilding of the Greenwood District in the wake of the massacre?*

- *Residents of the Greenwood District who endured the massacre and remained committed to their community are said to have been resilient. What is resilience? How do we prepare to be resilient?*

- *How might historical trauma be addressed in positive, affirming ways?*

- *What was (and is) the role of religion in terms of fostering diversity, equity, and inclusion?*

- *What was (and is) the role of government in terms of fostering diversity, equity, and inclusion?*

- *What was (and is) the role of the media in terms of diversity, eauity, and inclusion?*

- *How did segregation help and/or hinder diversity, equity, and inclusion efforts?*

- *We often speak of mentoring in an educational and business context. Should we mentor others in diversity, equity and inclusion, too?*

- *What institutional barriers to diversity, equity, and inclusion remain today?*

On Your Own: A Chapter Three Activity

1. You are an eyewitness to history. The date is June 2, 1921. The place is Tulsa, Oklahoma. You have just witnessed the massacre. Magically, a protective bubble enveloped you during this period. You emerged unscathed. Based upon what you have learned about that catastrophic

event, and from your vantage point as an eyewitness:

- What did you see on the night of May 31 and the morning of June 1, 1921?
- What do you see now?
- How do you feel?
- What did you learn about humanity?
- What will you do on June 2?

2. Research the rebuilding of communities following major catastrophes. Compare those rebuilding efforts with the reconstruction of the Greenwood District. Examples might include the rebuilding of Europe after World War II pursuant to the Marshall Plan or the clean-up and rebuilding of an American city in the aftermath of a natural disaster (*e.g.*, post-Hurricane Katrina [2005] New Orleans). Consider the factors that may be at work in terms of how a community responds to and begins to heal from trauma and tragedy.

3. In 1925, just four years after the devastation of the massacre, the National Negro Business League ("NNBL"), Booker T. Washington's "Black Chamber of Commerce," held its annual conference in Tulsa. How significant was this? What message(s) might the NNBL have been trying to convey about resilience and regeneration by its presence in Tulsa?

4. Research the phenomenon of "historical trauma." Cite some examples of events that triggered historical trauma. What coping mechanisms/cures have been proposed and by whom?

5. Think of three situations in which resilience was key; where you had to persevere to reach your goal(s). List them, together with the resources and support that enabled you to be successful.

6. Critically analyze the case for massacre reparations. Consider the following questions:

- What does it mean to make "reparations"?
- List some examples of reparations, domestically or internationally.
- What is the most compelling argument in favor of reparations for the massacre?
- What is the most compelling argument against reparations for the massacre?
- Assume you have been authorized to provide reparations for the massacre. You have been given carte blanche—you have no constraints in terms of scope or budget. Devise a plan for making some type of reparations. Consider all the pertinent questions, among them:

  ◊ *Who would pay for the reparations?*

  ◊ *Who would receive the reparations?*

  ◊ *What would be the logistical hurdles to making reparations?*

  ◊ *What would be the timeline for making reparations?*

  ◊ *What would be the political consequences of making reparations?*

  ◊ *What would be the economic consequences of making reparations?*

  ◊ *What would be the social consequences of making reparations?*

  ◊ *How would the making of reparations impact the way people view the historical event that spawned them (i.e., the massacre)?*

7. On June 13, 2005, the United States Senate passed Resolution 39 apologizing for its failure to enact federal anti-lynching legislation first proposed by an African American congressman one-hundred-and-five years prior. This marked the first time the Senate apologized for the nation's treatment of African Americans. The apology expressed regrets to the nearly five-thousand documented lynching victims (1880 - 1960) as well as survivors and their descendants, several of whom watched from the gallery.

These ghastly spectacles happened without the benefit of trials, principally in the South, and often with the complicity of local officials. Mob lynchings became picture-taking, public spectacles.

Read Senate Resolution 39 in its entirety, and then respond to the following questions:

- Is Senate Resolution 39 a form of reparations for lynchings in America?

- What is the effect of such a formal, legislative apology?

- Should such an apology be forthcoming for the Riot from lawmakers at the local, state, and/or federal levels?

- What is the most convincing argument in favor of such an apology for the massacre?

- What is the most compelling argument against such an apology?

Source: S. Res. 39 (109th Congress, 1st Session); Avis Thomas-Lester, "A Senate Apology for History on Lynching," *Washington Post*, June 14, 2005; "Senate Apologizes for Inaction on Lynching," http://www.nbcnews.com/id/8206697/ns/us_news-life/t/senate-apologizes-inaction-lynchings/#.WUwCRVTyu70, June 13, 2005 (last visited June 22, 2017).

8. Count your blessings—literally. List some of the many things for which you can be thankful. List any obstacles you overcame (and how you managed to overcome them) to get to where you are today.

A post-massacre view of the Greenwood District, *circa* 1930s, looking north on Greenwood Avenue from Archer Street.

Post-massacre scenes on Greenwood Avenue, *circa* 1950s.

Chapter Four
Renaissance

'Impossible' is a word found only in the dictionary of fools.
Napoleon

Chapter Four: Key Points

- Breaching the "conspiracy of silence" surrounding the massacre.

- Reversing decline in the Greenwood District.

- The vision of Oklahoma State Senator Maxine Horner and Oklahoma State Representative Don Ross.

- The Renaissance begins with Greenwood Cultural Center in 1983.

- The Greenwood District: Who is in the neighborhood?

- Renewed interested in history and culture of the area; cultural tourism.

- Collaborative spirit among governmental, community, and private business interest across racial lines.

- Current plans for redevelopment by a consortium of public/private interests.

- The presence of educational institutions (*e.g.*, OSU-Tulsa and Langston-Tulsa) and entertainment venues (*e.g.*, ONEOK Field) in the Greenwood District.

- Significance of the revitalization of the Greenwood District for the greater Tulsa community.

Chapter Four: Talking Points

- *What is diversity? What is equity? What is inclusion?*

- *Would things have been different in 1921 if there had been an understanding of diversity and inclusion?*

- *Define "forgiveness." Is it possible to forgive the perpetrators, direct and indirect, of the massacre? If so, on what terms would such forgiveness take place?*

- *Define "reparations." To what extent have reparations been made for the massacre? What, if any, additional reparations are needed?*

- *We often speak of the need for reconciliation. What would a reconciled Tulsa look like?*

- *Is race still the main issue when it comes to diversity, equity, and inclusion? Why or why not?*

- *What diversity, equity, and inclusion factors other than race have come to the forefront since 1921?*

- *How can we work to bring diverse people together—to be totally inclusive?*

- *Who is responsible for promoting diversity, equity, and inclusion?*

- *Is it possible to recreate Black Wall Street, a black entrepreneurial mecca, in a place like Tulsa today?*

On Your Own: Chapter Four Activities

1. Create a timeline using a long sheet of butcher's paper and colored markers. Draw a long, horizontal line on the paper using a black marker. Once again, using a black marker, draw vertical hatch marks to indicate the year, beginning with 1900 and ending in the current year. Above the horizontal black line, note significant events in American history with a different color marker, placed near the appropriate year. Below the horizontal black line, note significant events in Greenwood District history using yet another color marker. Once again, place these events near the appropriate dates. (You may use another format if this is not workable.) Once completed, use the timeline to emphasize that history occurs in a context, not in a vacuum. Discuss how what happened in Tulsa is interconnected with other people, places, and events in America and beyond.

2. Arguably, too many social, economic, and political dynamics have changed in Tulsa for one to realistically envision a rebirth of the famed Black Wall Street. If that is true, what might the Greenwood District—Black Wall

Street--aspire to be in the modern era?

3. Cultural tourism, sometimes called heritage tourism, remains strong in America. What might the Greenwood District do to make the community more accessible and appealing to those who would use their leisure time to explore history and culture?

4. Define the word "reparations." What, if any, reparations have been made with respect to the massacre? What form(s) of reparations might lead the Tulsa community to reconciliation? What are the possible challenges to efforts in behalf of reparations?

5. Renaissance is not possible without hope. Consider the social movements inspired by leaders like Mohandas ("Mahatma") Gandhi (India), Dr. Martin Luther King, Jr. (United States), and Nelson Mandela (South Africa). What role did hope play in their personal lives and in the social movements they led?

6. The namesake for Tulsa's John Hope Franklin Reconciliation Park, Dr. John Hope Franklin, reached the pinnacle of academic success as a historian. Test your knowledge of some of the seminal moments in Dr. Franklin's life with the following quiz.

Dr. John Hope Franklin
Know the History; Know the Historian

1. On March 25, 2009, America lost a trailblazing historian and scholar in the person of Dr. John Hope Franklin. At the time of his death, Dr. Franklin, a noted academician, was the John B. Duke Professor Emeritus of History at _____ University.

2. Born in 1915, Dr. Franklin spent his early years in the all-black town of _____, Oklahoma.

3. His family moved to Tulsa in 1925, just a few years after the massacre. They joined John Hope's father, _____ _____, a Tulsa lawyer who assisted many massacre victims with their legal claims.

4. John Hope Franklin graduated valedictorian of his 1931 Tulsa Booker T. Washington High School class. He and Tulsa Central High School valedictorian, _____, were honored at Tulsa's posh Mayo Hotel. Both men went on to become nationally renowned scholars and historians.

5. John Hope Franklin completed his undergraduate work at historically-black _____ University.

6. He earned his Ph.D. in History from _____ University. He received more than 100 honorary degrees during his lifetime.

7. Dr. Franklin's 1947 book, _____, became the seminal resource on African American history for generations of Americans. It has sold 3.5 million copies.

8. A lifelong advocate of positive race relations, Dr. Franklin marched with Nobel Laureate _____ from Selma to Montgomery, Alabama, during the Civil Rights Movement.

9. In the late 1990s, Dr. Franklin chaired President

_____'s One America in the 21st Century: Forging a New Future—The President's Initiative on Race.

10. In his final book, an autobiography entitled _____, Dr. Franklin recounted his life story with remarkable equanimity—without rancor or bitterness. Befitting his middle name, hope sprang eternal.

KEY: 1. Duke; 2. Rentiesville; 3. Buck Colbert Franklin; 4. Daniel J. Boorstin; 5. Fisk; 6. Harvard; 7. From Slavery to Freedom; 8. Dr. Martin Luther King, Jr.; 9. Bill Clinton; 10. Mirror to America.

John Hope Franklin Reconciliation Park in Tulsa, Oklahoma.

A Final Examination

The Superintendent of Tulsa Public Schools ("TPS"), with the unanimous support of the Tulsa School Board, has decided to implement a new Tulsa history course next year. This non-elective course will be required in grade eleven in all TPS schools. The TPS Superintendent has solicited your advice on the nature and extent of the course's treatment of the massacre and, by implication, the pre- and post-massacre Greenwood District (*e.g.*, Black Wall Street entrepreneurship; community resilience).

Specifically, you have been asked for your insights on the following questions:

1. When students ask our teachers about the reasons behind revisiting such an "unfortunate" period in Tulsa history, how might they respond?

2. What is the core message we want our students to take away from their study of the massacre?

3. What connections might we make between the factors that contributed to the massacre and the social, psychological, political, and economic conditions that prevail in modern Tulsa?

4. We want to teach our children coping skills. What lessons about forgiveness, reconciliation, and/or healing might we derive from this history?

5. How might we encourage a sense of hope while teaching, honestly, about the massacre and the pre- and post-massacre Greenwood District in Tulsa?

Please be thoughtful and concise. Your wisdom will help mold the leadership of the future.

Black Wall Street

Exploring Leadership, Diversity and Inclusion, and Community

The iconic Williams Dreamland Theatre, owned by John and Loula Williams, in the heart of early Black Wall Street (original location, 129 - 133 North Greenwood Avenue).

The following guide is intended for a two-hour, stand-alone workshop that explores leadership, diversity and inclusion, and community through the lens of Black Wall Street.

Two-Hour Black Wall Street Workshop Agenda

I. Welcome & Overview (20 minutes)

- An Introduction to *Black Wall Street**
- Short video footage (optional; several such videos are available via YouTube)

II. Reading: *The Ghosts of Greenwood Past* (10 minutes)

III. Lessons in Leadership, Diversity/Inclusion, and Community; Developing a Personal Leadership Action Plan (30 minutes)

IV. Roundtable (60 minutes)

- *Is it possible to heal from a tragic historical wound like the massacre and, if so, what would a healed community look like?*

- *Identify the forces in the Tulsa community (or in your community) that are constructive and destructive in terms of building positive race relations, and then discuss how to neutralize the destructive forces and leverage the constructive forces.*

- *What is your personal responsibility for initiating and moving forward conversation about race relations in Tulsa (or in your community)?*

* The introduction to *Black Wall Street* might include: (1) excerpts from Walter White's article that appeared in *Nation* magazine just after the massacre; and (2) a recitation of the key findings of the Oklahoma Commission to Study the Tulsa Race Riot of 1921 ("Commission"). Both pieces appear below.

'The Eruption of Tulsa:' An NAACP Official Investigates the Tulsa Race Riot of 1921

The years following World War I in the United States saw devastating race riots around the nation: in small cities like Elaine, Arkansas, and Knoxville, Tennessee as well as in larger ones such as Chicago, where a four-day riot in 1919 left two dozen African Americans dead and more than 300 injured. But the Tulsa race riot was perhaps the worst. In fact, white Tulsans' 24-hour rampage was one of the most vicious and intense race riots in American history before or since, resulting in the death of anywhere from 75 to 250 people and the burning of more than 1,000 black homes and businesses. Walter White, an official of the NAACP, traveled to Tulsa in disguise to survey the damage caused by the 1921 race riot. His report, one of many articles on the riot, was published in the *Nation* in the summer of 1921.

A hysterical white girl related that a nineteen-year-old colored boy attempted to assault her in the public elevator of a public office building of a thriving town of 100,000 in open daylight. Without pausing to find whether or not the story was true, without bothering with the slight detail of investigating the character of the woman who made the outcry (as a matter of fact, she was of exceedingly doubtful reputation), a mob of 100-per-cent Americans set forth on a wild rampage that cost the lives of fifty white men; of between 150 and 200 colored men, women and children; the destruction by fire of $1,500,000 worth of property; the looting of many homes; and ever-lasting damage to the reputation of the city of Tulsa and the State of Oklahoma.

This, in brief, is the story of the eruption of Tulsa on the night of May 31 and the morning of June 1. One could travel far and find few cities where the likelihood of trouble between the races was as little thought of as in Tulsa. Her reign of terror stands as a grim reminder of the grip mob violence has on the throat of America, and the ever-present possibility of devastating race conflicts where least expected.

Tulsa is a thriving, bustling, enormously wealthy town of between 90,000 and 100,000. In 1910 it was the home of 18,182 souls, a dead and hopeless outlook ahead. Then oil was discovered. The town grew amazingly. On December 29, 1920, it had bank deposits totaling $65,449,985.90; almost $1,000 per capita when compared with the Federal Census figures of 1920, which gave Tulsa 72,076. The town lies in the center of the oil region and many are the stories told of the making of fabulous fortunes by men who were operating on a shoe-string. Some of the stories rival those of the 'forty-niners' in California. The town has a number of modern office buildings, many beautiful homes, miles of clean, well-paved streets, and aggressive and progressive business men who well exemplify Tulsa's motto of 'The City with a Personality.'

So much for the setting. What are the causes of the race riot that occurred in such a place? First, the Negro in Oklahoma has shared in the sudden prosperity that has come to many of his white brothers, and there are some colored men there who are wealthy. This fact has caused a bitter resentment on the part of the lower order of whites, who feel that these colored men, members of an 'inferior race,' are exceedingly presumptuous in achieving greater economic prosperity than they who are members of a divinely ordered superior race. There are at least three colored persons in Oklahoma who are worth a million dollars each; J.W. Thompson of Clearview is worth $500,000; there are a number of men and women worth $100,000; and many whose possessions are valued at $25,000 and $50,000 each. This was particularly true of Tulsa, where there were two colored men worth $150,000 each; two worth $100,000; three $50,000; and four who were assessed at $25,000. In one case where a colored man owned and operated a printing plant with $25,000 worth of printing machinery in it, the leader of the mob that set fire to and destroyed the plant was a linotype operator employed for years by the colored owner at $48 per week. The white man was killed while attacking the plant. Oklahoma is largely populated by pioneers from other States. Some of the white pioneers are former residents of Mississippi, Georgia, Tennessee, Texas, and other States more typically southern than Oklahoma. These have brought with them their anti-Negro prejudices. Lethargic and unprogressive by nature, it sorely irks them to see Negroes making greater progress than they themselves are achieving.

Source: Walter White, "The Eruption of Tulsa," *Nation* 112 (June 29, 1921): 909–910.

Key Fact-Finding: The Oklahoma Commission to Study the Tulsa Race Riot of 1921

The Oklahoma Legislature formed the Riot Commission in 1997. The Riot Commission's February 28, 2001, final report chronicled the facts, including:

- *Black Tulsans had every reason to believe that Dick Rowland would be lynched after his arrest on charges later dismissed and highly suspect from the start.*
- *They had cause to believe that his personal safety, like the defense of themselves and their community, depended on them*

alone.

- *As hostile groups gathered and their confrontation worsened, municipal and county authorities failed to take actions to calm or contain the situation.*

- *At the eruption of violence, civil officials selected many men, all of them white and some of them participants in that violence, and made those men their agents as deputies.*

- *In that capacity, deputies did not stem the violence but added to it, often through overt acts themselves illegal.*

- *Public officials provided firearms and ammunition to individuals, again all of them white.*

- *Units of the Oklahoma National Guard participated in the mass arrests of all or nearly all of Greenwood's residents, removed them to other parts of the city, and detained them in holding centers.*

- *Entering the Greenwood [D]istrict, people stole, damaged or destroyed personal property left behind in homes and businesses.*

- *People, some of them agents of government, also deliberately burned or otherwise destroyed homes credibly estimated to have numbered 1,256,[473] along with virtually every other structure—including churches, schools, businesses, even a hospital and library—in the Greenwood district.*

- *Despite duties to preserve order and to protect property, no government at any level offered adequate resistance, if any at all, to what amounted to the destruction of the neighborhood referred to commonly as "Little Africa" and politely as the "Negro quarter."*

- *Although the exact total can never be determined, credible evidence makes it probable that many people, likely numbering between one and three hundred, were killed during the riot.*

- *Not one of these criminal acts was then or ever has been prosecuted or punished by government at any level, municipal, county, state, or national.*

- *Even after the restoration of order, it was official policy to release a black detainee only upon the application of a white person,*

and then only if that white agreed to accept responsibility for
that detainee's subsequent behavior.

- As private citizens, many whites in Tulsa and neighboring
  communities did extend invaluable assistance to the riot's
  victims, and the relief efforts of the American Red Cross, in
  particular, provided a model of human behavior at its best.

- Although city and county government bore much of the cost
  for Red Cross relief, neither contributed substantially to
  Greenwood's rebuilding; in fact, municipal authorities acted
  initially to impede rebuilding.

- In the end, the restoration of Greenwood after its systematic
  destruction was left to the victims of that destruction.

The Ghosts of Greenwood Past
A Walk Down Black Wall Street

Hannibal B. Johnson

African American boosters like E.P. McCabe touted pre-statehood Oklahoma, at the time divided into Indian Territory and Oklahoma Territory, as a virtual "promised land" for African Americans. McCabe dreamed of an all-black state carved out of Oklahoma Territory. He and others in the late 1800s lured Deep South African Americans to Southwestern/Midwestern Beulah Land.

Oklahoma attracted hordes of weary Southerners fleeing the oppression of the Jim Crow South. They went in search of full citizenship, land ownership, and economic opportunity. Though McCabe's "black state" dream never materialized, Oklahoma boasts more than fifty all-black towns throughout its history—more than any other state.

The promise of Oklahoma faded precipitously when she entered the Union in 1907. The newly-minted Oklahoma Legislature passed as its first measure Senate Bill Number 1. That law, a railroad facilities measure, welcomed Jim Crow to Oklahoma, and firmly ensconced segregation as the law of the land.

Meanwhile, a seeming contradiction emerged in Tulsa's African American community. In the early part of the twentieth century, the "Greenwood District" or simply "Greenwood," became a nationally renowned entrepreneurial center because of the proliferation of successful black-owned enterprises there. Legendary African American statesman and educator, Booker T. Washington, reportedly dubbed Greenwood Avenue, the nerve center of the community, "The Negro Wall Street" for its now-famous bustling business climate.

The Greenwood District pioneers deftly parlayed Jim Crow into an economic advantage. They seized the opportunity to create a closed market system that defied Jim Crow's fundamental premise: African American incompetence and inferiority.

Legal segregation forced African American Tulsans to do business with one another. This economic detour—the diversion of dolars away from the white community—allowed the roughly thirty-five-square-block Greenwood District, bounded by Detroit Avenue on the west, the Midland Valley tracks to the east, Pine Street to the north, and Archer Street to the South, to prosper as dollars circulated repeatedly within the community. Greenwood's insular service economy rested on a foundation of necessity. This necessity, in turn, molded a talented cadre of African American businesspersons and entrepreneurs.

Savvy entrepreneurs like Simon Berry developed their businesses around the needs of the community, niche marketing by today's standards. Berry created a nickel-a-ride jitney service with his topless Model-T Ford. He successfully operated a bus line that he ultimately sold to the City of Tulsa. He owned the Royal Hotel. He shuttled wealthy oil barons on a charter airline service he operated with his partner, James Lee Northington, Sr., a successful black building contractor. Simon Berry reportedly earned as much as $500 a day in the early 1920s.

Prominent professionals like Dr. A.C. Jackson transcended, if only temporarily, the color line. Dr. Jackson, christened the most able Negro surgeon in America by the Mayo brothers (of Mayo Clinic fame), treated patients of both races. Dr. Jackson died tragically in the 1921 Tulsa Race Riot (the "Riot"), the worst of the so-called race riots in early twentieth century America. Gunned down by a white teenager while surrendering at his residence, Dr. Jackson, lacking medical attention, bled to death.

Industrious families like the Williams found economic success in multiple ventures, including a theatre, a confectionery, a rooming house, and a garage.

Capable, confident women like Mabel B. Little operated thriving beauty salons and other enterprises. Women likewise added elegance and allure to the fabled thoroughfare. Greenwood Avenue bustled on Thursday, the traditional "maid's day off." African American women, many of whom worked in the homes of affluent whites, took advantage of the day's opportunity to "gussie up" and stroll down Greenwood way.

Brilliant educators like E.W. Woods, principal of the original, 1913 Booker T. Washington High School where he remained for some thirty-five years, gained respect and renown throughout the city. Woods arrived in Oklahoma from Memphis by foot, settling first in Sapulpa, then moving to Tulsa to accept the principal position at Booker T. Washington. Initially answering a call for "Colored" teachers, he eventually became known as "the quintessential Tulsan" for his preeminent leadership in the realm of public education. The Tulsa Convention Hall—the only facility large enough to accommodate the throngs of mourners—hosted Mr. Woods' 1948 funeral.

From movie theatres to professional offices, from grocery stores to schools, from beauty salons to shoeshine shops, Greenwood had it all. The community was so developed and refined that Greenwood Avenue, the heart of the Greenwood District, drew comparisons to such historic thoroughfares as Beale Street in Memphis and State Street in Chicago.

The success of the Greenwood District, given the prevailing racial pecking order, could scarcely be tolerated, let alone embraced, by the larger community.

Over time, fear and jealousy swelled. African American success, including home, business, and land ownership, caused increasing consternation and friction. Black World War I veterans, having tasted true freedom only on foreign soil, came back to America with heightened expectations. Valor and sacrifice in battle earned them the basic respect and human dignity so long denied in America—or so they thought. But America had not yet changed. Oklahoma proved no exception.

The underlying climate of racial oppression for African Americans in the United States prior to and during 1921 and the physical intimidation associated with it seems almost unfathomable today. It was open season on African Americans.

In 1919, more than two dozen major "race riots" erupted in America. In 1921, vigilantes lynched at least fifty-seven African Americans. Despite these atrocities, the American government did little to protect her dark-skinned denizens. Indeed, the United

States Senate three times failed to pass measures making lynching a federal offense.

In Tulsa, a seemingly random encounter between two teen-agers lit the fuse that would set Greenwood alight. The alleged assault on Sarah Page by Dick Rowland triggered unprecedented civil unrest. The interracial incident became the immediate cata-lyst for the massacre. Fueled by sensational reporting by *The Tulsa Tribune*, jealousy over African American economic success, land lust, and a racially hostile climate in general, mob rule held sway.

Authorities arrested the young African American man, Dick Rowland. A white mob threatened to lynch him. African Ameri-can men, determined to protect the teen from the rumored lynch-ing, marched to the courthouse that held young Rowland. Law en-forcement authorities asked them to retreat, assuring Rowland's safety. They left. The lynch talk persisted.

A second group of African American men from the Greenwood District proceeded to the courthouse, where they encountered and exchanged words with a swelling and boisterous group of white men gathered on the lawn. A gun discharged. Soon, throngs of weapon-wielding white men, some of them deputized by local law enforcement, invaded the Greenwood District.

In a span of about sixteen hours, people, property, hopes, and dreams vanished. The Greenwood District burned to the ground. Mobs prevented firefighters from extinguishing the flames. Prop-erty damage ran into the millions. Hundreds of people died. Scores were injured. Many African Americans fled Tulsa, never to return.

Ever courageous, the Greenwood District pioneers rebuilt the community from the ashes. Official Tulsa leadership hindered the rebuilding of Greenwood, blaming black citizens for their own plight, turning away charitable contributions for rebuilding, and creating reconstruction roadblocks. Some individuals and in-stitutions in the greater Tulsa community stepped up, however, providing much needed assistance. For example, Holy Family Cathedral and First Presbyterian Church offered refuge to Afri-can Americans. The American Red Cross, called "Angels of Mer-cy" by many, provided succor—medical care, food, shelter, and clothing—for massacre victims, some of whom lived for months in tents.

The law firm of Spears, Franklin & Chappelle provided legal assistance to riot victims. These African American lawyers lodged claims against the City of Tulsa and insurance companies for damage occasioned by the massacre. Beyond that, they counseled and consoled riot victims and made urgent appeals to African Americans nationwide for assistance. One of these men, B.C. Franklin, the father of famed historian Dr. John Hope Franklin, helped lead the charge.

Mount Zion Baptist Church provides yet another example of the remarkable courage and determination of the people of post-Riot Greenwood. The $85,000 church, only six weeks old when the Riot broke out, had been built with the help of a $50,000 loan from a single individual. Pre-massacre rumors included a fictitious but persistent story that Mount Zion housed a stash of arms for the looming racial conflict. The mob torched Mount Zion during the massacre, leaving nothing but a dirt floor basement.

Church members, still dazed by the devastation of the Riot, made several key decisions. They elected to continue to meet, often in private homes. When presented with the option of extinguishing the $50,000 mortgage through bankruptcy, the church leadership balked. While the legal obligation could perhaps be eliminated, they felt a moral obligation to pay off the loan, even absent the building. Decades later, Mount Zion did just that. The church paid off the loan and raised enough money to build a new structure. Mount Zion remains a vital and vibrant part of Greenwood.

Remarkably, and in stunningly short order, the Greenwood District came alive once again, bigger and better than ever. In 1925, the area hosted the annual conference of the National Negro Business League. By 1942, more than 200 businesses called the Greenwood District home.

The Greenwood story speaks to the triumph of the human spirit. It resonates with the timeless, universal virtues so many of us cherish: faith, determination, integrity, humility, and compassion.

Integration, urban renewal, a new business climate, and the aging of the early Greenwood pioneers caused the community to decline through the years, beginning in the 1960s, and continuing throughout the 1970s and early 1980s. Now, as the area sits poised for a renaissance, the ghosts of the Greenwood District past loom large on the horizon.

Describe one positive aspect of the *Black Wall Street* **story that stood out to you and/or held special significance for you.**

_____

_____

_____

_____

_____

_____

_____

What positive lessons about leadership, diversity and inclusion, and community does the *Black Wall Street* **saga offer?**

Lessons in Leadership

_____

_____

_____

_____

_____

_____

_____

Lessons in Diversity/Inclusion

_____

_____

_____

_____

_____

_____

_____

Lessons in Community

_____

_____

_____

_____

_____

_____

Personal Leadership Action Plan[474]

Introspection, awareness, compassion, and empathy rank among the key elements needed to foster diversity and promote an inclusive community. Transformational change, however, requires a personal commitment to positive action. Transformational change requires leadership.

Mindful of the lessons about leadership, diversity and inclusion, and community you derived from *Black Wall Street* and identified above, consider how you might apply those lessons to improve your community. You may also wish to consult the list of important leadership traits at the end of this document.

Please take a few moments to respond to the following questions:

☐ *What action(s) do I want to take to challenge racism, discrimination, and inequality and/or to promote diversity and inclusion in my community?*

_____

_____

_____

_____

_____

☐ *How will my action(s) impact my community?*

_____

_____

_____

_____

_____

_____

☐ *What resources or materials do I need to achieve my goal(s)?*

_____

_____

_____

_____

_____

☐ *How might I access those resources?*

- -

- -

- -

- -

- -

- -

☐ *What specific behaviors or steps will be involved in securing those resources?*

- -

- -

- -

- -

- -

☐ *What's a realistic timeline for implementing this action plan?*

- -

- -

- -

- -

- -

☐ *What are the risks involved in implementing this action plan?*

_____

_____

_____

_____

_____

_____

_____

☐ *Is the action that I contemplate worth the risk entailed? (If not, go back to the first question or think through what might be done to minimize the perceived risk.)*

_____

_____

_____

_____

_____

_____

☐ *What obstacles might I encounter?*

_____

_____

_____

_____

_____

☐ *What might I do to overcome these obstacles?*

_____

_____

_____

_____

_____

_____

☐ *What are my support systems?*

_____

_____

_____

_____

_____

_____

_____

☐ *Where might I find additional support?*

_____

_____

_____

_____

_____

_____

_____

☐ *How will I measure success? How will I know if my personal leadership action plan has made a difference? (Consider whether slow, incremental change might sometimes represent "success.")*

_____

_____

_____

_____

_____

_____

_____

Start where you are. Use what you have. Do what you can.
Arthur Ashe

Some Critical Leadership Traits

Self-Awareness* Empathy *

Communication Skills*Listening Skills

*Personal Responsibility *

creativity*Intellectual Curiosity*Courage*

Focus*respect*Humor*

DETERMINATION

adaptability*

Self-discipline * HUMILITY*Passion

Supplemental Materials & Resources

Documentaries & Performance Media

- *In Search of History: The Night Tulsa Burned* (The History Channel, 1999)
- *Burn: The Evolution of an American City* (Harold Jackson III, 2009)
- *Boomtown: An American Journey* (Kirkpatrick & Kinslow Productions, 2015)
- *Before They Die!: A Documentary About the Tulsa Race Riot Survivors* (Reggie Turner, 2008).
- *The Tulsa Lynching of 1921: A Hidden Story* (Michael Wilkerson, 2000).
- *Big Mama Speaks* (Hannibal B. Johnson, 2005) (one-woman play featuring Vanessa Harris-Adams; remembrance and reminiscence about the Black Wall Street).
- *Hate Crimes in the Heartland* (Rachel Lyon and Bavand Karim, 2014).
- *Race Riot Suite* (Jacob Fred Jazz Odyssey, 2011) (jazz suite on Kinnara Records, recorded at Tulsa's Church Studio).
- *Terror in Tulsa: History Uncovered* (in association with FullMind, 2008).
- Solomon Sir Jones film footage, http://beinecke.library.yale.edu/collections/highlights/solomon-sir-jones-films-1924-1928 (rare moving footage from the Yale University Library, *Beinecke Rare Book & Manuscript Collection of 1920s Greenwood District* shot by Solomon Sir Jones, a Baptist preacher and amateur filmmaker) (last visited June 30, 2017).

Books

- Scott Ellsworth, *Death in a Promised Land: The Tulsa Race Riot of 1921* (Baton Rouge, LA: Louisiana State University Press, 1982).
- Mary E. Jones Parish, *Events of the Tulsa Disaster* (Tulsa, OK: 1923).
- Eddie Faye Gates, *They Came Searching: How Blacks Sought the Promised Land in Tulsa* (Fort Worth, TX: Eakin Press 1997).
- Hannibal B. Johnson, *Black Wall Street: From Riot to Renaissance in Tulsa's Historic Greenwood District* (Fort Worth, TX: Eakin Press, 1998).
- Hannibal B. Johnson, *Up from the Ashes* (Fort Worth, TX: Eakin Press, 2000) (children's book).

- Hannibal B. Johnson, *Tulsa's Historic Greenwood District* (Charleston, SC: Arcadia Publishing 2014)
- Hannibal B. Johnson, *Acres of Aspiration: The All-Black Towns in Oklahoma* (Fort Worth, TX: Eakin Press 2002).
- Hannibal B. Johnson, *Apartheid in Indian Country?: Seeing Red Over Black Disenfranchisement* (Fort Worth, TX: Eakin Press 2012).
- Oklahoma Historical Society, *Tulsa Race Riot: A report by the Oklahoma Commission to Study the Tulsa Race Riot of 1921* (Oklahoma City, OK: Oklahoma Historical Society, February 28, 2001).
- Alfred Brophy, *Reconstructing the Dreamland—The Tulsa Race Riot of 1921: Riot, Reparations, and Reconciliation* (New York, NY: Oxford University Press, 2003).
- James S. Hirsch, *Riot and Remembrance: The Tulsa Race War and its Legacy* (New York, NY: Houghton, Mifflin Company, 2002)
- Rilla Askew, *Fire in Beulah* (New York, NY: Penguin Group, Penguin Putnam Inc., 2001)
- Anna Myers, *Tulsa Burning* (New York, NY: Walker Publishing Company, 2002)
- Tim Madigan, *The Burning: Massacre, Destruction and the Tulsa Race Riot of 1921* (New York, NY: St. Martin's Press, 2001).
- Bob Hower, *1921 Tulsa Race Riot, Angels of Mercy* (Tulsa, OK: Lucky Eight Publishing, 1993).
- Eddie Faye Gates, *Riot on Greenwood: The Total Destruction of Black Wall Street* (Fort Worth, TX: Eakin Press, 2003).
- John Hope Franklin and John Whittington Franklin, editors, *My Life in an Era: The Autobiography of Buck Colbert Franklin* (Baton Rouge, LA: Louisiana State University Press, 1997).
- John Hope Franklin, *Mirror to America: The Autobiography of John Hope Franklin* (New York, NY: Farrar, Straus and Giroux, 2006).
- Danney Goble, *Tulsa!: Biography of the American City* (San Francisco, CA: Council Oak Books, 1995).

Photographs & Artifacts

- Department of Special Collections and University Archives, McFarlin Library, University of Tulsa, Tulsa, Oklahoma
- Greenwood Cultural Center, Tulsa, Oklahoma
- National Museum of African American History and Culture, Smithsonian Institution, Washington, D.C.

- Oklahoma History Center, Oklahoma City, Oklahoma
- Oklahoma State University-Tulsa, Tulsa, OK
- Tulsa City-County Library, Tulsa, OK
- Tulsa Historical Society and Museum, Tulsa, Oklahoma
- *Tulsa World*, Tulsa, Oklahoma

Endnotes

1. The mission of the 400 Years of African American History Commission is to "develop and facilitate activities throughout the United States to commemorate the 400th anniversary of the arrival of Africans in the English colonies at Point Comfort, Virginia, in 1619, recognizing and highlighting the resilience and contributions of African Americans from that seminal moment forward, while simultaneously acknowledging the painful impact of slavery, racial discrimination, and racism on our Nation." The author serves as a Commissioner on that body.

2. Walter White investigated numerous "race riots" throughout the county in the early twentieth century, including the 1919 Red Summer events in Washington, D.C., Elaine, Arkansas, and Omaha, Nebraska. His work began in earnest when on September 22, 1906, the Atlanta Race Riot threatened the safety of his own family. *See., e.g.,* Adrian Margaret Brune, *The Awareness of Walter White,* THIS LAND, May 5, 2011, http://thislandpress.com/2011/05/05/the-awareness-of-walter-white/(last visited June 27, 2019).

3. According to his foster mother, the woman who raised him, Dick Rowland was born Jimmy Jones. He adopted the name "Dick," a personal favorite, and paired it with his foster mother's surname, Rowland. He registered in school under as Dick Rowland. As a teen, Dick worked odd jobs and socialized with a racially-mixed group of friends. When he purchased a diamond ring as a birthday gift to himself, some of his friends nicknamed him "Diamond Dick." After the Riot, authorities spirited Dick out of town to Kansas City. He later moved to Portland, Oregon, where he worked in shipyards along the Oregon coast. He died in a work-related accident. *See* Interview with Damie Rowland Ford, conducted by Ruth Sigler Avery, Ruth Sigler Avery Collection, Oklahoma State University-Tulsa Library, Special Collections and Archives, July 22, 1972, https://osu-tulsa.okstate.edu/library/specialcollections.php (last visited July 20, 2019).

4. "Greenwood Avenue" appears as early as 1902 on the Map of Original Townsite, Tulsa, Oklahoma; Tulsa, Creek Nation, Indian Territory (filed in the Northern District, Indian Territory, June 13, 1902, Chas. A. Davidson, Clerk, United States Courts) (on file with author). Two theories about the naming remain plausible: (1) The thoroughfare is named after Greenwood, Mississippi, which is itself named for Choctaw Chief Greenwood LeFlore; and (2) The road is named after Greenwood, Arkansas, the home of one or more or the persons who originally platted the area. Greenwood, Arkansas, is named after Sebastian County Circuit Judge Alfred Burton Greenwood. *See* THE CITY OF GREENWOOD, MISSISSIPPI, http://www.greenwoodms.com/about-greenwood/history (last visited July 3, 2019); City of Greenwood, https://www.greenwoodar.org/Visitors/Greenwood-History/In-the-Beginning (last visited July 3, 2019).

5. A slight variant on this account appears in a contemporaneous account of the Tulsa tragedy. *See* Mary Elizabeth Jones Parrish, EVENTS OF THE TULSA DISASTER (Tulsa, OK: John Hope Franklin Center for Reconciliation, 2009) (Limited Edition, First Printing, as originally published in 1923) (statement of an unnamed survivor, June 24, 1921, noting: " [T]he ruffians ordered [Dr. Jackson] out of his beautiful home. He came out with his hands up and said, 'Here I am boys, don't shoot,' but they shot him just the same."), at 41.

6. Walter White, *The Eruption of Tulsa,* NATION 112 (June 29, 1921): 909–910, cited in History Matters, http://historymatters.gmu.edu/d/5119 (last visited October 25, 2017). White, a NAACP official, visited Tulsa after the 1921 Tulsa Race Riot. As a Negro who could "pass"

for white, Walter White went "incognegro," surreptitiously intercepting interactions and conversations meant for whites only.

7. *See, e.g.*, John Hope Franklin, FROM SLAVERY TO FREEDOM (New York, NY: Alfred A. Knopf, 7th edition, 1994), cited in https://library.duke.edu/exhibits/johnhopefranklin/slavery.html (last visited July 9, 2019):

> Where slavery was growing, as in the lower South, in the late eighteenth and early nineteenth centuries, new and more stringent laws were enacted. All over the South, however, there emerged a body of laws generally regarded as the Slave Codes, which covered every aspect of the life of the slave. There were variations from state to state, but the general point of view expressed in most of them was the same; slaves are not people but property.

8. *The 1619 Project, 1619.*, THE NEW YORK TIMES MAGAZINE, August 18, 2019 (Editor's Note by Jake Silverstein), at 4.

9. Glenn C. Loury, *An American tragedy: The legacy of slavery lingers in our cities' ghettos,* BROOKINGS, March 1, 1998, https://www.brookings.edu/articles/an-american-tragedy-the-legacy-of-slavery-lingers-in-our-cities-ghettos/ (last visited June 19, 2019).

10. Oklahoma Slave Narratives, http://freepages.rootsweb.com/~ewyatt/genealogy/_borders/Oklahoma%20Slave%20Narratives/Franklin,%20Richard.html (last visited July 23, 2019).

11. Historical trauma and cultural healing, https://extension.umn.edu/mental-health/historical-trauma-and-cultural-healing (last visited March 1, 2019).

12. W.E. Burghardt Du Bois, THE SOULS OF BLACK FOLK: ESSAYS AND SKETCHES (Chicago, IL: A.C. McClurg & Co., 1903).

13. *King Praises Civil Rights Plank; "Strongest Since Reconstruction"*, TULSA WORLD, July 29, 1960, at A-1. Dr. King also counted among his friends Clara Luper, Oklahoma City civil rights icon. Ms. Luper led the nation's first sit-in at Katz Drug Store in Oklahoma City, where, in 1958, thirteen teenagers whom she advised for the NAACP sat at the lunch counter, refusing to leave until they were served. *See* Paul R. Lehman, *Quilt of Democracy: An Interview with Clara Luper*, OKLAHOMA HUMANITIES (Spring/Summer 2019), at 39.

14. Maria Yellow Horse Brave Heart, Ph.D., identified four stages of healing historical trauma in Native American communities. Her taxonomy applies equally well to addressing other collective traumas: (1) confront it; (2) understanding it; (3) release the pain of it; and (4) transcend it. *See, e.g.,* http://www.healingcollectivetrauma.com/ http://www.healingcollectivetrauma.com/ (last visited August 13, 2019).

15. W.E.B. Du Bois, BLACK RECONSTRUCTION IN AMERICA, 1860 - 1880 (New York, NY: Free Press, 1999), pp. 711 - 714 (chapter entitled *The Propaganda of History*).

16. Tulsan Ed Wheeler, a writer and intelligence officer for the Tulsa-based infantry battalion of the Oklahoma Army National Guard 45th Thunderbird Infantry Brigade, wrote a then-groundbreaking piece about the Riot in 1971, the fiftieth anniversary of the event. The Wheeler piece breeched the wall of silence and obscuring that had theretofore surrounded the Riot. *See* Ed Wheeler, *Profile of a Riot*, IMPACT MAGAZINE, *circa* 1971, https://nmaahc.si.edu/object/nmaahc_2011.60.18 (last visited July 21, 2019) (a magazine insert likely timed to coincide with fiftieth anniversary of the Riot).

17. The Greenwood District emerged as the name of Tulsa's original African American community after other monikers, some neutral or flattering, some derogatory, and some downright offensive, lost currency. These included: East End, Negro Quarter, Negro Business District, Negro Wall Street, Little Africa, and Niggertown.

18. *Meet The Last Surviving Witness To The Tulsa Race Riot Of 1921*, Code Switch, NPR https://www.npr.org/sections/codeswitch/2018/05/31/615546965/meet-the-last-surviving-witness-to-the-tulsa-race-riot-of-1921 (last visited November 26, 2018); *People & Stories Oral History Project: Dr. Olivia J. Hooker*, WHITE PLAINS PUBLIC LIBRARY HTTPS://WHITEPLAINSLIBRARY.ORG/2015/09/PEOPLE-STORIES-ORAL-HISTORY-PROJECT-DR-OLIVIA-J-HOOKER// (last visited November 26, 2018).

19. *See, e.g., Olivia Hooker, 103, Dies; Witness to an Ugly Moment in History,* THE NEW YORK TIMES, (SPRING/SUMMER 2019). (last visited November 26, 2018); *Olivia Hooker: 1921 Tulsa race riot survivor dies aged 103*, BBC NEWS, HTTPS://WWW.BBC.COM/NEWS/WORLD-US-CANADA-46332474 (LAST VISITED NOVEMBER 26, 2018); *Meet The Last Surviving Witness To The Tulsa Race Riot Of 1921*, Code Switch, NPR https://www.npr.org/sections/codeswitch/2018/05/31/615546965/meet-the-last-surviving-witness-to-the-tulsa-race-riot-of-1921 (last visited November 26, 2018); *People & Stories Oral History Project: Dr. Olivia J. Hooker*, WHITE PLAINS PUBLIC LIBRARY HTTPS://WHITEPLAINSLIBRARY.ORG/2015/09/PEOPLE-STORIES-ORAL-HISTORY-PROJECT-DR-OLIVIA-J-HOOKER/ (last visited November 26, 2018).

20. *Meet The Last Surviving Witness To The Tulsa Race Riot Of 1921*, Code Switch, NPR https://www.npr.org/sections/codeswitch/2018/05/31/615546965/meet-the-last-surviving-witness-to-the-tulsa-race-riot-of-1921 (last visited November 26, 2018); *People & Stories Oral History Project: Dr. Olivia J. Hooker*, WHITE PLAINS PUBLIC LIBRARY HTTPS://WHITEPLAINSLIBRARY.ORG/2015/09/PEOPLE-STORIES-ORAL-HISTORY-PROJECT-DR-OLIVIA-J-HOOKER/ (last visited November 26, 2018).

21. *See, e.g., Olivia Hooker, 103, Dies; Witness to an Ugly Moment in History,* THE NEW YORK TIMES, (SPRING/SUMMER 2019). (last visited November 26, 2018); *Olivia Hooker: 1921 Tulsa race riot survivor dies aged 103*, BBC NEWS, HTTPS://WWW.BBC.COM/NEWS/WORLD-US-CANADA-46332474 (LAST VISITED NOVEMBER 26, 2018); *Meet The Last Surviving Witness To The Tulsa Race Riot Of 1921*, Code Switch, NPR https://www.npr.org/sections/codeswitch/2018/05/31/615546965/meet-the-last-surviving-witness-to-the-tulsa-race-riot-of-1921 (last visited November 26, 2018); *People & Stories Oral History Project: Dr. Olivia J. Hooker*, WHITE PLAINS PUBLIC LIBRARY HTTPS://WHITEPLAINSLIBRARY.ORG/2015/09/PEOPLE-STORIES-ORAL-HISTORY-PROJECT-DR-OLIVIA-J-HOOKER/ (last visited November 26, 2018).

22. Additional thoughts include:

- o *Ayana Baraka*, Cinematographer: "Part of healing is recognizing the hurt, calling it by its name, and remembering it so not to ever make the same mistake again."

- o *Monica Basu*, George Kaiser Family Foundation: "Tulsa's landscape is tainted by continued segregation stemming from the 1921 event. Using the upcoming 100th anniversary to do all we can improve race relations will be important to create a brighter future for the city."

- o *David Blatt, Ph.D.*, former Executive Director, Oklahoma Policy Institute: "As the 100th anniversary of the 1921 Tulsa race massacre approaches, there is much work left to fully acknowledge this great moral stain on our state's history and repair its enduring traumas and divisions. We have an opportunity and a responsibility to honor the legacy of Olivia Hooker and all the victims and survivors, including providing some justice for the wealth that was stripped from them and their descendants who live today."

- o *Mechelle Brown*, Program Manager, Greenwood Cultural Center: "The 100th year commemoration of the 1921 Tulsa Race Riot turned massacre is imperative because it allows us the opportunity to not only remember our past, but to learn from it, to explore how it has impacted us, to acknowledge how we have transformed and hopefully, to continue the healing process."

o *Eddie Evans*. President, 100 Black Men of Tulsa: "Our young people need to understand and know the significance of our heritage—what our ancestors accomplished
economically--our rich heritage. We must learn to appreciate that. We can't let our
ancestors down."

o *Burt B. Holmes*, Businessman and Co-founder of QuikTrip: "The shame of this event
began the much-too-slow change in race relations in central and south Tulsa."

o *Toby Jenkins*, Executive Director, Oklahomans for Equality: "As a descendant of the
white and Native American residents of Tulsa, I can't help but feel my family participated in the massacre and destruction of Greenwood. Racism and bigotry have
been an inherent family trait. My parents broke that curse and alienated their own
family when they embraced integration and equality in the 1960s. While I have no
official record of what role my family had in the Greenwood Massacre, I do believe
it is a collective and generational guilt I share with my ancestors. I must prove I will
not forget. I must atone for the evil that was done. I am responsible--my children
and grandchildren are responsible--for the healing that must happen."

o *Arlene Johnson,* Arlene Johnson & Associates, Public Relations: *"Those who cannot remember the past are condemned to repeat it,'* according to George Santayana, late 19th
century poet and philosopher. Celebrating the 100th Anniversary of the 1921 Tulsa
Race Massacre is not only critical to the city›s cultural and racial history, it is also an
important milestone that reminds us of the national tragedy that left a permanent
stain. During the anniversary year, our challenge and our hope is to unite Tulsans
and find permanent healing."

o *Quraysh Ali Lansana*, Poet, Educator, and Author: "There is no questioning the significance of the destruction of Black Wall Street, where over thirty-five blocks of
African American prosperity was turned to rubble in less than 48 hours. But, the
evolution and rebuilding of Greenwood is of equal, if not greater, importance. The
centennial of the Massacre is also a 100-year-old recognition of the resilience, grit
and spirit of Black Tulsans in the face of despair and Jim Crow."

o *Glenda Love*, Community Volunteer and Nonprofit Consultant: "This anniversary
acknowledges 100 years since the tragedy in 1921. Our community has overcome
many challenges since that time. We need to look back, acknowledge our pain, mark
our accomplishments, and chart our course for a positive, shared future."

o *Jessica Lowe-Betts*, Diversity and Inclusion Consultant, ONEOK: "Commemorating
the 100th anniversary of the 1921 Tulsa Race Riot will shine a light on Tulsa's history and its people.   The commemoration will piece together a story about a legacy of
giants who changed a traumatic narrative to one of forgiveness, hope and longevity."

o *David Phillips, Esq.:* "There are few days in history that mark significant events, particularly for African Americans. The Black Wall Street massacre was one of them. It
was an African American 9/11."

o *S. Michelle Place*, Executive Director, Tulsa Historical Society & Museum: "Adequate
space has not always been provided for multiple viewpoints of recorded history.
Usually it's only the *winners* who get to tell the story. The 1921 attack on Greenwood
was one of the most significant events in Tulsa's history and almost no one talked
about for eighty years. One hundred years after the horrific Tulsa Race Riot/Massa-
cre, it's imperative that multiple perspectives are recorded and shared. 2021 is about
telling all of the story."

o   *Patricia Samuels*, Community Volunteer: "Commemorating the 100th Anniversary of the Tulsa Race Riot honors the strength and sacrifices of African American Tulsans, past, present and future, and ensures that our unique story of sacrifice is never forgotten."

o   *Norman M. Simon, M.D.*, retired physician: "The Tulsa Race Massacre was one of the darkest moments in our collective history. We mark the 100th anniversary of this shameful event in our past, as a new generation of young activists inspires a global movement against racism and violence against black lives. Remembering the Tulsa Race Massacre is a necessary step in rededicating ourselves to healing racial divides, to working together for greater understanding, equity, and creating a more just society for future generations."

o   *Jeff Van Hanken*, Wellspring Associate Professor, Department of Film Studies, University of Tulsa: "I feel we often make the mistake of thinking events happened, that they are in the past. But Black Wall Street, or more specifically, the absence of Tulsa's Black Wall Street, is with us, with all of us, everywhere every day. Imagining what those entrepreneurs might have built in the 100 years that have passed since June 1, 1921, is crushing."

23. Representative Ross's full response to the author's question about why it is important to mark the 100th anniversary of the 1921 Tulsa Race Riot, on file with the author, is as follows:

Going Backwards?
Don Ross

The 1921 Tulsa Race Riot was cloaked in a conspiracy of silence for fifty years by both blacks and whites. Blacks were afraid it could happen again and whites, with their continuing racism, offered no evidence that it couldn't.

In June of 1971, *Oklahoma Impact Magazine* published a full account of the deadliest day in American history during which as many as 300 persons were murdered. Praise and condemnation were heaped upon the publication. There was not one marker in or near the 'Black Wall Street of America' noting the tragedy.

Later, inspired by riot survivors and black pioneers, the Greenwood Cultural Center, the Black Wall Street Memorial, John Hope Franklin Reconciliation Park, and plaques noting the locations of Black Wall Street businesses were installed. All those efforts were led by blacks.

A museum to be named for Dr. John Hope Franklin was proposed, with $5 million offered by the state. Instead of a museum, the state supported John Hope Franklin Reconciliation Park, but provided less than $2 million, reneging on the balance of the initially-offered $5 million without protest from black lawmakers.

The Mayor of the City of Tulsa proposed using $4 million in sales tax revenues for the museum project. It did not gain the support of the black County Commissioner, the two black City Councilors, or the Chamber of Commerce. It failed for lack of leadership.

A baseball park proposed long after the museum has been built and is in use.

There is still no marker downtown or at the intersection of Sixth Street and Boulder Avenue where the first shots of the Riot were fired.

Having been very involved in earlier efforts and having been thwarted by insincere blacks and indifferent whites—and having missed some golden opportunities—I have chosen to retire from commemorations. I am indifferent about continuing celebration. For me, it's applauding "going backwards." What are the goals? A museum?

24. Wyonia Murray Bailey (June 13, 1913 - January 14, 1988) was an educator, activist, and civil rights advocate. She worked with the Metropolitan Tulsa Urban League, serving for a time as its executive director. Born in Little Rock, Arkansas, and graduated from Booker T. Washington High School in Tulsa, she earned Bachelor's and Master's Degrees from the University of Tulsa. She worked as a speech pathologist at both Children's Medical Center and Tulsa Public Schools, the first African American to hold that post in both cases. Ms. Bailey is buried in Tulsa's Crown Hill Cemetery in Tulsa. *See Civic leader, civil rights activist dies,* THE TULSA TRIBUNE, January 15, 1988; *Wyonia Bailey services held Saturday,* THE OKLAHOMA EAGLE, January 21, 1988; *Rites Set for Wyonia Bailey, Former Urban League Chief,* TULSA WORLD, January 16, 1988.

25. Ms. Bailey's poem adorns a granite monument outside the Greenwood Cultural Center in Tulsa.

26. *See* Chapter 2 for a discussion of the term of art "race riot" and its application to the 1921 event in Tulsa.

27. For information on Tulsa historic African American community, the Greenwood District, and the 1921 Tulsa Race Riot, *see, e.g.,* Hannibal B. Johnson, BLACK WALL STREET—FROM RIOT TO RENAISSANCE IN TULSA'S HISTORIC GREENWOOD DISTRICT (Austin, TX: Eakin Press 1998); Hannibal B. Johnson, UP FROM THE ASHES (Austin, TX: Eakin Press 2000); Hannibal B. Johnson, TULSA'S HISTORIC GREENWOOD DISTRICT (Charleston, SC: Arcadia Publishing 2014); Hannibal B. Johnson, UP FROM THE ASHES (Austin, TX: Eakin Press 2000); Scott Ellsworth, DEATH IN A PROMISED LAND: THE TULSA RACE RIOT OF 1921 (Baton Rouge, LA; Louisiana State University Press, 1982); TULSA RACE RIOT: A REPORT BY THE OKLAHOMA COMMISSION TO STUDY THE TULSA RACE RIOT OF 1921(Oklahoma City, OK: Oklahoma Historical Society, February 28, 2001); Mary Elizabeth Jones Parrish, EVENTS OF THE TULSA DISASTER (Tulsa, OK: John Hope Franklin Center for Reconciliation, 2009) (Limited Edition, First Printing, as originally published in 1923); Alfred L. Brophy, RECONSTRUCTING THE DREAMLAND (New York, NY: Oxford University Press 2002); James S. Hirsch, RIOT AND REMEMBRANCE (Boston, MA: Houghton Mifflin Harcourt 2002); BOB HOWER, 1921 TULSA RACE RIOT AND THE AMERICAN RED CROSS: "ANGELS OF MERCY" (Tulsa, OK: Homestead Press 1993; Eddie Faye Gates, THEY CAME SEARCHING: HOW BLACKS SOUGHT THE PROMISED LAND IN TULSA (Fort Worth, TX: Eakin Press 1997); Eddie Faye Gates, RIOT ON GREENWOOD: THE TOTAL DESTRUCTION OF BLACK WALL STREET, 1921 (Fort Worth, TX: Eakin Press 2003).

28. Bob Hower, 1921 TULSA RACE RIOT--"AMERICA'S DEADLIEST: "ANGELS OF MERCY," (Tulsa, OK: Homestead Press, 1993), at 228 (compiled from the memorabilia collection of Maurice Willows, Director of Red Cross Relief, and the grandfather of Bob Hower), at 163 ("The real truth regarding the underlying causes of the short-lived civil war which turned Tulsa, Oklahoma, into a bedlam on the morning of June 1st, 1921, may come to the surface in the future." Tulsa County Chapter American Red Cross Disaster Relief Report, Maurice Willows); *see also*, the use of the descriptor "disaster" in Mary Elizabeth Jones Parrish, EVENTS OF THE TULSA DISASTER (Tulsa, OK: John Hope Franklin Center for Reconciliation, 2009) (Limited Edition, First Printing, as originally published in 1923), the use of the label "holocaust" in John Hope Franklin and John Whittington Franklin, editors, MY LIFE IN AN ERA: THE AUTOBIOGRAPHY OF BUCK COLBERT FRANKLIN (Baton Rouge, LA: Louisiana State

University Press, 1997), at 198, 201, and the discussion of the terms "riot," "massacre," "ethnic cleansing," and "pogrom" in John Thompson, *Tulsa Race Riot of 1921: Curriculum launched*, February 27, 2018, https://nondoc.com/2018/02/27/tulsa-race-riot-of-1921-curriculum-launched/ (last visited February 2, 2019).

29. These definitions are drawn from OXFORD DICTIONARIES, online.

30. The author frequently, though not exclusively, uses the term of art "1921 Tulsa Race Riot," sometimes shortened to simply "Riot," throughout this text. This is the nomenclature used in much of the historical record, including interviews with survivors. The use of this historical referent for the events that transpired in Tulsa, Oklahoma, on May 31 and June 1, 1921, should not be construed as an endorsement of its descriptive accuracy. Rather, the reader should, as suggested, think critically about all aspects of this long-used label to determine, on balance, the appropriate word choice.

31. Randy Krehbiel, *1921 centennial commission to replace 'riot' with 'massacre' in official title*, TULSA WORLD, November 27, 2018, HTTPS://WWW.TULSAWORLD.COM/HOMEPAGELATEST/CENTENNIAL-COMMISSION-TO-REPLACE-RIOT-WITH-MASSACRE-IN-OFFICIAL-TITLE/ARTICLE_128D9304-6D59-5B5F-872A-F72509D3ECD8.HTML (last visited December 2, 2018).

32. As noted, the author generally uses the term "Riot" for what has historically been known as the 1921 Tulsa Race Riot. The shortened "Riot" acknowledges the historical referent "riot" as a term of art created and used by white chroniclers of history to describe violent racial events, often white-initiated, that targeted African Americans. As mentioned in the text, may other nouns may be used to describe these incidents. Choice of terminology in this context merits a robust discussion about power, politics, and nomenclature.

33. For a listing of the race riots of the early twentieth century and other examples of race-centric history, *see, e.g., American Racial History Timeline*, http://www.occidentaldissent.com/american-racial-history-timeline-2/american-racial-history-timeline-1900-1960/ (last visited June 27, 2019).

34. http://www.occidentaldissent.com/american-racial-history-timeline-2/american-racial-history-timeline-1900-1960/ (last visited January 23, 2019).

35. Original poem by the author, included in Hannibal B. Johnson, INCOGNEGRO: POETIC REFLECTIONS ON RACE AND DIVERSITY IN AMERICA (Fort Worth, TX: Eakin Press, 2019).

36. Educator and statesman Booker T. Washington is widely credited with coining the phrase "Negro Wall Street," which, at some indeterminate future point morphed into "Black Wall Street" in popular parlance. *See, e.g.,* Alexander Chavers, *Untold Story: Black Wall Street and the Tulsa Race Riots,* INTERNATIONAL POLICY DIGEST, September 26, 2017, https://intpolicydigest.org/2017/09/26/untold-history-black-wall-street-tulsa-race-riots/(last visited August 5, 2019); For an early use of the moniker "Negro Wall Street," *see* Mary Elizabeth Jones Parrish, EVENTS OF THE TULSA DISASTER (Tulsa, OK: John Hope Franklin Center for Reconciliation, 2009) (Limited Edition, First Printing, as originally published in 1923), at 7 (Speaking of a time 1919, Parrish used a variant of "Negro Wall Street": "On leaving the Frisco station, going north on Archer Street one could see nothing but Negro business places. Going east on Archer Street for two or more blocks there you would behold Greenwood Avenue, the Negro's Wall Street....").

37. For a closer look as trust-building in communities, *see, e.g.,* Rob Corcoran, TRUSTBUILDING: AN HONEST CONVERSATION ON RACE, RECONCILIATION, AND RESPONSIBILITY (Charlottesville, VA: University of Virginia Press, 2010).

38. After an extensive, community-involved process, those schools were renamed in 2018. Robert E. Lee Elementary became Council Oak Elementary. Jean Pierre Choteau Elementary became Wayman Tisdale Fine Arts Academy. Andrew Jackson Elementary became

Unity Learning Academy. Christopher Columbus Elementary became Delores Huerta Elementary. *See, e.g.,* Samuel Hardiman, *Lee School renamed Council Oak,* TULSA WORLD, August 21, 2018, at A-1; *Jackson Elementary name to Unity Learning Academy; Tulsa school board votes to adopt the name 'Lee School,'* TULSA WORLD, May 7, 2018, https://www.tulsaworld.com/news/education/lee-school-to-retain-surname-school-board-changes-jackson-elementary/article_bf88b8e8-4b06-5001-a656-b49ebfd45236.html (last visited August 21, 2018); *Tulsa Public Schools Board Approves Renaming 2 Elementary Schools,* NewsOn6.com, June 19, 2018 (last visited August 21, 2018); Samuel Hardiman, *New year, new names,* TULSA WORLD, August 23, 2018, at A1.

Similarly, back in 2016, the University of Tulsa removed the name John Rogers from one of its college of law buildings. John Rogers, a prominent attorney, a trustee at the University of Tulsa for forty years, and the founding dean of the institution's law school. Rogers also belonged to the Ku Klux Klan and another vigilante organization in the 1920s. Randy Krehbiel, *TU trustees vote to remove name with KKK ties from college of law building,* TULSA WORLD, May 5, 2016, https://www.tulsaworld.com/news/local/tu-trustees-vote-to-remove-name-with-kkk-ties-from/article_7b173495-d6bb-5c48-b6d0-93ae5418c6bd.html (last visited July 2, 2019).

39. *See, e.g.,* Richard DeSirey, MORNING STAR: LET US MAKE A NEW WAY (Columbia, SC: Richard DeSirey, 2018).

40. Kevin Canfield, *Fundraising campaign aims to expand, remodel Greenwood Cultural Center,* TULSA WORLD, April 1, 2019, A1.

41. Kendrick Marshall, *Alabama source of ideas for 1921 memorial: City leaders, centennial commission visit sites in planning future race massacre center,* TULSA WORLD, May 19, 2019, at A11. *See also,* Joseph Holloway, *Plans Revealed for Memorial Honoring Black Wall Street, Tulsa Race Massacre,* NEWSON6.COM, https://www.newson6.com/story/40494655/plans-revealed-for-memorial-honoring-black-wall-street-tulsa-race-riot (last visited May 19, 2019) (noting that the Tulsa Community Remembrance Coalition, a group separate from the Centennial Commission, plans to erect an outdoor memorial on the grounds of historic Vernon AME Church in the Greenwood District); *Massacre memorials planned: Black voices must be key in how the story is told,* TULSA WORLD, May 26, 2019, at G4 (editorial).

42. SB 17 (1921 Tulsa Race Riot; creating revolving fund; repealers; Effective date), http://www.oklegislature.gov/BillInfo.aspx?Bill=sb17&Session=1700 (last visited March 21, 2019).

43. E-mail from Oklahoma Senator Kevin Matthews to the author, March 20, 2019 (on file with author).

44. HANNIBAL B. JOHNSON, BLACK WALL STREET—FROM RIOT TO RENAISSANCE IN TULSA'S HISTORIC GREENWOOD DISTRICT (Fort Worth, TX: Eakin Press 1998).

45. *See, e.g.,* https://www.gilderlehrman.org/content/historical-context-go-west-and-grow-country; http://www.skagitriverjournal.com/US/Library/Newspapers/Greeley1-GoWest.html (last visited August 14, 2018).

46. *See, e.g.,* Hannibal B. Johnson, APARTHEID IN INDIAN COUNTRY?: SEEING RED OVER BLACK DISENFRANCHISEMENT (Fort Worth, TX: Eakin Press 2012).

47. *See, e.g.,* Hannibal B. Johnson, APARTHEID IN INDIAN COUNTRY?: SEEING RED OVER BLACK DISENFRANCHISEMENT (Fort Worth, TX: Eakin Press 2012).

48. Henry Louis Gates, Jr., *The Truth Behind '40 Acres and a Mule,'* originally posted on THE ROOT. http://www.pbs.org/wnet/african-americans-many-rivers-to-cross/history/the-truth-behind-40-acres-and-a-mule/ (last visited August 13, 2018).

49. *See* William T. Sherman, Military Division of the Mississippi; 1865 series - Special Field Order 15, January 16, 1865, http://www.georgiaencyclopedia.org/articles/history-archaeology/shermans-field-order-no-15 (last visited August 13, 2018); http://www.blackpast.org/primary/special-field-orders-no-15 (last visited August 13, 2018).

50. Henry Louis Gates, Jr., *The Truth Behind '40 Acres and a Mule,'* originally posted on THE ROOT. http://www.pbs.org/wnet/african-americans-many-rivers-to-cross/history/the-truth-behind-40-acres-and-a-mule/ (last visited August 13, 2018).

51. Henry Louis Gates, Jr., *The Truth Behind '40 Acres and a Mule,'* originally posted on THE ROOT. http://www.pbs.org/wnet/african-americans-many-rivers-to-cross/history/the-truth-behind-40-acres-and-a-mule/ (last visited August 13, 2018).

52. *See, e.g.,* Hannibal B. Johnson, APARTHEID IN INDIAN COUNTRY?: SEEING RED OVER BLACK DISENFRANCHISEMENT (Fort Worth, TX: Eakin Press 2012).

53. https://www.archives.gov/research/native-americans/dawes (last visited April 8, 2019).

54. Dawes Commission hearing notice for Cherokee Freedmen, https://search.aol.com/aol/image?p=map+of+cherokee+freedmen+allotments&s_it=img-ans&v_t=comsearch&fr (last visited August 17, 2018).

55. *See, e.g.,* Oklahoma Historical Society description of the measure at https://www.okhistory.org/publications/enc/entry.php?entry=SE017 (last visited July 31, 2019).

56. *See, e.g.,* Hannibal B. Johnson, ACRES OF ASPIRATION: THE ALL-BLACK TOWNS IN OKLAHOMA (Fort Worth, TX: Eakin Press, 2002).

57. Grayson explained that the Oklahoma economy of the early twentieth century centered on agriculture and fossil fuels. These Freedmen allotments, like so much other Oklahoma land, served as farms and sometimes yielded oil and gas. Land thus produced income and, for some, wealth. Telephone conference with Eli Grayson, June 27, 2019. Author's note: The portion of the Greenwood District with ties to the Muscogee (Creek) Nation is small in comparison to that linked to the Cherokee Nation, although it includes the present-day commercial sector of the Greenwood District.

58. E-mail correspondence with Eli Grayson, November 18, 2018 (on file with author).

59. Gurley, born in Huntsville, Alabama, on December 25, 1868, to formerly enslaved parents, spent most of his youth on a farm in Pine Bluff, Arkansas. He worked on the farm, taught school, and worked for the post office before staking a claim to land in Oklahoma during the opening of the Cherokee Strip Land Run in 1893. He worked his own farm in Perry, Oklahoma, served a stint a school principal, then open a successful mercantile enterprise. Gurley moved his business to Tulsa in July 1906. He built the first building in the "East End" *(i.e.,* the Greenwood District), constructed a number of other businesses and residences, and added the Gurley Hill Addition to the City of Tulsa. He also owned an 80-acre farm in Rogers County. Upon his parents' deaths in Arkansas in 1913, Gurley inherited a share of a 320-acre farm and timber property. TULSA STAR (Special Edition), August 19, 1914, at 14.

60. J.B. Stradford, an attorney, made the bulk of his money in real estate investments, http://blackwallstreet.org/jbstradford (last visited June 27, 2019).

61. Efforts to substantiate B.C. Franklin's recollections of Gurley land purchases proved unsuccessful. George A. Farrar, Jr., Project Manager at the Tulsa County Clerk's Office, conducted a search on records for O.W. Gurley dating back to 1897. The earliest land transaction he found occurred on October 18, 1910, at which time H.S. Hall sold "Lot No. Eleven (11) in Block No. Six (6) in the North Side Addition to the City of Tulsa according to the recorded plat thereof" to Gurley for $150. Deed Record, No. 68, Tulsa County Clerk's

Office. Lot 11, Block 6 is in the heart of Tulsa's Historic Greenwood District in what is now denominated on Tulsa County Assessor maps as "University Center at Tulsa." Records show Greenwood District deed and mortgage activity in first half of 1906 in the name of E. Gurley and E. Gurley *et al.*, grantee, E. Gurley being Emma Gurley, wife of O.W. Gurley. Several other land purchases by O.W. Gurley and/or Emma Gurley occurred in the 1920s, notably, that of a parcel sold by the Tate Brady Realty Company, Henry T. Brady, President, in 1926. *See* e-mail correspondence from George A. Farrar, Jr., Project Manager, Tulsa County Clerk's Office, June 26, 2019 (on file with author). Gurley had been a well-off landowner in Arkansas prior to his participation in an 1889 Oklahoma land run. http://www.blackwallstreet.org/owgurly (last visited June 27, 2019).

62. Buck Colbert Franklin, My Life and An Era: The Autobiography of Buck Colbert moved Franklin, John Hope Franklin and John Whittington Franklin, eds., (Baton Rouge, LA: LSU Press, 1997), at 199 - 200.

63. *See e.g.,* Leroy Vaughn, M.D., M.B.A., *The Black 'Negro' Wall Street,* OpEd.com, May 15, 2009, https://www.opednews.com/articles/The-Black-Negro-Wall-Str-by-Dr-Leroy-Vaughn--090511-890.html (last visited July 3, 2019); *Greenwood, Okla.: The Legacy Race Riot,* The Root, February 24, 20111, https://www.opednews.com/articles/The-Black-Negro-Wall-Str-by-Dr-Leroy-Vaughn--090511-890.html (last visited July 3, 2019); Alexander Chavers, *Untold History: Black Wall Street and the Tulsa Race Riots,* International Policy Digest, September 26, 2017, (last visited July 3, 2019).

64. For more on the all-black towns in Oklahoma, *see* Hannibal B. Johnson, Acres of Aspiration: the All-Black Towns in Oklahoma (Fort Worth, TX: Eakin Press, 2002).

65. Mabel B. Little, Fire on Mount Zion: My Life and History as a Black Woman in America (Melvin B. Tolson Black Heritage Center, Langston University, Langston, Oklahoma, 1990), at 26, 32.

66. Mary Elizabeth Jones Parrish, Events of the Tulsa Disaster (Tulsa, OK: John Hope Franklin Center for Reconciliation, 2009) (Limited Edition, First Printing, as originally published in 1923), at 7.

67. During this period, "racism in the country is deemed to have been worse than in any other period after the American Civil War.…African Americans lost many civil rights gains made during Reconstruction. Anti-black violence, lynching, segregation, legal racial discrimination, and expression of white supremacy increased." https://www.theroot.com/greenwood-okla-the-legacy-of-the-tulsa-race-riot-1790862897 (last visited June 27, 2019).

68. *See, e.g.,* David F. Krugler, 1919, The Year of Racial Violence: How African Americans Fought Back (Cambridge, England: Cambridge University Press 2014).

69. "Negro Wall Street" morphed into the more modern-sounding "Black Wall Street" at some indeterminate point. The Wall Street reference suggests business in a general sense, not the presence of a well-defined financial hub. Perhaps a more apt moniker for the community would have been "Black Main Street," as most of the businesses were Mom-and-Pop, sole proprietorship operations. The first full-fledged black-owned bank in Tulsa's African American community did not appear until 1970. American State Bank operated from 1970 - 2011. *See, e.g.,* Tim Stanley, *State's first black-owned bank served north Tulsa,* Tulsa World, February 26, 2019, A1. Note: American State Bank was not Oklahoma's first black-owned bank. That honor belongs to Farmers & Merchants Bank in the all-black town of Boley, Oklahoma, established in 1906. *See* Hannibal B. Johnson, Acres of Aspiration: The All-Black Towns in Oklahoma (Fort Worth, TX: Eakin Press 2002), at 84 .

70. Mary Elizabeth Jones Parrish, Events of the Tulsa Disaster (Tulsa, OK: John Hope Franklin Center for Reconciliation, 2009) (Limited Edition, First Printing, as originally pub-

lished in 1923), at 7.

71. Tulsa Race Riot: A report by the Oklahoma Commission to Study the Tulsa Race Riot of 1921 (Oklahoma City, OK: Oklahoma Historical Society, February 28, 2001), at 23 - 24, https://archive.org/details/ReportOnTulsaRaceRiotOf1921 (last visited June 23, 2019).

72. *See, e.g.,* Tim Stanley, *Walking into a legacy: Memorial to Booker T. Washington's founding principal to be unveiled,* Tulsa World, August 11, 2019, at A1; *Ellis Walker Woods Memorial,* https://www.ewwoods.org/ (last visited June 16, 2019); Eddie Faye Gates, They Came Searching: How Blacks Sought the Promised Land in Tulsa (Fort Worth, TX: Eakin Press, 1997), at 238 - 240 (excerpt from article by Homer Dexter Woods, son of Ellis Walker Woods).

73. *How lynching was used by whites to destroy competition from black business owners,* April 28, 2018 https://www.latimes.com/opinion/readersreact/la-ol-le-lynching-memorial-business-20180428-story.html (last visited June 27, 2019).

74. *See, e.g.,* https://www.brainyquote.com/quotes/ida_b_wells_295205 (last visited June 27, 2019); https://www.lifesayingsquotes.com/quote/city-memphis-demonstrated-neither-charac-ter-178/ (last visited June 27, 2019); Lee D. Baker, *Ida B. Wells-Barnett and Her Passion for Justice,* April 1996, http://people.duke.edu/~ldbaker/classes/aaih/caaih/ibwells/ibwbkgrd.html (last visited June 27, 2019); Damon Mitchell, *The People's Grocery Store Lynching, Memphis, Tennessee,* January 24, 2018, https://daily.jstor.org/peoples-grocery-lynching/ (last visited June 27, 2019).

75. *Wed, 03.09.1892: Lynching in Memphis!,* https://aaregistry.org/story/lynching-in-memphis/ (last visited June 27, 2019).

76. Mary Elizabeth Jones Parrish, Events of the Tulsa Disaster (Tulsa, OK: John Hope Franklin Center for Reconciliation, 2009) (Limited Edition, First Printing, as originally published in 1923), at 7.

77. Black soldiers served, perhaps most notably, in France. *See, e.g.,* Chris Pleasance, *Fighting for respect: Fascinating images show the black soldiers who fought for America during the First World War while facing discrimination at home,* Mailonline, November 2, 2017, https://www.dailymail.co.uk/news/article-5042937/The-black-soldiers-fought-America-World-War-One.html (last visited June 28, 2019); Phil Gregory, *Black Soldiers in WWI,* The Black Presence in Britain, November 11, 2013, https://blackpresence.co.uk/remembrance-day-black-asian-soldiers-in-ww1/ (last visited June 28, 2-019).

78. *United Confederate Veterans,* https://snaccooperative.org/ark:/99166/w6k97466 (last visited July 31, 2019).

79. *Throwback Tulsa gallery: Confederate veterans gathered in Tulsa for 1918 reunion,* Tulsa World, November 2, 2017, https://www.tulsaworld.com/photovideo/slideshows/throwback-tul-sa-gallery-confederate-veterans-gathered-in-tulsa-for-reunion/collection_7fd26fde-ecc4-5fce-902d-6f81687223f4.html#1 (last visited November 27, 2018).

80. Born in Pine Bluff, Arkansas, George Haynes was a social worker, educator, and co-founder and first executive director of the National Urban League. He earned a Bachelor's Degree at Fisk University in Nashville, Tennessee. In 1904, he earned a Master's Degree from Yale University. While studying at the University of Chicago during the summers of 1906 and 1907, Dr. Haynes became increasingly interested in social problems affecting black migrants from the Deep South. This fascination led him to the New York School of Philanthropy, from which he graduated in 1910. Two years later, he earned his Ph.D. from Columbia University. Columbia University Press published his doctoral dissertation, *The Negro at Work in New York City.* NASW Foundation, http://naswfoundation.org/pioneers/h/haynes.htm (last visited August 9, 2018).

81. *Red Summer of 1919,* http://www.knowpia.com/pages/Red_Summer_of_1919 (last vis-

ited August 9, 2018).

83. *See, e.g.*, Lauren Jackson, *On the Meaning of 'Race Riot*,' essence, February 25, 2019, https://www.essence.com/black-history-month-2019/on-the-meaning-of-race-riot/ (last visited July 31, 2019).

84. Jesse J. Holland, *Murders of blacks in 1919 now remembered: Hundreds of African Americans died at the hands of white mobs during "Red Summer*," Associated Press, TULSA WORLD, July 24, 2019, at A5.

85. Femi Lewis, *The Red Summer of 1919: Race Riots Rock Cities Throughout the United States*, https://www.thoughtco.com/red-summer-of-1919-45394 (last visited May 2, 2019); *see also*, Cameron McWhirter, RED SUMMER: THE SUMMER OF 1919 AND THE AWAKENING OF BLACK AMERICA (New York, NY: St. Martin's Griffin, 2012); Rosalind Bentley, *Bloody race riots of 1919 explored*, ATLANTA JOURNAL CONSTITUTION, https://www.ajc.com/entertainment/calendar/bloody-race-riots-1919-explored/nCHunD5YQNJgMLxCIW4UvO/ (last visited May 13, 2019).

86. *See, e.g.*, 1911: *Laura and Lawrence Nelson lynched*, http://www.executedtoday.com/2011/05/25/1911-laura-and-lawrence-nelson-lynched/ (last visited July 31, 2019). Dianna Everett, *Lynching*, ENCYCLOPEDIA OF OKLAHOMA HISTORY, Oklahoma History Center, https://www.okhistory.org/publications/enc/entry.php?entry=LY001 (last visited July 31, 2019).

87. *See, e.g.*, NAACP, https://www.naacp.org/naacp-history-dyer-anti-lynching-bill/ (last visited June 16, 2019).

88. https://search.aol.com/aol/image?p=lynching+flyers&s_it=img-ans&v_t=comsearch&-fr=comsearch&imgurl=http%3A%2F%2Fwww.amistadresource.org%2FLBimages%2Fim-age_07_06_010_a_flyer.jpg#id=7&iurl=https%3A%2F%2Fthebluereview.org%2Fwp-con-tent%2Fuploads%2F2013%2F08%2FNAACP-ad.jpg&action=click (last visited August 21, 2018).

89. https://www.history.com/topics/roaring-twenties (last visited September 17, 2018).

90. https://www.azquotes.com/author/7202-Washington_Irving/tag/history (last visited September 17, 2018), from Washington Irving, THE LEGEND OF SLEEPY HOLLOW AND OTHER STORIES FROM THE SKETCH BOOK, at 144 (City of Westminster, London, England: Penguin 2006).

91. *See, e.g.*, Michael S. Givel, *Sundown on the Prairie: The Extralegal Campaigns and Efforts from 1889 to 1967 to Exclude African Americans from Norman, Oklahoma*, THE CHRONICLES OF OKLA-HOMA, vol. XCVI, number three, Fall 2018, at 260, 264.

92. Statement of James Leighton Avery, Ruth Sigler Avery Collection, Oklahoma State University-Tulsa Library, Special Collections and Archives, undated, https://osu-tulsa.okstate.edu/library/specialcollections.php (last visited July 20, 2019). *See also*, Steve Gerkin, *Beno Hall: Tulsa's Den of Terror*, THIS LAND, September 3, 2011, https://osu-tulsa.okstate.edu/library/specialcollections.php (last visited July 20, 2019).

93. Eddie Faye Gates, THEY CAME SEARCHING: HOW BLACKS SOUGHT THE PROMISED LAND IN TULSA (Fort Worth, TX: Eakin Press, 1997), at 253 (transcript of interview with Tony Pringer, grandson of Molly and Herbert Johnson).

94. Eddie Gates, THEY CAME SEARCHING: HOW BLACKS SOUGHT THE PROMISED LAND IN TULSA (Fort Worth, TX: Eakin Press, 1997), at 253 -255 (transcript of interview with Tony Pringer, grandson of Molly and Herbert Johnson).

95. *See, e.g.*, Mary Elizabeth Jones Parrish, EVENTS OF THE TULSA DISASTER (Tulsa, OK: John Hope Franklin Center for Reconciliation, 2009) (Limited Edition, First Printing, as original-

ly published in 1923), at 30, 35 (statements of Dr. R.T. Bridgewater, Assistant Tulsa County Physician, June 22, 1921 [citing race prejudice and the national lack of confidence in law enforcement as causes of the Riot], and E.A. Loupe, plumber, June 22, 1921 [citing "a growing racial hate by the lower Whites because of Negro prosperity and independence…."]).

96. Post-Riot actions by the Tulsa Chamber of Commerce suggest that monied and powerful interests in Tulsa targeted the Greenwood District for rail system projects. Just weeks after the disaster, the Tulsa Chamber of Commerce unanimously passed a resolution that endorsed the taking of a portion of the burned area:

> WHEREAS, there exists in this City the necessity for a Union Station and joint terminal, both for railroads and interurban systems,
>
> WHEREAS, the recent fire in the northeast portion of the City has made available a thoroughly feasible and practicable site for the Union Station and joint terminal,
>
> NOW, THEREFORE, Be it Resolved, that it is the unanimous sentiment of the Chamber of Commerce and Federation of Allied Interests of Tulsa, Oklahoma, that the railroads and interurbans of the City of Tulsa immediately take steps toward the erection of a Union Station and railroad and interurban terminal….

Minutes of the July 1, 1921, meeting of the Tulsa Chamber of Commerce (on file with author).

97. *Nab Negro for Attacking Girl In an Elevator*, Tulsa Tribune, May 31, 1921.

98. *See, e.g.,* James Allen, Without Sanctuary: Lynching Photography in America (Sante Fe, NM: Twin Palms Publishers 2000).

99. A white mob lynched Roy Belton (*a.k.a.*, Tom Owens) on August 28, 1920, while thousands of onlookers gawked at the spectacle.

> Hi-Jacker Maintains He Is Not Guilty in His Final Breath of Existence
>
> Aroused with indignation [*sic*] at the murder of Homer Nida, taxi driver, a mob of 400 citizens visited the county jail about 11 o'clock last night, took T.M. Owens from his cell and hanged him to a signboard about three miles southwest of Tulsa on the Jenks road, and about three-quarters of a mile south off the Tulsa-Sapulpa highway.

MOB LYNCHES TOM OWENS: Thousands Participate In Vengeance for Nida, Tulsa World, August 29, 1920, front page.

100. *See, e.g.,* Tulsa Race Riot: A report by the Oklahoma Commission to Study the Tulsa Race Riot of 1921 (Oklahoma City, OK: Oklahoma Historical Society, February 28, 2001), at 62, https://archive.org/details/ReportOnTulsaRaceRiotOf1921 (last visited June 23, 2019).

101 *See, e.g.,* Stephen P. Kerr, J.D., LL.M., Tulsa Race War: 31ˢᵀ May 1921, at 23 (1999, unpublished manuscript by the grandson of First Presbyterian minister, Dr. Charles William Kerr on file in the archives of First Presbyterian Church). Kerr noted that 500 members of what he describes as a white lynch mob were given "special commissions" to act as "emergency Police deputies." This gave them authority to invade the Greenwood District on the premise of suppressing a non-existent "armed insurrection" by African Americans.

102. *See, e.g., Redfearn v. American Central Insurance Company,* 116 Okla. 137 (1926), finding, among of things, that: (1) Tulsa officials failed to act to protect the Greenwood District denizens; (2) uniformed local law enforcement officers deputized men who set alight the

black community; (3) Tulsa officials interned African Americans at various locations, including the Tulsa Convention Center and fairgrounds, while their homes burned; (4) Tulsa officials obstructed the delivery of private assistance to African Americans following destruction of the Greenwood District; and (5) The City of Tulsa attempted to prevent rebuilding in the Greenwood District by enacting a stricter fire code that would have made reconstruction cost-prohibitive for most African Americans. William Redfearn, a white man, lost two Greenwood District businesses, the Dixie Theater and the Red Wing Hotel, in the 1921 Tulsa Race Riot. He watched the fully-insured properties go up in smoke. His insurance policy contained a common exclusionary clause, forswearing coverage occasioned by riot or civil unrest. The Standard Fire Policy and many other property insurance policies, then as now, contained a "riot exclusion" clause that excepts coverage for losses caused by riot or civil commotion. *See, e.g.,* https://www.realestateagent.com/real-estate-glossary/insurance/riot-exclusion.html (last visited May 2, 2019). Attaching the label "riot" to the Tulsa disaster proved intentional, at least seemingly, and incontrovertibly consequential. *See, e.g.,* https://tulsarenaissancehistory.blogspot.com/2018/10/1402-south-birmingham-avenue-penny-and.html?m=1 (last visited February 25, 2019).

103. *See generally,* Tulsa Race Riot: A report by the Oklahoma Commission to Study the Tulsa Race Riot of 1921 (Oklahoma City, OK: Oklahoma Historical Society, February 28, 2001), https://archive.org/details/ReportOnTulsaRaceRiotOf1921 (last visited June 23, 2019).

104. First Presbyterian Church, Tulsa, Oklahoma, Oral History Series, Interview with George "Bill" & Eve Morrow, February 5, 2000, No, 16, at 8; *see also,* Mary Elizabeth Jones Parrish, Events of the Tulsa Disaster (Tulsa, OK: John Hope Franklin Center for Reconciliation, 2009) (Limited Edition, First Printing, as originally published in 1923), at 23 (statement of P.S. Thompson, Ph.C., President, Tulsa Medical, Dental & Pharmaceutical Association, June 22, 1921, noting, "Immediate Cause: There was a report in the Tulsa Tribune that threats were being made to lynch a Negro for attempted criminal assault upon a White girl, which was wholly without foundation or cause." *See also,* Randy Krehbiel, *1921 Tulsa newspapers fueled racism, and one story is cited for sparking the burning of Greenwood: Massacre.,* Tulsa World, May 31, 2019, at A11.

105. Orville D Menard, *Tom Dennison, The Omaha Bee, and the 1919 Omaha Race Riot,* Nebraska History 68 (1987), at 152-16, http://www.nebraskahistory.org/publish/publicat/history/full-text/1987-4-Dennison_Riot.pdf (February 10, 2010) (last visited July 2, 2019). *See also, Girl Identifies Assailant: Officers Keep Mob Off Negro,* The Omaha Daily Bee, September 27, 1919; *Omaha Mob Hangs and Burns Negro Who Assaulted Girl: Lynching Committee of 30 Receives Will Brown From Other Court House Prisoners,* The Omaha Daily Bee, September 29, 1919; *Colored Assailant Of Agnes Lobeck Pays For His Crime: Omaha Mob Hangs and Burns Negro Who Assaulted White Girl After Court House Is Destroyed By Fire And Many Are Injured,* The Omaha Daily Bee, September 29, 1919.

106. Alonzo Smith, *The Omaha Courthouse Lynching of 1919,* January 22, 2007, https://www.blackpast.org/african-american-history/omaha-courthouse-lynching-1919/ (last visited June 30, 2019).

107. *See, e.g.,* Alan Royle, *Historical Movie Info, Movie Trivia, Fascinating Hollywood Facts,* http://filmstarfacts.com/2018/04/22/henry-fonda-1905-82/(last visited July 1, 2019); Frederick H. Lowe, *Museum that memorialized black lynching victims opens in Montgomery, Alabama,* April 27, 2018, http://www.stlamerican.com/news/local_news/museum-that-memorial-izes-black-lynching-victims-opens-in-montgomery-alabama/article_b6071e20-4a2a-11e8-927e-739c3a67bf84.html (last visited July 1, 2019); Sean Hogan, Turning On The Light: Henry Fonda and Will Brown, January 31, 2018, https://www.rogerebert.com/balder-and-

dash/turning-on-the-light-henry-fonda-and-will-brown (last visited July 1, 2019).

108. First Presbyterian Church, Tulsa, Oklahoma, Oral History Series, Interview with Dan & Jean Davisson, May 18, 1999, No. 4, at 16.

109. Mary Elizabeth Jones Parrish, EVENTS OF THE TULSA DISASTER (Tulsa, OK: John Hope Franklin Center for Reconciliation, 2009) (Limited Edition, First Printing, as originally published in 1923), at 9.

110. Mary Elizabeth Jones Parrish, EVENTS OF THE TULSA DISASTER (Tulsa, OK: John Hope Franklin Center for Reconciliation, 2009) (Limited Edition, First Printing, as originally published in 1923) (statement of Mrs. Carrie Kinlaw, June 23, 1921), at 36.

111. B.C. Franklin, *The Tulsa Race Riot and Three of its Victims*, August 22, 1931, https://nmaahc.si.edu/object/nmaahc_2015.176.1 (last visited October 7, 2018) (manuscript recovered from a storage area in 2015 and donated to the National Museum of African American History and Culture by Tulsa Friends and John W. and Karen R. Franklin) ; *see also*, Allison Keyes, *A Long-Lost Manuscript Contains a Searing Eyewitness Account of the Tulsa Race Massacre of 1921*, May 27, 2016, https://www.smithsonianmag.com/smithsonian-institution/long-lost-manuscript-contains-searing-eyewitness-account-tulsa-race-massacre-1921-180959251/ (last visited October 7, 2018); Mary Elizabeth Jones Parrish, EVENTS OF THE TULSA DISASTER (Tulsa, OK: John Hope Franklin Center for Reconciliation, 2009) (Limited Edition, First Printing, as originally published in 1923) (statement of Mrs. Carrie Kinlaw noting that "an aeroplane shot down a man right in our path," June 23, 1921), at 37; Mary Elizabeth Jones Parrish, EVENTS OF THE TULSA DISASTER (Tulsa, OK: John Hope Franklin Center for Reconciliation, 2009) (Limited Edition, First Printing, as originally published in 1923) (statement of anonymous witness, noting that amidst the "looting and burning of Negro homes…aeroplanes flew over head, some very low," June 24, 1921) at 42.

112. TULSA RACE RIOT: A REPORT BY THE OKLAHOMA COMMISSION TO STUDY THE TULSA RACE RIOT OF 1921 (Oklahoma City, OK: Oklahoma Historical Society, February 28, 2001), at 71, https://archive.org/details/ReportOnTulsaRaceRiotOf1921 (last visited June 23, 2019); *see also*, http://digitalprairie.ok.gov/cdm/ref/collection/race-riot/id/182 (last visited September 21, 2018).

113. Bob Hower, 1921 TULSA RACE RIOT--"AMERICA'S DEADLIEST: "ANGELS OF MERCY," (Tulsa, OK: Homestead Press, 1993), at 10 (compiled from the memorabilia collection of Maurice Willows, Director of Red Cross Relief, and the grandfather of Bob Hower).

114. Bob Hower, 1921 TULSA RACE RIOT--"AMERICA'S DEADLIEST: "ANGELS OF MERCY," (Tulsa, OK: Homestead Press, 1993), at 7 - 9 (compiled from the memorabilia collection of Maurice Willows, Director of Red Cross Relief, and the grandfather of Bob Hower).

115. Mary Elizabeth Jones Parrish, EVENTS OF THE TULSA DISASTER (Tulsa, OK: John Hope Franklin Center for Reconciliation, 2009) (Limited Edition, First Printing, as originally published in 1923), at 14 - 19. The notion of having a white person vouch for an African American harks back to the post-slavery "Black Codes," laws enacted by Deep South state legislatures to restrict the freedom of African Americans and ensure their availability as a cheap labor force. Among such laws, vagrancy provisions and other measures routinely required African Americans to have a white person speak to their entitlement to be out and about. *See, e.g.*, https://www.history.com/topics/black-history/black-codes (last visited July 25, 2019); https://www.thoughtco.com/the-black-codes-4125744 (last visited July 25, 2019).

116. Mary Elizabeth Jones Parrish, EVENTS OF THE TULSA DISASTER (Tulsa, OK: John Hope Franklin Center for Reconciliation, 2009) (Limited Edition, First Printing, as originally published in 1923), at 30 (statement of James T.A. West, Teacher in High School, June 20, 1921).

117. *See, e.g.*, TULSA RACE RIOT: A REPORT BY THE OKLAHOMA COMMISSION TO STUDY THE TULSA RACE RIOT OF 1921 (February 28, 2001), at 37, https://archive.org/details/ReportOnTulsaRaceRiotOf1921 (last visited June 23, 2019). Author and historian Scott Ellsworth, in his chapter entitled *The Tulsa Race Riot*, noted: "In the week following the riot, nearly all Tulsa's African American citizenry had managed to win their freedom, by one way or another, from the internment centers. Largely homeless, and in many cases now penniless, they made their way back to Greenwood,. However, Greenwood was gone."

118. Mary Elizabeth Jones Parrish, EVENTS OF THE TULSA DISASTER (Tulsa, OK: John Hope Franklin Center for Reconciliation, 2009) (Limited Edition, First Printing, as originally published in 1923), at 30 (statement of P.S. Thompson, Ph.C., President, Tulsa Medical, Dental and Pharmaceutical Association, June 22, 1921).

119. *See, e.g.*, Stephen P. Kerr, J.D., LL.M., TULSA RACE WAR: 31ST MAY 1921 (1999, unpublished manuscript by the grandson of First Presbyterian minister, Dr. Charles William Kerr on file in the archives of First Presbyterian Church):

> Grandfather Kerr rang up his First Church Sexton and told him to open the First Presbyterian Church basement…to refugee Blacks fleeing the original Courthouse Lynch Mob given 'special commissions' by the City to act as 'emergency deputies.'

> Grandfather Kerr also authorized Church funds to be used to feed and care for the Blacks. Then, Grandfather Kerr rang up various Black Ministers and leaders telling them that his Church basement will welcome all who need refuge. He tells the Greenwood leaders, 'I think the rioters will respect the sacred character of a Christian Church.'

120. *See, e.g.*, James D. White, TULSA CATHOLICS (New York, NY: Carlton Press, 1978), noting: "During the Tulsa race riot in May, 1921, the church basement [of Holy Family Cathedral] was used as a shelter for some two hundred women and children refugees. (Most of the men who had lost their homes in the burning and looting in the northside ghetto were sent to Muskogee until the riot was brought under control.); *see also*, Michael A. Malcom, THE TRI-SPIRED GEM: HOLY FAMILY CATHEDRAL: A COLLECTION OF ESSAYS, DIARIES, AND REFLECTIONS (Tulsa, OK: Holy Family Cathedral, 2014) (containing an essay by African American Tulsa attorney James O. Goodwin highlighting the two white downtown Tulsa churches that opened their doors to black refugees, First Presbyterian Church and Holy Family Cathedral).

121. Georgia Lloyd Jones Snoke, granddaughter of Richard Lloyd Jones, publisher of THE TULSA TRIBUNE, noted, "[T]he night of the riot, blacks sheltered in Grandmother and Grandfather's Northside home, as they did with other white families. My aunt Bis, then about nine, told me of taking sandwiches and drink to riot victims as they huddled there." Transcript of remarks of Georgia Lloyd Jones Snoke to All Souls Unitarian Church, June 25, 2017, from the archives of First Presbyterian Church.

122. Adapted from *Final 1921 Tulsa Race Riot Reconnaissance Survey*, November 2005, National Park Service, U.S. Department of the Interior, http://cdm15020.contentdm.oclc.org/cdm/ref/collection/p15020coll6/id/200 (last visited September 15, 2018); *see also*, TULSA RACE RIOT: A REPORT BY THE OKLAHOMA COMMISSION TO STUDY THE TULSA RACE RIOT OF 1921 (Oklahoma City, OK: Oklahoma Historical Society, February 28, 2001), http://www.okhistory.org/research/forms/freport.pdf (last visited June 2, 2016).

123. Bob Hower, 1921 TULSA RACE RIOT—"AMERICA'S DEADLIEST: "ANGELS OF MERCY," (Tulsa, OK: Homestead Press, 1993), at 228 (compiled from the memorabilia collection of Maurice Willows, Director of Red Cross Relief, and the grandfather of Bob Hower), at

7 - 9.

124. *African-American Damie Rowland Ford: Oral History, 'Mother of Dick Rowland,' on July 22, 1972* (interview by Ruth Avery of Damie Rowland Ford on July 22, 1972), *cited in*, Bob Hower, 1921 Tulsa Race Riot--"America's Deadliest: "Angels of Mercy," (Tulsa, OK: Homestead Press, 1993), at 228 (compiled from the memorabilia collection of Maurice Willows, Director of Red Cross Relief, and the grandfather of Bob Hower).

125. *Dead Estimated at 100: City is Quiet*, June 2, 1921, Tulsa World, front page.

126. John Hope Franklin and Scott Ellsworth, *History Knows No Fences: An Overview*, Tulsa Race Riot: A report by the Oklahoma Commission to Study the Tulsa Race Riot of 1921 (Oklahoma City, OK: Oklahoma Historical Society, February 28, 2001), at 22 - 23,, https://archive.org/details/ReportOnTulsaRaceRiotOf1921 (last visited June 23, 2019).

127. *See, e.g.*, *State Troops in Charge*, Tulsa World, June 1, 1921, front page; *Dead Estimated at 100: City is Quiet*, June 2, 1921, Tulsa World, front page.

128. Mary Elizabeth Jones Parrish, Events of the Tulsa Disaster (Tulsa, OK: John Hope Franklin Center for Reconciliation, 2009) (Limited Edition, First Printing, as originally published in 1923), at 25.

129. Mary Elizabeth Jones Parrish, Events of the Tulsa Disaster (Tulsa, OK: John Hope Franklin Center for Reconciliation, 2009) (Limited Edition, First Printing, as originally published in 1923), at 14.

130. *NAACP legal file. Extradition--A.S. [sic] Smitherman, 1922;* Papers of the NAACP, Part 8, Series A, Discrimination in the criminal justice system, 1910 - 1955, Legal Department and Central Office records, 1910 - 1939; reel 3, fr. 0041 - 0059 (Frederick, MD: University Publications of America, 1988) (Description: Correspondence documenting the NAACP's fight against the extradition of A.J. Smitherman from Massachusetts to Oklahoma. Mr. Smitherman escaped a race riot in Tulsa and fears being lynched if he returns.), http://www.worldcat.org/title/naacp-legal-file-extradition-assic-smitherman-1922/oclc/26366328&referer=brief_results (last visited October 30, 2018), *cited in A Descriptive Poem of the Tulsa Riot and Massacre*, http://www.personal.utulsa.edu/~marc-carlson/riot/smithermanpoem.html (last visited October 30, 2018).

131. *See, e.g.*, First Presbyterian Church, Tulsa, Oklahoma, Oral History Series, Interview with Betty Payne and Elizabeth Mapes, March 20, 1999, and April 17, 1999 No. 1, at 32; First Presbyterian Church, Tulsa, Oklahoma, Oral History Series, Interview with Joan "Johnnie" Coe, September 18, 1999, No. 13, at 37 – 38.

132. First Presbyterian Church, Tulsa, Oklahoma, Oral History Series, Interview with George "Bill" & Eve Morrow, February 5, 2000, No, 16, at 8 – 10.

133. Stephen P. Kerr, J.D., LL.M., Tulsa Race War: 31ˢᵀ May 1921, at 23 (1999, unpublished manuscript by the grandson of First Presbyterian minister, Dr. Charles William Kerr on file in the archives of First Presbyterian Church, at 49.

134. Internal, untitled First Presbyterian Church document (available in Church archives) created as background for Dr. James Miller, circa 1993; *see also, Commemorating a Half Century of Christian Service in Oklahoma, First Presbyterian Church, Tulsa, Oklahoma*, November 26, 1948.

135. *Deacon/session notes 1921 files; Notes taken on Wednesday, July 18, 2018, by Jane Wright & Joan Hoar*, First Presbyterian Church archives. [Special note: Deacons provide service (*e.g.*, attending to the sick and the afflicted). Session members (*i.e.*, elders) provide financial and program support, and leadership (*e.g.*, chairing committees such as personnel and building & grounds).]

136. Stephen P. Kerr, J.D., LL.M., Tulsa Race War: 31ˢᵀ May 1921, at 23 (1999, unpublished

manuscript by the grandson of First Presbyterian minister, Dr. Charles William Kerr on file in the archives of First Presbyterian Church, at 153 - 167.

137. *See, e.g.*, I. Marc Carlson, *The Tulsa Race Massacre*, https://tulsaraceriot.wordpress.com/tag/kkk/

138. Stephen P. Kerr, J.D., LL.M., TULSA RACE WAR: 31ST MAY 1921, at 23 (1999, unpublished manuscript by the grandson of First Presbyterian minister, Dr. Charles William Kerr on file in the archives of First Presbyterian Church, at 168 - 174.

139. *See, e.g.*, Ginnie Graham, *From the Ashes: Tulsa Race Massacre history still unraveling*, TULSA WORLD, June 2, 2019, at G1.

140. *See, also*, Mary Elizabeth Jones Parrish, EVENTS OF THE TULSA DISASTER (Tulsa, OK: John Hope Franklin Center for Reconciliation, 2009) (Limited Edition, First Printing, as originally published in 1923), at 12. Ms. Parrish noted the deployment of airplanes during the Tulsa disaster:

> The aeroplanes continued to watch over the fleeing people like great birds of prey watching for a victum [*sic*], but I have not heard of them doing any harm to the people out in the direction where we were. I have been reliably informed, however, that they fired on the people who were gathered in groups in the colored park close to town.

141. It is near certain that planes flew in and around the Greenwood District during the onslaught. It is less certain whether the planes engaged in reconnaissance or strafed and bombed this community under siege:

> It is within reason that there was some shooting from planes and even the dropping of incendiaries, but the evidence would seem to indicate that it was of a minor nature and had no real effect in the riot. While it is certain that airplanes were used by the police for reconnaissance, by photographers and sightseers, there probably were some whites who fired guns from planes or dropped bottles of gasoline or something of that sort. However, they were probably few in number. It is important to note, a number of prominent African Americans at the time of the riot including James T. West, Dr. R.T. Bridgewater, and Walter White of the NAACP, did not speak of any aggressive actions by airplanes during the conflict.

Richard S. Warner, "Airplanes and the Riot," *Final Report of the 1921 Tulsa Race Riot Grand Jury, cited in* TULSA RACE RIOT: A REPORT BY THE OKLAHOMA COMMISSION TO STUDY THE TULSA RACE RIOT OF 1921 (Oklahoma City, OK: Oklahoma Historical Society, February 28, 2001), at 107, https://archive.org/details/ReportOnTulsaRaceRiotOf1921 (last visited June 23, 2019).

142. Letter on file at the Greenwood Cultural Center, 322 North Greenwood Avenue, Tulsa, Oklahoma.

143. Letter on file with the author.

144. T.P. Scott, NEGRO CITY DIRECTORY (The Greenwood Chamber of Commerce, 1941), at xiii-xiv.

145. BOOKER T. WASHINGTON HIGH SCHOOL YEARBOOK, 1921, available at Rudisill Library, Tulsa, Oklahoma.

146. https://www.nytimes.com/1921/06/02/archives/85-whites-and-negroes-die-in-tulsa-riots-as-3000-armed-men-battle.html (last visited September 14, 2018).

147. For June 1 - 2, 1921, newspaper headlines, see generally, https://search.aol.com/aol/image (last visited September 28, 2018).

148. *Painful Past*, editorial, TULSA WORLD, November 19, 2008, https://www.tulsaworld.com/opinion/editorials/painful-past/article_b2ab58ea-bf19-5cfd-b3c3-492a28b752a1.html?utm_medium=social&utm_source=email&utm_campaign=user-share (last visited September 10, 2018).

149. Minutes of the Tulsa City Commission, June 14, 1921.

150. https://search.aol.com/aol/image?p=black+wall+street+rebuilding+photo&s_it (last visited August 21, 2018).

151. *Final Report of the 1921 Tulsa Race Riot Grand Jury, cited in* TULSA RACE RIOT: A REPORT BY THE OKLAHOMA COMMISSION TO STUDY THE TULSA RACE RIOT OF 1921 (Oklahoma City, OK: Oklahoma Historical Society, February 28, 2001), at 89, https://archive.org/details/ReportOnTulsaRaceRiotOf1921 (last visited June 23, 2019).

152. *Report by Maurice Willows, Director, Tulsa County Chapter, American Red Cross Disaster Relief Committee, cited in* Bob Hower, 1921 TULSA RACE RIOT AND THE AMERICAN RED CROSS: "ANGELS OF MERCY" (Tulsa, OK: Homestead Press, 1993), at 160.

153. *Report by Maurice Willows, Director, Tulsa County Chapter, American Red Cross Disaster Relief Committee, cited in* Bob Hower, 1921 TULSA RACE RIOT AND THE AMERICAN RED CROSS: "ANGELS OF MERCY" (Tulsa, OK: Homestead Press, 1993), at 146.

154. *Report by Maurice Willows, Director, Tulsa County Chapter, American Red Cross Disaster Relief Committee, cited in* Bob Hower, 1921 TULSA RACE RIOT AND THE AMERICAN RED CROSS: "ANGELS OF MERCY" (Tulsa, OK: Homestead Press, 1993), at 156.

155. *Report by Maurice Willows, Director, Tulsa County Chapter, American Red Cross Disaster Relief Committee, cited in* Bob Hower, 1921 TULSA RACE RIOT AND THE AMERICAN RED CROSS: "ANGELS OF MERCY" (Tulsa, OK: Homestead Press, 1993), at 157.

156. *Report by Maurice Willows, Director, Tulsa County Chapter, American Red Cross Disaster Relief Committee, cited in* Bob Hower, 1921 TULSA RACE RIOT AND THE AMERICAN RED CROSS: "ANGELS OF MERCY" (Tulsa, OK: Homestead Press, 1993), at 157.

157. *It Must Not be Again*, THE TULSA TRIBUNE, June 4, 1921, at 8.

158. Ordinance No. 2156, June 7, 1921, published in the TULSA WORLD June 10, 11, and 12, 1921; Minutes of the Tulsa City Commission, June 7, 1921, at 3.

159. *See, e.g., Burned District in Fire Limits*, TULSA WORLD, June 8, 1921, https://chroniclingamerica.loc.gov/lccn/sn85042345/1921-06-08/ed-1/seq-2/ (last visited September 14, 2018).

160. *See generally*, Buck Colbert Franklin, MY LIFE AND AN ERA: THE AUTOBIOGRAPHY OF BUCK COLBERT FRANKLIN, John Hope Franklin and John Whittington Franklin, eds., (Baton Rouge, LA: LSU Press, 1997); Allison Keyes, *A Long-Lost Manuscript Contains a Searing Eyewitness Account of the Tulsa Race Massacre of 1921: An Oklahoma lawyer details the attack by hundreds of whites on the thriving black neighborhood where hundreds died 95 years ago*, May 27, 2016, https://www.smithsonianmag.com/smithsonian-institution/long-lost-manuscript-contains-searing-eyewitness-account-tulsa-race-massacre-1921-180959251/ (last visited September 19, 2018).

161. John Hope Franklin and John Whittington Franklin, editors, MY LIFE IN AN ERA: THE AUTOBIOGRAPHY OF BUCK COLBERT FRANKLIN (Baton Rouge, LA: Louisiana State University Press, 1997), at 198.

162. H.A. Guess, OKLAHOMA SUN, August 3, 1921, *cited in* TULSA RACE RIOT: A REPORT BY THE OKLAHOMA COMMISSION TO STUDY THE TULSA RACE RIOT OF 1921 (Oklahoma City, OK: Oklahoma Historical Society, February 28, 2001), at 173, https://archive.org/details/ReportOnTulsaRaceRiotOf1921 (last visited June 23, 2019).

163. Rev. G. Calvin McCutchen (1927 - 2019), served as senior pastor of Mount Zion Baptist Church for fifty years, from his installation on October 4, 1957, to his retirement into pastor emeritus status in November 2007. Rev. McCutchen doubled as a Tulsa civil rights leader, leading youth sit-ins at whites-only restaurants and shepherding a youth delegation from Tulsa to the 1963 March on Washington. Rev. McCutchen died on March 30, 2019. *See* Tim Stanley, *Rev. G. Calvin McCutchen, longtime north Tulsa pastor, civil rights leader, dies at 92,* TULSA WORLD, April 3, 2019, http://tracking.bhmedia.whatcounts. com/t?r=40&c=160797&l=85&ctl=304666:662BA2D7A9FCE51F212264E44ADBBBB-149CA475AD5540ABF& (last visited April 4, 2019).

164. Mary Elizabeth Jones Parrish, EVENTS OF THE TULSA DISASTER (Tulsa, OK: John Hope Franklin Center for Reconciliation, 2009) (Limited Edition, First Printing, as originally published in 1923), at 7.

165. Mary Elizabeth Jones Parrish, EVENTS OF THE TULSA DISASTER (Tulsa, OK: John Hope Franklin Center for Reconciliation, 2009) (Limited Edition, First Printing, as originally published in 1923), at 7.

166. Mary Elizabeth Jones Parrish, EVENTS OF THE TULSA DISASTER (Tulsa, OK: John Hope Franklin Center for Reconciliation, 2009) (Limited Edition, First Printing, as originally published in 1923).

167. Mary Elizabeth Jones Parrish, EVENTS OF THE TULSA DISASTER (Tulsa, OK: John Hope Franklin Center for Reconciliation, 2009) (Limited Edition, First Printing, as originally published in 1923), at 93.

168. John Hope Franklin and John Whittington Franklin, editors, MY LIFE IN AN ERA: THE AUTOBIOGRAPHY OF BUCK COLBERT FRANKLIN (Baton Rouge, LA: Louisiana State University Press, 1997), at 201 - 202.

169. Crisis, XXXI (New York, NY: N.A.A.C.P., April 1926), at 269.

170. DIRECTORY OF THE COLORED SECTION, TULSA, OKLAHOMA, FIRST EDITION: ALPHABETICAL LIST OF HOMES OF COLORED IN TULSA, OKLAHOMA; CERTIFIED BUSINESS AND PROFESSIONAL; A COMPLETE MAILING LIST OF MERCHANTS, COMPLIED BY POWELL AND STEVENSON, *circa* 1935 (on file with author).

171. Tulsa Medicine History: Charles J. Bate, M.D., http://tcmsok.org/mc/wp-content/ uploads/2012/08/Charles_Bate.pdf (last visited January 27, 2019).

172. Eddie Faye Gates, THEY CAME SEARCHING: HOW BLACKS SOUGHT THE PROMISED LAND IN TULSA (Fort Worth, TX: Eakin Press, 1997), at 46 -47.

173. Oral interview with Dr. Charles Bate, http://cdm15020.contentdm.oclc.org/cdm/ref/ collection/p15020coll10/id/140 (last visited January 27, 2019).

174. United States Commission on Civil Rights, Oklahoma Advisory Committee, SCHOOL DESEGREGATION IN TULSA, OKLAHOMA: A REPORT (Ann Arbor, MI: United States Commission on Civil Rights, Oklahoma Advisory Committee, August 1977, reprints from the collection of the University of Michigan Library) (report by the United States Commission on Civil Rights, Oklahoma Advisory Committee; Committee members: State Rep. Hannah Atkins of Oklahoma City [chair]; Earl D. Mitchell of Stillwater [vice chair]; William C. Brown, Mrs. William V. Carey, and Richard Vallejo, Oklahoma City; Nancy G. Feldman, Patty P. Eaton, and June Echo-Hawk, Tulsa; William R. Carmack, Patricia A. Davis, and Jerry Muskrat, Norman; John H. Nelson, Lawton; Caryl Taylor, Okmulgee; and Stephen Jones, Enid), at 2 - 4.

175. Don Thompson and Eddie Faye Gates, *Reverend Benjamin S. Roberts (B.S.): 'Shepherd of the Prairie and Secular Leader, Too'* (part of a collection of photographs and captions celebrat-

ing Tulsa's African American pioneers on display in the B.S. Roberts Room on the campus of Oklahoma State University, Tulsa).

176. Eddie Faye Gates, THEY CAME SEARCHING: HOW BLACKS SOUGHT THE PROMISED LAND IN TULSA (Fort Worth, TX: Eakin Press, 1997), at 161 - 165.

177. Don Thompson and Eddie Faye Gates, *Reverend Benjamin S. Roberts (B.S.): 'Shepherd of the Prairie and Secular Leader, Too'* (part of a collection of photographs and captions celebrating Tulsa's African American pioneers on display in the B.S. Roberts Room on the campus of Oklahoma State University, Tulsa).

178. Mike Strain, *The day MLK came to Tulsa: 'We must all live together as brothers or we will die together as fools,'* TULSA WORLD, January 16, 2017, http://www.tulsaworld.com/news/local/the-day-mlk-came-to-tulsa-we-must-all-live/article_4b0ab51a-8080-568d-a738-5ea6114958e2.html (last viewed January 18, 2017).

179. Jonathan Cooper, *Tulsa Man Who Met Dr. King Reflects On The Civil Rights Icon,* January 21, 2019, http://www.newson6.com/story/39827562/tulsa-man-who-met-dr-king-reflects-on-the-civil-rights-icon (last visited January 22, 2019).

180. https://search.aol.com/aol/image?p=green+book&s_it=img-ans&v_t=comsearch&fr=comsearch&imgurl=https%3A%2F%2Fupload.wikimedia.org%2Fwikipedia%2Fcommons%2Fthumb%2F7%2F70%2FThe_Negro_Motorist_Green_Book.jpg%2F1200px-The_Negro_Motorist_Green_Book.jpg#id=2&iurl=https%3A%2F%2Fs.newsweek.com%2Fsites%2Fwww.newsweek.com%2Ffiles%2Fstyles%2Fembed-lg%2Fpublic%2F2018%2F01%2F04%2F0104greenbook1940.jpg&action=click

181. *See, e.g.,* https://blackpast.org/aah/negro-motorist-green-book-1936-1964; https://www.biographies.net/bio/m/0crhh5q (last visited January 8, 2019).

182 *Green Book* (2018), https://www.imdb.com/title/tt6966692/ (last visited April 8, 2019).

183. Schomburg Center for Research in Black Culture, Manuscripts, Archives and Rare Books Division, The New York Public Library. "The Negro Motorist Green Book: 1947," *The New York Public Library Digital Collections.* 1947. http://digitalcollections.nypl.org/items/29219280-892b-0132-4271-58d385a7bbd0 (last visited January 8, 2019).

184. Schomburg Center for Research in Black Culture, Manuscripts, Archives and Rare Books Division, The New York Public Library. "The Negro Motorist Green Book: 1939," *The New York Public Library Digital Collections.* 1939. http://digitalcollections.nypl.org/items/911d3420-83da-0132-687a-58d385a7b928 (last visited January 8, 2019).

185. Schomburg Center for Research in Black Culture, Manuscripts, Archives and Rare Books Division, The New York Public Library. "The Negro Motorist Green Book: 1947," *The New York Public Library Digital Collections.* 1947. http://digitalcollections.nypl.org/items/29219280-892b-0132-4271-58d385a7bbd0 (last visited January 8, 2019).

186. Schomburg Center for Research in Black Culture, Manuscripts, Archives and Rare Books Division, The New York Public Library. "Green Book: 1962," *The New York Public Library Digital Collections.* 1962. http://digitalcollections.nypl.org/items/786175a0-942e-0132-97b0-58d385a7bbd0 (last visited January 8, 2019).

187. https://legal-dictionary.thefreedictionary.com/eminent+domain (last visited April 8, 2019).

188. *See, e.g.,* https://sociologydictionary.org/urban-renewal/ (last visited April 8, 2019); Bob Weeks, Urban Renewal: A Flawed Idea That Failed 50 Years Ago, https://wichitaliberty.org/free-markets/urban-renewal-a-flawed-idea-that-failed-50-years-ago/ (last visited April 8, 2019).

189. Steven Lackmeyer, *Urban Renewal,* Oklahoma Historical Society, http://www.okhistory.org/publications/enc/entry.php?entry=UR006 (last visited September 4, 2018).

190. *See* Department of City Development Recommendations to the Tulsa City Commission, presented and approved on May 2, 1986, on file with author; *see also*, http://www.tulsadevelopmentauthority.org/about/ (last visited September 7, 2018).

Urban renewal funding ended in 1974. Still, the role of Tulsa Development Authority ("TDA") expanded to cover diverse areas including neighborhood improvement, code enforcement, flood area acquisition, and home rehabilitation. Today, TDA focuses on land acquisition and sales for targeted economic development. TDA collaborates with planning bodies, city government, and local developers. It drives the improvement of targeted, deteriorated areas that offer potential for residential and commercial redevelopment.

TDA (1) restores land value by removing blighted buildings; (2) creates opportunities for revitalization by selling surplus land; (3) assists the City of Tulsa in selling unused lands; (4) improves infrastructure and beautification processes by managing tax increment funds ("TIFs"); (5) drives new multi-family residential projects by administering downtown development funds; and (6) provides vision and planning for areas targeted for improvement. TDA's mission includes a focus on safety and sanitation.

TDA's involvement in a project does not end with a land sale. It becomes a working partner with developers who purchase lands or buildings. TDA ensures ideas become reality by participating in the building process every step of the way. With its mantra of "the highest and best use" for each property, TDA works to assure each project meets the city's needs for new housing, retail service and office space. Developers are required to present an architectural plan and any plan changes to the TDA board for approval. Developers must complete projects within a reasonable time.

191. *Resolution 2339*, Board of Commissioners of the City of Tulsa, Oklahoma, November 17, 1959; *Minutes of the regular meeting of the Board of Commissioners of the City of Tulsa, Oklahoma*, July 31, 1959.

192. Photo courtesy of Shannon West, Selser Schaefer Architects, Tulsa, Oklahoma.

193. Kevin M. Kruse, "A traffic jam in Atlanta would seem to have nothing to do with slavery. But look closer....", *The 1619 Project*, THE NEW YORK TIMES MAGAZINE, August 18, 2019.

194. Author James Baldwin famously quipped in 1963 that "urban renewal means Negro removal." *See* youtube.com/watch?v=T8Abhj17kYU (last visited August 27, 2019) (clip of interview of James Baldwin by Kenneth Clark, conducted immediately after Baldwin met with United States Attorney General Robert F. Kennedy).

The notion of Tulsa Development Authority overseeing black removal remains entrenched. Hundreds of black Tulsans attended a City Council meeting on March 27, 2019, at which two "sector plans" (urban renewal plans) were on the agenda, the Unity Heritage/Greenwood Neighborhood Sector Plan and the Crosbie Heights Sector Plan. Black residents complained of the failure of Tulsa Development Authority to provide adequate notice to glean community input on the plans. Residents also voiced fear of the use of eminent domain to acquire properties and displace community members. The Tulsa City Council tabled the sector plans indefinitely.

One woman voiced the fears gentrification through eminent domain cogently and compellingly:

> Charlotte Combs, 65, was one of the 213 people allowed in City Council Chambers for the hearing. Hundreds more never made it inside.
>
> 'Immediately, it was a flashback, and the first thing that came to my mind, if they are allowed to do it (by eminent domain), where would I move? Where

would I relocate?' said Combs, who lives in the Heritage Hills neighborhood. 'At my age, and like some of my other neighbors ... we're at the age now we really don't have a desire to relocate to any other area.'

Combs' flashback was to decades-old city urban renewal projects north of downtown that helped clear the way for highways, private commercial development and higher-education facilities.

In the process, she said, homes and private businesses, including some on Black Wall Street, were cleared and their owners relocated. Some businesses survived, some didn't.

Kevin Canfield, *'Where would I move?': Tulsa homeowners voice concern about possible effects of eminent domain*, TULSA WORLD, April 7, 2019, https://www.tulsaworld.com/news/local/government-and-politics/where-would-i-move-tulsa-homeowners-voice-concern-about-possible/article_35931eea-4127-5c2d-94c7-a3465841eed5.html (last visited April 7, 2019); See also, Kevin Canfield, TDA responds to concerns, Tulsa World, April 7, 2019, at A8.

195. *See, e.g.*, Sherwood Ross, *Integration's Side Effects Hit Businesses In Black Areas*, January 26, 1987, http://articles.sun-sentinel.com/1987-01-26/business/8701060249_1_black-merchants-black-business-black-poverty (last visited September 6, 2018).

196. *Interstate 244*, Oklahoma, Interstate-Guide.com, http://www.interstate-guide.com/i-244_ok.html (last visited September 5, 2018).

197. *See, e.g.*, Michael Wall, *Succession Planning for Small Businesses*, May 2, 2018, https://www.forbes.com/sites/impactpartners/2018/05/02/succession-planning-for-small-businesses/#53e894d77a7d (last visited September 8, 2018).

198. https://search.aol.com/aol/image?p=black+wall+street+rebuilding+photo&s_it (last visited August 21, 2018).

199. Original poem by the author, included in Hannibal B. Johnson, INCOGNEGRO: POETIC REFLECTIONS ON RACE & DIVERSITY IN AMERICA (Fort Worth, TX: Eakin Press, 2019).

200. Minutes of the Tulsa City Commission, June 14, 1921; Dexter Mullins, *Survivors of infamous 1921 Tulsa race riot still hope for justice, see also* http://america.aljazeera.com/articles/2014/7/19/survivors-of-infamous1921tulsaraceriotstillhopeforjustice.html (last visited August 6, 2018).

201. Kendrick Marshall, *"Signs of Gentrification": Greenwood community worries black people are being pushed out, history disrespected*, TULSA WORLD, June 16, 2019, A1.

202. Scott Ellsworth, DEATH IN A PROMISED LAND (Baton Rouge, LA; Louisiana State University Press, 1982).

203. TULSA RACE RIOT: A REPORT BY THE OKLAHOMA COMMISSION TO STUDY THE TULSA RACE RIOT OF 1921 (Oklahoma City, OK: Oklahoma Historical Society, February 28, 2001), http://www.okhistory.org/research/forms/freport.pdf (last visited June 2, 2016).

204. Remarks by M. Susan Savage at John Hope Franklin Reconciliation Park groundbreaking on November 17, 2008, the last public appearance of Dr. John Hope Franklin before his death on March 25, 2009) (E-mail correspondence from M. Susan Savage, October 17, 2018, on file with author).

205. Sam Howe Verhovek, *75 Years Later, Tulsa Confronts Its Race Riot*, THE NEW YORK TIMES, May 31, 1996, https://www.nytimes.com/1996/05/31/us/75-years-later-tulsa-confronts-its-race-riot.html (last visited April 8, 2019).

206. Remarks by M. Susan Savage at reconciliation services hosted by Rev. G. Calvin McCutcheon, Pastor, Mount Zion Baptist Church, on June 4, 2000 (E-mail correspondence from M. Susan Savage, October 17, 2018, on file with author).

207. TULSA RACE RIOT: A REPORT BY THE OKLAHOMA COMMISSION TO STUDY THE TULSA RACE

RIOT OF 1921 (Oklahoma City, OK: Oklahoma Historical Society, February 28, 2001), http://www.okhistory.org/research/forms/freport.pdf (last visited June 2, 2016).

208. TULSA RACE RIOT: A REPORT BY THE OKLAHOMA COMMISSION TO STUDY THE TULSA RACE RIOT OF 1921 (Oklahoma City, OK: Oklahoma Historical Society, February 28, 2001), http://www.okhistory.org/research/forms/freport.pdf (last visited June 2, 2016).

209. TULSA RACE RIOT: A REPORT BY THE OKLAHOMA COMMISSION TO STUDY THE TULSA RACE RIOT OF 1921 (Oklahoma City: OK, Oklahoma Historical Society, February 28, 2001), http://www.okhistory.org/research/forms/freport.pdf (last visited June 2, 2016); *see also*, *Tulsa Race Riot Commission Recommends Reparations*, DEMOCRACY NOW!, February 8, 2000, http://www.democracynow.org/2000/2/8/tulsa_race_riot_commission_recommends_ reparations (last visited May 20, 2016); *Reparations for the 1921 Tulsa, OK race Riot: 2001 Action of Immediate Witness*, UNITARIAN UNIVERSALIST ASSOCIATION, http://www.uua.org/statements/reparations-1921-tulsa-ok-race-riot (last visited May 20, 2016); Expat Okie, *The Tulsa Race Riot of 1921 – justice delayed, but the fight goes on*, DAILY KOS, June 30, 2012, http://www.dailykos.com/stories/2012/6/30/1104681/-The-Tulsa-Race-Riot-of-1921-and-justice-delayed-but-the-fight-goes-on (last visited May 20, 2016).

210. *See, e.g.*, Kimberly C. Ellis, H-Net, *The Tulsa Reparations Coalition Call for Endorsements*, HUMANITIES AND SOCIAL SCIENCES ONLINE, July 24, 2001, http://h-net.msu.edu/cgi-bin/logbrowse.pl?trx=vx&list=H-Afro-Am&month=0107&msg=8dwEh5cWPFL90c-Q2pKNFUA (last visited May 21, 2016) (The Tulsa Reparations Coalition, sponsored by the Center for Racial Justice, Inc. formed on April 7, 2001 to obtain restitution for the damages suffered by Tulsa's Black community, as recommended by the Oklahoma Commission on February 21, 2001.); National Coalition of Blacks for Reparations in America, http://ncobra.org/aboutus/index.html (last visited May 21, 2016). The National Coalition of Blacks for Reparations in America, founded September 26, 1987, is a grassroots group organized for the sole purpose of obtaining reparations for African descendants in the United States.

211. *Race Relations Survey*, John Hope Franklin Center for Reconciliation, http://www.jhfcenter.org/the-centers-work/community-outreach/ (last visited June 8, 2016).

212. Correspondence with Pete Churchwell, November 28, 2018 (responses to author's ten questions; on file with author).

213. E-mail correspondence with Dr. Vivian Clark-Adams, December 17, 2018 (on file with author).

214. 1921 Riot Reconciliation Act of 2001, 74 Okla. St. Ann. Sec. 8000.1.2 - 1.3 (West 2002).

215. *See, e.g.*, *Tulsa Park Named for John Hope Franklin*, DUKETODAY, November 24, 2008, http://today.duke.edu/2008/11/tulsa_franklin.html (last visited May 13, 2016); *Tulsa's John Hope Franklin Park Dedicated*, NewsOn6.com, October 27, 2010, http://www.newson6.com/story/13396011/tulsas-john-hope-franklin-reconciliation-park-to-be-dedicated (last visited May 13, 20116).

216. John Hope Franklin Center for Reconciliation, http://www.jhfcenter.org/about/ (last visited May 23, 2016).

217. Randy Krehbiel, *Fostering Hope*, TULSA WORLD, October 4, 2013, http://www.tulsaworld.com/archives/fostering-hope/article_6003f519-7a80-5f59-a9a2-21dc6b090eaa.html (last visited May 23, 2016).

218. Greenwood Area Redevelopment Authority, 74 OK Stat § 74-8223 (2014), http://law.justia.com/codes/oklahoma/2014/title-74/section-74-8223/ (last visited May 23, 2106).

219. Added at 19 Ok. Reg. 1505, effective May 28, 2002; Amended at 20 Ok. Reg. 2679, effective July 25, 2003; *see also*, Oklahoma Regents for Higher Education, http://okhighered.

org/news-center/tulsa-recon-scholars.shtml (last visited May 23, 2016).

220. Oklahoma Regents for Higher Education, http://okhighered.org/news-center/tulsa-recon-scholars.shtml (last visited May 23, 2016).

221. https://www.facebook.com/saynotohate (last visited January 4, 2019).

222. April 21, 2003 Press Release: NCCJ Racial Reconciliation Project to Release Final Report, Thursday, April 24, 2003; 11:30 a.m., Greenwood Cultural Center (on file with author). The author served as facilitator/consultant for the Racial Reconciliation Project.

223. Brian Ford, *Memories of riot evoked as survivors win medals*, TULSA WORLD, April 25, 2001, file:///D:/Users/Hannibal%20Johnson/Downloads/memories%20evoked%20survivors%20win%20medals%204-25-01.pdf (last visited May 23, 2016); Alex Tresniowski, *Burned Into Memory: Survivors of the Bloody 1921 Tulsa Race Riot Band Together to Get Their Story Told*, PEOPLE 59:14, April 14, 2003.

224. Brian Ford, *Memories of riot evoked as survivors win medals*, TULSA WORLD, April 25, 2001, file:///D:/Users/Hannibal%20Johnson/Downloads/memories%20evoked%20survivors%20win%20medals%204-25-01.pdf (last visited May 23, 2016).

225. *Interfaith ministry mails checks to race riot survivors*, CHURCH CENTRAL, April 28, 2002 http://www.churchcentral.com/news/interfaith-ministry-mails-checks-to-race-riot-survivors/ (last visited May 11, 2016); *Tulsa group pays race riot survivors*, CHICAGO TRIBUNE, April 26, 2002, http://articles.chicagotribune.com/2002-04-26/news/0204260127_1_race-riot-tulsa-latter-day-saints (last visited May 11, 2016).

226. *Tulsa group pays race riot survivors*, CHICAGO TRIBUNE, April 26, 2002, http://articles.chicagotribune.com/2002-04-26/news/0204260127_1_race-riot-tulsa-latter-day-saints (last visited May 11, 2016).

227. *Third and final reparations gifts made: Tulsa Race Riot survivors receive almost $50,000*, TULSA METROPOLITAN MINISTRY UPDATE, fourth quarter 2003(on file with author).

228. *Third and final reparations gifts made: Tulsa Race Riot survivors receive almost $50,000*, TULSA METROPOLITAN MINISTRY UPDATE, fourth quarter 2003(on file with author).

229. Meeting minutes, Tulsa Metro Chamber and Community Race Riot Task Force, July 23, 2002, Tulsa Metro Chamber, 616 South Boston Avenue, Tulsa, Oklahoma (on file with author).

230. Tulsa Metro Chamber Race Riot Task Force minutes, June 27, 2001 (on file with author).

231. Tulsa Metro Chamber Race Riot Task Force minutes, June 27, 2001 (on file with author).

232. Tulsa Metro Chamber Race Riot Task Force minutes, June 27, 2001 (on file with author).

233. http://www.zoominfo.com/p/John-Gaberino/76303467 (last visited June 16, 2016).

234. Tulsa Metro Chamber Race Riot Task Force minutes, September 19, 2001 (on file with author).

235. Telephone conference with John Gaberino, June 16, 2016.

236. *16th Annual Buck Colbert Franklin Memorial Civil Rights Lecture*, The University of Tulsa, https://calendar.utulsa.edu/event/16th_annual_buck_colbert_franklin_memorial_civil_rights_lecture_3777#.V1LR-qQrKM8 (last visited June 4, 2016).

237. *See Alexander v. Oklahoma*, 382 F.3d 1206 (10th Cir. 2004).

238. Adrian Brune, *A Long Wait for Justice*. VILLAGE VOICE, April 30, 2003.

239. Daren Briscoe, *A Day of Reckoning*, NEWSWEEK, March 10, 2005.

240. *See Alexander v. Oklahoma*, 382 F.3d 1206 (10ᵗʰ Cir. 2004).

241. *Supreme Court refuses '21 Tulsa race riot suit*, THE CHARLESTON GAZETTE, May 17, 2005.

242. *See, e.g.*, Testimony of Charles J. Ogletree, Jr. Before the Inter-American Commission on Human Rights, Organization of American States, On the Petition Alleging Violations of the Human Rights Of John Melvin Alexander, *et al.*, by the United States of America, http://www.charleshamiltonhouston.org/wp-content/uploads/2013/11/OAS-03-02-07-Ogletree-Statement.pdf (last visited May 10, 2016).

243. *See, e.g.*, Randy Krehbiel, *Group to hear case for damages in Tulsa Race Riot*, TULSA WORLD, February 26, 2007.

244. Jim Myers, *Race riot bill gets House hearing but source indicates floor vote unlikely*, TULSA WORLD, April 25, 2007.

245. *See* the bill at http://www.theorator.com/bills110/text/hr1995.html (last visited May 9, 2016); *see also*, https://www.gpo.gov/fdsys/pkg/CHRG-110hhrg34924/pdf/CHRG-110hhrg34924.pdf.

246. Jim Myers, *U.S. House bill would extend statute of limitations*, TULSA WORLD, April 21, 2007.

247. Jim Myers, *Race riot bill gets House hearing but source indicates floor vote unlikely*, TULSA WORLD, April 25, 2007.

248. Jim Myers, *Race Riot survivors bill fails to advance*, TULSA WORLD, April 3, 2009.

249. *See* the bill at https://www.govtrack.us/congress/bills/111/hr1843/text/ih; see also, https://www.govtrack.us/congress/bills/111/hr1843/text (last visited December 2, 2018).

250. https://www.govtrack.us/congress/bills/112/hr5593/text (last visited December 2, 2018).

251. Expat Okie, The Tulsa Race Riot of 1921--justice delayed, but the fight goes on, Daily Kos, https://www.dailykos.com/stories/2012/6/30/1104681/-The-Tulsa-Race-Riot-of-1921-and-justice-delayed-but-the-fight-goes-on (last visited December 2, 2018).

252. https://www.congress.gov/bill/113th-congress/house-bill/98.

253. Marc Parry, Congress Is Taking On Reparations: At the First Hearing, Academic Historians Were Absent, The Chronicle of Higher Education, June 19, 2019, https://www.chronicle.com/article/Congress-Is-Taking-On/246527 (last visited June 19, 2-019). The bill is H.R. 40--116th Congress (2019 - 20), https://www.congress.gov/bill/116th-congress/house-bill/40/text (last visited June 19, 2019).

254. Kendrick Marshall, *Reparations debate has Tulsa ties: U.S. House subcommittee hears about lasting legacy of Tulsa Race Massacre*, TULSA WORLD, June 20, 2019, at A1.

255. 1921 Tulsa Race Riot Memorial of Reconciliation Design Committee Preamble, on file with author.

256. JOHN HOPE FRANKLIN, THE COLOR LINE: LEGACY FOR THE TWENTY-FIRST CENTURY, (Columbia, Missouri: University of Missouri Press 1994).

257. *See, e.g.*, A.G. Sulzberger, *As Survivors Dwindle, Tulsa Confronts Past*, THE NEW YORK TIMES, June 19, 2011, http://www.nytimes.com/2011/06/20/us/20tulsa.html?_r=0 (last visited May 26, 2016).

258. *See, e.g., Oklahoma Clears Black In Deadly 1921 Race Riot*, THE NEW YORK TIMES, http://www.nytimes.com/1996/10/26/us/oklahoma-clears-black-in-deadly-1921-race-riot.html, October 26, 1996 (last visited May 26, 2016); Steve Gerkin, *First Charged, Last Freed*, THIS LAND, March 20, 2014, http://thislandpress.com/2014/03/20/first-charged-last-freed/ (last visited May 26, 2016).

259. Carrie Golus, *Legal precedent: Jewel C. Stradford Lafontant broke many barriers as a lawyer and*

public servant, THE UNIVERSITY OF CHICAGO MAGAZINE, July – August 2013, http://mag.uchicago.edu/law-policy-society/legal-precedent (last visited May 27, 2016).

260. *Race Riot Charges Dropped*, NewsOn6.comOM, December 11, 2007, http://www.newson6.com/story/7722806/race-riot-charges-dropped (last visited May 26, 2016).

261. Excerpts from remarks of Tim Blake Nelson at the 2010 Greenwood Cultural Center Legacy Award Dinner, April 15, 2010 (excerpted remarks prepared May 27, 2010), on file with author.

262. Letter from Rick L. Oglesby to the Honorable Kevin L. Matthews, 1921 Tulsa Race Massacre Centennial Commission, May 27, 2019 (on file with author).

263. The John Hope Franklin Center for Reconciliation created "The Curriculum Resource Portal," an online compilation of materials that provides educators with resources chronicling Tulsa's Historic Greenwood District, including interviews, lesson plans discussion guides, photographs, and a virtual tour of John Hope Franklin Reconciliation Park. *See* www.jhfcenter.org/curriculum (last visited June 21, 2019).

264. Barbara Hoberock, *Senate passes bill requiring teaching of Tulsa Race Riot History*, TULSA WORLD, March 16, 2012.

265. John Paul Brammer, *Oklahoma Bill Would Have Required Teaching the Tulsa Race Riot*, Blue Nation Review, http://bluenationreview.com/oklahoma-bill-require-teaching-tulsa-race-riot/ (last visited May 18, 106).

266. Randy Krehbiel, *Lessons of history: Tulsa Race Riot now included in state academic standards*, TULSA WORLD, May 31, 2016, at 1.

267. E-mail correspondence from Catherine Mathis, Senior Vice President, Chief Communications Officer, McGraw-Hill Education, June 17, 2016 (on file with author); *see also*, A.G. Sulzberger, *As Survivors Dwindle, Tulsa Confronts Past*, NEW YORK TIMES, June 19, 2011, http://www.nytimes.com/2011/06/20/us/20tulsa.html? r=0 (last visited June 17, 2016).

268. E-mail from Danielle Neves, Deputy Chief of Teaching and Learning, Tulsa Public Schools, to author, March 11, 2019 (on file with author); *see also*, Kyle Hinchey, *TPS teachers learn how to talk about massacre*, TULSA WORLD, July 20, 2019.

269. E-mail correspondence from Senator Kevin Matthews, June 20, 2018 (on file with author).

270. lasilljuneteenth.org/history/ok-state-juneteenth-legislation/ (last visited May 23, 2019).

271. "North Tulsa," often left ambiguous and ill-defined, is the north quadrant of the City of Tulsa. Tulsa's Historic Greenwood District, adjacent to downtown, sits in what might be called near-North Tulsa. The City's black residents have consistently and predominately lived in sectors of North Tulsa, a large land mass, in part pushed by the Riot and subsequent developments out of the Greenwood District to points farther north.

272. North Tulsa Economic Development Initiative, Inc., http://www.ntedi.net/ (last visited June 4, 2016).

273. LEAD North, http://www.leadnorthtulsa.org/; http://www.leadershiptulsa.org/programs/leadnorth/ (last visited June 4, 2016).

274. NorthTulsa100, http://www.northtulsa100.com/about-us.html (last visited June 4, 2016).

275. NorthTulsa100, http://www.northtulsa100.com (last visited June 16, 2019).

276. www.langston. Edu (last visited May 19, 2016).

277. *Langston University-Tulsa*, TULSA CITY-COUNTY LIBRARY, http://www.tulsalibrary.org/tos/langston-university-tulsa (last visited May 19, 2016).

278. United States Commission on Civil Rights, Oklahoma Advisory Committee, *School Desegregation in Tulsa, Oklahoma* (abstract from report; abstract author unnamed), https://eric.ed.gov/?id=ED145054 (last visited June 25, 2019); for full report, *see* United States Commission on Civil Rights, Oklahoma Advisory Committee, SCHOOL DESEGREGATION IN TULSA, OKLAHOMA: A REPORT (Ann Arbor, MI: United States Commission on Civil Rights, Oklahoma Advisory Committee, August 1977, reprints from the collection of the University of Michigan Library) (report by the United States Commission on Civil Rights, Oklahoma Advisory Committee; Committee members: State Rep. Hannah Atkins of Oklahoma City [chair]; Earl D. Mitchell of Stillwater [vice chair]; William C. Brown, Mrs. William V. Carey, and Richard Vallejo, Oklahoma City; Nancy G. Feldman, Patty P. Eaton, and June Echo-Hawk, Tulsa; William R. Carmack, Patricia A. Davis, and Jerry Muskrat, Norman; John H. Nelson, Lawton; Caryl Taylor, Okmulgee; and Stephen Jones, Enid). The report also noted that the Attorney General of the United States filed suit against the Tulsa Independent School District on July 30, 1968, alleging failure to comply with the constitutional mandate to maintain and operate a unitary school system. SCHOOL DESEGREGATION IN TULSA, OKLAHOMA: A REPORT, at 37.

279. Sam Hardiman, *Tulsa Public Schools is pledging to fix 'pervasive racial disparities' in indicators of student success*, TULSA WORLD, August 2, 2018, https://www.tulsaworld.com/news/education/tulsa-public-schools-is-pledging-to-fix-pervasive-racial-disparities/article_35adf06a-b513-55bc-8d63-f403b53c5e60.html (last visited September 5, 2018).

280. The strategic plan for Tulsa Public Schools lists equity among the District's core values, noting: "All children deserve the opportunity to develop their full academic and social potential. Valuing equity means that we must provide resources and supports matched to student need, for every student in every school. Our diversity is a community treasure, and we must foster an inclusive environment by examining biases and resolving unfair practices." *See* https://www.tulsaschools.org/about/strategic-plan/core-values (last visited April 11, 2019).

281. *See* Sam Hardiman, *Tulsa Public Schools is pledging to fix 'pervasive racial disparities' in indicators of student success,* TULSA WORLD, August 2, 2018, https://www.tulsaworld.com/news/education/tulsa-public-schools-is-pledging-to-fix-pervasive-racial-disparities/article_35adf06a-b513-55bc-8d63-f403b53c5e60.html (last visited August 2, 2018).

282. *See* https://greenwoodleadershipacademy.org/our-story/ (last visited August 7, 2018).

283. *See* http://tulsalegacy.org/index.php (last visited August 7, 2018).

284. *See* https://www.facebook.com/pg/Langston-Hughes-Academy-for-Arts-and-Technology-1570959033178537/about/?ref=page_internal (last visited August 7, 2018).

285. *See, e.g.,* https://kipptulsa.org/; https://www.schoolandcollegelistings.com/US/Tulsa/195038060513666/KIPP-Tulsa (last visited August 1, 2019).

286. *Uncommon Schools,* https://uncommonschools.org/faq/ (last visited March 27, 2019).

287. *See, e.g., Farewell Weekend at Driller's Stadium: Drillers To Conclude 29 Regular Seasons At Their 15th & Yale Home,* September 2, 2009, http://tulsa.drillers.milb.com/news/article.jsp?ymd=20090902&content_id=6754122&vkey=pr_t260&fext=.jsp&sid=t260 (last viewed May 14, 2016); *ONEOK Field Opens Next Week,* April 2, 2010, http://www.fox23.com/news/local/oneok-field-opens-next-week/254455561 (last viewed May 14, 2016).

288. Robert Evatt, *GreenArch brings apartments, retail to Greenwood,* TULSA WORLD, July 14, 2012, http://www.tulsaworld.com/business/realestate/greenarch-brings-apartments-retail-to-greenwood/article_04374996-ea94-5034-817b-7940ad3400dc.html (last viewed May 14, 2016)

289. *See, e.g., P.J.,* Lassek, *Drillers site: Greenwood,* TULSA WORLD, June 26, 2009; P.J. Lassek, *City*

breaks ground on downtown ballpark, TULSA WORLD, December 19, 2008,. *P.J.* Lassek, *Baseball park named ONEOK Field*, TULSA WORLD, anuary 13, 2009; Barry Lewis, *Downtown debut: Drillers Lose First Game at New ONEOK Field*, TULSA WORLD, April 9, 2010, *(last viewed June 7, 2016)*.

290. Michael Paul Williams, *Painful parallels--Williams: Tulsa ballpark offers lesson for Richmond*, RICHMOND TIMES-DISPATCH, October 18, 2013, https://www.richmond.com/news/local/michael-paul-williams/williams-tulsa-ballpark-offers-lesson-for-richmond/article_111da5b4-5e78-5f7f-a31a-f583ecd71737.html (last visited April 9, 2019).

291. Kendrick Marshall, *"Signs of Gentrification": Greenwood community worries black people are being pushed out, history disrespected*, TULSA WORLD, June 16, 2019, A1.

292. Kendrick Marshall, *"Signs of Gentrification": Greenwood community worries black people are being pushed out, history disrespected*, TULSA WORLD, June 16, 2019, A1.

293. *See, e.g.*, Robert Evatt, GreenArch brings apartments, retail to Greenwood, Tulsa World, July 14, 2012; updated September 30, 2013, http://www.tulsaworld.com/business/realestate/greenarch-brings-apartments-retail-to-greenwood/article_04374996-ea94-5034-817b-7940ad3400dc.html (last visited June 7, 2016).

294. *USA BMX Moving to Tulsa – Evans-Fintube to Serve as Preferred Site for Arena and Headquarters,* https://www.cityoftulsa.org/press-room/usa-bmx-moving-to-tulsa-evans-fintube-to-serve-as-preferred-site-for-arena-and-headquarters/ (last visited March 27, 2019).

295. *Proposed BMX Facility Sparks Concerns From Residents*, NEW ON 6/KOTV, July 10, 2017, https://www.youtube.com/watch?v=8WmlyVoyMJM (last visited June 28, 2019).

296. Rhett Morgan, *Banking on growth*, TULSA WORLD, November 17, 2018, at A-13.

297. Mike Averill, *Committed to Tulsa*, TULSA WORLD, June 29, 2019, at A1.

298. Kendrick Marshall, *WPX HQ may boost minority ventures: WPX Energy presence in Greenwood District could spark surge in black entrepreneurship*, TULSA WORLD, June 30, 2019, at A1.

299. E-mail correspondence with Tyrance Billingsley, Chairman, Student Advisory Board for OSRHE; President of Student Government, Metro Campus, Tulsa Community College; and CEO of Phi Beta Lambda, January 25, 2017.

300. https://www.forbes.com/pictures/feki45igde/no-1-tulsa-okla/#fbfc7a317996 (last visited May 22, 2018).

301. https://www.dreamtulsa.com/ (last visited May 22, 2018).

302. *See* http://www.blackenterprise.com/dream-tulsa-black-entrepreneurs-rebuild-black-wall-street/ (last visited March 26, 2018).

303. http://rise1922.org/ (last visited May 28, 2018).

304. Rhett Morgan, *A path to a start: Pop-up school for black entrepreneurs coming to Tulsa in July*, TULSA WORLD, June 8, 2019, at A13.

305. E-mail correspondence with Robinne Burrell, June 8, 2018 (on file with author).

306. *Five Years of Progress on North Tulsa Area-Wide Plan Brownfields Projects,* October 7, 2017, https://www.cityoftulsa.org/press-room/five-years-of-progress-on-north-tulsa-area-wide-plan-brownfields-projects/ (last visited January 4, 2019).

307. *See* "National Track Stadium, BMX Headquarters Moving To Tulsa," NewsOn6.com, April 6, 2016, http://www.newson6.com/story/31660855/national-track-stadium-bmx-headquarters-moving-to-tulsa (last visited July 23, 2018); see also "USA BMX Moving to Tulsa – Evans-Fintube to Serve as Preferred Site for Arena and Headquarters," City of Tulsa, August 5, 2017, https://www.cityoftulsa.org/press-room/usa-bmx-moving-to-tulsa-evans-fintube-to-serve-as-preferred-site-for-arena-and-headquarters/ (last visited July 23, 2018).

308. Mikeal Vaughn, MBA, PMP, https://www.linkedin.com/in/mikeal-vaughn-mba-pmp-2178301b/ (last visited August 22, 2018).

309. Rhett Morgan, *Tulsan seeks teacher for new Urban Coders Guild*, TULSA WORLD, August 25, 2018, at A13.

310. *See* https://www.facebook.com/urbancodersguild/?timeline_context_item_type=intro_card_work&timeline_context_item_source=5712415&fref=tag (last visited August 22, 2018).

311. *See* Paighten Harkins, *New north Tulsa grocery store will help shrink area's food desert*, TULSA WORLD, December 18, 2016, https://www.tulsaworld.com/news/local/new-north-tulsa-grocery-store-will-help-shrink-area-s/article_fb1e3f0d-de3e-5465-89e3-a248dc6a6917.html (last visited August 30, 2018); see also, North Tulsans Talk Solutions to Food Desert Problem, NewsOn6.com, http://www.newson6.com/story/26356033/north-tulsans-talk-solution-to-food-desert-problem (last visited August 30, 2018).

312. Telephone conference with Bill White, Director of Development, Greenwood Cultural Center, August 30, 2018.

313. E-mail from Jamaal Dyer, Project Manager, 1921 Tulsa Race Massacre Centennial Commission, September 4, 2018 (on file with author).

314. E-mail from Jamaal Dyer, Project Manager, 1921 Tulsa Race Massacre Centennial Commission, September 4, 2018 (on file with author).

315. https://www.typros.org/diversity; https://www.facebook.com/pg/typros/about/?ref=page_internal (last visited September 7, 2018).

316. *North Tulsa 'turning point,'* (editorial), TULSA WORLD, February 14, 2019, at A10.

317. E-mail from Wendy Thomas to the author, July 15, 2016.

318. BEFORE THEY DIE! (2008), IMDb, http://www.imdb.com/title/tt1549724/ (last visited May 27, 2016).

319. *See, e.g.,* A. G. SULZBERGER, *As Survivors Dwindle, Tulsa Confronts Past,* THE NEW YORK TIMES, June 19, 2011, http://www.nytimes.com/2011/06/20/us/20tulsa.html?pagewanted=all (last visited May 13, 2016); *Mayor culpa: Climbing aboard the apology bandwagon,* THE OKLAHOMAN, November 3, 2008 (editorial), http://newsok.com/article/3318505 (last visited May 13, 2016).

320. *In Search of History: The Night Tulsa Burned* (1999), IMDb, http://www.imdb.com/title/tt1421039/ (last visited May 27, 2016).

321. Smithsonian National Museum of African American History & Culture, https://nmaahc.si.edu/; The 1921 Tulsa Race Riot is explored at https://nmaahc.si.edu/explore/collection/search?edan_q=tulsa&edan_local=1&edan_fq[]=topic:%22Violence%22 (last visited February 26, 2017).

322. *See Smithsonian Acquires Rare 'Black Wall Street' Film,* http://americanhistory.si.edu/press/releases/smithsonian-acquires-rare-%E2%80%9Cblack-wall-street%E2%80%9D-film; *see also,* americanhistory.si.edu (Reverend Harold Anderson's Black Wall Street Film, National Museum of American History Archives Center), (last visited February 26, 2017).

323. Doug Collette, *Jacob Fred Jazz Odyssey: Race Riot Suite*, September 19, 2011, https://www.allaboutjazz.com/race-riot-suite-jacob-fred-jazz-odyssey-kinnara-records-review-by-doug-collette.php (last visited May 27, 2016).

324. *Jacob Fred Jazz Odyssey: The Race Riot Suite*, WEXNER CENTER FOR THE ARTS: PERFORMING ARTS, May 12, 2012, http://wexarts.org/performing-arts/jacob-fred-jazz-odyssey-race-riot-suite (May 27, 2016).

325. *The Cherokee Nation v. Raymond Nash, et al*, Civil Action 13-01313 (TFH) (D.C.D.C.,

August 30, 2017).

326. *See generally*, Hannibal B. Johnson, APARTHEID IN INDIAN COUNTRY?: SEEING RED OVER BLACK DISENFRANCHISEMENT (Fort Worth, TX: Eakin Press, 2012).

327. *See* Hannibal B. Johnson, APARTHEID IN INDIAN COUNTRY?: SEEING RED OVER BLACK DISENFRANCHISEMENT (Fort Worth, TX: Eakin Press, 2012).

328. The Cherokee Nation Election Commission certified the 2019 General Election results on June 3, 2019. Tribal citizens elected Chuck Hoskin, Jr. as Principal Chief and Bryan Warner as Deputy Chief. Hoskin became the 18th constitutionally-elected Principal Chief of the Cherokee Nation in tribal history, and seventh elected Principal Chief in the modern era. *See* https://www.tulsaworld.com/communities/skiatook/news/official-cherokee-nation-principal-chief-deputy-chief-election-results-name/article_ffa8d768-531c-51f0-aa72-0cfd81fc4c82.html (last visited June 5, 2019).

329. Greenwood Cultural Center Legacy Award recipients have included--

- 2004: Alfre Woodard
- 2005: N/A
- 2006: Orlando "Tubby" Smith
- 2007: Dr. John Hope Franklin
- 2008: Judy Eason-McIntyre; Betty Price; and Mayor M. Susan Savage
- 2009: Wayman Tisdale
- 2010: Tim Blake Nelson
- 2011: N/A
- 2012: N/A
- 2013: N/A
- 2014: N/A
- 2015: John Gibson
- 2016: Nolan Richardson
- 2017: Governor Frank Keating
- 2018: Mayor Rodger A. Randle
- 2019: Chief Bill John Baker, Cherokee Nation; Marilyn Vann; and David Cornsilk

330. *Creek Nation Freedmen file lawsuit against Oklahoma tribe*, TULSA WORLD, July 27, 2018, https://www.tulsaworld.com/creek-nation-freedmen-file-lawsuit-against-oklahoma-tribe/article_766c679f-3bf7-5268-8fe9-8f9fa34f6a3a.html (last visited August 4, 2018).

331. *Muscogee Creek Indian Freedmen Band, Inc. v. David Bernhardt*, Case 1:18-cv-01705-CKK, Document 29 (U.S.D.D., D.C., May 6, 2019) (memorandum opinion).

332. Lenzy Krehbiel-Burton, *Creek freedmen descendants' lawsuit dismissed*, TULSA WORLD, May 10, 2019, at A14.

333. The author wrote the storyboard for the Black Wall Street Airport Exhibit and assisted Bill White in raising the necessary funding to create and sustain it.

334. http://www.tulsaworld.com/news/local/mural-near-greenwood-cultural-center-honors-black-wall-street/article_589ad151-5847-502a-9dae-b22583fdd352.html (last visited June 2, 2018).

335. "6 In The Morning Talks About 'Greenwood Avenue: A VR Experience,'" July 30, 2018, NewsOn6.com, http://www.newson6.com/story/38764326/6-in-the-morning-talks-about-greenwood-avenue-a-virtual-reality-experience (last visited July 30, 2018).

336. Mitchell Willetts, *'It's been almost 100 years, and people still don't know': Virtual reality project to bring Black Wall Street history to life*, TULSA WORLD, July 31, 2018, https://www.tulsaworld.com/news/local/it-s-been-almost-years-and-people-still-don-t/article_cc220f33-5b7c-5813-9ac3-2a7b3e1d5625.html (last visited July 31, 2018).

337. James D. Watts, Jr., *ARTS: 'Tulsa '21: Black Wall Street' returns for one show only*, TUL-SA WORLD, August 19, 2018, https://www.tulsaworld.com/scene/artsandentertainment/arts-tulsa-black-wall-street-returns-for-one-show-only/article_7067d1a4-6efd-58f2-b929-e7e2fe5f5690.html (last visited August 27, 2018).

338. Rhett Morgan, *'It's goosebump-worthy': Gathering Place crowds get their first look at $465 million, riverfront park*, TULSA WORLD, September 8, 2018, https://www.tulsaworld.com/news/gatheringplace/it-s-goosebump-worthy-gathering-place-crowds-get-their-first/article_265de9f1-a74b-5b05-9f24-2148735af53e.html (last visited September 9, 2018).

339. *Transforming Tulsa, Starting with a Park*, THE NEW YORK TIMES, August 10, 2018, https://www.nytimes.com/2018/08/10/arts/design/tulsa-park-gathering-place.html (last visited August 10, 2018); *see also*, Janna A. Zinzi, *Tulsa Built a Park That It Hopes Will Heal Historic Wounds*, DAILY BEAST, https://www.thedailybeast.com/tulsa-builds-a-park-that-it-hopes-will-heal-historic-wounds (last visited July 29, 2019).

340. A Gathering Place For Tulsa, https://www.gatheringplace.org/our-story (last visited July 18, 2018).

341. Michael Overall, *George Kaiser: Tulsan of the century*, TULSA WORLD MAGAZINE, Issue 20, January – February 2019, at 27, 28.

342. Michael Overall, *George Kaiser: Tulsan of the century*, TULSA WORLD MAGAZINE, Issue 20, January – February 2019, at 27, 29.

343. Michael Overall, *George Kaiser: Tulsan of the century*, TULSA WORLD MAGAZINE, Issue 20, January – February 2019, at 27, 29.

344. *Gathering Place Named Best New Attraction In Nation,* January 18, 2019, http://www.newson6.com/story/39815407/gathering-place-named-best-new-attraction-in-nation (last visited January 18, 2019); Kevin Canfield, *USA's best of the best: Gathering Place named Best New Attraction*, TULSA WORLD, at A9.

345. Osage Prairie Trail, https://stepoutside.org/place/osage-prairie-trail-tulsa-ok.html (last visited August 2, 2019).

346. *See Senator Lankford Recognizes 95ᵗʰ Anniversary of the Tulsa Race Riot with Senate Speech* (May 25, 2016), https://www.lankford.senate.gov/news/press-releases/senator-lankford-recognizes-95th-anniversary-of-the-tulsa-race-riot-with-senate-speech (last visited June 18, 2019); *see also*, U.S. *Senate Sen. James Lankford on 1921 Tulsa Massacre* (May 23, 2019), https://archive.org/details/CSPAN2_20190523_150000_U.S._Senate_Sen._James_Lankford_on_1921_Tulsa_Massacre (last visited June 18, 2019) (Senator Lankford again addressed the Riot on the Senate floor in recognition of its impending 98ᵗʰ anniversary).

347. Chris Casteel, *Tulsa race riot story told in exhibit at new African American museum in DC*, December 11, 2016, https://newsok.com/article/5530239/tulsa-race-riot-story-told-in-exhibit-at-new-african-american-museum-in-dc (last visited August 5, 2018).

348. https://tulsahistory.org/visit/exhibits/1921-race-riot-virtual-exhibit/; *see also*, https://tulsahistory.org/learn/online-exhibits/the-tulsa-race-riot/ (last visited August 6, 2018).

349. http://cdm15887.contentdm.oclc.org/cdm/landingpage/collection/p15887coll1 (last visited August 6, 2018).

350. For more information, *see* http://www.greenwoodculturalcenter.com/ (last visited August 6, 2018).

351. *Historic Markers and Monuments in Tulsa County, Images and Coordinates*, TULSA CITY-COUNTY LIBRARY, http://guides.tulsalibrary.org/content.php?pid=137405&sid=2884210 (last visited May 19,. 2016).

352. https://www.niche.com/k12/search/best-public-high-schools/s/oklahoma/ (last visited December 27, 2018).

353. https://btw.tulsaschools.org/ (last visited December 27, 2018).

354. *New Historical Marker Cites Role Standpipe Hill Played In Race Riot*, NewsOn6.com, June 12, 2014, http://www.newson6.com/story/25761541/historical-marker-dedicated-on-standpipe-hill (last visited May 19, 2016).

355. Oklahoma Center for Community and Justice ("OCCJ"), http://www.occjok.org/ (last visited May 27, 2016).

356. Hannibal B. Johnson, *Curriculum Counts*, THIS LAND, May 10, 2011, http://thislandpress.com/2011/05/10/curriculum-counts-the-importance-of-teaching-about-the-1921-tulsa-race-riots/ (last visited May 27, 2016).

357. *A Resolution Supporting The Completion of the John Hope Franklin Reconciliation Park; The Establishment of the John Hope Franklin Center for Reconciliation; The Establishment of the Tulsa Reconciliation Education Program; And The Establishment of the Mayor's Community Race Relations Committee*; approved by the Tulsa City Council October 9, 2008; approved by the Mayor of the City of Tulsa October 13, 2008; on file at the Office of the City Clerk, City of Tulsa, Oklahoma, file stamped October 10, 2008.

358. *A Resolution Supporting The Completion of the John Hope Franklin Reconciliation Park; The Establishment of the John Hope Franklin Center for Reconciliation; The Establishment of the Tulsa Reconciliation Education Program; And The Establishment of the Mayor's Community Race Relations Committee*; approved by the Tulsa City Council October 9, 2008; approved by the Mayor of the City of Tulsa October 13, 2008; on file at the Office of the City Clerk, City of Tulsa, Oklahoma, file stamped October 10, 2008.

359. https://www.facebook.com/pg/CompassionateTulsa/about/?ref=page_internal (last visited October 25, 2017).

360. Tulsa's Still She Rises is profiled in: Sarah Stillman, *America's Other Family-Separation Crisis: Sending a mother to prison can have a devastating effect on her children. Why, then, do we lock so many women up?*, THE NEW YORKER, October 30, 2018, https://www.newyorker.com/magazine/2018/11/05/americas-other-family-separation-crisis (last visited October 31, 2018) (November 5, 2018 issue, titled *Separated*).

361. Endnote: https://www.bronxdefenders.org/programs/still-she-rises-tulsa/; https://www.stillsherises.org/our-mission/ (last visited May 27, 2018).

362. https://theblackwallsttimes.com/2017/03/26/the-black-wall-street-times-mission-a-letter-from-the-editor-in-chief/

363. https://www.linkedin.com/in/devondouglass/ (last visited January 25, 2019).

364. The City's "New Tulsans Welcoming Plan," unveiled on September 20, 2018, seeks to improve the lives of immigrants in five core areas: civic engagement, economic development, education, health, and public safety. Kevin Canfield, City to welcome, support immigrants: *The New Tulsans Welcoming Plan is said to help improve immigrants' lives*, TULSA WORLD, September 20, 2018, at A1.

365. https://www.cityoftulsa.org/press-room/mayor-gt-bynum-unveils-tulsa-s-first-resilience-strategy/.

366. https://cityoftulsa.org/press-room/mayor-bynum-selects-krystal-reyes-to-lead-tulsa-s-resilience-efforts/ (last visited June 4, 2019).

367. http://www.mosaictulsa.com/ (last visited August 21, 2018).

368. Bill Sherman, *Greater Tulsa Area African-American Affairs Commission begins mission: Greater Tulsa Area African-American Affairs Commission convenes for first time*, December 15,

2017, Tulsa World, https://www.tulsaworld.com/homepagelatest/greater-tulsa-area-african-american-affairs-commission-convenes-for-first/article_b995d2b5-dd9a-5792-a2b4-3de86d95b497.html (last visited August 27, 2018).

369. http://www.thetulsaartsdistrict.org/first-friday-art-crawl (last visited September 9, 2018).

370. Telephone interview with Dr. Ricco Wright, September 9, 2018.

371. http://allsoulschurch.org/about-us/ (last visited September 24, 2018).

372. Rev. Marlin Lavanhar, Pastor, All Souls Unitarian Church, Facebook post, September 23, 2018.

373. http://allsoulschurch.org/about-us/ (last visited September 24, 2018).

374. Rev. Dr. Martin Luther King, Jr., Strength to Love (New York, NY: Harper & Row, 1963) (a collection of sermons illuminating Dr. King's convictions in the context of the civil rights struggle and contemporary American society).

375. https://www.tulsa-health.org/sites/default/files/page_attachments/Life%20Expectancy%20Report.pdf (last visited January 2, 2019).

376. https://www.tulsa-health.org/sites/default/files/page_attachments/Life%20Expectancy%20Report.pdf (last visited January 2, 2019).

377. Tulsa Development Authority--Progress As Promised: Project Areas and Current Development Opportunities (1990), on file with author.

378. Vision2025, https://vision2025.info/ (last visited January 3, 2019).

379. *Tulsa's North Cincinnati Avenue Renamed Martin Luther King Jr. Boulevard*, September 18, 2012, NewsOn6.com, http://www.newson6.com/story/19572265/tulsas-north-cincinnati-avenue-renamed-martin-luther-king-jr-boulevard (last visited January 3, 2019).

380. Arianna Pickard, *Emerson's conversion to Montessori school detailed at Tulsa school board meeting*, Tulsa World, January 5, 2017, https://www.tulsaworld.com/news/education/emersons-conversion-to-montessori-school-detailed-at-tulsa-school/article_c28fb3c6-0fa3-5182-a293-cb4a61c319ff.html (last visited January 3, 2019).

381. Kevin Canfield, *Art 'outside the box,'* Tulsa World, January 18, 2019, at A1.

382. Michael Overall, *Tulsa's MLK parade grew from 60 in 1979 to more than 7,000 expected this year: MARKING CHANGE*, Tulsa World, January 21, 2019, A1.

383. Tulsa Mayor Kathy Taylor issued an apology to Riot survivors in 2001 as part of a celebration of conscience ceremony.

384. The police inaction deemed to constitute dereliction of duty by some includes the failure or refusal to: (1) arrest the publisher of The Tulsa Tribune for incitement to riot for publishing inflammatory May 31, 1921, piece entitled "To Lynch a Nigger Tonight"; (2) confiscate copies of said edition of The Tulsa Tribune; (3) amass sufficient officers to quell the disturbance; (4) prevent the assemblage of a thousands-strong white lynch mob at the courthouse; (5) disburse the lynch mob once it had convened; and (6) call immediately upon the Governor of Oklahoma for military assistance once an impending conflict became clear. *See, e.g.*, Stephen P. Kerr, J.D., LL.M., Tulsa Race War: 31st May 1921 (undated, unpublished manuscript by the grandson of First Presbyterian minister, Dr. Charles William Kerr on file in the archives of First Presbyterian Church).

385. On Good Friday, April 6, 2012, a string of killings occurred in North Tulsa, leaving three people dead and two others injured. Suspects Alvin Lee Watts and Jacob Carl England ultimately accepted plea agreements on December 16, 2012, calling for the life-without-parole sentences. Prosecutors dropped their requests for death sentences with respect to both defendants. *Good Friday Shootings in Tulsa*, https://www.tulsaworld.com/good-friday-shoot-

ings-in-tulsa/collection_ae83ec02-66a7-11e3-89b9-001a4bcf6878.html (last visited March 27, 2019).

386. Remarks of Tulsa Police Chief Chuck Jordan, September 21, 2013, on file with author; *see also* Dave Harper, *TPD police chief apologizes for police inaction in Tulsa Race Riot during Saturday event*, TULSA WORLD, September 21, 2013.

387. John A. Gustafson served as Tulsa's Chief of Police from April 27, 1920, to June 25, 1921. https://www.tulsapolice.org/content/history/chiefs.aspx (last visited May 25, 2016).

388. *See State Rests Case Upon 2 Remaining Counts of Gustafson Accusations*, THE MORNING TULSA DAILY WORLD (Tulsa, Okla.), Vol. 15, No. 291, Ed. 1, Tuesday, July 19, 1921, The Gateway to Oklahoma History, http://gateway.okhistory.org/ark:/67531/metadc77830/m1/1/zoom/?q=tulsa%20police%20chief%20gustafson%20convicted (last visited May 25, 2016).

389. *See, e.g., The Questions That Remain: A conversation about Tulsa's Race Riot and racism today*, TULSA WORLD, http://www.tulsaworld.com/app/race-riot/timeline.html (last visited May 25, 2016).

390. *Chief Found Guilty on Two Counts*, THE MORNING TULSA DAILY WORLD (Tulsa, Okla.), Vol. 15, No. 295, Ed. 1, Saturday, July 23, 1921, The Gateway to Oklahoma History, http://gateway.okhistory.org/ark:/67531/metadc77726/m1/1/?q=tulsa%20police%20chief%20gustafson%20convicted (last visited May 25, 2016) noting: "While the conviction carries no criminal conviction with it, the chief is automatically ousted from office."

391. *See, e.g., TULSA RACE RIOT JURY INDICTS POLICE CHIEF; He, With Others, Is Accused of Dereliction of Duty and Laxity on Dry Laws and Vice*, THE NEW YORK TIMES, June 25, 1921.

392. Dave Harper, *TPD police chief apologizes for police inaction in Tulsa Race Riot during Saturday event*, TULSA WORLD, September 21, 2013.

393. Rev. Andrew Bozeman, *Oklahoma police chief apologizes for 1921 attack on Black Wall Street*, SAN FRANCISCO BAY VIEW, NATIONAL BLACK NEWSPAPER, *October 2, 2013*, http://sfbayview.com/2013/10/oklahoma-police-chief-apologizes-for-1921-attack-on-black-wall-street/ (last visited May 11, 2016);
See also, Okla. Police Chief Chuck Jordan Apologizes for Police Role in 1921 Race Riot, OPPOSING VIEWS, September 23, 2013, http://www.opposingviews.com/i/society/okla-police-chief-chuck-jordan-apologizes-police-role-1921-race-riot (last visited May 11, 2016).

394. *Chief Jordan's apology is a symbolic and meaningful gesture*, TULSA WORLD (editorial), September 25, 2013.

395. *The Tulsa Star*, August 19, 1914, accessed from Library of Congress Chronicling America: Historic American Newspapers, http://chroniclingamerica.loc.gov/lccn/sn86064118/1914-08-19/ed-1/seq-15/ (last visited May 12, 2016); Art T. Burton, BLACK GUN, SILVER STAR: THE LIFE AND LEGEND OF FRONTIER MARSHAL BASS REEVES (Lincoln, Nebraska: University of Nebraska Press 2006).

396. *Tulsa Police on the right track with training changes*, TULSA WORLD, October 17, 2018 (TULSA WORLD editorial from the Tulsa World editorial writers), https://www.tulsaworld.com/opinion/editorials/tulsa-world-editorial-tulsa-police-on-right-track-with-training/article_3a348558-da72-5d9d-a758-b66c3e990f06.html (last visited October 18, 2018).

397. E-mail from Sarah Guardiola, Chief Executive Officer, SKYWAY Leadership Institute, Home of TPAL @ HelmZar Challenge Course, to the author, June 10, 2019 (on file with author).

398. *See* Michael Overall, *Despite Good Friday shootings last year, Tulsa tried to come together*, TULSA WORLD, March 29, 2013; *Tulsa's 'Good Friday' Murder Suspects Plead Guilty*, http://www.newson6.com/story/24234704/tulsas-good-friday-murder-suspects-plead-guilty; http://www.tulsaworld.com/good-friday-shootings-in-tulsa/collection_ae83ec02-66a7-11e3-89b9-001a4bcf6878.html; http://www.tulsaworld.com/news/local/despite-good-friday-shootings-last-year-tulsa-tried-to-come/article_d2a3d084-3c2b-5ea7-8c21-21e3ee7c-d6ef.html?mode=print

399. Randy Krehbiel, *Fragile peace the work of many*, TULSA WORLD, September 25, 2016, A-1.

400. Arianna Pickard and Corey Jones, *Robert Bates convicted of manslaughter in shooting of Eric Harris*, TULSA WORLD, April 28, 2016.

401. Arianna Pickard, *Terence Crutcher family attorneys allege 'misinformation' from police*, TULSA WORLD, http://www.tulsaworld.com/news/courts/terence-crutcher-family-attorneys-allege-misinformation-from-police/article_392556ce-f698-54ed-9db9-fa9736493874.html (last visited September 21, 2016).

402. Samantha Vincent and Corey Jones, *Justice will be achieved in the Terence Crutcher shooting, Tulsa police chief assures community*, TULSA WORLD, http://www.tulsaworld.com/news/crimewatch/justice-will-be-achieved-in-terence-crutcher-shooting-tulsa-police/article_ceb93e3d-2ce1-539b-bb89-b849a224e16f.html (last visited September 21, 2016)/

403. Lenzy Krehbiel-Burton, *Tulsa officer charged with manslaughter for fatal shooting seen on video*, TULSA WORLD, http://www.aol.com/article/news/2016/09/22/tulsa-officer-charged-with-manslaughter-for-fatal-shooting-seen/21477477/ (last visited September 22, 2016).

404. Bill Sherman, *North Tulsa pastors praise city leaders' actions*, TULSA WORLD, September 24, 2016, http://www.tulsaworld.com/news/religion/north-tulsa-pastors-praise-citys-handling-of-terence-crutcher/article_7073b2ac-11c1-51c9-8aab-457c1ff69316.html?mode=print (last visited September 24, 2016).

405. Ashley Parrish, *From The Editor*, TULSA WORLD MAGAZINE, issue 08, December/February 2017, at 8.

406. *We the People Oklahoma to discuss Tulsa Police policy in wake of officer involved fatal shooting*, September 19, 2016 (updated September 20, 2016, https://www.kjrh.com/news/local-news/we-the-people-oklahoma-to-discuss-tulsa-police-policy-in-wake-of-officer-involved-fatal-shooting (last visited April 10, 2019).

407. *See, e.g.*, Samantha Vincent, *Verdict: Not Guilty*, TULSA WORLD, May 18, 2017, A1; *Protesters block traffic, chant at hotel*, TULSA WORLD, May 18, 2017, A5..

408. Clayton Youngman, *Mayor after Shelby verdict: 'Greatest issue' facing Tulsa is racial disparity*, May 18, 2017, http://ktul.com/news/local/live-mayor-police-chief-hold-press-conference-on-betty-shelbys-acquittal (last visited May 18, 2017).

409. Rick Maranon, *Bynum announces new Tulsa community policing commission*, FOX23 (December 16, 2016), https://www.fox23.com/news/bynum-announces-new-tulsa-community-ty-policing-commission/476704206 (last visited June 15, 2018).

410. *Mayor Appoints Community Policing Commission*, KWGS NEWS, December 15, 2015, http://publicradiotulsa.org/post/mayor-appoints-community-policing-commission#stream/0 (last visited December 17, 2016).

411. *Findings and Recommendations of the Tulsa Commission on Community Policing*, https://blox-images.newyork1.vip.townnews.com/tulsaworld.com/content/tncms/assets/v3/editorial/e/c4/ec4c93b2-0f63-53ba-b650-ac19d4f96d02/58d70bcc45fee.pdf.pdf (last visited June 18, 2018).

412. *President Obama Announces Task Force on 21ˢᵗ Century Policing*, https://obamawhite-

house.archives.gov/the-press-office/2014/12/18/president-obama-announces-task-force-21st-century-policing (last visited June 18, 2018).

413. Kevin Canfield, *Changes sought in equality meetings: Group says talks on police treatment of minorities need more accountability*, Tulsa World, April 12, 2019, at A1.

414. Kevin Canfield, *Mayor outlines proposal for independent police monitoring*, Tulsa World, April 10, 2019, https://www.tulsaworld.com/news/local/government-and-politics/mayor-outlines-proposal-for-independent-police-monitoring/article_eb60a8de-7693-5de1-9848-396b00470e99.html?utm_source=WhatCountsEmail&utm_medium=NEWS%20-%20Morning%20Headlines&utm_campaign=Morning%20Headlines&utm_content=Morning%20Headlines (last visited April 12, 2019).

415. https://terencecrutcherfoundation.org/about-us (last visited August 20, 2018).

416. Ginnie Graham, *Launch of Terence Crutcher Foundation coincides with birthday and anniversary of his death: Twin sister establishes Terence Crutcher Foundation*, Tulsa World, http://www.tulsaworld.com/news/columnists/ginniegraham/launch-of-terence-crutcher-foundation-coincides-with-birthday-and-anniversary/article_4780ce9b-9577-5a40-b6de-a78b93eeaba7.html (last visited August 16, 2017).

417. Corey Jones, *Out of loss, hope*, Tulsa World, August 20, 2018, at A-7.

418. Kevin Canfield, *NAACP Legal Defense Fund along with community leaders demand changes to Tulsa's policing practices*, Tulsa World (May 31, 2018), http://www.tulsaworld.com/news/local/naacp-legal-defense-fund-along-with-community-leaders-demand-changes/article_9c76d005-68a6-54a1-80a9-013539509882.html (last visited June 14, 2018).

419. http://www.newson6.com/story/38421856/terence-crutchers-dad-urges-tulsa-city-council-implement-policing-reforms (last visited June 14, 2018).

420. Kevin Canfield, *Minister calls for reforms: Terence Crutcher's father delivers emotional plea to city councilors, mayor*, Tulsa Word (June 14, 2018).

421. http://www.newson6.com/story/38421856/terence-crutchers-dad-urges-tulsa-city-council-implement-policing-reforms (last visited June 14, 2018).

422. CLEET Continuing Education: Classroom Training, https://www.ok.gov/cleet/CLEET_Training/Continuing_Education_-_Classroom_Training/ (last visited August 26, 2018).

423. Corey Jones, *Betty Shelby teaching course for officers on "surviving the aftermath of a critical incident,"* Tulsa World, August 24, 2018, https://www.tulsaworld.com/homepagelatest/betty-shelby-teaching-course-for-officers-on-surviving-the-aftermath/article_9388a019-cd03-5890-9757-069a5bf9706d.html (last visited August 26, 2018); Matt Trotter, *Betty Shelby to Teach Course at Tulsa County Sheriff's Office on Surviving a Critical Incident*, Public Radio Tulsa, August 24, 2018, http://www.publicradiotulsa.org/post/betty-shelby-teach-course-tulsa-county-sheriffs-office-surviving-critical-incident (last visited August 26, 2018); *see also* Isaac Stanley-Becker, *She fatally shot an unarmed black man. Now she's teaching other police officers how to 'survive' such incidents.*, August 28, 2018, https://www.washingtonpost.com/news/morning-mix/wp/2018/08/28/she-fatally-shot-an-unarmed-black-man-now-shes-teaching-other-cops-how-to-survive-such-incidents/?noredirect=on&utm_term=.bdff34e002b7 (last visited August 28, 2018)..

424. Samantha Vicent, *Former Tulsa Police Officer Shannon Kepler convicted of manslaughter Panel chooses lesser manslaughter conviction*, Tulsa World (October 18, 2017), http://www.tulsaworld.com/news/courts/former-tulsa-police-officer-shannon-kepler-convicted-of-manslaughter/article_6317fe90-68ef-55d1-b3dc-287d5342f35e.html (last visited October 19, 2017).

425. *See, e.g.,* Robin Young, HERE & NOW, National Public Radio, July 23, 2019, https://www.wbur.org/hereandnow/2019/07/23/tulsa-race-massacre-centenary (last visited July 24, 2019) (In this interview with Brenda Alford, **whose grandparents survived the** 1921 massacre, but lost their businesses--a shoe shop, a record store, a dance pavilion, and a community skating rink--Ms. Alford recalls driving by Oaklawn Cemetery as a child and hearing relatives in the car talking about a mass grave for black Riot victims there.)

426. TULSA RACE RIOT: A REPORT BY THE OKLAHOMA COMMISSION TO STUDY THE TULSA RACE RIOT OF 1921 (Oklahoma City, OK: Oklahoma Historical Society, February 28, 2001), http://www.okhistory.org/research/forms/freport.pdf (last visited July 19, 2019), at 140.

427. Walter White, *The Eruption of Tulsa,* NATION 112 (June 29, 1921): 909–910, cited in History Matters, http://historymatters.gmu.edu/d/5119 (last visited October 25, 2017). White, a NAACP official, visited Tulsa after the 1921 Tulsa Race Riot. As a Negro who could "pass" for white, Walter White went "incogNegro," surreptitiously intercepting interactions and conversations meant for whites only.

428. Kendrick Marshall, *Mass graves probe a "homicide investigation,"* TULSA WORLD, June 28, 2019, at A1.

429. TULSA RACE RIOT: A REPORT BY THE OKLAHOMA COMMISSION TO STUDY THE TULSA RACE RIOT OF 1921 (Oklahoma City, OK: Oklahoma Historical Society, February 28, 2001), http://www.okhistory.org/research/forms/freport.pdf (last visited October 3, 2018), at 133 - 142; *see also,* Stephen P. Kerr, J.D., LL.M., TULSA RACE WAR: 31ST MAY 1921, at 23 (1999, unpublished manuscript by the grandson of First Presbyterian minister, Dr. Charles William Kerr on file in the archives of First Presbyterian Church, at 35 - 36, noting Oaklawn Cemetery and Rose Hill Cemetery, 4161 East Admiral Place, as mass grave sites and Newblock Park as a place where black bodies were burned in the Sand Springs municipal trash incinerator; also contending that black bodies were dumped into the Arkansas River and buried in North Tulsa trenches.

Dr. Scott Ellsworth, a history professor at the University of Michigan, worked with the Oklahoma Commission to Study the Tulsa Race Riot of 1921 on the original investigation of mass graves and is working with the current mass graves initiative to follow up on that preliminary work. In the summer of 2019, Dr. Ellsworth indicated there may be a fourth site meriting investigation and scientific testing. The area, located close to Newblock Park, was captured in a now-lost photograph showing the burial of Riot victims in a trench on June 3, 1921. The photo came to the attention of the Commission back in 2002, but by that time the Commission had officially disbanded. E-mail from Dr. Scott Ellworth to the author, July 22, 2019 (on file with author).

430. Kevin Canfield, *Mass graves to be sought again,* TULSA WORLD, October 3, 2018, at A-1; *see also* Randy Krehbiel, *Burial site possibilities,* TULSA WORLD, October 15, 2018, at A-1.

431. G.T. Bynum, Facebook post, October 2, 2018.

432. Kevin Canfield, *Search for 1921 Race Massacre graves in plans,* TULSA WORLD, April 25, 2019, at A1.

433. *See, e.g.,* Randy Krehbiel, *Public input key in search for graves,* TULSA WORLD, May 23, 2019, at A11.

434. *Research Project for 1921-9021 Race Massacre Centennial Commission; Project Title: Mapping Historical Trauma in Tulsa, 1921 to 202; Funding Source: Private Funds to Centennial Steering Committee,* on file with author.

435. The Brady Heights Neighborhood (now simply "The Heights"), with residential construction spanning from 1906 to 1925, likely derives its name from Tate Brady and from the

addition which bears his name. The houses of Brady Heights are on a larger scale and of a more sophisticated design than those of adjacent neighborhoods. Bay windows with leaded glass, servants' quarters, and broad porches suggest the elegance of earlier days. From territorial days until the 1920s, Brady Heights was an important part of a then-fashionable residential area. Young professional businessmen and oilmen, including G. Y. Vandever, I. S. Mincks and "Diamond Joe" Wilson, owned homes there. The Brady Heights Historic District joined the National Register of Historic Places on June 27, 1980. It is the first Tulsa district to be so listed. *See, e.g.,* https://web.archive.org/web/20070824061300/http://www.tulsapreservationcommission.org/nationalregister/districts/bradyheights/ (last visited January 1, 2019).

436. Lee Roy Chapman, *The Nightmare of Dreamland*, THIS LAND, April 18, 2012.

437. *See, e.g.,* Lee Roy Chapman, *The Nightmare of Dreamland*, THIS LAND, April 18, 2012, http://thislandpress.com/2012/04/18/tate-brady-battle-greenwood/ (last visited May 9, 2016).

438. Emory Bryan, *Tulsa's Brady District Tax Reaches Successful End*, NEWSON6, June 21, 2017, www.newson6.com/story/35720169/tulsas-brady-district-tax-reahces-successful-end (last visited April 10, 2019).

439. *Tulsa city council changes a street's name from 'Brady' the KKK member to honor 'Brady' the photojournalist,"* NEW YORK DAILY NEWS, August 16, 2013, http://www.nydailynews.com/news/national/tulsa-street-honored-kkk-member-article-1.1428937 (last visited May 8, 2016).

440. Kyle Hinchey, *Councilor Blake Ewing proposes changing name of Brady Street to Reconciliation Way*, TULSA WORLD, October 19, 2018, https://www.tulsaworld.com/news/government/councilor-blake-ewing-proposes-changing-name-of-brady-street-to/article_59c8c984-00e4-5d49-adca-faca460d3590.html (last visited October 21, 2018).

441. Kevin Canfield, *Brady Street name to change*, TULSA WORLD, November 29, 2018, at A-1.

442. See https://bradytheater.com/venue-info/ (last visited December 6, 2018); James D. Watts, Jr., *Brady Theater to change its name to Tulsa Theater next year*, TULSA WORLD, December 6, 2018, https://www.tulsaworld.com/news/local/brady-theater-to-change-its-name-to-tulsa-theater-next/article_74dc2190-8e2d-5020-9923-1261aea52ca1.html?fbclid=IwAR2gRfnt0-nJ8ePr3Tvg3NjF01ifgjG8QBpC14_vG12EKU89ftjXLdAl6t4 (last visited December 7, 2018).

443. E-mail from Twan Jones, President, The Heights Neighborhood Association, to the author, August 30, 2019 (on file with author).

444. James Leighton Avery, son of Cyrus Avery, recalled his father's feelings about the handling of the Riot aftermath. According to James Leighton Avery, the elder Avery noted that Tulsans failed to take financial responsibility for the tragedy, as they could have done by levying additional taxes to cover the damages. Moreover, the Chamber of Commerce, bent of boosterism and fiercely independent, refused offers of financial assistance that came in from throughout the country. Cyrus Avery spoke of his personal involvement, which included beseeching Governor Robertson, successfully, to pay the guardsmen who quelled the Riot from a state emergency fund, as Tulsa lacked the financial wherewithal to do so. Cyrus Avery also served on the Chamber of Commerce Reconstruction Committee, only to be summarily replaced when Mayor T.D. Evans ousted the Chamber group in favor of another group of his choosing. Avery viewed the replacement a politically-motivated, as he was a leading Democrat and the Mayor a Republican. Avery and others were ultimately successful in transferring monies and leadership to the American Red Cross, hailed by many Tulsans for its relief work. *See* statement of James Leighton Avery, son of Cyrus Avery, Ruth Sigler Avery Collection, Oklahoma State University-Tulsa Library, Special Collections

and Archives, undated, https://osu-tulsa.okstate.edu/library/specialcollections.php (last visited July 21, 2019).

445. *A public act of atonement: Chamber regrets what it did, didn't do after race massacre,* TULSA WORLD, May 29, 2019, at A9 (editorial).

446. Kendrick Marshall, *Chamber shares race massacre minutes: It also apologizes for the organization's historic inaction against racism,* TULSA WORLD, May 29, 2019, at A11.

447. After the formation of the Commission, The Black Wall Street Chamber of Commerce ("BWSCC") emerged. BWSCC, formed in March 2018, bills itself as "a professional organization created to educate, create, and inspire economic vitality in the African American and North Tulsa community." Its mission is: "To create and build the quality of life and business opportunities for the African American and North Tulsa community through business education, African American cultural values, legislative advocacy, and economic development." While the Commission maintains no formal relationship with BWSCC, it has reached out to BWSCC members and sought to include them in its work. *See* https://www.facebook.com/pg/bwschamber/about/?ref=page_internal (last visited January 1, 2019).

448. Letter on file with the author.

449. Mayor G.T. Bynum letter on file with the author.

450. *See* https://www.facebook.com/officialblackwallstreet/info/?tab=page_info (last visited May 17. 2016).

451. *See, e.g., Teaching With Capitol Art,* OKLAHOMA ARTS COUNCIL, http://arts.ok.gov/Teaching_with_Capitol_Art.php?c=cac&res=vs (last visited May 21, 2016); Graham Lee Brewer, *Ralph Ellison portrait is now visible at Oklahoma Capitol,* THE OKLAHOMAN, http://newsok.com/article/3940449, published March 7, 2014; *updated: March 6, 2014 (last visited May 21, 2016);* Portrait of John Hope Franklin Unveiled at Oklahoma State Capitol, The Journal of Blacks in Higher Education, March 1, 2012. https://www.jbhe.com/2012/03/portrait-of-john-hope-franklin-unveiled-at-oklahoma-state-capitol/ (last visited May 21, 2016).
John Hope Franklin's professional career has been summarized as follows:

> John Hope Franklin was a historian specializing in Southern and African American history. He wrote From Slavery to Freedom, the seminal work on African American history, which was first published in 1947. In the course of his career, Franklin had professorships at St. Augustine College, North Carolina College, Howard University, Brooklyn College, University of Chicago, and Duke University. He served as president of numerous historical and community organizations throughout his career. President Clinton awarded him the Presidential Medal of Freedom in 1995. Franklin also served on President Clinton's Advisory Board for the President's Initiative on Race from 1997 to 1998.

Duke University Libraries, https://library.duke.edu/rubenstein/collections/creators/people/johnhopefranklin (last visited April 13, 2019).

453. The portraits of prominent African Americans in the Capitol Rotunda include:

- **Roscoe Dunjee** (1883 - 1965, by Simmie Knox): Oklahoma journalist and publisher Roscoe Dunjee founded the nationally-known OKLAHOMA CITY BLACK DISPATCH newspaper in 1915. A courageous and vocal champion of African American civil rights, he helped shape modern American history.

- **Ada Lois Sipuel Fisher** (1924 - 1995, by Mitsuno Ishii Reedy): Ada Sipuel Fisher challenged the University of Oklahoma's discriminatory admission policy for graduate students. A leading activist, attorney, and educator, she opened higher education to African-American students in Oklahoma and laid the foundation for the land-mark *Brown v. Board of Education* decision.

- **Dr. John Hope Franklin** (1915 - 2009, by Everett Raymond Kinstler): Dr. John Hope Franklin's prodigious scholarship and prolific writing made him a legend among those who know and care about history. His seminal work, FROM SLAVERY TO FREEDOM, was first published in 1947 and has since sold millions of copies world-wide.

- **Ralph Ellison** (1914 - 1994, by Tracey Harris): Ralph Ellison, critically-acclaimed author, was raised in the "Deep Deuce" area of Oklahoma City. Most famous for the novel, INVISIBLE MAN, he won the National Book Award in 1953 for that seminal work.

- **Albert Comstock Hamlin** (1881 – 1912, by Simmie Knox): A. C. Hamlin, a Re-publican, was the first African-American elected to the Oklahoma State Legislature, elected in 1908 and serving until 1910. Hamlin lost his re-election bid as a direct re-sult of a constitutional amendment known as the "grandfather clause" that prevent-ed many African Americans in Oklahoma from voting. The United States Supreme Court declared the amendment unconstitutional in *Guinn v. United States.*

- **Benjamin Harrison Hill** (1904 – 1971, by Simmie Knox): Benjamin Harrison Hill, a religious leader, state lawmaker, and journalist, served Tulsa's African American community for more than three decades. At the time of his death in 1971, Ben Hill was a member of the Oklahoma State House of Representatives, having served two terms, initially elected in 1968.

- **Edward P. McCabe** (1850 – 1923, by Simmie Knox): Edward P. McCabe, dubbed "the father of the all-black town movement" by some, established the all-black town of Langston, Oklahoma, as well as the LANGSTON HERALD newspaper. He also led black migration to Oklahoma in the late 1800s and early 1900s.

454. Oklahoma State Capitol Art Collection, https://www.arts.ok.gov/Art_at_the_Capi-tol/Capitol_Collection.php?c=cac&n=People (last visited August 2, 2019).

455. Stacy Ryburn, *Tulsa Race Riot: Symposium on Reconciliation—Tulsa gets a preview of upcom-ing Smithsonian African American history exhibit*, TULSA WORLD, May 26, 2016, http://www.tulsaworld.com/news/local/tulsa-gets-preview-of-upcoming-smithsonian-african-ameri-can-history-exhibit/article_08bcc34c-ac71-55c8-99c5-57d520692026.html (last visited June 2, 2016).

456. National Museum of African American History and Culture, http://nmaahc.si.edu/About/Mission (last visited June 2, 2016).

457. Veneice Sims (then Veneice Dunn) missed the 1921 Booker T. Washington High School prom, slated for the Stradford Hotel ballroom, on account of the Riot. She was then a sixteen-year-old high school junior. When students at Booker T. Washington High School learned of her story decades later, they invited her to the 2000 prom. Overjoyed, Ms. Sims, 95 years old at the time, finally checked that adolescent rite of passage off her bucket list. She noted: "In those days, I never left our neighborhood. Blacks and whites did not talk to each other, unless you had some kind of working relationship. Blacks and whites together at a prom—in 1921, you never would have thought it possible." Randy Krehbiel, *Prom-goer swings back into time*, TULSA WORLD, April 13, 2000, http://www.tulsaworld.com/archives/prom-goer-swings-back-into-time/article_de88099a-3315-55a6-bd3e-d701f2bf712b.html (last visited May 13, 2016).

458. The Zarrow photographic Survivors exhibit is on display at the Greenwood Cultural

Center in Tulsa.

459. *See, e.g.*, Donielle Prince, *Racism as Trauma: Clinical Perspectives from Social Work and Psychology*, March 9, 2016, https://www.acesconnection.com/g/california-aces-action/blog/racism-as-trauma-clinical-perspectives-from-social-work-and-psychology (last visited March 5, 2019).

460. The Winter Institute, http://winterinstitute.org/about/mission-vision-values/ (last visited March 5, 2019).

461. Hope in the Cities, https://us.iofc.org/hope-in-the-cities (last visited July 1, 2019).

462. https://chicago1919.org/about (last visited May 13, 2019).

463. Correspondence and conversation between author and Richard DeSirey, M.S., L.P.C., August 12, 2019.

464. *See* Michael Hill, *Black Wall Street, Durham, North Carolina*, NCPEDIA, https://www.ncpedia.org/black-wall-street-durham-north-carolina, 2003 (last visited October 26, 2018).

A NOTE ON DURHAM'S "BLACK WALL STREET"

Tulsa's Black Wall Street shared that billing with a community about 1,000 miles to the east. Both insular economic enclaves thrived amidst the forced separation of the races.

Parrish Street in Durham, North Carolina, once resembled a black enterprise zone. In the early 1900s, this area earned the moniker "Black Wall Street." The four-block black business district on Parrish Street served the Hayti community just to the south. Hayti hosted Durham's black residential district and served as the center of its educational, cultural, and religious life.

As in America generally, race relations in North Carolina and, specifically, Durham, left much to be desired at the time. Nonetheless, Durham's black businessmen, with little resistance, and some measure of support, from their white counterparts, proved successful.

John Merrick, Dr. Aaron Moore, and C. C. Spaulding, the "Triumvirate," headed North Carolina Mutual Life Insurance Company, the nation's largest black-owned insurance company, and dabbled in real estate and textiles. North Carolina Mutual moved its headquarters to Parrish Street in 1906. The next year, Mechanics and Farmers Bank, founded by R. B. Fitzgerald and W. G. Pearson, followed suit.

Booker T. Washington visited in 1910, taking note of the ambition and thrift of Durham's black denizens. Dr. W. E. B. Du Bois visited in 1912, marveling at the unparalleled level of black entrepreneurship he witnessed. Dr. Du Bois credited Durham's white leadership for its general progressivity, noting: "[I]t is precisely the opposite spirit in places like Atlanta."

As with many other communities of color across the United States (including Tulsa's "Black Wall Street"), urban renewal initiatives in the 1960s hobbled Durham's black business community, especially Hayti. By this time, though, the heyday of Parrish Street had passed.

465. https://nmaahc.si.edu/object/nmaahc_2011.60.18 (last visited January 1, 2019).

466. Scott Ellsworth, DEATH IN A PROMISED LAND: THE TULSA RACE RIOT OF 1921 (Baton Rouge, LA: LSU Press, 1982).

467. Hannibal B. Johnson, BLACK WALL STREET: FROM RIOT TO RENAISSANCE IN TULSA'S HISTORIC GREENWOOD DISTRICT (Fort Worth , TX: Eakin Press, 1998).

468. https://www.jhfcenter.org/reconciliation-park (last visited January 1, 2019).

469. Representative Sheila Jackson Lee introduced H.R. 40--Commission to Study and Develop Reparation Proposals for African-Americans Act, in the 116th Congress on January 3, 2019. *See* https://www.congress.gov/bill/116th-congress/house-bill/40; https://www.

congress.gov/bill/116th-congress/house-bill/40/all-info. Versions of the bill have been introduced in prior years. Former United States Representative John Conyers, Jr. (D-Mich.) proposed this legislation unsuccessfully every year from 1989 until his resignation in 2017. The federal government made slavery-related reparations in the nineteenth century--to former slave owners for the loss of their "property." *See, e.g.*, Tera W. Hunter, *When Slaveowners Got Reparations: Lincoln signed a bill in 1862 that paid up to $200 for every enslaved person freed*, NEW YORK TIMES, April 16, 2019, https://www.nytimes.com/2019/04/16/opinion/when-slave-owners-got-reparations.html (last visited June 10, 2019) (The District of Columbia Emancipation Act, signed April 16, 1862, by President Lincoln, emancipated enslaved individuals in Washington, D.C., and paid Union-loyal slaveholders up to $300 for every enslaved person freed.). *See also*, National Archives https://www.archives.gov/exhibits/featured-documents/dc-emancipation-act (last visited June 10, 2019) ("[This pre-Emancipation Proclamation Act] provided for immediate emancipation, compensation to former owners who were loyal to the Union of up to $300 for each freed slave, voluntary colonization of former slaves to locations outside the United States, and payments of up to $100 for each person choosing emigration. Over the next 9 months, the Board of Commissioners appointed to administer the act approved 930 petitions, completely or in part, from former owners for the freedom of 2,989 former slaves."

470. *See* Chad V. Johnson, Ph.D., *Tulsa Area Race Relations and History Survey*, https://www.researchgate.net/publication/307857984_Tulsa_Race_Relations_and_History_Survey (last visited June 22, 2019).

471. *See Chad V. Johnson, Ph.D., Tulsa Area Race Relations and History Survey, https://www.researchgate.net/publication/307857984_Tulsa_Race_Relations_and_History_Survey (last visited June 22, 2019).*

472. Gurley, an Alabama-born Arkansas transplant, participated in the 1889 Oklahoma land run. In 1906, he purchased property in what is now the Greenwood District, selling some lots and establishing several businesses. He is a founder of Vernon A.M.E. Church in the Greenwood District. Gurley lost it all in the 1921 Tulsa Race Riot. He moved to Los Angeles where, presumably, he died. Records of his life in Los Angeles date at least to 1930, when he is listed in the city directory as living at 364 East 33rd Street. *See Uncrowned Community Builders: Biography for Ottowa (O.W.) Gurley*, https://www.uncrownedcommunitybuilders.com/person/ottowa-o-w (last visited January 3, 2019).

473. Mary Elizabeth Jones Parrish, in her chronicle of the ravages wrought by the 1921 Tulsa Race Riot, EVENTS OF THE TULSA DISASTER, lists several destroyed churches: "Methodist Episcopal, African Methodist Episcopal, Colored Methodist Episcopal, Mount Zion Baptist, Paradise Baptist, Metropolitan Baptist, Union Baptist, and Seventh Day Advent[ist]". *See* Mary Elizabeth Jones Parrish, EVENTS OF THE TULSA DISASTER (Tulsa, OK: John Hope Franklin Center for Reconciliation, 2009) (Limited Edition, First Printing, as originally published in 1923), at 106; *see also*, http://paradisebc.net/story (last visited December 30, 2018). St. Monica Catholic Church and School opened in 1925, a mere four years after the conflagration. The church and school, both white-run, helped shore up Tulsa's black community in its greatest moment of need. *Graduates Of Tulsa's First Black Catholic School Reunite*, August 23rd 2013, http://www.newson6.com/story/23244445/graduates-of-tulsas-first (last visited December 31, 2018).

474. Adapted from Maurianne Adams, Lee Ann Bell, and Pat Griffin, TEACHING FOR DIVERSITY AND SOCIAL JUSTICE—A SOURCEBOOK (New York and London: Routledge, 1997), p. 140.

Index

About the Author

Hannibal B. Johnson, a Harvard Law School graduate, is an author, attorney, and consultant specializing in diversity and inclusion issues, human relations, leadership, and non-profit leadership and management. He has taught at The University of Tulsa College of Law, Oklahoma State University, and The University of Oklahoma. Johnson serves on the federal 400 Years of African-American History Commission, a body charged with planning, developing, and implementing activities appropriate to the 400th anniversary of the arrival, in 1619, of Africans in the English colonies at Point Comfort, Virginia. He is the education chair for the 1921 Tulsa Race Massacre Commission. His books, including *Black Wall Street, Up from the Ashes, Acres of Aspiration, Apartheid in Indian Country,* and *The Sawners of Chandler,*

J. Shelton Photography

chronicle the African American experience in Oklahoma and its indelible impact on American history. The 2011 National Black Theatre Festival showcased Johnson's play, *Big Mama Speaks—A Tulsa Race Riot Survivor's Story. Big Mama Speaks* has also been staged in Caux, Switzerland. Johnson has received numerous awards and honors for his work and community service.

CPSIA information can be obtained
at www.ICGtesting.com
Printed in the USA
LVHW081912090322
713038LV00003B/122